The Vitruvian Inspiration

HENRI PATRIK

The Vitruvian Inspiration

The victorious write the history
(Napoleon)

Translated by Patrick Depreitere

Clusteruitgeverij Schrijverspunt

Title: The Vitruvian Inpiration

First edition: 1 April 2020
Second edition: 20 July 2020
Translated by Patrick Depreitere

Issued by: Henri Patrik & Falcon books
Printing: schrijverspunt.nl
Henri.d.patrik@gmail.com
http://www.henripatrik.nl
Cover design: Henri Patrik
Code: 2020.07.20
ISBN 978-94-6266-417-3
NUR: 332

For the people who mean everything in my life
Marie-France, my wife,
Katja and Jack, my children

THE ATMOSPHERE OF LAWLESSNESS

In the summer of 1995, *Médecins Sans Frontières* has commissioned me in the eastern Bosnian city of Tuzla. MSF was the only non-governmental humanitarian organisation on the ground. While NATO bombed the Serbian positions on the outskirts of the town, I spoke to the refugees from the Srebrenica enclave who had survived the journey of more than one hundred kilometres through the inhospitable mountain region.

I wrote a book about this intense period: "*Srebrenica. Witnesses to a massacre.*" When Henri Patrik invited me to write a foreword to his fact-based thriller "*The Vitruvian Inspiration*" which takes place in 2002 in Sarajevo, I reread some chapters of my book. To my surprise and shame, I noticed how many facts I had forgotten.

How could that be? The atrocities and the tragic fate of the refugees had seized me so profoundly at the time.
I was embarrassed to death.

Coincidentally, however, Isaac Bashevis Singer"s excellent novel "*Enemies: A Love Story*" I've read, describes the same phenomenon. The Jewish survivors of the Holocaust who just arrived in New York noticed that they already had forgotten a large part of their traumatic past.
We live in a world that is forgetting ever more quickly. At a furious rate, one astonishing and terrible fact follows another. Opinions and visions about life and forms of society fall apart into fragments. On the rebound, there is a growing group of people who yearn for Oneness, a community in which there are no ethnic, linguistic, or religious differences.

That is how the Balkan War began. In the course of the 1990s, it made the bankruptcy of the international institutions painfully clear.
But that too was quickly forgotten, despite the thick books that well-known sociologists have written on the subject.

Stories can form a barrier against this dangerous amnesia. They remain in our memory much longer because they affect us through our emotions.
That is why Henri Patrik has cast his account of the international institutions that managed the chaos in Bosnia after the war but failed miserably, into a shocking and exciting story. The high value of the novel lies in the indictment of incompetence, corruption, and abuse of power of these institutions. As a liaison officer in Bosnia, Henri Patrik experienced the chaos in Sarajevo up close. Crime, murder, prostitution and human

trafficking were the reality of everyday life. "The Vitruvian Inspiration" is compelling and well founded, but more important is the atmosphere of the novel, warning against short-sighted politics, blind profit-seeking, and growing fundamentalism.
And against representatives of the international community who feel that they are above the law.

Bob Van Laerhoven
4 May 2015

PROLOGUE

Paris, 2000

LUCAS'S EXCITEMENT WAS GROWING. SLOWING DOWN HIS PACE, HE SCRUTINISED A quiet neighbourhood under a clear blue sky. A faint wind was blowing through the trees and bushes in the gaps between the few houses lined up on both sides. He let his gaze run around the street and houses, spotting twenty metres farther ahead three vehicles parked along the sidewalk. Four passing pedestrians gave him a short, uninterested look. Any neighbour watching him from behind drawn curtains might consider him as another official arsehole going to harass the poor widow.

He rang the bell. Behind the closed door, he heard a dull sound of an electric gong slowly fading away while frantic footsteps were approaching. Then the door swung open, and a good-looking black-haired woman wearing blue jeans and a white silk blouse with decent cleavage appeared.

He laughed charmingly. "Mrs Dumont, Denise Dumont?"

She looked him up and down. "That's me," she answered hesitantly.

Without a briefcase, I am not looking like a salesman.

Her features relaxed.

He showed a brown card with three-coloured slanted bands over the corner. "Ministry of Defence, Lucas Dupont." His voice sounded hoarse. "It's about your late husband, Commander Marcel Dumont."

She frowned. "Julien, one of my husband's colleagues, has been here yesterday. Is there anything new?" Her features betrayed her concern.

Indeed, this Julien was the reason for his visit. Lucas returned her a neutral smile. As an experienced womaniser, he hoped she would succumb to his charms. He gave her a seductive smile.

"Perhaps we should go inside," he proposed.

She let him in, shut the door, and guided him to a spacious room. *Soberly furnished.* His nose caught the scent of beeswax. At one end was a tall window bordered by grey curtains whereas the most exquisite lace filtered sunlight, at the other end a large television, with on each side a bookshelf. A long leather-covered couch, two armchairs, and a small coffee table occupied the centre. On the rear wall hung four framed paintings, he immediately identified as *Tahitian Women on the Beach*, *Two Tahitian Women*, *The Yellow Christ and the Post-Sermon Vision. Cheap replies by Paul Gauguin*, he thought. The sunlight on the brown parquet shone with a beckoning warmth.

"Anything new about my husband's death? Please have a seat," she said invitingly.

He coughed softly in his hand. "Uh, first, I'd be pleased if you tell me why Mr Julien Cartier has been visiting you."

Denise Dumont took a seat on the large couch, and he settled down across from her in an armchair. *She's handsome.* Prettier than on the pictures he'd seen. Friendly features, grey-blue eyes, little seesaw nose, and a mouth to be kissed. Sturdy grapefruit-sized tits with long nipples beyond that transparent blouse. He liked small tits. Everything a hand was unable to hold, he considered as wasted. In other circumstances, he would have tried her.

"Julien claimed that Marcel's death wasn't an accident, but cold blood murder," she retorted. "By a hitman."

He shook his head. "Ma'am, you reckon that your husband ought to have blackmailed a superior?" He leaned in, muffling his voice. "Julien Cartier has PTSD. During that shooting out in Mitrovica, he witnessed his two friends dying. It was a terrible shock for him. Unfortunately, his chiefs found out too late that he was psychologically disturbed. Pretending that high-ranking officers have conspired is going to increase the suffering of the concerned families. So, we have to stop him."

Denise's big eyes started flickering in disbelief and distrust. "You guys are going to cover up the whole affair, aren't you?"

What else could he have expected from a Judicial Police Inspector? But he kept smiling. "Ma'am, the Minister ordered an additional investigation, examining Cartier's statements. After checking any inconsistency, he appointed three independent psychiatrists who diagnosed PTSD. Moreover, we gathered dozens of statements from natives witnessing your husband's killing. Don't forget the countless casualties among the citizens. All witnesses are unanimously claiming that the killing of the two brave policemen was just bad luck; they were at the wrong place at the wrong time."

"Bollocks," retorted Denise. "Julien isn't traumatised, he has been very persuasive to me. He mentioned photographs that might substantiate his allegations."

Lucas chuckled. "Do you believe that nonsense, ma'am? Has he shown you those pictures?" Lucas looked in her eyes, aware of the effect his blue eyes had on women. But Denise Dumont's features betrayed nothing but disdain. *She's still suffering from her husband's loss.* Devoured by anger, Denise refused to accept fatality as the cause of death. No, she was not going to give up until she knew the truth.

She straightened her back and riposted. "My husband and Leduc owned several photos. Where are they?"

He shrugged with an apologetic smile. "It's a pity that the authorities haven't found any of that stuff, isn't it?"

"The authorities might have destroyed all evidence," she snarled.

"You are a bright woman and a good inspector. Don't be guided by emotions. Have you told anyone else about this ridiculous theory?"

"No, I haven't. First, I'm going to do my proper investigation. Then I'm going to discuss the issue with the Leduc family. Together we're going to decide what to do next."

He nodded. "Good idea, perhaps it's the best thing you can do, and hopefully, the Leduc family have a more realistic view on the matter."

After gazing at him for a moment, she glanced away.

"Don't you think," continued Lucas sternly, "that your husband would have informed you if he had discovered a conspiracy or whatever. Why tell a friend and not his wife?" Embraced by a euphoric sense of power, he stared at her with an expressionless face.

She hesitated. "My husband and I had an agreement. We discussed neither our job nor our assignments; we avoided domestic conflicts. However, Marcel hated hypocrites, and I think he would have denounced any corrupt official."

It's hopeless.

"Well, there's nothing left for me, but let get one thing straight, keep it discreet for the time, and do not talk to the media. Think about National Security."

"What do you think?" she hissed.

"I hope you're going to regain your inner peace as soon as possible." This stubborn woman wasn't going to accept any arguments. *The families of the victims have decided to go on.* He liked this woman. *Too bad.* He'd failed.

She got up.

"Mrs Dumont, if you'd like some advice during your investigation," began Lucas while straightening up himself from his seat, "I'd recommend that you call my office at the Ministry. We doubt there's anything shady about your husband's death, however, what if we were wrong? Don't play the hero and let *us* handle the affair." He rumbled into his inner pocket and took out a business card.

He stretched out his hand. "My card with the phone number and email." But as Denise reached for the card, his other hand grabbed her wrist, twisting her arm while moving around her, immobilising her arm against her spine and jabbing her body forward on the couch. The card fell on the floor, as her astonishing scream got smothered in the fabric cushion. Holding her quiet with one hand, pushing his knee on her spine, his other hand took a small pistol out of his pocket. He stabbed the thin cylinder against her occiput. A slight humming noise indicated that the gun was doing its job, and a few seconds later, her body stopped twitching. He took a pair of rubber gloves from his pocket and pulled them on. Then he picked up the business card, shoving it in his pocket.

After having found the bathroom next to the kitchen, he paced back to the living room where he threw the motionless body over his shoulder. *What a pity*, he thought while moving to the bathroom. There he undressed the unconscious woman before lowering her naked body into the tub. To dissimulate the needle mark, he smashed the back of her skull several times against the edge of the bathtub until it started bleeding. After that, he turned on the taps, regulated the temperature, and waited until the tub was almost full. Finally, he held the head underwater until her heart stopped beating.

Death by drowning. No traces of third person involvement.

When he left the house minutes later, a passing young woman glanced up at him. Fortunately for her too short of making a future identification possible. He scrutinised either side of the road, let his eyes roam over the house facade across the street, and stiffened. *Someone is watching me behind the curtain on the second floor*.

He kept staring at the window for at least two minutes, but couldn't discover any suspect movements. He sighed with relief, turned toward the street, and walked away toward his car.

Lucas had ceased to exist.

Sunday, 6 October 2002

ONE

Srebrenica, 11 July 1995

SHE WAS EXHAUSTED, DESPERATELY GASPING FOR BREATH. HER BURNING LUNGS were calling for more air. But she kept stumbling through the close-knit trees, while low-hanging branches tore her clothes, causing bleeding injuries in her face and legs. She glanced over her shoulder, and although she didn't see her pursuers, she could hear their laughter getting louder.

They're playing with me.

Her breasts bounced above the ripped upper part of her dress, but she didn't have time to spend on her appearance.

You must run faster to stay alive.

Her naked feet were a bloody mass. Every step on a root or a cobble caused an unbearable sharp pain shooting through her whole body, torturing her brain. Her heart was throbbing against her ribs. *Sit down and have a rest.* But she was too anxious to obey that inner voice. Fear was conquering all her pain. *If those monsters catch me, they'll do what they did to my sister.*

The sound of breaking branches mixed up with the horny shouting, made her run faster. *Allah, give me strength and time.* Then she called out her lover's name, damning that monstrous man who'd betrayed him.

At last, she was going to escape those monsters.

"We're coming, Turkish whore, you have nowhere to go," echoed a shrill voice through the trees. Shivering all over her body, she didn't manage to increase the pace. Then her eyes caught the edge of the abyss. Suddenly realising that her chasers wouldn't get her, she felt a lot lighter, and the pain started to fade away. Footsteps rushed closer, whereas the abyss was just a few yards ahead.

Zumra looked over her shoulder, desperately taking deep gulps of air. The largest man of the five chasers was going to reach her.

"Free," she yelled, the moment his fingers were going to grab her. Stepping over the edge, she gave him a triumphant grin.

"Fuck you," she called out, plunging into salvation.

Sarajevo, 6 October 2002

Zumra Abdic shot up completely confused, waving wildly with her arms. Her thin nightgown adhered to her skin. She felt cold and glanced around the room, starting to recognise her environment: almost bare walls, the doorway, the wardrobe, and the bedside table. The heavy heart beating was diminishing. She drew a deep breath. Always the same nightmare. *Is there a link with my past?* The doctors had diagnosed severe trauma that caused her memory loss, especially all memories before the 12th of July 1995. She'd even forgotten her name. Her rescuer had declared her as her sister who'd lost her identification papers during the Serb attack. Convincing enough for the Red Cross to provide her with new documents. Officially she was her saver's sister. After the end of the war, both travelled to Sarajevo.

When will it stop?

The place next to her was empty. Panic emerged. *Where did Lazar go?*

Then Lazar appeared in underpants between the doorposts.

"Those lousy dreams again?" he asked worriedly.

"Was I yelling something?"

"You only produced unintelligible sounds," answered Lazar, approaching along her side.

"Do you have to go on working?"

He sat down on the edge of the bed. "It's Sunday, sweetheart." His hand stroked through her short black hair. "I had to go to the toilet. You can talk to me about your dreams if you wish."

She felt safe with him. They had been lovers for three months, and their relationship seemed to be going in the right direction. Although she didn't doubt his feelings, she feared for the future. She was not prepared yet for a steady relationship. Too early. Too many obscure things were haunting her mind; the war had carved deep scars into her heart and soul. Even though she usually stayed in his house, she regularly headed back to her apartment. *To be alone for a moment*, she told him. However, he was a good policeman, and she wondered how long it would take him to find out the truth. She kissed the palmetto of his hand, his chest and cheek. How handsome he was with his long fair hair and deep blue eyes. When those eyes had crossed hers for the first time, she immediately had fallen in love. She couldn't remember ever having known that feeling before. But often an unknown man with gloomy features was flashing through her mind, causing her a tingling sensation inside her belly. Just as it was with Lazar. Had she been in love back then? Maybe that mysterious man was searching for her. Could that be the reason why a new relationship frightened her?

Lazar bowed and softly kissed her mouth. She smiled, listening to his accelerating breath, while a pleasant fire started growing deep in her belly. She moved up and pulled him next to her, his hand slipping over her clammy nightgown.

"Wait," she murmured, pulling the thing over her head and throwing it on the floor. Then she fell backwards. His rough hand slid gently over her boobs, causing the nipples hardening. Her eyes closed, and she surrendered. He was a good lover. She noticed his impatience when he pulled her knickers off. His hand slid over her shaven pubic area, making her breathing faster. Enjoying his tender caresses, she unwittingly groaned, pushing her belly against his tights. Their lovemaking was short but intense, and they reached the zenith of pleasure together.

Lazar remained immobilised while his heartbeat stabilised. Then he turned to face her. She smiled, kissed him softly on his mouth, and he stretched out on his back next to her. Feeling happy and satisfied, she closed her eyes, wondering if the moment was opportune to confess.

Why not tell him everything?

He'd got a rough time in the war, and even though he didn't tell much about it, she guessed he'd done terrible things. War transforms people into animals. Had he been guilty of inhumanities? Torture, murder, rape?

Her nightmares made her afraid. What had she been doing in the war? She laughed sadly as she heard light snoring.

By Allah, what shall I do? Living in sin, Allah had turned away from her. Although she was in love, she feared for the future. *You can only build a future if there's mutual trust.*

"I don't deserve you, my dear Lazar," she whispered in his ear.

My existence is a big lie.

TWO

"I AM GOING TO KILL CEES VISSER," EXCLAIMED BRAM RUYTER ANGRILY, PUTTING his beer glass in front of him. He slowly wiped the foam off his beard and leaned in, slapping his fist on the table. "It's a shame." He quickly glanced over his shoulder, taking a deep breath. They were the only guests in the pub. His eyes observed the man across to him while scratching his black circle beard.

"You can't be serious," countered Edhem Hasic sarcastically, "you're such a gentle person." He was a tall, rugged man with Slavic features, big green eyes, thick eyebrows, and a firm chin, wearing a worn pair of jeans and a blue T-shirt.

They were seated at their usual table in the far corner, drinking local beer. Central Café was Sarajevo's most famous pub. Usually, when being alone, Bram sat quietly at the same table, dreaming, thinking, and drinking beer. Or he was making notes. As soon as his friend joined him, they were talking about the current situation in Bosnia, carefully avoiding *the theme* that could hurt, although it had brought them together.

"That jerk destroyed my life," groaned Bram. "And now he's in Sarajevo as a military attaché. It's a shame." Thinking of Cees made him always resentful.

Edhem's features kept emotionless, although he undoubtedly knew the man's name.

"That jerk refused to protect the relatives of our Bosnian employees," Bram continued bitterly. "Visser was Franken's right-hand man, his ears and eyes. The executioner of dirty tasks. But he was also making his own decisions. I didn't believe him when he claimed that Thom Karremans ordered it. However, I am no longer convinced either that Karremans was innocent. A pity I never got the opportunity to clear those things out with him. I want to question Cees about that contested order. He provoked my arrest, after which I've been threatened and treated as a mentally ill person. I'll never forget the months of therapy in a mental institution. My former colleagues do not talk to me, convinced I'm disturbed."

Edhem was rocketing in his armchair. "Since when do you know Visser is in town?"

Bram straightened his back. "Since yesterday. That guy is a shameless prick. I can't accept he can be a military attaché after all the things he did in Srebrenica. There must be a lot of Bosniaks around eager to cut off his head."

"Who's been telling you he's here?"

"I've read it on the internet." Why tell Edhem everything? They'd been friends for six months, and Bram trusted him like nobody else in his life. But he thought it too early to reveal all his secrets. Other opportunities would come.

Edhem had a sip of beer, and his features became somewhat softened. "Bram, Dutchbat was powerless against Mladic's supremacy."

Bram raised his eyebrows. "You should hate all the Dutch people being in Srebrenica in 1995," he mumbled, quickly glancing over his shoulder. Although they spoke English, the word *Srebrenica* was taboo for either the Bosniaks as the Dutch.

"Why should I hate you? You're a victim just like me."

Bram straightened his shoulders. "I'll put it bluntly, Naser Oric stayed in Tuzla as shortly after the hell broke loose in Srebrenica. Do you call that coincidence?"

Edhem had been Oric's friend, although they hadn't met since the war.

Edhem let out a deep breath. "You're upset, but I don't blame you. After Naser had returned in April from his gathering with the high command in Sarajevo, he cancelled his Zepa-flight at the last minute, because he had to meet with the commander of the second Corps, Sead Delic. A last instant decision. An hour later, the helicopter flying to Zepa got shot down. After that incident, he knew touts were among his confidants, and he refused to head on to Srebrenica. The Serbs had put a high price on his head. But believe me, his presence in the enclave would have changed little."

Bram had learned that in the early days of the war, Oric and his warriors had been carrying out numerous hit-and-run operations, killing hundreds of innocent people in the neighbouring Serb villages. Could the Serbs be blamed for taking revenge? He checked his watch, reluctant to elaborate on this sensitive subject, although many questions kept unanswered.

"I'll have to leave you alone, Edhem," he groaned. "Winston Chambers has invited me for dinner. Imagine, after all these months, my boss wants to learn more about me."

On Sunday, they usually went to a restaurant before Edhem started his shift. After the pub closed, they headed into the city for a quiet drink in some quiet bar. Most of the time, they went ahead until the early morning.

Edhem leaned in with a frown. "What do you think of your boss?"

Bram shrugged. "He's quite acceptable." He got along well with Winston, without searching for a more intimate relationship. He did his job as requested in his contract. However, outside the organisation, he wished to be independent and free. International solidarity was not for him. Most of the time, the EU and UN aid workers gathered in one of the two Irish Pubs or the Country Club. *They are just concerned about partying and screwing around*, Bram thought, as he just wanted to discover different faces and places, learn as much as possible about the country and the people, improving his knowledge of the local language.

"Winston thinks I'm too individualistic, having a lack of team spirit," he said with a shrug. "He doesn't understand that after my daily job, I want to be free."

"You're living alone, aren't you?"

"Yes, but I'm also an author. I write novels."

"You're a fucking writer. You're writing about what?"

"Regarding the fucking war. About what I've seen here. About all the lies that the International press is telling their readers."

"Do you write about what happened in Srebrenica?"

"Yes, I do. Don't worry, one day I'll tell you more about it." Bram took another quick look at his watch. "It's time to go," he said with a smouldering smile. "I just wanted to say hello." He laughed apologetically, rose from his chair, and picked up his wallet.

"Never mind," Edhem replied, "I'll take care of the bill."

"If it's not getting too late this evening, I'll pop in." Bram got a warm pat on his back and walked out, heading to the Parrot Building where he'd parked his car, thinking of his first meeting with Edhem.

Months ago.

Bram was standing at the bar, drinking beer while admiring the courage of several young people sitting on the terrace. Too cold for having a seat outside. His eyes wandered through the room, searching for a suitable place. He counted only a few guests and plenty of free tables. From the corner of his eye, he saw someone standing next to him, and he turned to face the man.

He caught the view of a tall athletically native with a hooky face, crochet nose, green eyes, thick eyebrows, and a strong chin, wearing jeans, a blue T-shirt, brown jacket and Nike sports shoes.

The man chuckled. "New here?"

"Yes, I arrived a few weeks ago," Bram answered reluctantly.

"I'm Edhem, and I work here as a bouncer."

"Bram, nice to meet you. Your English is perfect." The waiter placed a big glass of beer in front of him. "Do you drink a beer with me?" asked Bram with a slight smirk.

"I'd love to."

At first, they talked about unimportant matters. Edhem was a qualified engineer who's employed as a bouncer in the basement of the Central Café's disco.

"For personal reasons," he said. "Besides, I am a single without any family."

"In the current world, I'm alone too," replied Bram with a sad smile.

After a while, Edhem ordered a new round. The barroom filled up, but they were staying at the far end of the counter.

"How long have you been in Bosnia?" asked Edhem curtly.

"A few weeks. It isn't my first visit. In 1995, I was in Srebrenica."

"So, you're a Dutchman," said Edhem with a vehement kind of bitterness.

Bram glanced up to him thoughtfully, aware that the Dutchmen had left unpleasant memories to the Bosniaks.

Edhem swallowed, looking over his shoulder while leaning toward him.

"I was also in Srebrenica," he groaned. "I've lost my whole family there."

Sarajevo, 6 October

Bram kept his eyes focussed on the road, but his thoughts were still on that first meeting with Edhem. They had been talking all night long while drinking until they could hardly stand on their feet. That night they had become friends. Since then they regularly went to a restaurant or did sightseeing. Sometimes they visited the Irish Pub close to the Glass Tower. In his current function, it was always good to meet other humanitarian workers and EuPol officials.

"Damned!" Bram braked abruptly. The car was losing grip on the tarmac, sliding few metres ahead before it drew to a halt. Bram glanced over his shoulder, noticing a narrow dark gap between tall pines. He shifted, drove backwards, and turned onto the unpaved path. The car bumped over pebbles, stones and potholes, forcing him to slow his pace. After a long bend, he caught sight of a tall building on his right, almost wholly tucked away among the trees. He drove through an open gate where the path was merging into a broad tarmac road bordered by lighting poles and ending on an abundant unpaved and grassy parking lot that stretched out across the entire width of the grey facade. On each corner were tall metallic lighting poles. He parked his car facing the building and got out, his eyes wandering over the surrounding dense forest and the house, a grey nineteenth-century, two-story mansion. He was wondering why Winston had chosen this godforsaken environment. Foreigners usually felt safer in an inhabited world. He gazed around while strolling to the front door, where he pulled the antique draw bell. Somewhere in the belly of the house resonated a flat gong.

Winston Chambers was inviting him for the first time to his dwelling space. He wished to catch up on Bram's future, he'd said.

Bram's thoughts got interrupted by the almost silent opening of the massive front door. Between the doorposts appeared a friendly-looking, sixty-year-old bald man with a round face, small eyes, a full grey beard and a thick moustache. But that grandfatherly appearance didn't fool Bram.

A strong personality.

Winston laughed exuberantly, and they shook hands.

Bram followed him through a hall with a staircase into a large room where a strong smell of pine, resin, and blossoms filled the air. A modern living and dining room consisted of bar furniture, white leather armchairs, a four-person couch, a large plasma screen, and two loudspeaker boxes. The dining space contained a sideboard and in the centre a long wooden table and ordinary wood chairs with high backrest.

That does not match the style of the house. The original furniture probably got stolen during the war. A large and tall window bordered by black drapes in the front facade allowed enough sunlight entering the interior. Several paintings in gold frames, erotic casts of young, half-naked women, covered the more significant part of the white walls. His gaze went to the sideboard and the three thick round glasses in which a little flame flashed. *Scented candles*. He wondered if a woman was living in the house.

Winston observed his exploratory glances with a slight smile.

"I like exciting things," he said, pointing at the sofa. "Please have a seat."

Bram sat down. "What an idea to come living here."

"This house has a spacious meeting room upstairs," Winston replied while he walked away, stepping through a doorway in the rear wall. Barely a minute later, he was already back with a large serving tray with two bottles of Dutch beer, glasses, and all kinds of refreshments on it.

Bram's nose caught the smell of roast. *Who's doing the cooking?*

"How do you feel at *Last Hope*?" Winston asked.

"Excellent."

"How long have you been with us? Six months?"

"That's right." Bram grabbed a handful of chips.

"What are you searching in Sarajevo?"

"Making money."

"I know you've been already in the country in the past. Srebrenica, isn't it?"

"Is that in my file? Did the file mention that my wife has died here?"

"Yes, it did."

Hypocrite. This pleasant get-together began to look like an interrogation. They faced each other.

Winston kept smiling. "Is that the reason why you stay so isolated?"

"Do you think so?"

"Or do you prefer the company of Muslims above that of your international colleagues?"

Bram did not stir.

"Rumours are going fast," continued Winston.

"I love lamb, and what I'm doing during my off-duty time is none of your business. Edhem and I have a lot in common because we've got witnessed the same mass murder."

Winston shook his head. "You're a Catholic, aren't you?"

"I'm not. I'm an atheist."

"A monkey who's sympathising with Islam."

Bram knew fundamentalist Muslims called disbelievers *monkey*.

"Religion has nothing to do with it," he replied sharply. "Edhem was once a moderate Muslim, but he lost faith in Srebrenica. "*A true god would never have let that happen*," he told me once, and I agree."

Winston emptied his glass, put it on the tray, and leaned back.

"Europe made a big mistake, letting almost half of Bosnia in Muslim hands," he said coldly.

Bram frowned in disbelief, thinking he'd heard wrong. He firmly believed in a multicultural society, as long as a secular society got assured.

Winston leaned in with a frown. "How do you feel about Islam?"

"Muslims, Catholics, Orthodox, I leave them in peace. Everyone is free whether to believe in a superior being or not to believe. As long as those God-worshippers leave me out of their faith, as long as they don't try to convert me, I've got no problem with them. I do respect people, but I don't care about religion. Anyway, religion isn't part of my job description, is it?"

"Have you forgotten on the 11th of September 2001? You're wrong when thinking that terrorism is far behind us and that we're not concerned. Our politicians are blind, Bram, liars." Winston had raised his voice.

Bram shook his head. "It sounds as terrorists are going to strike in Europe?"

"Be convinced they will. All those mujahidin who were staying in Bosnia are unifying and getting stronger and stronger. European leaders are closing their eyes. Al-Qaeda is a small fry, compared to what's coming next."

"Populist talk. Do you believe that nonsense? I'm not a specialist in matters of terrorism, but I have a solid military background. Just to set up small acts of terrorism requires a lot of resources. The essential logistical support makes them vulnerable. Money transfers, weapons, and equipment always leave traces, making the tracking and seizing of most terrorists possible, even before they're able to trigger a bomb."

Winston indignantly hit his fists on his thighs. "Apparently, you believe the nonsense our politicians are preaching! They're all blind, Bram." His voice was rising. "They mistakenly equate Muslim immigration with the immigration of popular groups with a Catholic background. An enormous distinction. Spanish, Italian, Greek, and South American immigrants don't commit terror attacks. Neither do the people from the east or the north. Don't deny that Islam is dangerous."

"I know more about Islam than you might think. Most Muslim-immigrants coming to the west are Sunnis, a movement within Islam with the most followers. Their tradition gets its strength from the Qur'an and the Hadith."

Winston raised his eyebrows. "The Hadith? What's that?"

"The Hadith contains the traditions of Muhammad and his followers, his statements and actions. Don't you know the difference between Sunnis and Shiites?"

Winston didn't answer.

"Sunnis do not interpret the Qur'an, contrary to the Shiites," Bram continued with impatience.

Winston cautiously rubbed his bald skull. "I'm talking about those fucking mujahidin, jihadists, and Salafists."

Bram knew that Westerners called all fundamentalists in one breath.

"I agree. Salafism originates from Sunnism." Bram laughed mockingly. "A movement inspired by the first generation of muslins. Initially, they were against violence, nor did they want an armed struggle against the infidels."

Winston sat up straight, stimulated. "Do I hear admiration for Islam in your voice? Do you also believe that jihadists are not real Muslims, but just criminals?"

"I'm not that naive. Every religion can become a dangerous doctrine if politicised. Politicians set their own goals; they are trying to convince us that they do so for our well-being, convincing the voters that there are good and bad Muslims. The jihadists are fundamentalists who take up arms to defend Islam and to safeguard its domination, extending Islam to an ideal Muslim world. Muhammad believed being the last prophet, and he was predicting peace and love in his early preacher years. But fast enough, he learned that living from religion wasn't possible, and he became a military leader and politician, starting to understand that religion was giving him the power he could use to control his people. In the 7th century, he began to conquer the world in the name of God. Not the religion is bad, but the people using it to achieve their goals. The Catholics evolved through centuries, but Islam didn't because Muhammad prevented that through the *divine revelations: no one is allowed to question God's words.* The Qur'an mentions that humans cannot change the word of God. Fundamentalists use the literal text of the Qur'an as the only law. But not all Muslims agree with, preferring the peace proclaiming verses which Muhammad preached in his early years. The Bosniaks are moderate Muslims because they have adapted to the norms and laws of a secular state. That's why the Arab Wahabis are looking at them with great disdain."

"You've learned all that stuff during these six months with us?"

"No, I've studied the culture of Islam before."

"And you're not afraid of what's coming at us?"

"Not yet. Why should I be afraid? From a handful of fundamentalists who interpret the Qur'an all too literally?"

Winston shook his head.

"You are misinformed, Bram," he snarled. "During the Bosnian War, there were many mujahidin in the country. And that's another word for jihadists. They had caused a furore as allies of the Americans when they fought against the Russians in Afghanistan. Do you know that Osama bin Laden has fought in Bosnia? By the way, a lot of al-Qaeda fighters have fought in Bosnia, most of them staying in the country after the war. Qatar and Saudi Arabia finance them. And their objectives are clear, aren't they?"

Bram didn't go into it any more, judging that it would be wiser, not to refute Winston's arguments. After a while, Winston got that.

"Well, let's stop talking about politics. Time for the meal."

They didn't talk much at dinner. Winston played the excellent host, serving a simple meal: a slice of special pastry as a starter, marinated steak, fried potatoes with French beans, followed by a refreshing fruit cocktail. They drank coffee in the sitting room, with a glass of Winston's best Irish Whisky, Bushmills 21, enjoying a few minutes of silence.

"As far as your work is concerned," began Winston, "I'm more than satisfied. However, I don't understand how you can cling so tightly to a file as if your life depends on it." He cut off the tip of a thick cigar and stabbed it with a lot of fuss.

Bram didn't smoke. However, he appreciated the specific smell of a burning cigar.

"As far as your evaluation note is concerned," Winston went on, "I can reassure you that the company will renew your contract."

Bram chuckled. "Thank you." He was on good terms with Winston, and sometimes he stayed with him in the evening to talk about the current situation in Bosnia, or he accompanied him on occasion to the Irish Pub 2, where they had a few beers. There were always customers, mainly international aid workers, the staff of embassies and consulates. Himself preferred a quiet restaurant. During the past six months, he had seldom been out with his colleagues, afraid that they would ask him about his former life.

Colleagues knew that he'd served in Srebrenica. That's why he favoured Edhem's company. For both the past was a closed book, concealing personal wounds. He had also asked his friend to talk to him in the local language so he could learn it faster.

Winston blew a few circles of smoke to the ceiling.

"After what you've got experienced in Srebrenica, it must be special working again in this country."

"It is."

"You know, during the events of 1995, I was safe at home. Later I heard all the possible nonsense about it on television." Three grey circles detached themselves from his tufted lips.

Bram nodded. "It was worse than anything you've ever seen on television. Nobody wants to hear the truth, and I have learned to live with it."

"Did you witness those atrocities?"

"Indirect. But I've witnessed powerlessness, political hypocrisy, cowardice and deceit. Some of my colleagues behaved like heroes after washing the shit of fear out of their pants."

Winston listened attentively, filling the short breaks with blowing circles.

"Was Mladic as terrifying as they say?" he asked when Bram paused.

Bram shrugged. "He's an arrogant, narcissistic personality who despises non-Serbs, hating the politicians as well, and behaving like a Roman general. Mladic is a good strategist and commander, respected and loved by his men. Yes, he radiates vitality and self-confidence. But his word is not worth a penny."

There was a short silence that Winston used to refill the glasses, although Bram shook his head violently.

"I've seen Mladic facing Karremans," Bram continued, suddenly driven by unusual emotions. "Thom shit in his pants, only worried about himself. Later he claimed that he'd been worried about his men's lives. Bullshit, he knew that Mladic wouldn't offend the Blue Helmets, because he didn't want to risk NATO intervention. But what would NATO have done if Mladic had just shot a bullet in Thom Karremans's head, claiming that he had given his troops orders to shoot at the Serbs?"

Winston's cigar was almost gone, and he didn't make any more circles. "That's a hard talk about your former commander. You don't respect that fellow, do you?" Winston gave him a look of disapproval.

"Why should I? And, Winston, Srebrenica belongs to the past."

"Bram, you're avoiding the International Community. Do you blame her for what happened to you?"

Bram felt like a hungry wolf preparing to attack his prey. "The Europeans let the massacre happen in Srebrenica." His voice was trembling. "Whatever is said or whatever excuses and justifications invoked, it does not alter the fact that the Westerners have done nothing to prevent the drama. Isn't it strange that political and military analysts couldn't predict the disaster? The Serbs would never have allowed that the three enclaves Zepa, Srebrenica and Gorazde fell in Bosnian hands. Saying that the Western politicians and NATO *couldn't foresee that Mladic would kill 8000 to 10000 people* is bullshit. The Serbs had to occupy those enclaves before attending the peace negotiations. Today Zepa and Srebrenica are part of *Republica Srpska*."

"Is that the reason why you handle your cases so frantically? How much time did you spend on the Emma Badora case?"

Bram shrugged but didn't answer. Emma Badora had occupied him completely. As if he'd felt an innate need to protect her. She was so young, and yet she'd shown more courage than older victims. Emma had hated what she did, refusing to accept being called a whore.

"Your commitment is to your credit, Bram," Winston said with a shrug. "But what is your true motivation? Why help these young women and endanger your own life? What are you trying to prove here? That you're more courageous now than you were in 1995?"

Bram leaned forward, putting his clenched fists on the tabletop.

"Am I a humanitarian worker or not?" he whispered. "When I open a case, I want to handle it neatly. When a girl trusts us, she deserves our protection. It's our task to make sure that she can safely return to her family. All those so-called aid workers who have a good life here and who make a lot of money while the population is starving, make me throw up, Winston. That's why I avoid the company of those hypocrites."

Winston briefly bit his upper lip. "Watch out with hubris and enthusiasm. Don't start a crusade against injustice here, Bram." His tone was threatening. "Don't forget that all the information about the girls is confidential. You signed a contract, remember. We don't want to find any data in the media. Reporters always make a twisted story out of it. And we need donors."

Bram shook his head pityingly.

"I don't know what evil we could do with all those so-called confidential data," he countered vehemently. "Who is interested in the welfare of young prostitutes who are only called victims in the statistics?"

Winston laughed. "Sometimes, I get the impression that this job is an excuse to hide another motivation. You don't want to write a novel about *Last Hope*, do you?"

Bram shuddered, looking his chef straight in the eyes. "Who told you that I want to write a book?"

Winston smiled innocently. "Come down. I'm joking, man. The way you treat everything and put it on paper in such detail..." He paused for a few seconds. "You're not writing a book, are you?"

"Where would I get the time?" Bram was wondering if Winston knew more than he said. Nobody knew he was writing a book, except Edhem. Moreover, the book was about Mayke, not about *Last Hope*.

He's just guessing.

"Did your wife, uh Mayke, discover something here that you want to investigate further?"

Bram held out the fierce gaze.

"My wife wanted to interview Karadzic. But I don't think she caught a glimpse of him."

"I've always wondered if there wasn't more to that accident."

"She had bad luck. Her driver was an old rally driver who probably underestimated the risks on Bosnian roads."

Bram paused for an instant. "Winston, I've been thinking about Emma's transfer to the airport. Tim Watson takes her there. Do you mind if I accompany them?"

Winston pulled his forehead in wrinkles. "You've done your job. The judge sentenced the bar owner, and our best man will take Emma to the airport. Nobody knows about her departure."

"Still, I want to be there."

"No, you're not a field officer. Tomorrow you will close the case. Discussion closed."

Bram knew Winston enough to take his words seriously. He looked at his watch and stood up.

"Thanks for dinner," he said. "I still have something on my schedule."

Winston gave him a look of surprise and disbelief but said nothing. He guided Bram outside, and they said goodbye with a handshake. Walking to his car, Bram glanced over his shoulder, seeing Winston closing the door.

Back at the wheel, he turned the ignition key, and the engine burbled into life with a gentle hum. He made a turn backwards, then headed to the exit, watching through the side window. To his surprise, someone on the first floor was hiding behind a curtain. But not fast enough.

He had seen a young woman with long dark hair.

THREE

BROTHER LYNX SIGHED WHEN SHORTLY IN THE AFTERNOON, THE DISPLAY OF HIS cell phone lit up. He read the text without picking up the device.

Send Smaug to Tartarus.

The brotherhood had sent him to Sarajevo as a discrete protector of significant people, exceptionally not for killing enemies. He picked up his cell phone and started typing:

Request ACK.

Ten seconds later, a new message lit up.

Send Smaug to Tartarus, and resume your duties.

He got up, stuck his cell phone in his pocket, and gazed at his watch; he had still a lot of time for preparing himself, exactly knowing what to do. *Smaug the Dragon* had been spatting too much fire, and Brother Lynx had to take him out before he did irreversible damage. He got the feeling of being a dragon slayer, as described in Tolkien's The Hobbit.

Discretion above anything else, and there was no space for failures. Not even for the *Chosen*. Brother Lynx had been tasked as a *Protector*, not an *Executioner*. Just another few weeks more and his assignment would have come to an end. It was the first time he'd been in the same place for so long. He was protecting a *Chosen* and informing the Council whenever a problem was arising. A *Protector* remained invisible, and he only employed violence when his protégé was in immediate danger. An executioner, though, getting his assignment directly from the Council, travelled to the location under fictitious identity, eliminated the target, and left the country immediately with a new passport. A matter of erasing as many traces as possible. It was exceptional that the brotherhood had been changing the rules, proof of absolute trust. But after this task, he would reinstate his previous identity until his replacement: *Protector*. He was a rising star, but the way to the top was still long and dangerous.

He grabbed the briefcase standing next to his chair, put it on the desk, opened the leather flap, and removed the false bottom. Moments later, he was holding an almost brand-new Glock 17 in his hand. For the first time in his career, he would use a Glock. Perpetually changing the modus operandi, the instructors had taught him during the training sessions. It could be a matter of life and death.

After physically checking the weapon, he unclipped the magazine and moved the slide several times back and forth. An extra check because he cleaned his handgun every night. He took a silencer from the case and screwed it onto the barrel. Then he removed the cartridges from the magazine. After inspecting them, he loosened the bottom plate, checked the spring, replaced the base plate and the rounds, and pulled the slide back and forth. Then he put the weapon back into the case and attached the cover.

Although he was an expert on firearms, he rarely used them. They were traceable. But he couldn't take any chances against *Smaug*.

Never underestimate an opponent.

He was in no hurry, brewed some coffee, and drank two cups while considering various scripts. *Tartarus* would be the dragon's last destination. However, approaching the target was going to be the most difficult. He needed a good excuse to leave his actual job for a few hours.

Recalling the short text, he grinned, wondering if the *Messenger* was a fan of Tolkien and the Greek mythology. Computers were able to decipher most mathematical codes. That's why the brotherhood used *myths and sagas*. During his training, he'd read numerous literary works to understand the art of interpreting quotations. Each imported word in the message had to be meaningless for casual readers. Make sense of the text was not always easy, but all the brothers had university degrees and got specialised in various fields. They'd spent a lot of time encoding and decoding messages. Important information or assignments got hidden in an innocent sentence being an allusion to a literary work or a historical event. Worthless for criminal investigators, magistrates, and other enemies.

Tartarus belonged to Greek mythology, being a part of the Underworld. The shadowy realm where *Hades*, the brother of Zeus, was in charge. *Tartarus* was the place where the spirits of the deceased, having done horrible things in life, or challenged the gods, were severely punished.

Send Smaug to Tartarus.

The message was bringing death.

Monday, 7 October 2002

FOUR

GREG STONE REACHED THE HEIGHT OF RAPTURE. HIS WHOLE BODY WAS SHUDDERING as he exploded inside her hot, almost burning tightness, vaguely hearing her screaming of supreme delight.

"I love you, Daria," he murmured in her ear.

The waves of passion slowly faded away. Stone smiled happily, listening to his pounding heart and her panting against his cheek. He remained motionless with her arms wrapped around his neck. Until she gave him two lovingly taps on his back; becoming too heavy, he rolled beside her and sighed deeply.

Daria turned to face him and placed her arm over his bulging belly. *She's beautiful.* She had an oval face, long pitch-black hair, sensual mouth, slim figure, and small tits.

"What's the matter, sweetheart?" she murmured in his ear.

He turned his head. Her magical dark eyes were radiating a melancholy glow. "I love you," he whispered, kissing her fleetingly on her lips. As if he wanted to stifle the words he hadn't uttered since Lea's death.

She smiled. "Me too. But why make such a serious face?"

He didn't answer, closing his eyes, overwhelmed by memories.

Belgium, Bosnia 2000

They considered him as an activated time bomb, not knowing when it would go off. His colleagues feared that he would take every opportunity to reveal their dark secrets. They had wronged him and were searching for a way out to save their necks. Mercilessly he'd destroyed several marriages by his astute revelations at parties. They had nothing to stop him.

But since a few months, he was no longer enjoying this Monte Cristo staging. Therefore, he'd accepted a mission to Bosnia, although the end of his career was imminent. Everyone in the headquarters had breathed a sigh of relief, while he hoped to find inner peace in Bosnia at last.

And his plan seemed to succeed.

First, he served for eighteen months at the EUMM. Then he signed a contract with EuPol. After a few days working for the police lords, as he called those high-ranking policemen, he'd observed at the market in Ilidza a young woman being harassed by a vagrant. Without hesitation, he intervened, chasing the troublemaker, an unforeseen event with consequences. The woman, accompanied by a girlfriend, was surprised that he spoke Serbo-Croatian so fluently and to prove her gratitude, she offered him a coffee. He followed the two girls into a café, where they drank several cups of coffee.

Her name was Daria, she was thirty-two, married, had three children and worked as a pole dancer in a bar where she ended up against her will. Her girlfriend kept silent, giving him a suspicious look. Before both parted in the late afternoon, he and Daria exchanged their phone numbers.

During the next few days, they communicated through short messages until they gathered in the same café at the tram station in Ilidza. This time she told him how she'd ended up in Sarajevo through deception.

Two years earlier, she'd heard by chance that certain travel agencies were searching for workers to be employed abroad. Her sister disapproved, but she did not listen and visited one of those travel offices. A nice-looking fellow immediately proposed a job in Austria. She'd accepted. Everything was fake, but how could she have known? She'd been dreaming of earning enough money abroad to settle in the capital with her children.

But she didn't end up in Vienna, as was promised. In Belgrade, she'd to get a visa for Austria. Unfortunately, there was no employment left. However, they offered her an alternative place in Mitrovica.

There she arrived the next day with two other girls. She'd been fooled by women traffickers who used travel agencies as a cover-up.

After her revelation, he understood he was walking on a dangerous path. It would be better for him using his common sense and forgetting her as soon as possible. But the three-month jail after Lea's death had affected his brain. Everything he'd learned, everything he'd believed in, had been banished from his memory. Now he was living according to his proper principles and laws, only doing what he liked.

Fuck the world and its hypocrites. Dangers didn't frighten him any more. He sympathised with Daria and decided to help her. He freed her out of the bar and immediately got into trouble with Slavic women traffickers. These ruthless criminals demanded payment for Daria's debts, alleging she hadn't paid her rent. He asked the caller for a postponement. However, the barkeeper with whom he was negotiating on the phone refused his proposal, threatening to come over getting her. But Greg insisted and in turn threatened to involve IPTF if the bar owner did not accept his bid. His language skills and fearless approach made an impression. The mafioso probably didn't want to risk a storm, while Greg didn't want any problems with his employer. Greg was playing a dangerous game but had no choice. He worked for EuPol and risked his job, or his life if it went wrong.

They made a deal, and he settled Daria's debt. The young mother of three children was free again. But when he wanted to take her to the airport, she decided to live with him for a while until she felt mentally strong enough to face her family. She was ashamed and needed time to digest her unhappy adventure. Anyway, she was free and happy.

He agreed and brought her to his dwelling place.

First, they slept in separate rooms. However, something was growing between them, a mutual affection followed by infatuation and physical attraction. Whatever it was, two weeks later, they lay in each other's arms.

He was no longer alone. A new life could start.

Sarajevo, 7 October 2002

Daria will make me forget the past. But since she'd shown up in his life, he felt continually being watched. Last Friday morning in the cafeteria, he'd watched the political advisor Mycroft Follum talking to operations director Derek Fleming, who kept staring in his direction. However, this odd couple was only part of his concerns; he was primarily thinking of the newcomer who'd been walking around in the Glass Tower for a few months: a French police officer who'd emerged from nowhere. Nobody had introduced him to the other group members, and Greg still didn't know what his position was. At first, he'd paid little attention to the man. But coming home Thursday afternoon, he'd parked next to a vehicle in front of his dwelling place, discovering a man at the steering, turning his head away. But not fast enough.

Greg got suspicious as he, the next morning in the cafeteria, noticed that man talking to Deputy Commissioner Normand Montpetit. Both had been gazing in his direction. He hadn't yet informed Daria. But the longer he thought about that Frenchman, the more he rejected coincidence.

It has to do with Daria!

He'd been leaving his country to come to terms with himself, searching for a new challenge and getting Lea out of his mind. He also wanted to forget those who'd been disappointing him. The mission to the Balkans had to be his salvation.

But what about Daria? As he saved her from the clutches of women traffickers, he'd been convincing himself doing the right thing. Any normal human being would have done the same. They were friends, although no one around him believed that. Knights and damsels existed only in literature, not in real life.

But what he'd never thought possible, had happened. Cupid's arrows had touched his heart. An old gentleman in love with a twenty years younger girl, he was aware of the gossip about him. Sometimes conversations abruptly stopped when he joined a group. Nobody told him anything wrong. But their eyes spoke volumes.

Let them think what they want.

In the meantime, months had passed.

He took a deep breath, enjoying the slender fingers stroking his chest.

"Daria Bazila," he whispered, "what have we done?"

She chuckled, softly touching his growing penis. But his mind wasn't quite synchronised. A shiver flashed through his body when it occurred to him that sooner or later, she would go back to her country.

She gave him a fleeting kiss on his neck.

"What's going on, sweetheart?" she asked, while her caresses drove him crazy.

But he still resisted. "I'm thinking," he murmured. As Chief Information Technology at EuPol, he had unlimited access to the server. The suspicious British jerks weren't happy about it, fearing he could reveal some secrets. In any case, they wanted him replaced by one of their spooks. He groaned unconsciously when her fingers became very naughty.

"There's a new French officer at headquarters," he mumbled. "Weird bird. I saw him in front of the house last Thursday afternoon. When I got parked next to him, he turned his face away. I think he was spying on this house."

She withdrew her hand. The spell was gone, and Greg's proud pole relaxed as a deflated balloon. His body stiffening, he glanced up at her and spotted fear in her eyes.

"What does he look like?" Her voice trembled.

Greg described the Frenchman. "Do you know this man?"

She nodded almost imperceptibly. "I have a confession to make," she said softly.

He barely understood her.

"What the hell does that man want from you?" he asked with impatience.

"He has come to kill me!"

FIVE

THERE WERE FEW BIZARRE THINGS IN LIFE CHIEF INSPECTOR LAZAR MAGAS HADN'T seen before. Like the corpse lying on the bed in the hotel suite. A completely naked man sprawled on his back seemed to be sleeping, arms stretched out at a right angle. Lazar stood at the footboard, putting on a pair of rubber gloves while studying the sinister scene. Smooth shaved armpits and pubic area. On top of the joined legs, in the middle of two remarkably large testicles, lay a shrivelled penis like a dried-out earthworm. This stage looked familiar to Lazar, but he couldn't remember where he had seen something similar.

The blankets had fallen alongside the bed on the right, and the brown body was in stark contrast to it. The skin was getting pale, while the wide-open eyes staring at the ceiling, resembled glass marbles with a shattered core.

Lazar studied the face, eyes, arms, and legs.

"He must have been dead for hours," he said. "The rigor mortis is as good as finished." During the war, he had become acquainted with the most horrible killings, learning how to get someone talking.

'It's part of any war,' he always said. *'The human has an incredible imagination to express his cruelty.'*

After Tito died in 1980, Lazar and his older brother emigrated to America at their parent's insistence. There he obtained a university degree and applied to the Federal Bureau of Investigation, becoming a Special Agent.

His parents had been right. Tito's death marked the end of Yugoslavia because there was no worthy successor. Shortly before his death, Tito ordered the killing of his successor, the man he'd appointed himself. After Tito's death, a struggle for power started between the leaders of the six constituent republics. Slovenia declared itself independent, and the war with Serbia was short-lived because there were only a few Serbs living. But when Croatia also declared its independence, Milosevic had no choice but to go down the path of war: too many Serbs lived there. In Bosnia, the Muslim fundamentalist Izetbegovic saw his chance, and after a referendum, he declared Bosnia independent. Radovan Karadzic, the leader of the Bosnian Serbs, refused a Muslim government and declared war. The next day, the siege of Sarajevo began.

Lazar and his brother returned to Bosnia to support their parents. But they arrived too late and were told that the neighbours had killed them. Both joined a particular unit of the Bosnian army. Shortly after, Lazar's brother was shot by a sniper on the sniper's alley; after which Lazar became a ruthless adversary of the Serbs. He interrogated and killed numerous četniks. A bloody period that dragged on for three years, during which he learned more about death than when he served in the FBI.

Fortunately, the international community is not aware of the secrets I'm carrying with me. The painful memories blurred when Senad, his chubby assistant and best friend, joined him. A loyal bachelor, bon vivant and joker with an oval face, thick grey hair, round cheeks, big blue eyes, and thick lips.

Senad frowned. "I have never seen anyone die like this before."

"No one dies like that."

On his first glance at the naked body, he'd realised that it wasn't a natural death. Therefore, he'd asked the police doctor and the technicians to wait until he'd examined the body by himself. His gaze wandered slowly over the body while he walked to the headboard. He bent over the head and scrutinised the eyes, the nose, the face, and the neck. There were no discolourations of lips or skin indicating neither poison nor strangulation marks. Even the balding head showed no signs of violence.

His eyes wandered over the empty bedside table. He squatted, tilted his head over the surface, and narrowed his eyes.

"There were two glasses here recently," he said. He glanced through the room, and his face brightened. Then he waved to the bar cabinet.

"Get those glasses to the lab," Lazar called out sharply, heading back to the body.

"Not so easy to kill without leaving traces," he said with vigour while bowing over the bed until his eyes were above the pale face. "And so fast that the victim didn't have the time to move," he continued, being aware that the technicians were impatiently waiting for the end of his inspection. Lazar scrutinised every inch of the corps.

"Given the position of the body," he explained, "I assume the man has been sexually active as his partner killed him. However, the expression in his eyes suggests that in a split second, he has understood what was going on. Could it be either a man or a woman? And how did he or she kill him?"

No one answered.

Not that Lazar had expected they would. He grinned, bowed again, looked in the left ear, whistled between his teeth, and turned around to face analyst Ferid Munic. "Look for sperm and hairs, including pubic hairs. The visitor may have drunk something from one of those glasses."

Ferid was medium-sized, a hundred kilos heavy, but he still moved quite fast. Lazar considered him to be the only expert who performed his task with enthusiasm. Being a renowned chemist in the past, he was now working as a forensic analyst at the National Forensic Institute in Sarajevo, leading a small group of forensic researchers with a steady hand and professional knowledge. Despite the lack of resources, he achieved exceptional results with his fingerprint specialist, photographer, and three inexperienced forensic detectives.

Lazar waved to the house bar. "Look around and take any drinking glass with or without liquid, any bottle or whatever else, getting it to the lab to have it checked for fingerprints. Also, look for fingerprints on the door of the bar cabinet."

The obese trace analyst gestured to one of his men to search the suite.

Lazar examined the stiff cold legs, but couldn't move them. He tilted his head and discovered purple spots on the buttocks. When pushing on it, the skin turned white. With a satisfied smile, he looked at the technicians.

"The rigor mortis is almost complete," he said, "so I guess death occurred around 1 a.m. On the other hand, the livor mortis is not yet complete, but I think that the discolouration will be complete between 9 a.m., and 10 a.m. There are only spots on the back and the buttocks. The murder is at least ten hours old, and the body hadn't been moved in the last eight hours."

The listeners looked at each other, and he enjoyed their confused facial expression. Those forensic technicians had probably expected to get that analysis from the coroner or the police doctor.

He paced to the living room area and stopped beside a chair. A white robe lay over the backrest, which he moved to the underwear and double-folded pants on the other armchair. Then he pulled a wallet out the pocket of the jacket lying on the first chair and opened it.

"By the beard of the Prophet," he murmured, quickly putting the wallet back. *A member of the Dutch embassy. Damned, the military attaché.* There was little time left. The Chief of Police would take the investigation away from him as soon as the embassy was informed. Then the EuPol would take over.

"Get those clothes to the lab," he called out. "Put them immediately in a plastic bag. Hurry up."

The trace analyst, standing at the house bar, nodded startled.

Milan Delic was still busy, pulling on his white uniform when Lazar grabbed him by the arm, taking him to the bedside. The police doctor had a round face with bulging cheeks, thick tip brows, and a red nose.

"I'm pretty sure our perpetrator is a woman," he told Milan. "While playing the dominant role, she had him extend his arms and close his eyes. Then she did some exciting things to distract him while riding him. Maybe she left some traces. Concentrate your research on the pubic area. Have the body removed and do an external and internal autopsy immediately. She might have put something in his drink."

"Did she do that?" The man rubbed his nose.

"That's up to you to find out." Lazar beckoned his assistant to join him and left the suite. In the corridor, he bumped into two police officers keeping watch.

"Who found the body?" he asked the first one.

"The chambermaid. She's downstairs in the lobby," the man replied.

The drawn drapes on the window and the sparsely lit lobby created a mysterious atmosphere while the smell of fresh coffee betrayed the presence of some staff personal. On the other side of the reception hall, against the farthest wall, sat a middle-aged woman; slim, small and not particularly handsome. She was wearing a light-brown hotel dress, of which the edge came halfway up her thighs. She held her knees together, and her hands folded in her lap. In front of her was a cup of coffee. She didn't look particularly affected. *She has seen corpses before.*

"Chief inspector Magas," he said, "and Inspector Mujdza. You're the maid?"

She nodded.

Lazar and Senad sat down, one on each side.

"You have found the body?" ~~asked~~ Lazar asked with a faint smile.

"Yes, I did."

"Was the door unlocked?"

"It was locked."

"But you walked into the room anyway?"

"Only after I've got knocked three times. Assuming that the man was gone, I went inside using my card. What a shock. At first, I thought he was asleep. But, uh, who sleeps like that now? I've got informed the desk immediately." She didn't seem impressed at all. Certainly not shocked.

Lazar leaned in. "Do you know if the man had got visitors?"

"No, sir."

"Did you touch anything in the room?"

"I didn't touch anything, sir. Uh, just the door."

"Well, I may have to ask you a few more questions later."

Lazar got up and walked to the reception desk where a young blonde receptionist had a cup of coffee, a beautiful woman with lush shapes hidden by a two-piece hotel uniform and a buttoned-up jacket. Long hairs hung along her face. *Her lips are too red.*

Lazar gave her a stiff smile. "What can you tell me about the victim?"

Senad joined him.

The receptionist opened the guest register on her computer monitor. "Cees Visser," she said formally. "He's been living here for eight months. Every day after breakfast, a driver comes picking him up and brings him back in the evening. Sometimes, before joining his room, he has a drink in the bar."

"A man without problems?"

She smiled vaguely. "Yes, a quiet man, but also a whore lover. Twice a week, he orders a young, very young prostitute. Some of them may still have gone to primary school."

"Where do you order these girls?"

"We don't order; he does," she retorted. "Probably in the *Florida Bar*. We don't care what visitors are doing in their rooms. Mr Visser pays an extra fee for our discretion and what happens beyond closed doors is none of our business as long as they don't bother other guests."

"I suppose your other guests aren't blind and see what kind of women are walking through the lobby, are they? Ought to provide bad publicity."

She laughed. "A supervisor guides the girl to the client, and he also comes picking her up when the client has finished, very discreetly."

"Are you sure the girls were from the *Florida Bar*?"

"The *Florida Bar* is the only luxury brothel, where wealthy Europeans are the best customers. The owners get protection, and who'll risk trouble with the mafia? Chief Inspector Magas, despite the prostitution ban, not only do the bar owners make a lot of money out of it but also do the city administration. So why shouldn't we also earn something by glancing at the other way if internationals break the rules? These guys are untouchable anyway." *She expresses herself very carefully.*

Lazar knew that the *Florida Bar* got protection, which wasn't his problem, but that of Migration and the Special Brigade that fought the Organized Crime. He let his eyes wander through the hall toward the elevators, which were out of sight from the reception desk. A purser in uniform was standing near the door in the entrance hall. But nowhere a lift boy.

He turned to face the young woman again. "Thus, anyone might go unseen to the rooms?" His features became agitated.

She shrugged. "Customers don't like registering their visitors."

The customer's requirements are more important than security. "Did the guest in 308 receive a visit last night?"

"Yes, I saw the usual supervisor with a young girl. Must have been around 11 p.m."

"And did you see that man when he came back picking up the girl?"

"I did, around 1 a.m. But that man wasn't alone."

"What do you mean by *not alone*?"

"He was with a friend."

"Did you recognise that friend?"

"I didn't." While walking toward the elevators, both were engaged in an intense conversation.

"Can you describe that friend?"

"Uh... I didn't get a perfect look at him. He walked with bowed head and wore a cap or something. He stepped on the other side of the supervisor."

"Did you see that...whore when she left the hotel?"

"I did, and I recognised her. It wasn't the first time she came here."

"Did she behave as usual?"

"What do you mean?"

"Did she seem to be in a hurry? Was she looking around?"

"She was talking to her companion, and their behaviour seemed normal to me."

"Was that second fellow there too?"

"I only peered in their direction for a short time," she answered in a defensive tone. "They were among a group of foreigners. I only paid attention to that whore and her supervisor, not to the others. I'm not that curious."

"Okay, I'd like to believe that. Perhaps you know that girl's name?"

She shook her head. "She's young, I guess about twenty-five. I reckon she came here for the fifth time. Before, there was another one who came here twice a week."

Lazar cursed internally. The killer might be a young prostitute, her supervisor, or someone else. Or that second person? He had to wait for the autopsy, which could reveal the exact time the attaché had died. If the murder happened after 1 a.m., he could cancel the prostitute and her companion as possible perpetrators.

Lazar gave her a stern look. "What did the supervisor look like?"

Suddenly she didn't seem so confident any more. She'd spoken about the usual supervisor, so she had seen him several times already.

"He is big, slim but muscular and has a short military haircut."
"Round or long face?"
"Angular."
"Colour of his hair?"
"Uh, dark brown."
"Eyes?"
"I don't know, dark, I guess."
"Curved, straight, thick nose?"
"Straight nose."
"Special features? Scars? Beard?"
She contemplated for a few seconds. "Smoothly shaved, no scars." She answered curtly.
Lazar looked at Senad, who was writing everything down.
"I think that's it for the time being," Lazar said with a shrug, turning to the woman. "Is there anything else we need to know?"
She shook her head without saying anything.
"Thank you for your cooperation, madam. But maybe I'll have to ask you a few more questions later. Give your name and address to my colleague."
Lazar nodded to Senad and walked to the exit.

SIX

BRAM RUYTER TOOK A DEEP BREATH OF RELIEF; EMMA BADORA WAS SAFE. A HEAVY burden lifted from his soul. So much could have gone wrong. His resolve had paid off; Emma sat safely in the plane, flying back to her family. Although he'd been working with *Last Hope* for months, this was his first great success.

Meanwhile, he had interviewed dozens of girls, but none of them had been willing to testify so far. After Kathryn Bolkovac's disappearance in 2001, the hope of so many women forced into prostitution had evaporated into smoke. But despite Bolkovac's revelations to the press, nothing had changed. Women traffickers, corrupt police officers and UN officials had become even more cautious.

But Emma had trusted him, only willing to talk to him. Was it because of her youthfulness or her almost childish naivety? Or had she believed international justice?

He recalled the events that had brought him into this small office. But although Mayke's death had caused his return to Bosnia, Jasmina was still haunting through his mind. Even more, since he had taken care of Emma.

Srebrenica, 11 July 1995.

Madness. Jasmina was the sun in his life he'd been looking for so long. *Fuck the war, Mladic, and his troops which are playing cat and mouse with UNPROFOR and the Dutch Battalion.* Only his foolish commander believed they were safe in Srebrenica.

Jasmina grabbed his hand, pulling him insistently into the obscurity of the shed. *'Enjoy, tomorrow it might be over,'* murmured an inner voice. Bram doubted the future of those besieged Muslim communities. But at that instant, he contemplated what he was doing while Mladic prepared his final offensive. *Thom is a coward.* He despised his commander. Was that the result of stress? *How long can I still conceal our relationship?* Several colleagues were already gossiping, and he wondered if the commander knew. *If he finds out,* he did not dare thinking any further. This job was all he had, why play with fire?

Jasmina seemed impatient. She knew where to go and took him to the farthest corner where the emergency rations were stacked. Their love corner, with Wim's complicity; the non-commissioned logistics officer was a close friend. The heavy boxes stacked to 2,5 m high walls bounded an empty place. In the middle of the front wall was a column of empty boxes attached with adhesive tape, melting together with the cartons, producing easy access to the interior space.

"Sesame, open you." He pushed the improvised door forward, and they quickly slipped in. Then he shoves the pile back into place. They stood a bit uneasily in the two by two spaces, with several filled up cartons settled as a couch against the farthest wall. Not very comfortable but better than nothing. Bram turned to face Jasmina who wore sports shoes, faded jeans, and a light woollen jacket with a hood. He pointed to the couch, and they sat down next to each other.

Looking into her amber eyes, Bram grabbed her finely cut face in both hands and under her long black hair, the remaining piece of the earlobe, painful memory from her childhood of an aggressive dog that almost had bitten her to death.

His hands softly brought her face toward him, and she kissed him passionately as if she wanted to say goodbye, closing her eyes.

'Stop it,' screamed some voice deep in his mind. Hopeless love could lead to complications. However, his passion was more substantial than his fear of getting discovered.

His heart was pounding like a drum. "Jasmina," he whispered.

"Volim te," she returned between two kisses. "I love you."

"Volim te, Jasmina," he gasped in a language he barely understood. He was in love as he'd never been before. That's why he feared for the future. How would he ever find her after the war?

"Tomorrow I may be dead," she whispered in his ear with a shaky voice, giving him a look of despair while her body was fiercely trembling.

Is she looking for an apology for the inevitable?

There were regularly grenade impacts in the distance. Nothing new, Ratko Mladic bombed the enclave daily. Bram wondered when finally a grenade would fall on their camp. Only Thom Karremans refused to believe that Mladic was preparing an attack, refuting the possibility that the arrogant Serb general was testing whether or not NATO would carry out air raids if he started an offensive against the Muslims. Thom was so concerned with his proper safety that he kept blind to reality.

"Let's not waste any time," she panted in his ear. "I don't want to die without knowing what could have been between us."

She stood up and got rid of her jeans and grey panties. They had been here several times without consuming their relationship, just half-dressed kissing and caressing, satisfying each other with hands and tongue, afraid to be discovered. He left it to her whether to continue or not.

But her body language didn't cheat, while he still hesitated.

"*Bram, jebi me*," she panted. "Fuck me."

He wasn't used to that kind of language from her. Holy shit, he didn't have any condoms. He could never have imagined that he would need those things in a war zone during a mission. His blood was bubbling. *Fuck the rules*. He got up, loosened his belt, lowered his pants and underpants onto his desert boots. He turned around and grabbed one of the full cartons, sliding it to the middle of the space. He had never undressed so quickly. The height was right, and he sat down.

She smiled seductively and spread her legs over his thighs. His hard penis rubbed her dark pubic hair, while their open mouths found each other in an endless wet kiss. He had some difficulty manoeuvring his belly in the right position. She sighed when he finally entered her, pushing her pubic mound forward while her hands swirled through his hair. Her lips kissed every place on his face. He couldn't understand the words she whispered, but they sounded like heavenly music.

He moved slowly, wanted this moment last forever, while outside the shooting continued. The bombs did not fall far from the camp. *Fuck the war*.

Jasmina was helping him to forget the war for a few minutes. She clasped his body like a drowning person desperately holding a piece of the ship's wood. Her contracting muscles made him crazy.

"Volim te," he called out, pouring his seed into her.

"Volim te," she whispered, just before her belly began to shake. He covered her mouth with his trembling lips to mute her screaming.

The interval between the grenade impacts was decreasing.

Sarajevo,7 October 2002

Bram blinked his eyes, looking around in confusion. A screeching tone tried to get him back into the present, blowing the disturbing pictures out of his mind. The phone was ringing.

He picked up the receiver.

"Winston," he heard. "Come over immediately with the Badora file."

"What's wrong with her?"

"Bring her file, and then we'll talk about it." Winston hung up.

Bram shook his head, putting down the receiver. Then he rubbed the sweat off his forehead with his arm. After a short moment of hesitation, he took a file out of the top drawer and opened it.

Emma Badora was a nineteen-year-old girl from Romania who'd found a safe place at *Last Hope* and who was flying back to her country. Why did Winston want that file? Wasn't the case closed?

Did I make a mistake?

Emma got lured to Belgrade, where criminals were waiting for her. They took her against her will by car to Sarajevo and sold her to a bar owner.

A new life into prostitution began. But she didn't give up, waiting for an opportunity to escape. One day, the local police raided the bar under the supervision of IPTF, and international observers took her to the regional office in Ilidza for interrogation, where she immediately requested for help. A classic case. But Emma wasn't an ordinary girl. She wished to fight those criminals, and she agreed to testify against the bar owner. In return, Emma requested her repatriation. The International Organisation for Migration had promised protection, ensuring that she would be safe and go home after the trial.

The local police arrested the brothel owner. Emma kept living in a shelter until the trial two weeks ago. She testified in court, and the accused got convicted of five years in prison. IOM kept its promises, and she was now flying back.

Case closed.

Bram slammed the folder, got up, and stepped into the corridor smashing the door. Winston's tone was worrying him. He walked down the hallway, entered the office without knocking, and stopped abruptly in the middle of the room. His boss sat at his desk, facing four uniformed men: two IPTF observers and two local police officers. The door to the adjoining secretariat was open, and he nodded briefly to secretary Peter Camden sitting behind his desk. A man with opulent black hairdo, neutral Caucasian features with dark eyes, wearing dark-framed spectacles. An inconspicuous, quiet person, mastering six languages. The man nodded and returned to his activity.

"There you are at last," Winston's voice sounded displeased. "I introduce Captain Alistair Cook and Lieutenant Elmer Drake from IPTF." Then he pointed to the local police officers. "Inspectors Hassan Krisnic and Slobodan Bratovic from the Immigration Police."

Bram shook their hand and threw the file on the desk.

"I'm Bram Ruyter," he said, glancing shortly toward his boss.

"Bram," Winston hissed, "I reckon you have nothing to do with this affair, but I have to ask you anyway. Have you outside these walls been telling anyone about Emma Badora's return?"

Bram turned to face his boss with growing anger.

"Are you nuts?"

Winston pulled up an eyebrow. "Yes or no?" he snarled.

"No, of course not! Why ask?"

"Bram, you've been here for several months, doing a good job. But any man might feel the need to talk about his work," answered Winston in a soothing tone. "Didn't tell your friend?"

"My name is Bram, not everybody. And leave my friend out of this. I'm not a rookie."

That starts badly.

Winston's eyes were glistening as cat eyes in the dark. It seemed apparent he was considering Bram's reaction inappropriate.

Bram shook his head, gazing furiously at his boss like a captured lynx preparing to attack its prey. Although he usually got on well with the elderly man, he never felt very comfortable in his presence. '*Winston's smile is hiding something mysterious*,' Bram didn't stop telling himself. However, he didn't find out yet what it was. Last day's invitation had made him feel uncomfortable. Something was going on, but what?

"Emma Badora has vanished," Winston exclaimed. "And with her Tim."

Bram shuddered; he had recruited Tim Watson, an ex-SAS.

"Did Watson run off with her?" His attempt to be funny failed, he could read from their features. *Damned, do they believe I know where Tim and the girl are?*

Seconds ticked away, and the excitement was palpable. Finally, Winston cleared his throat.

"Tim had to take her to the gathering point," he said, pointing at the two police officers. "These people had to put that girl discreetly on a direct flight to Bucharest. But Tim did not appear at the rendezvous. I've checked, Tim and the woman left the safe house as planned."

The security man in the safe house had confirmed Tim's and Emma's departure to the airport by e-mail. Bram was wondering if Winston would blame him and he reacted irritated.

"Don't blame me, Winston," he called out. "Tim is the field officer, not me. Didn't you clarify that yesterday?" A good thing he'd asked Winston to accompany Tim. '*You're not a field officer*,' Winston had repeatedly retorted.

Captain Alistair Cook began to lose his patience and his gaze dimmed. "Where's that woman now?" he yelled at Winston.

Winston shrugged. "The brothel owner, Miomir Milic, has been convicted of five years of imprisonment. It's naive to think that he'll leave the witness unpunished."

Bram had never seen his boss so cynically. Could Tim have anything to do with Emma's disappearance? He recalled that Winston had introduced this SAS veteran to him. However, Bram had eventually recruited him and would be held responsible.

Emma Badora had always expressed her fear, claiming that she would never get on the plane in one piece. Perhaps she'd been using her charms to convince Tim taking her to Romania by car. Tim spoke Serbo-Croatian well.

Bram stared at the officer. "Captain Crook..."

"Cook is my name," interrupted the man with a violent hand movement. "Without R, sir." He looked like a heavyset Maori rugby player. But that didn't intimidate Bram at all.

"All right, Captain Cook without R. I think that concludes your task. We'll set up an internal investigation, and you'll get a report from me. Please, if you'll excuse me now. Or does anyone have anything useful to ask me?" He looked fleetingly at the uniformed men one by one, give his boss a last dark look, turned around and hurried back to his office, slamming the door shut behind him.

There he sat down in his chair, sniffing through his computer folders, wondering why he should have handed over Badora's file. Usually, he kept every folder in his built-in safe after making a digital copy of it. The content of Emma's record was stuck in his head. He still felt responsible for her. This affair awakened memories. *Holy shit, what has happened?*

He didn't find an answer in Emma's file. The young Romanian had only accused the brothel owner. Nowhere had she named corrupted international police observers. After her testimony, Tim had taken her back to the safe house where she stayed until the afternoon.

He found a short notice about her departure.

Tim Watson will take Emma Badora to the airport at 0200 p.m. and entrust her to two IPTF observers.

In the column next to it was written:

Third parking space in front of the main entrance.

She should have landed in Bucharest by now. He shut the file and leaned back, closing eyes. But that short rest got abruptly interrupted by an open swinging door. Disturbed, he opened his eyes again and saw his boss stepping furiously to his desk.

"Tim is in the German field hospital," Winston said.

"What?" yelled Bram in horror. "Did he have an accident? Where's

Emma?"

"An ambush. Criminals have stopped Tim's car. When he got out, they knocked him unconscious. Tim doesn't know how long he'd been unconscious, but he managed to get back into his car and to drive to the hospital, where he collapsed in the reception hall."

"How bad is he?"

"He'll have to stay overnight. But apart from a slight head concussion, some blue spots, and a bruised rib, he'll be fine. I've already spoken to him by phone."

"What has he been telling you?"

"Little. It all happened very quickly, Tim said. A passing car has forced him to stop. When he'd stepped out, a few men from a second car attacked him. He saw these guys only briefly. Slavic appearance, locals. They beat him up before he understood what was happening."

"Was it that easy? SAS? According to your explanation, Tim has been acting like a rookie. That smells like incompetence."

"It was a routine job, Bram. Nobody could have foreseen that the convicted bar owner would react so quickly. Very professionally done. Tim didn't stand a chance."

"And no trace of Emma?" Bram's fist hit hard on the tabletop. "I should have accompanied her. We'll never see her again."

Winston narrowed his eyes. "And what would you have done to avoid the abduction?"

"Two of us would have had a chance. I am surprised that Tim was so easy to trap. He's supposed to be an experienced SAS soldier," retorted Bram.

"Those guys aren't amateurs either."

"We have promised Emma that we would get her on the plane safely. I suggest we check out the nightclubs in Ilidza as soon as possible."

Winston grimaced, bowing toward Bram.

"Stop," he yelled. "It's a simple whore, not the Queen of England."

"I thought those women are victims," returned Bram with a furious air. "Emma had been taken to the *Florida Bar* against her will." He felt an almost uncontrollable desire to jab his boss, but he held back. His temperamental character had already got him into trouble.

"Let's forget about this case," Winston groaned. "This Emma has never been here!"

"You're not serious, are you?"

Winston gave him a look of anger.

"I'm very serious, Bram," he said fiercely. "If this is going public, we might close our shop. The board of directors will never accept that we're not able to protect the girls IOM brings to us. Fortunately, their office commander agrees to forget about this matter. We almost lost one of our men. We were lucky. Tim was lucky. Let's stick to that. Bad luck for that girl. From now on, we'll have to be more careful. We learned our lesson, don't you think?"

"I got it," Bram growled.

Go to hell. He had come to Bosnia to save the girls forced into prostitution. All illusion. Nobody cared about those women. He had a well-paid job that without human trafficking would have no reason to exist. Aid organisations are earning from human misery.

'*Why should we solve problems and lose the well-paid job?*' said many of his colleagues. Their primary motivation was a generous monthly salary.

Bram stood up. "Tomorrow I'll take a day off. I have to get a clear head again."

Winston frowned. "Well, if a day-off can bring you to better thoughts. Take a few days if you have to."

"Why not? I'll take off right away until Monday."

Winston nodded, turned around, and stepped to the door. Something else must have crossed his mind because he turned around abruptly.

"But don't forget, Bram, Emma has never been here," he said.

SEVEN

LAZAR MAGAS MISTRUSTED EGZON SUBIC, POLICE CHIEF OF CANTON 9. HE SUSPECTED Egzon that he knew something about his past. On every morning meeting, after repeating the need for exemplary behaviour, Egzon grinned at him, a creepy, confrontational smile. A silent warning?

What does he know? When is he going to use it against me?

Every invitation to Egzon's office sent an adrenaline rush through his veins. Today was no different. Although the call wasn't a surprise, it came sooner as he'd expected. A shiver went through his body as he recalled his police debut. He'd never thought his first act was going to be an illegal one. Did Egzon know about it?

Coincidence?

Fate?

No one had come out of the war innocently. Neither *Good* nor *Bad* exist. Killing either for pleasure, a principle or an idea, what was the difference? Any murder remains murder, regardless of motive or circumstance.

Despite too many police officers, he'd applied for the Homicide Department. No problem with his FBI experience, because there was a desperate lack of competent inspectors. In no time, he'd risen to the rank of chief inspector. Political friends in the right place, especially at the Ministry of Home Affairs, had been an excellent help. The war had wiped out his family and brothers in arms, and he hoped through his new job to be able to bury the past. However, some dead faces out of the past were still haunting him in his nightmares.

Shedding these dark thoughts away, he stepped into the corridor, and his footsteps sounded hollow on the grey tiles belonging to another era. In his mind, the chief of police was a parasite with mafia connections. EuPol was watching him, and Special Envoy of the Secretary-General Klein had told EuPol Commissioner Ivar Ragnarsson that he wanted Egzon Subic out of the police. Many colleagues wondered how Egzon had passed the screening process.

After the war, the police force had quickly increased up to 45,000 men, which was one police officer for seventy-five inhabitants. Moreover, the police had become mono-ethnic and war criminals in particular thought they had found a safe refuge there. For that reason, the Bonn-Petersburg Agreement provided for a European-style police force, a contingent which enjoys the confidence of the population. The government decreased the number of police officers down to eleven thousand, and each new police officer had to pass a thorough screening process before being registered. This check was one of the IPTF's tasks. But its practical implementation so far proved to be a failure. Numerous war criminals still were part of the police force.

When Lazar joined the police, there was no database of personnel. Corruption was rampant at all levels, while many police chiefs feared they might get arrested. Politicians exerted considerable influence on police and magistrates. Besides, corruption in the IPTF ranks was one of the reasons why the International Police Force made little progress with its reorganisation plan. The Americans were in charge, while a private organisation under contract from the US Department of State provided the necessary policemen. Meanwhile, Lazar knew that a large number of police observers kept a double agenda, that this group did much more than observe and that spies and Special Forces were carrying out secret missions. It was no secret that SAS was chasing war criminals, especially looking for Karadzic and Mladic.

Although the international police observers had to implement the police reform enshrined in the Dayton Peace Agreements, the local police were still as corrupt as they used to be and still dependent on political power. The citizens lost their trust in the police, while the promises of EuPol only made them sceptically grin.

Lazar knew the ropes. *'Don't wake up sleeping dogs,'* he said to himself. Live and let live; he was an unwritten leaf yet, and he wanted to keep it that way. *Let the past rest, avoid that The Hague get interested in my acts of war.* Interrogations and executions were a thing of the past. But the International Court of Justice remained a threat.

Fuck the western hypocrites.

Despite all the violence he'd dealt with during the war, he had never lost his sense of justice. According to him, the judge did not have to punish the thief stealing bread to satisfy his hunger, but the politician provoking the people to steal to fill its stomach. In his mind, he pointed toward all the corrupt authorities who were more interested in their power and dark side activities than in the well-being of the population.

In a corrupt system, being honest could be dangerous. However, Lazar was smart enough to leave his corrupt colleagues alone as long as they stayed out of his way. Nevertheless, he was afraid of being shot one night in front of his house.

EuPol Commissioner Ivar Ragnarsson, nicknamed the Viking, had already tried several times to recruit him, but each time he'd been refusing. He didn't like to spy on his people by order of the Western European Police Lords, as he called the European police observers.

He knocked on the door and went inside. Egzon was sitting behind his desk, writing in a file. He was a heavyset, broad-shouldered man with an angular pockmarked face, stinging eyes, wild haircut and striking black mujahidin beard, a terrifying appearance.

He didn't glance up. "Sit down," he said. "What have you discovered in the hotel-murder case?"

"I'm waiting for the result of the autopsy,"

Egzon now straightened his back and carefully laid down his writing pen as if it were a hand grenade igniter. His dark eyes coldly gazed toward his subordinate.

But Lazar didn't tear his eyes away.

"I suppose you know that a military attaché has diplomatic status?" Egzon called out.

"You can't be serious," replied Lazar astonished.

Egzon kept fiercely staring at him.

Lazar shrugged. "I didn't know. I immediately ordered an autopsy. As I always do."

"Whether you knew it or not, you aren't involved any more. At the request of the Dutch embassy, EuPol took the body. Tomorrow a Dutch medical team will fly over. After that, the corpse flies to Schiphol in a zinc box. End of story."

"I made the first observations. It's about murder."

"Lazar, EuPol is now in charge. However, the corpse remains in the forensic institute, but we leave it untouched. What did you discover?"

"Too early." Lazar wondered if the pathologist anatomist had already performed the external autopsy.

"What did the hotel staff have to say?" asked Egzon impatiently.

"Nothing!" Giving in meant writing a report. Probably a "heart attack" would be registered as the cause of death. After what he'd discovered about the victim, the Dutch Ministry of Foreign Affairs would benefit significantly from closing the investigation as soon as possible.

Egzon leaned over the desk. "I want your report on the Hotic case today," he said in a threatening tone. "Did I make myself clear?"

Lazar nodded.

"You can go."

Lazar stepped into the corridor, slamming the door shut.

The Hotic case must distract me.

He hated Egzon as he hated unresolved cases. And the attaché affair was an unusual murder case which has aroused his curiosity.

And Egzon can go to hell.

EIGHT

NORMAND MONTPETIT STEPPED INTO THE HALLWAY, FEARING THAT THE NOISE OF the growling dog might disturb the neighbourhood's peacefulness. He already had ignored the electronically generated growling twice, not being in the mood to receive visitors at this late evening.

But the late visitor persistently kept pressing the button, causing every time a terrifying growling that echoed through the bare corridor. On his way toward the door, he muttered a series of obscene French words getting lost in the noise made by those terrifying watchdogs. At the front door, he turned them off, opened the door and took a hard stance. But beneath the stairs, he recognised a falsely grinning little man with a sullen face, millimetre black hair, big eyes, elephant ears and a crooked pointed nose, wearing a dark jacket. Someone you didn't waste a second glance on when you passed him on the street. A guy for whom Normand felt little sympathy. However, he feared that powerful EuPol politician.

"Is it that urgent?" he snarled at Mycroft Follum.

Follum showed him a faint smile. "Sorry for this late disturbance."

Normand didn't believe a word of it but stepped aside.

"Did you tie up the dogs?" asked Mycroft with an ironic tone.

"The dogs are locked up," confirmed Normand coldly, allowing Mycroft pass by. "What gives me the honour of seeing you here at this late hour?"

Montpetit distrusted this slimy Briton as he distrusted all Britons. The islanders made no secret of the fact that they called the EU mission a waste of money and time. However, they were claiming as many vital positions for themselves as possible. Some called Mycroft *The Hobbit*, and it remained a mystery to him wherefrom they got this strange name. *Must be typically British*, he thought. Once he asked a colleague what *Hobbit* meant, and got only a broad grin in response.

Normand guided his late visitor to a soberly furnished living room, waved to one of the two fabric armchairs and sat down opposite him. Why offer Mycroft a drink if his red nose showed that he'd already consumed a considerable amount of alcohol?

"It's about your career," Mycroft announced some bad news.

"My career?" Mycroft crossed his right leg over his left, leaning back.

"Greg Stone may break your career," answered *The Hobbit* with a laugh.

Normand raised his eyebrows. Greg was a Belgian IT expert who enjoyed high prestige at the EUMM, where he'd served for a year and a half. After a successful reform, the EuPol coordinator had offered him a civilian contract. In the meantime, the IT expert had proved that he was worthy of the trust placed in him. Without him, EuPol would never have met its deadline.

Montpetit grinned. "What bothers you about Greg Stone?"

"He lives with a Moldavian whore."

Normand shrugged. '*Il est libre de baiser avec qui il veut.*' His English was terrible, and whenever he couldn't find the right sentence or word, he started speaking in French.

"That whore has been living with him for months," Mycroft yelled.

Montpetit gave him a look of cold disdain. "His private life is none of my business." His neurons were working at full speed. Mycroft hadn't come to bother him without reason.

"Indeed, it's your business. However, that whore illegally stays in the country," grunted Mycroft with a fake grin.

"How do you know?"

"Stone doesn't even bother to be discreet. At every official party, he parades with her like a peacock. Recently he attended a party at the EUMM building. I'm surprised you didn't see her there."

"Is there Moldavian written on her forehead?"

Mycroft snorted noisily "I don't know how the Commissioner will react if he finds out. But I'm afraid he'll not be happy."

"How do you know she's illegally staying in the country?" Although Normand hated people who were scrambling with whores, he didn't want to judge too hastily. Greg was a nice guy, and no law forbade him from living with a girlfriend. He was not the only foreigner doing so.

Mycroft features got angry. "Her passport is no longer valid. We've checked with the Immigration Department. In February, after IPTF did a raid in the *Florida Bar*, she was seized and interrogated by one of our police observers. Her visa was going to expire in April."

"Then why was she released?"

Mycroft grinned like a hungry hyena. "At that time, her visa was still valid for two weeks. But now she's illegally staying in the country. The police would already have arrested her, but the Immigration Police didn't find her in the *Florida Bar*. They are not yet aware that she lives with one of our employees. However, I won't be able to keep that information secret for long. The Commissioner is particularly sensitive in these matters. But he's now swamped with obligations. Good for you, I guess. In this way, you can, in all discretion, rectify this painful situation."

Montpetit didn't answer.

Mycroft Follum bowed deeper forward. "Do you know that Klein is following up on this case? He won't be happy if you keep passive. Our reputation is at stake, and after all that negative IPTF bullshit in the newspapers, a scandal would be disastrous for us. Certainly not good for you." He sighed briefly. "After all the shit you've been through in Mitrovica."

Normand felt as if he got a bucket of ice water over his head. A veiled threat. *They know.* Special Envoy of the Secretary-General Klein, the highest official jerk of the peace mission, had a lot of power.

Normand frowned. "Are you saying that I've got to fire that Belgian? But on what charge?"

The Briton smiled nastily. "Inappropriate behaviour. Accommodating an illegal person. Maintaining a whore. Shall I continue?"

Normand would have preferred throwing the Briton out. But Mycroft was an influential person in Sarajevo. He'd served with the EUMM for years. Despite rumours about his alcohol problem, his pro-Serbian statements and his intimate relationship with a Serbian interpreter, he remained at his post.

Normand was thinking about his career. His government and the brotherhood supported him, but he couldn't survive within EuPol if the Britons set him on fire. Amazing that the mighty Klein interfered. Did the arrogant bastard want to polish his blazon after the Kathryn Bolkovac case? Strange that Klein was so quick to expel a civilian employee out of the country. Greg Stone didn't belong to any billion-dollar company. He was an insignificant technical expert who didn't pose a threat to anyone. But as long as the UN-troops were in the country, Klein ruled over Commissioner Ragnarsson. He could also ruin his career.

He sighed deeply. "All right, I'll fire him, but what about his replacement?"

"We've got already a suitable person."

"What a coincidence. You've been thinking of everything."

"Klein would be happy when the problem got solved by tomorrow."

Normand had no choice. The British knew too much about him; they were in Mitrovica when the incident happened. Or did they know more? If so, they might become a severe threat.

"If it's Klein's wish, I'll fire Greg," he said in a resigning tone.

Mycroft nodded with a satisfied smile. "I didn't expect anything else, either. Our technician will contact Janus tomorrow. You make him sign his contract immediately."

The conversation was over. Without wasting time, Normand let his visitor out. He slammed the door shut and grabbed his cell phone.

What will the Brotherhood Commander do when he hears that the British are threatening me?

After leaving the academy with the highest distinction, the whole world was at his feet. But intelligence alone is not enough to make a career. He was young, ambitious and willing to do anything for reaching the summits, including selling his soul to the devil, what he had done.

Nemesis offered enormous advantages. He had been climbing the echelons faster than he'd expected, enjoying protection. And in return, he only had to do what they ordered him to do; he was appointed and received promotions. He also received a high salary. The fact that the Nemesis objectives did not match the EU's did not bother him.

I have to inform Nemesis. He thought of Dragon Borjan. A Nemesis soldier whose actions in Mitrovica had come to his ears. Strange, because Nemesis demanded the utmost discretion from its brothers. Probably the reason why the Supreme Command had transferred Borjan to Sarajevo as his direct guard angel, his protector. Officially, Dragon didn't occupy any office, but he possessed an admission ticket. Formally Montpetit was under his command. He had always thought that Nemesis-Brothers didn't have an identity.

Dragon was his unique solution.

But by requesting his support, he was taking a considerable risk. Always dangerous to take initiatives without involving the Council. Endangering the brotherhood was a severe offence that could be punished by death.

With a sigh, he typed in a number.

"Dragon," he said, seconds later, "I want you at my house immediately."

NINE

TWO LIGHTING POLES BARELY ILLUMINATED THE DESERTED STREET. SOMETHING had frightened Borjan Dragon, but there was nothing in the rear-view mirror. Engine noise? No, he couldn't see any other vehicle in the vicinity. While opening the door, he perpetually looked left and right. Nowhere any sign of life. On the other side of the street, the evening breeze was whispering mysterious messages through the trees.

He stepped out and tilted his head, trying to catch unusual noises. But he heard nothing suspicious. He slammed the door and started slowly to climb the narrow path toward the top of the slope. His shoes made barely any noise on the hard earth soil, and with his grey trousers, dark sweater and brown leather jacket, he immersed in his gloomy surroundings.

Since the events in Kosovo last year, he didn't feel safe anywhere. After having discovered that Daria Bazila, accompanied by another woman and her pimp had left for Bosnia, he immediately had started the pursuit. He hated defeats, considering her escape as a personal humiliation. No whore was going to humiliate him.

He'd signed out from the Civilian Police without consulting the Nemesis Council, leaving Mitrovica in a hurry. He couldn't trust his Serbian friends any more as they knew too much about him.

At the Serbian border, the Belgian border militia had confirmed that the three refugees had been crossing. In Belgrade, he finally contacted the Council, which had given him a new task: security advisor of EuPol deputy commissioner in Sarajevo. On his way to Sarajevo, he'd visited Banja Luka and discovered that Daria Bazila had got a visa for the federation. There was no other option than to catch that whore and secure the incriminating evidence she possessed. If he succeeded, he might avoid a severe sanction. He'd checked all the nightclubs in the Sarajevo area; Daria had vanished. According to the *Florida Bar* owner, she'd returned to Moldova.

His gaze roamed around without spotting suspicious movement. He rang the doorbell. *What does Montpetit want from me?*

He watched toward the main road, listening to a deadly silence until he heard the door swivels open. He turned around, sullenly looking at the man between the doorposts. Normand Montpetit was short and slim, had a military haircut and a pear-shaped unfriendly face accentuated by an unfashionable pair of glasses. He was wearing a far too full blue jogging suit, making him look ridiculous.

In an intimate French circle, colleagues named this nervous fellow Bonaparte. Clearly suffering from an inferiority complex, he tried to hide it by making quick decisions, which he usually had to withdraw or modify shortly afterwards. Dragon despised this man in whom the government saw so much future. He slipped past him, heading straight for the kitchen. As if he belonged there, he grabbed a can of beer from the refrigerator and returned to the living room. After drinking half of his tin, he started stepping around.

Normand had sat down on the couch. "We've something to discuss. Have you still not found that Moldavian whore?"

Dragon laughed coldly. "I know where she lives, but I haven't spotted her yet."

"Where is she?"

"She's with a Belgian guy who works for EuPol."

"Well, I'm aware Greg Stone lives with a Moldavian girl," Montpetit said thoughtfully. "But I didn't know she was the woman you're looking for."

"One of the *Florida Bar* girls revealed to me that Daria Bazila lives with

a Belgian. And I know, there's only one Belgian EuPol observer."
"I never thought Stone would be so careless."
Dragon made an impatient gesture. "If that whore told him..."
"Tomorrow I'll fire him," Montpetit interrupted. "After that, he'll have no other choice but to return to his country, while the girl ought to go back to the *Florida Bar*, the only place she knows in Bosnia."
"Someday your incompetence will be your end." Dragon's voice sounded reproachful. "Those two arseholes have to disappear. What that whore has in her possession can cost you your neck." Dragon sat down and put his empty can in front of him.
Montpetit jumped up. "Sarajevo is not Mitrovica," he called out. "And how can you be so sure that this Daria possesses the evidence?"
"Trust me, Normand. Let me take care of them, and tomorrow the sun will shine again over you. They'll disappear into dust."
They were staring furiously at each other.
"No," yelled Normand.
Dragon cursed inside. "That girl in the *Florida Bar* has told me more," he said vehemently. "Initially, Daria Bazila got protected by a general who promised to bring her to France, but he broke his word. Then Daria met that Belgian guy, with whom she's living for months now. He takes her everywhere, and everyone knows her. She's by no means a paid slave, which means that she may have revealed him everything."
"You're wrong. I will fire Greg, that's it. Once he's dismissed, his story will sound absolutely incredible. Do you think he's going to make a big deal out of it? Once that whore has returned to the *Florida Bar*, we'll raid the bar, and then we'll confiscate all of her possessions. If she has that evidence, we'll find it. You've told me that you've been killing that other whore in Mitrovica. So, everything will be fine. Stone's girlfriend can say everything she likes, but she won't be able to prove it any more. Case closed."
Dragon made a grim face. "Both must disappear."
Normand sat down again. "No," he retorted. "Greg Stone has many local friends, and some are dangerous. I am going on Wednesday to Brussels where I'll announce Stone's resignation to the EU Council. *Fin de l'histoire*.
"I think my solution is the only good one," Dragon insisted.
Norman's eyes twinkled.
"Here you can't just torture a Western European and make him disappear," he snarled. "Discretion, have you forgotten? We're going to do it the gentle way. The Viking is not an idiot; we have to prevent him from becoming suspicious."
Dragon shook his head. "It's about your head."
"That's the way you'll proceed. But I've another problem. The British know what happened in Mitrovica. Today Follum made that clear to me. Sooner or later they'll make that public to break me."

In Mitrovica, Dragon should have discreetly cleaned any traces of Montpetit's deeds. But that damn Daria had tricked him. She'd escaped taking with her some hard evidence against Montpetit. Although UNMIK authorities didn't know him, his sudden departure had been raising questions. At EuPol too, there were rumours. His identity did not worry him; Nemesis members were phantoms. But policemen in Mitrovica had secretly taken pictures of him so that he could be traced from now on. Too many people had seen him. He didn't want to be sent to another part of the world. Or to be killed. And now Normand asked him for help, violating the strict rules of the brotherhood.

"What do you want me to do?" asked Dragon, giving him a look of cold disdain. When a *Chosen* got jeopardised, he had to inform the Council. Nemesis had sent him to the Balkans because he was mastering the local language. Once he was a refuge, who'd entered France under a false name. During an offensive of the Arkan Tigers in Bosnia, he'd taken the identity of a dead citizen. A secret office had erased the data of his former existence. But the brotherhood's strict rules gave him goose bumps; disobedience endangering Nemesis institutions was punishable by death.

Normand looked at him closely.

"I think Follum belongs to MI6, just like Derek Fleming," he said.

"You're kidding," answered Dragon in an ironic tone. Ever since he worked in the Glass Tower, he'd observed everyone. '*Knowing your environment and the people might save your life*,' he'd learned. Follum and Fleming were at the top of his list of potential threats. Observing Fleming, he'd discovered that the man visited the British Embassy every morning with his briefcase. He rarely lingered there for more than a quarter of an hour. One day Dragon had spotted that briefcase on Fleming's desk in an empty office. Without hesitation, he'd made a scratch with his cutting knife at the bottom of the suitcase. Almost impossible to see. So he found out that Fleming was changing the briefcase at the embassy.

"For the time being, there's no immediate danger," he humbled. "I can't and shouldn't do anything against the British. We don't want a war with their Secret Service. However, I'll do what's necessary so that they don't bother you in the future." A promise he would probably not keep. What could he do to convince the British to stay away from the Deputy Commissioner? He doubted it was a good option to consult the Council either. The secretary would be furious. *Don't do anything that's making my case worse*. He would quietly wait for the arrival of his reliever to whom he would hand over the settlement of Montpetit's problems.

I'll visit that whore while the Belgian is in the Glass Tower. He would leave this cursed country for another task only after proving he was a worthy Nemesis-Brother.

"I don't think we'll meet again in the future," he sneered, getting up. He left the house, slamming the door shut behind him. After looking around for a while, he started walking down toward his car. *Nothing is going according to plan*, he thought. Tormented by a lousy hunch, he stopped in the middle of the slope looking over the houses on the ridge. All the windows were dark.

With peace of mind, he stepped steadily in the direction of his SUV, pressed the distance button, grabbed the door handle, and stiffened.

"Hello, Dragon, don't move and look ahead." The voice behind his back sounded icy. Could he reach his shoulder holster fast enough? *No, this guy is pointing a real firearm at me.*

"What do you want?" he asked with a trembling voice.

The stranger laughed softly. "I've pointed a 9 mm on your back, so no jokes. Carefully open the door, stand in front of the opening, spread your legs and put your hands on the roof."

Dragon hesitated for a moment. When he obeyed, he would entirely be at the mercy of the other. *Wait until he makes a mistake.*

He did what the other ordered.

"Your legs farther back and more spread. Stretch your arms completely apart, your hands flat on the roof," the man insisted.

It's a professional. The opponent had him entirely under control and could easily unbalance him on the slightest movement. *If he shoots now, I'll be in a wheelchair or dead.*

Dragon felt the hard barrel of a gun in his back and gave a cry of pain. A hand was sliding under his armpit along the inside of the jacket, grabbing his handgun.

"Do you want money?" he tried.

"Shut your mouth," whispered the man in his neck, standing between his spread legs. "I'll take a few steps back, and when I say "now", you get behind the wheel putting your hands on the top of it."

Dragon obeyed, heard the rear door go open and someone settling in the back seat.

"Pull the door shut and fasten your seatbelt."

Dragon sighed. As soon as they were moving, he was going to give the guy the scare of his life. At high speed, that arsehole would lose any control.

He glanced in the rear-view mirror and froze, feeling a sting in his neck as the man pulled the trigger of an injection gun.

"Send Smaug to Tartarus," the man whispered near his ear.

Dizziness was overwhelming him, and a haze appeared before his eyes. He tried to move but got obstructed by the safety belt. His arms sensed very heavy. He thought of the horn. However, it occurred to him that he hadn't yet inserted the key into the ignition slot. He could hardly breathe.

Send Smaug to Tartarus.

What did mean that message?

Smaug seemed familiar to him. He remembered having read something about a dragon, called *Smaug*.

The Lord of the Rings.

Smaug was a dragon, and his name was Dragon.

Everything started to dance before his eyes.

My replacement.

Then the light went out.

Tuesday, 8 October 2002

TEN

Srebrenica, 11 July 1995

BRAM WOULD HAVE SLIT CEES VISSER'S THROAT WITH GREAT SATISFACTION. HE hated Franken's slimy friend and had never been able to get along with him, but this time it was about the life and death of his lover's family.

"I want to speak to the superior," he said with clenched fists. He was one of the few officers who didn't fear this arrogant major. But envy was not the cause of their mutual dislike. Cees was a narcissistic prick without any empathy for his subordinates, whereas Bram was a negotiator between the local Bosnian government and his commander. Civil Affairs. For Cees, only orders and rules mattered. There was no room in his heart, for empathy. "*As a soldier, you have to get rid of your feelings*," was his motto.

Visser grinned provocatively. "The old man is ill," he snarled. "He handed over his command to the deputy commander. But it's his will to keep only the natives with a UN pass in the camp."

"All aid organisations shield the relatives of their personnel," reposted Bram, taking several steps toward him.

"That's not part of the Rules of Engagement, Captain. We're not aid workers, we're neutral military. It's already an exception that we are protecting our foreign employees. So watch your tongue," retorted Visser.

Bram pointed to the desperate young woman standing ten paces away from the fence.

"Please," he pleaded, "her parents are elderly people, and her sister is very young. Don't you understand what's happening beyond the fence?"

The major shrugged and his features darkened. "We've made a decision. We must respect our neutrality, and we do not wage war on the Serbs."

Bram cast a helpless glance at Jasmina who was looking at him beggingly.

"Bullshit," yelled Bram out of control, moving toward his superior. "You collaborate with the Serbs!" He was aware that Dutch crews from various observation posts had already surrendered to the Serbs; they preferred to stay with the Serbs rather than return to the battalion. Many soldiers were considering Rob Franken as a pro-Serb.

Major Visser stiffened. "I'll have you court-martialled," he shouted.

Bram got overwhelmed by despair, knowing what Jasmina was going to do if Cees stuck to his viewpoint; she would join her family. Jasmina was the eldest child, and she felt responsible for her sister and her parents.

The soldier at the gate was waiting for the major's sign.

Bram lost his temper and made a great mistake. He jumped forward and hit his superior.

Sarajevo, 8 October 2002

Bram Ruyter woke up, looked around dazed and realised that the taxi had stopped. He paid and got out. *Beautiful weather for walking.*

The morning news on the local station had positively influenced his mood. '*A Dutch diplomat has been murdered in a hotel room,*' the TV newscaster had reported. He had also mentioned that the military attaché loved bizarre sex, especially with young girls. Bram was not entirely satisfied. However, Visser's death closed a chapter from his past. Eventually, he had decided to visit Suada's sister.

Despite the blue sky and bright sun, temperatures remained around twenty-two degrees Celsius. He was lightly dressed, wore comfortable suede Timberland shoes, and a worn pair of jeans with matching blue cotton shirt of which two upper buttons were loose. He knew that many women were secretly staring at him. Every morning after shaving, he stared in the mirror for a while and remembered Mayke's words. *You do look like a magician.* His stinging green eyes, long black hair, and circle beard gave his face the mystical look of a sorcerer. He contemplated a long walk across the town. The Emma Badora file still bothered him. He had to think quietly. All those young women or even girls forced into prostitution touched him more than he was willing to admit. Or was it that inexorable hatred for the Serbs who'd been destroying his life twice? Two tragedies that almost had driven him into madness.

'*If evil spirits constantly disturb your night's sleep, you quickly become a different person,*' he'd said to a psychiatrist after his return from Srebrenica. '*Your words and advice can't dispel these demons either.*'

Then he'd met Wim, the non-commissioned officer from Srebrenica, who'd told him an interesting story. Bram had immediately understood that madness hadn't stopped yet. Without hesitation, he'd applied for a job in Sarajevo, where he hoped to bury his past forever if he eventually got answers to many questions. His body needed movement while his mind cried out for rest. The time was getting ripe to forget all the atrocities he'd seen in the past.

Winston had been right: Emma's abduction was not his fault. Life went on, and there was more in the world than violence, crime and inhumanity. Sarajevo offered countless opportunities to experience beautiful moments and to escape from reality for a while. Restaurants, terraces, and shops. It seemed a good idea to mingle among the crowd's cacophony of voices, walking across the winding streets around Bascarsija. In the old market place, he would enjoy the picturesque Turkish shops admiring the displayed craft products in the showcases. Thinking of something else, forgetting, living, and enjoying. Emma Badora belonged to the past.

He walked toward the cathedral, passed *Central Café*, and halted. Sarajevo's most famous establishment had a modern interior and a terrace across the entire width of the road. On one side there was a beautiful cathedral and, on the opposite side, barely twenty metres away, a taxi stand.

An empty table in front of the entrance was too tempting that he couldn't resist. He sat down and slammed his right leg over his left.

Immediately a waiter showed up.

"*Jedno Sarajevsko*, one Sarajevo beer," Bram ordered. "Edhem je ovdje? Is Edhem here?"

"*Veceras*, tonight," replied the young man.

"*Hvala*."

While the waiter was walking away, he considered a moment to call Edhem. He appreciated Edhem's company, especially when he, as part of his job, visited the brothels, which was not without danger because the mafia bosses knew who he was. But he'd made them clear he wasn't fighting prostitution, only helping abused girls. So they considered him as a classic hypocritical Westerner fighter against human traffickers, consuming their products. On the one hand, his visits were part of his research to write a book, and on the other hand, he wanted to remove the real victims of this environment.

He recalled Kathryn Bolkovac, well known in the International Environment. Her name was taboo but regularly whispered by aid workers. In 2001 she'd got the courage to accuse a group of international police observers of corruption, including some of her colleagues. But she had not understood the cruel world in which she'd ended up. Bram called this environment where money, power and sex were closely connected: *Hypocrita Mundi*. Bolkovac had been ignoring all the warnings until it was too late. She'd thought she could defy this corrupt elite because she stood on the right side. But the bad guys were more muscular and in the majority, so she was finally fired under a pretext. Too late Kathryn found out that the government, defending its organisations, was concealing the truth.

This knowledge convinced Bram that openly declaring war on the Mafia bosses and corrupt police observers would be suicidal. He did not send IPTF patrols to these houses when observing a violation of local laws. '*That's not my job*,' he'd told the new *Florida Bar* owner. '*As long as the girls are working voluntarily, you have nothing to fear from me. I'm not the Pope's emissary*.' That's how they accepted that he talked to the girls, a compromise solution. It took him not long to discover that many of those women voluntarily chose this life. They wanted to earn money quickly to start a new life in their homeland. He was only interested in the girls who were held against their will because that was equal to rape. He did not pity those who voluntarily chose this lifestyle. This point of view sometimes brought him into conflict with naive female aid workers who all too often incorrectly mentioned in their reports that *all* women were forced into prostitution.

Bullshit.

Although Badora was an exception: she'd been a victim. Her testimony had put the brothel owner behind bars for years. His condemnation made everyone happy, but the convicted person would be forgotten after a short time and soon be released.

His eyes wandered over hundreds of heads; young and old sitting at tables on the terraces which had been set up along the entire length of the pedestrian street between the Zelinih Beretki and the Ferhadija. Bram studied the entrance of the Catholic cathedral across the Ferhadija, a pedestrian zone interconnecting Marsala Tita in an east-west direction, the main road around the inner city, and the old Turkish market place called Bascarsija.

He sipped his beer. Like so many others, he was shamelessly peeking at the passing beauties in colourful ultra-short skirts and tops with raised bosoms and swaying hips. Who in the West would believe that most of them were Muslim women? Since he was working for *Last Hope*, he started realising that repatriating victims of trafficking had become more important to him than he wanted to admit. However, his original goal had not been repatriating women.

He took a deep breath, staring again at the cathedral. Then his cell phone started ringing.

An incoming message.

I am on my way to the parrot building. I'll be there in fifteen minutes. Urgent! If not possible, send a message.

Bram frowned, unaware of what to think. Annoyed and worried at the same time, he swallowed half of his beer. Then he thoughtfully glanced at the display of his cell phone, leaned back and let the golden rays of the sun caress his face. There was still some time left. Slowly the sounds around him faded away, his eyes closed, and images flashed through his mind.

Months Ago

The Irish delegation had organised a party in the downstairs room of EUMM headquarters. Like all representatives of various international organisations, Winston figured on the inventory list. However, he was on holiday and Bram replaced him.

Not knowing many people in the building, Bram was waiting for the right moment to disappear discreetly. After lunch, he headed toward the bar next to the exit, where he unobtrusively could leave the room. He ordered a large glass of Sarajevsko, looked aside and saw a young man observing him.

Bram was in a good mood. "Are you drinking one of mine?" he asked him.

The young man nodded.

"I'm Bram Ruyter," said Bram.

The young man grinned. "Emir Besic."

At first, they talked about their professional work while drinking a few beers. As the evening progressed, their tongues became looser. They talked about personal matters, family, hobbies, and more.

"Where do you live?" asked Bram hours later with a thick tongue.

"Near the Kosevo stadium, on the heights of Breka." The young man described where this place was.

At that moment, a man dressed in white appeared next to them, picking up two glasses of beer and heading back to his table.

"That's Derek Fleming," Emir said.

"Yes, I know him from the name."

"He's my neighbour."

Suddenly Bram was sober again.

Sarajevo, 8 October 2002

Bram opened his eyes. Around him sounded a cacophony of voices. His watch told him that fifteen minutes had passed. He beckoned to the waiter, paid and gave him a big tip. Then he hurried to the Obala Kulina Bana, the extension of the Sniper Alley leading to Pale. He thought of the snipers firing at civilians from the buildings on the flanks of the surrounding mountains. The war had been ruthless without fairness. But wasn't every war dirty and filthy? He moved fast, crossed the iron bridge, and stood indecisively along the right bank of the Miljacka. His gaze wandered fleetingly across the small parking space in front of the pharmacy.

Emir's car is not here. His eyes moved toward the narrow passage alongside the pharmacy, which led to the courtyard of the Parrot Building, Bosnia's ugliest building. He turned left on the road alongside the bank, leading to Bosnia's most famous bridge, the *Princip Bridge*, officially called *Latinski Cuprija*. There, on 28 June 1914, Gravilo Princip had shot the archduke François-Ferdinand of Austria and his pregnant wife Sophie with a handgun, which resulted in the Great War. Every time Emir requested a meeting, Bram usually parked on the grass along the bank, and he discretely met his friend on the opposite side of the park. But that place seemed deserted, as was the bush having the size of a football pitch, at the right. Despite the excellent weather, all the benches along the paths seemed deserted.

He slowly walked downstream, passing the first car of a long line. He was wondering where his friend was going to wait. Then he spotted Emir's green Volkswagen Golf down the road at the far end, parked on the grass strip.

Emir sat behind the wheel, staring foolishly at him.

Bram slowed his pace, turned around, but couldn't see anyone watching at him. Frowning, he turned toward Emir, noticing that the door was ajar. Looking around suspiciously, Bram unconsciously started walking faster. But as he reached the door, he halted in shock. Emir's big eyes reflected a mixture of horror and pain.

However, he didn't suffer. He was as dead as Pharaoh Ramses the Great.

ELEVEN

ZUMRA ABDIC JUMPED OUT OF THE ARMCHAIR, FOOLISHLY PEEKING AT THE flickering television screen. Still sleep drunk, she thought to hear a shrill sound, her eyes moving to the cell phone that was slowly spinning over the tabletop. She caught the thing just before it was going to slide over the edge.

Timka.

She'd been staying with Lazar for a few days without calling her friend. Timka had to worry, probably trying to find out when she was going to get back home. Zumra pressed the green icon and brought the phone to her ear.

"Hey, Timka, are you all right?" she whispered.

"I need you to jump in for me." Timka's voice sounded nervous.

"It's your week! However, if I have to watch out for the children, I'll be right with you."

"No, Zumra, I have my period, you know, and I don't feel well. You must go in my place. You have twenty minutes to get to the cemetery. Can you do that?"

Zumra glanced at her wristwatch. *Four o'clock*. Lazar certainly wouldn't get home before five.

"Yes," she answered quietly. "See you later." She broke off the connection.

How badly she wanted to end this impossible life right away. However, she thought that now confessing her sins to Lazar would not be the right thing to do. But someday she would have to tell him. First, she'd got to help her friend out of need. Her watch told her that she had enough time to disappear before Lazar came home and would ask awkward questions. Especially since they were going out to dinner that night. She was praying he would forgive her for that missed dinner, assuming she'd an excellent reason heading back to her apartment. Barely to believe that he gave her so much freedom without asking questions. She hated all those lies but feared the moment of truth. For days she'd been thinking about a solution without finding a way out. The longer she put it off, the harder it would be to explain her behaviour.

Seconds were ticking away, no more time for changing clothes. A quick glance into the bedroom mirror assured Zumra that she looked good in jeans and a top. She put on a light leather jacket, grabbed her cell phone, and called for a taxi.

Ten minutes later, she stepped into the cab next to the kindly smiling driver, a man in the fifties.

"As usual," she said with a faint smile.

Zumra was not a very chatty type, and the driver knew that if she didn't want a conversation, he'd better keep his mouth shut. He nodded and joined the traffic. The ride from Stup to the Kosevo-cemetery took fifteen minutes.

The north-south route was passing through a tunnel, ending at an intersection after a long bend. The taxi turned left and stopped along the pavement.

Zumra paid, crossed the road and stopped on the sidewalk, looking anxiously over the line of cars. But she couldn't spot Loverboy's vehicle. Whenever pedestrians approached, she feigned phoning or paced from left to right. Eventually, from the stadium side, she caught sight of a fast-approaching white car. She put the cell phone back in her purse while stepping to the roadside as the vehicle halted.

She got in, facing the dissatisfied features of the man behind the wheel.

"Damned, where is Timka?" snarled the man in Serb-Croatian with a heavy American accent.

"Timka has her period," she replied gruffly.

Loverboy was tall, athletically built and a friendly-looking, handsome guy. But this appearance was treacherous, and his friendly features hid a soulless arsehole. She hated him as she hated herself for being submissive.

"Where are you taking me?" she asked in better English than his Serbo-Croatian.

He was increasing speed. "As usual," he snarled. "Listen carefully, Zumra, you must say you're Timka, you got it?"

No, she did not understand that she'd to use her friend's name.

"As long as that goes well," she remarked with concern.

"It depends on you. Our client is new, and I guess he doesn't know Timka."

But why asking for a girl if you don't know her?

Eurotel was a well-appointed hotel where the most prominent international aid workers regularly organized parties. It was barely a hundred metres away from IPTF headquarters and about ten metres ahead of *Irish Pub 2*. The hotel also had a large meeting room, which was regularly booked out to international organisations. The EuPol Commissioner sometimes held conferences there.

She observed Loverboy from the corner of her eye, noting that he was submerged in thought, unconsciously drumming a melody with his fingers on the wheel. She'd met him through Timka who had always hung out in places where international aid workers came. '*They have money, Zumra, and we can use it,*' she'd emphasised.

They encountered no difficulties hooking men because both were very handsome. So, they'd been surviving the after-war economic crisis and were able to pay the rent, giving their children a normal upbringing. Their situation had improved when Timka met the generous Tommy Branson at a party in the *Irish Pub 2*. Tommy was a guy who knew what women like to hear. He feigned being a good father figure for the kids, and Timka had been dreaming of a permanent relationship. *'Financial security guaranteed,'* she'd told Zumra with a broad smile. When she realised her mistake, it was too late for both of them.

Zumra glanced at the man who had introduced them into this filthy world. Men with money and influence. Some were monsters like Branson who was calling himself a mediator. In her eyes, Loverboy was a ruthless pimp of the worst kind.

He gave her a look of hostility. "There we are, dear," he groaned.

Let's get this over quickly. Zumra followed the American to the entrance. *Maybe after that, I can still go out for dinner with Lazar.*

There was little movement in the lobby. The man behind the counter handed Loverboy a key, and she obediently followed him to the second floor, using the lift. For Bosnian standards, the suite looked comfortably furnished. They entered a small hall, facing the bathroom, while the other door gave access to the suite. The hotel earned well from the International Community.

"You wait here," Branson said. He squeezed her cheek slightly; every time the same ritual. The door got locked, and she sat down in an armchair, wondering who she was going to serve.

Lazar, forgive me.

But the waiting was short. Less than five minutes later, Zumra heard a light noise in the hall and got up. *Hardly time to relax.* A door slammed shut, and a big guy appeared between the doorposts. She held her breath. The man's angular face with cruel features made her tremble. Seeing her, his eyes narrowed.

"Who are you?" he snarled, moving towards her.

"Timka," she answered with a faint voice.

"Wrong answer, my dear."

The blow to her face brought her off balance, and she fell sideways on the brown carpet. In her fall, her head hit a hard object.

The world ceased to exist.

TWELVE

BRAM RUYTER STARED DAZED AT THE CORPSE IN THE CAR. *GET OUT OF HERE.* Getting involved in a criminal case meant the end of his plans. Could he be linked to this murder? Was he the cause of it? He slowly moved toward the door while his eyes scrutinised the surroundings. Then he focused on Emir's neck showing a large dark spot. The whole scene set off alarm bells in his head, and he twisted around.

No one. Bram sighed. What he was beginning to imagine seemed madness. Was the killer still around? He took his cell phone out of his pocket and punched in Emir's number. Seconds later, he heard the familiar sound. But it wasn't coming out of Emir's car. He held the mobile phone to his ear, peering secretly at the park while his thumb moved feverishly over the keyboard. Once the phone turned off, he feigned talking, slowly walking past the car.

"Listen carefully, Ruud," he said in a loud tone. "I can't right now, but I promise I'll come by as soon as I can." *Don't exaggerate, be reasonable.* But a new thought made his heart beat faster. By calling Emir, he'd left his phone number on Emir's phone. *The killer must be nearby*. The gazed across the park. No walkers and the benches were unoccupied. His eyes travelled to the edge of the forest. Suddenly he spotted a grey vehicle along the sidewalk on the connection road with two men in the front.

Holy shit. The driver was photographing him. He tried to protect his face with his right arm, walking with accelerated pace toward the next bridge while talking loudly to his imaginary interlocutor. Once the car was out his sight, he shoved the cell phone back in his pocket, suppressing the urge to look over his shoulder. As he rushes across the bridge, he heard in the distance a car door slam. He speeded up, crossed the road at the traffic lights and walked to the next intersection where he plunged into an alley. Out of sight of possible pursuers, he changed to a light running pace. He covered the distance to the next junction in less than ten seconds. Once around the corner, he marched at an average pace again. In no time, he reached Bascarsija, a hardened square providing connections to several alleys. In the middle stood the famous fountain where several walkers were feeding numerous pigeons.

Although he couldn't see or hear anyone, he was afraid of being followed. Melted among the crowd, he hastily crossed the square to the taxi rank. But after a few steps, he changed his mind, stopping in front of a small sports shop where he started searching through dozens of colourful football shirts of well-known international clubs while gazing over the edge of the stand.

Nothing. Bram refused to believe that he'd imagined anything. The two in the grey car had to be involved with Emir's death since they owned his cell phone. After some hesitation, he looked around one last time, headed for the first taxi in the line and opened the door.

"Kosevo stadium, Aleksandra Puskina 12," he said, settling down into the passenger seat.

The elderly man nodded and started his Volkswagen Golf.

Bram looked back over his shoulder through the rear window. No suspects. He breathed out deeply and checking his watch: 0450 p.m. The taxi entered the tunnel, and he leaned back.

What did Emir want to tell me? Should he be worried about his future? No matter how much Bram tormented his memory, he couldn't find a single clue linking him to the murder. He hoped no one had seen him near the body. Except for the two men in the car, no one could prove that he'd got an appointment with Emir. Could there be a link to *Last Hope*? He knew very little about Emir.

When the car emerged from the tunnel, he gazed through the side windows to a double-lane road in both directions of which the other side was still under construction. *Probably out of money to finish the works.* At the next intersection, the taxi turned onto the Patriotski Lige. During minutes they were driving past the big marketplace along with the cemetery. Then they turned right at the stadium. After a few kilometres going uphill on a narrow, winding road, the taxi stopped a hundred metres before the ridge. Bram paid and waited until the cab dropped out of sight over the top of the hill. He kept listening for a moment but didn't hear any noise of an engine. On the other side of the road opposite the hollow path, there were two garages with a paved parking lot behind it. The owner had built those garages since the winter did not allow access by car to the houses. Bram walked calmly along the hollow path up to the Y-junction, where he turned left on a paved alley toward his dwelling place. A similar house stood along the other side path, the owner of both dwells.

The covered terrace with a railing was built on a wooden pole construction, a few metres away from the path. He climbed the five steps, walked to the front door, listening to the slight cracking of the wooden floor under his shoes. Before putting the key into the lock, he gazed over his shoulder. There was nothing to see.

He unlocked the heavy wooden door, entered the short hall and closed behind him. The house had a lounge-kitchen combination in the front and at the rear side, two bedrooms with a bathroom in the middle. In the facade sat two high windows ensuring the space felt open and bright. The modern furniture consisted of a white leather couch and two armchairs, a coffee table, an ample cupboard with television, a DVD player, and a satellite decoder. In the dining area stood a bar and a long table with six pine chairs around it. A corridor, either accessible from the living room and the hall, cut the house into two blocks.

Bram headed toward the open kitchen and took a small hammer out of the top drawer of the cabinet. *Do not take any risks.* Replacing a SIM card was not enough to avoid being traced. Although he had no idea who could be behind the murder, he feared MI6, the British Secret Service, which monitored all communications in the country.

He shattered the phone, then wiped the shards in a plastic bag that he tucked in the freezer between the meat and the vegetables. In the end, he crossed the living room with a satisfied feeling, opened the hallway door and hurried to his bedroom which was furnished with a double bed, two bedside tables and a wardrobe from grandmother's era. A large window bordered with dark curtains provided good lighting. He took a small suitcase out the hidden compartment in the cupboard, threw it on the bed and searched among the clothes for a pair of rolled-up sports socks, which he rolled open. He pulled out a mobile phone, discovering with delight that the battery was still providing enough power.

Back in the living room, he poured himself a bourbon, sat down on the couch and turned on the television. But he didn't care about the images. After a large sip of whisky, he leaned back, closing his eyes. *Emir has sent me a message from EuPol's headquarters.* Then he'd driven to the park where a killer had been waiting for him. Or someone had been following him from EuPol. Had Emir seen or heard something that wasn't allowed? *If it has to do with Derek Fleming, I'm also involved.* Emir's phone's ringing tone had come out of that grey BMW.

Sipping more whisky, the dull, heavy sound of the gong took him brutally out of his mind. He wasn't expecting any visitor. That could only be the landlord. The landlord, a jovial but pushy man, regularly visited him to improve his poor English. Bram rushed to the hall, determined to get rid of him. He opened the door and frowned. In front of him stood two heavy men dressed in jeans with a matching jacket and a grey shirt with open collars. Clothing twins. Their cruel face features caused a weak feeling in his stomach.

He laughed kindly, staring from one to another. They were chewing gum and looked like American cowboys.

"We'd like to ask you a few questions," the biggest of the two said.

"And who are you?"

"We are English citizens."

"I don't know you."

"But we know who you are, Mr Ruyter. We kindly ask you to give us a few moments of your time. I can assure you that it will not take long."

Bram glanced up to the spokesman. "You didn't tell me whether who you are nor who gives you the right to disturb me," he said with a defensive look.

Their faces remained emotionless.

"Mr Ruyter, we are English SFOR agents, and we're investigating terrorist activities in Sarajevo."

"I can assure you that I am not a terrorist."

He knew they were lying. But it could be dangerous accusing him.

He'd seen these guys before, both sitting in a grey BMW while they were taking pictures of him.

THIRTEEN

LAZAR MAGAS SAT DAYDREAMING IN HIS OFFICE, GAZING AT THE TWO TOWERS through the window. He was in a bad mood because Egzon had imposed him to finish a boring criminal record. But his thoughts were with the Dutch attaché. What he'd discovered made him feel uneasy. That international arsehole had loved young prostitutes. Any international involvement in crime affairs usually resulted in complications, especially when it came to murder. *Fuck, that case is no longer my problem.*

Egzon didn't take any chances and had given him a hopeless investigation to distract him, requesting an urgent report on the Hotic affair. *Why should I care about that pimp?* The victim was a criminal who'd double-crossed his boss, after which a contract killer had executed him. A crime that might remain unresolved, as the most homicides cases related to the underworld.

Let them kill each other. It was a case for colleague Fakir, but Egzon liked to provoke him whenever an opportunity arose. *Who cares about a dead pimp?* A hitman pulled the trigger, then shoot another bullet between the eyes as a signature; no fingerprints nor murder weapon.

He browsed listlessly through the thin file. *Further investigation is a waste of time and money.* He sighed and started writing his conclusions.

As the EuPol observers were continually monitoring the actions of the local police, the Chief Commissioner insisted that any investigation be carried out according to the internationally imposed rules. In this way, he secured European Union subsidies for the reform of the Bosnian police and judicial system. Money that mainly disappeared into the pockets of high-ranking officials and politicians who supported the project, while ordinary field police officers saw no improvement.

His thoughts drifted off. The day was passing, and, in an hour, he would have dinner with Zumra. Afterwards, he was going to take her back to his apartment in Stup where they'd make love for hours. Life could be so beautiful.

He leaned back with closed eyes while his thoughts were drifting in the past. During and after the war, he'd got countless love affairs, which had helped him to control his inner anger. Due to an overflow of lonely women who'd lost their husbands or friends, embellishing girls had become comfortable. Thousands of young men died, and the ratio of women to men rose to ten to one. Then he'd met Zumra. After their first night, he'd felt she was more than a spontaneous sexual interlude. When she wasn't around, he was missing her, and for the first time in his life, he thought that he was in love. Evoking her image in his mind, put him in a beautiful trance over and over again. Hadn't he heard somewhere that love is causing pain?

They had a lot in common because she hadn't come out of the war unharmed either. He'd lost his parents and brother, she'd lost her whole family, although she couldn't remember where and when. She was suffering amnesia and refused to talk about her past, about what happened during the war. She'd forgotten everything.

Sometimes he was dubious about her amnesia. How to explain her nightmares? What about that name she called out occasionally? Were her dreams projecting experiences from her past? *Forget the past and live in the present.* Zumra was a wonderful woman. Her melancholy look made her appear so vulnerable that he wanted to protect her. Yet he was more concerned about her than he was showing. Sometimes Zumra vanished for a few days. '*Looking for peace in my lodge*,' she alleged when he asked. He found it strange that she refused to show him her dwell. '*Give me some more time*,' she begged every time he was insisting accompanying her. '*I'm living in a poor neighbourhood with my mother. I've got to prepare her.*' He assumed that she was ashamed to show him the poverty in which she was living.

He opened his eyes, looking around. The sun shining through the window behind his back was warmly illuminating his office. The doors on either side led respectively to the corridor and the storage room. On his left hand stood a bookshelf full of files, a fridge with a coffee maker on it, and a high bookcase full of colourful maps. Another entrance in front of him led to his server room.

Near the door toward the corridor, hung a laminated map of Sarajevo. In the corner stood a couch, table, and two armchairs. A room from the communist period that smelled like overcooked coffee.

Sometimes he was missing the luxury of his American office, where his job had got priority over private life. Here he was part of the human misery. Seventy per cent unemployment, while countless wretches survived thanks to an additional income on the black market. Poor losers, not criminals. A matter of survival, a view that Western police observers were not sharing. The Western European social model considered begging as a criminal offence, preferring to tax charity. *'No one is above the law. This parallel trade must stop,'* kept repeating observers. That without this illegal trade, hundreds of children and adults would be starving to death was not their business. In the Western European social model, justice considered begging as a criminal offence. A community that liked presenting itself as an example of humanity. Bullshit. How could someone survive properly without financial means?

Since the gruesome death of his parents, he doubted that the Western model of society should replace the Bosnian model. He was thinking of the growing Muslim fundamentalism. While the U.S. government denied that seven thousand mujahidin had fought in Bosnia, these assassins had been spreading across the country, discretely proclaiming the real and literal interpretation of the Qur'an. Back into the Dark Ages. Suddenly the number of radical followers grew day by day, as did increase the construction of mosques. Authoritarian Arab governments financially supported the more indigent population in remote places, far away from the media, what the EU had failed to do. The EU was only interested in projects getting visibility in the mainstream media. Nobody seemed to notice the growing radicalisation. Women with a headdress, hijab, niqab, burqa, and chador, while in public they got severely separated from the men. No more women in a football stadium. Was that the future of his country?

The West kept pretending that everything was okay. He let out a sigh, bowed over the file again and wrote the last sentences of his report. *Then I go home.*

But the phone decided otherwise. '*Egzon*' indicated the display.

Lazar took the call.

"Move your ass to the *Princip Bridge*. A murder," the chief of police snarled.

Lazar was not very enthusiastic. "Who is going there?" he asked.

"Two surveillance vans. Routine job."

"The technical team already been warned?"

"Yes, as the pathologist anatomist." The line went dead.

His romantic dinner tonight ended like the Titanic in the ocean. With a grim face, he slammed the map and threw it in the top drawer. Internally indulging Egzon, he left his office.

Moments later, when stepping into the adjoining office without knocking, four pairs of eyes glanced up. Izet Neoric and Nijaz Bolic were sitting in front of each other on the far side, the brown-headed Fadila Piric in front of Senad Mujdza, his partner. Her facial features softened. She was a handsome woman with dark eyes, narrow lips, and slightly curved mouth corners. The Serbs had exterminated her family and husband. After the war, Lazar had taken her to the police, where she became his most loyal employee.

Senad Mujdza dropped his newspaper. "Is there something wrong?" he asked with a frown.

"A homicide."

Senad stood up, pulling up his wide crumpled pants and followed him in the corridor. Their footsteps sounded harsh through the dark. They left the building on the side door near to the place where Lazar used to park his unmarked police car. As he sat behind the wheel, he called Zumra. But she didn't pick up. He left a short text message, wondering why she didn't pick up.

Senad gave him a mischievous smile. "When are you getting married?"

"There's still time for that," Lazar answered, giving him a look of disapproval.

"Make sure she doesn't go looking for a younger guy."

Lazar silenced his friend with a reprimanding glance.

Hardly five minutes later, they reached the crime scene. A crowd of onlookers were obstructing traffic. Lazar operated the horn violently.

"That's chaos," he called out, as the people slowly faded apart. He drove onto the green soil and parked. Annoyed, he got out, slammed the door and stepped up to two policemen talking to a small group of curious people. They seemed very relaxed, smoking a cigarette. He recognised a few TV reporters asking questions to the police officers.

"If in five minutes, you haven't closed this place off, you can take off your uniforms," he shouted. "And no comments to the press. Do I make myself clear?"

The eldest threw his half-smoked stalk on the ground and immediately started roaring at about ten people, while three policemen in his neighbourhood followed his example.

Lazar, with Senad who had joined him in the meantime, beside him, paced to the crime scene. Men with plastic headgear and white coats were already busy. They greeted each other with a small gesture and put on blue paper booties.

Lazar's studied the man behind the wheel, staring at him with empty eyes.

"Numerous traces already got lost," Ferid Munic complained. "Always the same with these rookies. It's time for a change."

"EuPol has to take care of that," replied Lazar sarcastically.

The photographer seemed to be ready with his task, while the fingerprint specialist was powdering inside the car.

Lazar shook his head in despair, putting on his latex gloves.

"Collecting traces at a crime scene is teamwork," he grunted, knowing that sharp remarks no longer elicited any reactions. Then he turned to face Ferid.

"Did you become wiser now?"

"Death by strangulation with a thin, metal string," replied Ferid without hesitation. "There's also a deep cut behind the right ear."

Lazar leaned forward and in the neck discovered a thin metal wire twisted together with the ends behind the headrest, holding the body upright. He also examined the wound and the scraped skin behind the right ear.

"The killer must have been a strong man," he remarked.

"I think so," replied Ferid. "But he must have used handles in which the wire was stuck. With his bare hands, even with gloves on, he would have cut himself. Our killer builds his instruments himself."

Lazar nodded. "Looks like a bicycle brake wire. Who found the body?"

"An old man walking his dog."

"Where is he?"

"Back to his apartment. One of the officers has noted his name and address. But he won't make us much wiser."

"Are there any other witnesses?"

"There aren't."

Lazar glanced across the river to the two blocks along the main road. Then he turned to Senad.

"Send an agent to those apartments. Perhaps someone was peeping out of the window. Witnesses rarely take the initiative to come and help us."

Senad nodded and rushed toward one of the cops. Moments later, Lazar saw the patrolman running across the street. Then he bowed over the body, knowing that in a murder investigation, the hours following the crime are crucial. He wanted to collect as much evidence as possible because waiting for the autopsy results decreased his chances of finding the culprit.

Ferid was inspecting the victim's hands and nails. "Oh yes," he said suddenly, "we've found two packs of heroin. Not much, but just enough to assume that the man dealt with drugs."

Lazar gave him a look of astonishment. He didn't trust the careless display of evidence. '*Never allow yourself to get deceived by appearances*,' he used to say to Senad. Hasty interpretations are dangerous as Lazar had all too often experienced in America where some thirty per cent of the prisoners were innocent.

"A clue is not proof of guilt," he said sternly. "Don't just look at what you find, but ask yourself why you find it. The white powder may belong to the victim. But why did we find it between the seats?" He ignored Ferid's frowned-up eyebrows and thoughtfully walked around the vehicle to the other side, where he opened the door and began investigating the interior. After a while, he got out and glanced around, but couldn't see the pathologist anywhere.

He sighed and glanced up to Ferid. "Damn, where is Milan?"

The scientist shrugged but didn't answer.

"Well, as soon as he's finished his job here, get the car to the lab for a thorough examination," he continued without addressing anyone in particular. In America, that order would be taken as insulting, but here every action had to be ordered. Taking the initiative was unknown to them. A consequence of communism, he assumed.

He crouched and searched the victim's clothes, finding a wallet in the back pocket from which he took out the identity papers.

"Emir Besic," he read with a loud voice. "And look at that, what a beautiful business card. *Digital Future*," he said to Senad, who perpetually

made notes.
Lazar put the wallet in one of the plastic bags he always carried with him. "Something is missing."
"What then?" asked Senad with a frown.
"He's an engineer, lives and works for Sarajevo's largest IT company, has business cards, an email address and a mobile phone number. All these details are printed on the card."
Senad smiled triumphantly. "But there's no cell phone here."
Lazar nodded with a smile. "Probably taken by the killer," he said. "Or by a casual passerby." He got out, let his eyes slowly wander over the vehicle, walked to the front, and checked the bumper. The slight dent in the middle did not escape his alertness. He stroked his fingertips over the grass, stood up again, and turned to Senad.
"Look, tyre marks left by the car colliding with this bumper."
"Or traces of a car that was there before the victim arrived."
"And what caused the dent in the bumper? Look at it, these traces are still fresh. They might explain how the killer could get on the backseat without the victim tried to drive away."
"What do you mean?"
"Our victim parked here, but before he could get out, another car deliberately hit his bumper. The perpetrator's car."
Lazar paused shortly. "The assassin threatens the surprised victim with a gun, drop in the backseat, gives Emir a crippling thump behind his right ear and puts a stranglehold cord around his neck. The headrest and the handles make the strangulation a child's play."
Senad set a thoughtful face. "Don't the drug point to the organised crime environment?" He was obviously not convinced by his chief's hypothesis.
"My dear Senad, think of a magic trick. Distract the attention and create an illusion. If it were about drugs, we wouldn't find two or three grams of heroin here. The perpetrator wants us to believe that's a drug matter."
He gestured to Ferid to get off the grass. "Man, watch where you're stepping."
Ferid came standing next to him on the road, while Lazar kept waving to the strip between the car and the asphalt.
"Grass," he said with a grin, "and the killer has been standing close to the car. But now you've been destroying those footprints. Stay on the road. The photographer should take pictures of the whole strip. Tell your trackers to take a good look at the soil on each side. Check also the front bumper."
He paused.
The team leader swallowed, stepped backwards, calling his photographer, assuming that the man hadn't yet photographed this piece of land.
"The killer walked around the hood," Lazar emphasised.
Ferid didn't argue and designated a technician.

“There’s more to this than we can see at first glance,” growled Lazar, turning toward the photographer. “Take discreet photographs of the crowd. Probably it won’t give us anything, but you never know.”

When he turned around to face Ferid, he saw in the distance the pathologist arriving. The little chubby man didn’t seem to be in a hurry at all. He got out his old Volkswagen Golf break at ease, briefly admiring the surroundings. Then he stepped toward the trunk, opened the lid, and calmly put on a white plastic jacket. Finally, he grabbed a suitcase and strolled to the crime scene.

“Dobar dan,” Lazar grumbled, and he picked up his nose for the alcoholic vapour escaping Milan’s mouth. Knowing that every remark was meaningless, he kept his opinion to himself.

“Dobar dan,” the physician answered almost inaudibly.

“All useful clues might be secured by now,” said Lazar with an ironic beat to his voice. “We’re done here, Ferid. If you find anything, give me a call, no matter what time it is.”

The technician nodded. “I’ll do that.”

Senad put his notebook away and walked next to Lazar. “What do you think?”

Lazar shrugged. “A murder during rush hour and nobody has seen something.” He cast an investigative glance around him, glancing for minutes toward the roads around the park, constructed for the residents of the Parrot Building, and the customers of the pharmacy.

“Those who are going to the centre, or Pale, coming from the south also use it. It’s an important abbreviation,” he remarked softly.

“The killer must have good nerves,” replied Senad with a grin. “Cars pass by here all the time.”

“Yeah, it was a very calculated act. The perpetrator intentionally hit the bumper to divert his victim.”

“That dent could have been there already,” insisted Senad categorically.

“Those tracks in the grass and that new dent convince me otherwise,” Lazar said insistently. “Before the victim understood what was happening, the killer already got in the backseat.” He paused. “Then he struck him with the butt of a gun, what’s proven by the scratched skin behind the ear. If by chance someone would’ve parked behind Emir’s car, he only would’ve seen the back of two people. But the killer struck the victim at the moment no witnesses being around. He strapped his victim to the headrest, and I’m guessing he didn’t stay in the car for more than a few minutes.”

“Apparently, a professional,” Senad admitted.

“Yes, and it’s not about drugs. Yet that powder is a disturbing clue. Who goes to all this trouble to lead us astray?”

Senad Mujdza shrugged and yawned demonstratively.

“Where else do you want to go?” he asked hopefully.

"Perhaps *Digital Future* might make us wiser." Lazar took his cell phone and called Zumra. When he heard the voicemail message again, he pensively put his cell phone back in his pocket.

Zumra, where are you hanging out?

FOURTEEN

BRAM RUYTER STARED FEARLESSLY AT THE MEN IN FRONT OF HIM. BOTH HAD GOT A broken nose at least once, while the scar on the neck of one of them came from a knife sting. The ice-cold glow in their dark eyes contradicted the jovial grin on their weathered faces.

Bram felt cornered, reluctant to let in these strangers. Even if they were what they alleged to be, it didn't make them less dangerous. He was unarmed, and if he refused them access, they might become violent. He'd heard about the SAS reputation. Or perhaps they belonged to MI6 or an even worse organisation. All those organisations produced well-trained killers. In defending national interests, they swept the most heinous crimes under the carpet. But he couldn't imagine they were considering him as a danger to their national security. He made himself even broader between the doorposts.

"May I see your ID?" he asked coldly.

"I was wondering when you were going to ask us," replied the spokesman with a mocking laugh.

Bram followed their movements carefully, ready to react if they pulled a weapon. But they took identical-looking wallets out of their inner pockets and showed their ID cards with stoic faces. The SFOR documents looked authentic. William Smith and Tom Jones.

"We avoid as much publicity as possible," the spokesman said. "We're not in the phone book."

"I didn't expect that either," Bram replied with a smirk, memorising their names. *Alias Smith and Jones*, he thought. The famous television series from his youth. *Play the naive social worker, curious and innocent but not afraid.*

He stepped aside, beckoned them theatrically inside, slammed the door and guided them to the living room.

"Sit down," he said calmly. "I'll listen, but honestly, I'm ignorant concerning terrorist matters."

The spokesman moved to the large sofa and sat down, while his partner remained upright, curiously studying every object in the living room.

"I'm William, and my colleague is Tom," said the sitting man, quoting the ID-card names. However, Bram considered those names as fake as the smile on their faces.

Bram just nodded and sat down opposite William.

"You work for *Last Hope*, don't you?" asked William, giving him a look of amused contempt.

"Are you clairvoyant?"

"What's your job?"

"What do you think?"

William's eyes sparkled, but he remained silent.

After a few seconds, Bram shrugged. "I'm not a terrorist."

Silence. Their facial expression kept unchanged.

Then Bram grinned. "I am Head of Office of a small cell that saves victims of the women trafficking. Has nothing to do with terrorism."

William's features got hard. "What were you doing in the Netherlands?"

"Irrelevant."

"You were military, I suppose."

"Why ask if you know?"

William kept a sharp eye on him.

Bram laughed, not at all disturbed.

"Do you have friends in the Glass Tower?" William asked.

"What do you think?"

"What have you done today?"

"Not enough to show off on the front page of *The Times*. A day of rest. The sun lured me out, and I went out walking around the city."

His remark did not provoke a reaction either.

William straightened his back. "Which pubs did you visit?"

"A voice in my head tells me that you already know. Central Café."

"The meeting point of the international elite, isn't it?" It sounded ironical.

"Are you also a member? There you'll not find mujahidin. And as far as I know, no other members of terrorist organisations in Bosnia." Bram shook his head, showing his irritation. "Okay," he said vehemently, "we're adults, I suppose. So, stop this childish game and tell me what you want to know." Convinced that they were armed, it was too late to go pick up his gun in the bedroom. Even though they let him go, he didn't feel like leaving them alone. At that moment, he saw Tom Jones walking toward the kitchen.

"Do you know the name Emir Besic?" asked William leaning back. Finally, the cat was out of the bag.

Bram made a thoughtful face. "Yes, I've already heard that name."

"You know damn well Besic is working for *Digital Future*."

He's talking about Besic as if he's still alive.

"Ah, so, that guy! Now I remember, I met him a few months ago. Emir. Here, first names are enough. I'd forgotten his last name. A good salesman, he sold me a laptop."

"Where did you meet that guy?"

"EUMM party in the headquarters. The companies with which EUMM is doing business, usually receive an invitation. To make it short, at the bar, I happened to have a conversation with Emir. We were bored to death, both waiting for the right moment to escape. You know how it goes, before you are aware, you're talking with an unknown person, complaining about insignificant things you will not remember later on. Suddenly you forget your intention to leave discreetly, spending most of the night drinking and telling each other about unpleasant experiences."

"What were your conversations about?"

"Do you have a hearing problem? I just told you, it was about our unhappy life. The war and human misery. Poverty. His work for *Digital Future* and a lot I can't remember. My unhappy relationships. Why this interest?"

Williams's face kept emotionless. "Didn't you meet him later?"

Bram wondered what they knew about him. *If you have to lie, stick to the truth as much as possible.*

"I think I bumped a few days, or weeks into him again. It happened in a restaurant," he answered. "Coincidentally. But in the end, we both felt so lonely that we had a good time together. Emir spontaneously invited me to his table. The residents here are nice people, you know."

"You keep saying it was a coincidence." William's voice betrayed disbelief.

"Do you think otherwise?"

"Of course not!"

"Sarajevo is so little," Bram said. "Now I remember having met him once again in the *Digital Future*, when I got my laptop, of course."

"But today you didn't meet him?" Williams's voice sounded like the hissing of a cobra, and his gaze didn't let him go for a second.

Bram shook his head. "We're not that intimate yet."

"What were you doing along the Miljacka, in front of that ugly yellow building?"

"You've got me watched?"

"Answer, please." William's facial expression radiated a mixture of restrained anger and frustration. He was visibly struggling to keep his composure.

Bram put his right leg over his left. "That's none of your business," he snarled. "Well, I often go for a walk, you know, and no one has come to ask me annoying questions about that, so far. I like to stroll through those little alleys around Bascarsija. Do you know that fountain that...?"

"You didn't happen to have an appointment with Emir?" interrupted William irritated.

"Why should I? I'm not a sissy. If you got me watched, you should know that I haven't met anyone."

"Neither did you receive a message from Emir Besic?"

Bram shook his head in astonishment. "Why would he call me?"

"Could you have missed his call?" William paused for a moment. "Can I have your cell phone for a moment?" he asked angrily.

If Bram had got a gun, he would've thrown out those two. Now he shrugged and handed him his cell phone. William put it on the corner of the tabletop, picked up his phone and called a number. While he was waiting impatiently, the corners of his mouth curled up slightly in a lousy attempt to smile.

Seconds passed. Gradually the corners of William's mouth sank back down, while his features betrayed despair, disbelief, and disillusionment.

Bram understood that William was using Emir's phone. William put the phone back in his pocket, grabbed Bram's phone from the table, and started checking the stored data. After a while, his lips narrowed to a line, and wrinkles appeared on his forehead. Then he slid the device over the tabletop toward Bram. Despite appearances, he seemed still to believe that his suspicion was justified.

Bram could hardly hide his triumph. "Is there something wrong with my cell phone?" he asked innocently.

"No, but it's strange that the *Digital Future* phone number doesn't figure in your contact list, although you maintain a business relationship with that company. Do you know its phone number by heart?"

"No, you're right, that number figures in my other cell phone."

As if stung by a wasp, William shot up. "Do you have another phone?" he called out with frustration.

Bram shrugged apologetically. "I had it a few days ago. Probably I've got lost it in a pub, or it's been stolen. Who cares?"

"Did you report the theft?"

"Why would I do that? Everyone knows it's futile to report a theft."

During Williams's theatrical performance, Tom Jones had entered the kitchen, and Bram had been watching him from the corner of his eye. Tom had thoroughly examined the kitchen, pulling open the doors of the cupboard, checking the fridge. To Bram's great relief, he hadn't checked the contents.

In the end, William seemed to understand that he couldn't continue this discussion forever. He made a dissatisfied sound as his eyes wandered desperately through the living room one last time in the hope of discovering something suspicious.

Bram thought they had been disturbing him long enough. He turned around to the kitchen to yell something unpleasant toward Tom, but an icy cold hug took his breath away; Tom was nowhere visible.

"Tom, we're done here," called William over his shoulder.

For a moment, Bram felt relieved when he saw Tom get up, but his facial expression worried him. The man was contemplating something, worrying.

William, however, didn't seem to notice it.

"I hope you enjoyed the promenade in town," he said with a breathless laugh.

Bram nodded. "Yes, I did. I wanted to cross that *Princip Bridge* again. Well, I'd be surprised you're aware where that name comes from," he said with a taunted laugh.

William's face features betrayed that he didn't know. Neither of those gorillas had probably heard the name Gravilo Princip before.

"He was a terrorist," Bram said with a loud voice. "He caused the First World War, and has been dead for more than eighty years."

William's features betrayed his displeasure. But apparently, he was at the end of his story. "Terrorism is not a subject to be taken lightly, Mr Ruyter. We know with certainty that Emir belonged to a terrorist organisation. Never heard of the Free Islamic State, or FIS for short?"

Bram shook his head. He had never heard of such an organisation, nor did he believe that it existed.

"Most likely, Besic was preparing an attack against my compatriots," William continued.

Bram drew a confused face. "You speak in the past tense. As if...?"

William shook his head. "We think Emir had an accident, but that's all I can say. The case is extremely delicate, Mr Ruyter. Please accept our apologies. Our visit was essential to get you off our suspect list. We wanted to make sure that your presence along the river had nothing to do with Emir."

"Am I a suspect? And why is that river so important?"

"Excuse me, but that's all we can say. We leave you alone now."

Bram felt relieved that they were leaving. He accompanied them to the exit.

"Good evening, Mr Ruyter," William Smith said with a fake smile. "We appreciate your cooperation."

The ironic undertone told a different story, and the expression in William's eyes gave Bram goose bumps.

He did not doubt that they would come back.

FIFTEEN

MAGAS SENSED AN ALARMING TINGLE WHEN HIS EYES CAUGHT A FERAL-LOOKING man behind the steering of a slowly driving car. He remained standing in front of the glass door while his friend entered the big building. His gaze was following a passing old Volkswagen with its irregularly spinning engine and defective exhaust. The smell of burned oil was irritating.

The driver was an unshaven, skinny man with strikingly large aqueous pig eyes peeking at him grimly. Reaching the end of the parking lot, the car turned right and vanished out of sight, while the greasy smoke slowly evaporated into the air. Sunken into thought, he stepped through the doorway. Senad stood at the reception desk gazing as bewitched by the striking blonde. Lazar estimated her mid-twenties. The round face, convex cheeks and red-dyed lips made her mouth look bigger. Her long thin hair fell loosely alongside her abundantly creamed face, ending under a pair of huge boobs bulging out of the deep cleavage. Senad seemed to enjoy the spectacle. Personally, Lazar found her make-up and tunic rather vulgar. Too plump to be sexy. As he joined Senad, the woman bowed even deeper, smiled very sultry, offering them a broader view of her treasures.

He ignored her.

"Have you seen that Volkswagen?" he asked at Senad.

"No, what about it?"

"When we arrived here, the car with loudly broken exhaust was entering the parking place. Behind the wheel sat an unsavoury looking individual who was perpetually staring in my direction. At first, he wanted to stop, but when he saw us, he drove on, turned around, and passing by, he peered in my direction again."

Senad grinned ambiguously. "He'll love blonde guys."

"I think I've read great fear in his eyes."

The receptionist cleared her throat.

"What do the gentlemen want?" she asked impatiently with a loud voice.

Lazar turned toward her. "My name is Magas, chief inspector, and that's my assistant Mujdza. A certain Emir Besic is working here." He fleetingly showed his proof of legitimacy.

"Indeed, but he's not here yet." She moved her upper body on the rhythm of her voice.

"That's why we're here. I want to speak to the manager."

"You mean Mr Pozderac?"

"Do you have several managers?"

She made an angry face and came around the edge of the desk with waving hips, surrounded by a cloud of cheap perfume that made Lazar sneeze. Her short white skirt barely covered her voluminous buttocks. *Awful.* She beckoned both inspectors to follow, leading them to an office at the far end of a short corridor. Two tall windows warmly illuminated the modestly furnished office with vanilla-coloured walls.

A 50-year-old man with a long black beard and wavy hair up to his shoulders was sitting behind a cheap-looking black desk. His angular face, dark eyes, and fleshy mouth gave him a sinister appearance.

Lazar could hardly suppress a grin. *A caricature of Rasputin. An exceptional couple.*

"The police, Mr Pozderac," she said, and it sounded like the announcement of a disaster.

The man frowned and looked from the one to the other. Lazar assumed the blonde had already forgotten their names.

"Chief inspector Magas and assistant Mujdza," he said. "We are here to have a talk about Mr Besic."

Pozderac waved the receptionist out. She turned around, causing her golden hair to fan out wide and her skirt to go up, producing an arousing image of a small pair of knickers cutting her fleshy buttocks in half. Head in the neck, she rocked her hip through the doorway, shutting the door behind her. Only the pungent scent of her perfume lingered.

"Did Emir anything illegal? He's our best collaborator," Pozderac said with a shrill voice.

"He *was* your best employee," Lazar corrected.

The substantial body shot out of the office chair, and Pozderac walked up to them.

"Do you mean that..." he stammered.

Lazar interrupted him. "Indeed, Mr Pozderac, I mean that someone has killed your best employee."

The manager seemed deeply affected. "Is there anything I can offer you? Tea or coffee?" He made a slow gesture to the two chairs opposite the desk.

"No, thank you. We won't keep you from your work for long. We heard that, uh, Emir has been living here, so we'd like to check out his accommodation. In anticipation of a more detailed investigation by our forensic team."

Pozderac seemed to panic, his eyes getting greater. "What? A team?"

"Take it easy, Mr Pozderac, that's the routine."

Lazar and Senad sat down while Pozderac fell into his leather armchair.

"What happened?" Pozderac's effeminate voice reminded Lazar of Demis Roussos.

"Emir got strangled in his car. Is it possible he dealt with drugs?"

Pozderac reacted indignantly. "How can you think of such a thing? Emir is uh was a computer freak, not a drug user."

"Did he have money worries?"

The man nervously lit a cigarette. *Foreign.*

"No," he answered, shaking his head. "He got a good salary." He inhaled deeply and blew the smoke out of his nostrils.

"Did he have enemies or friends?" Lazar saw that the man's index and the middle finger looked like sausages and were yellow-brown.

"Emir was a friendly young man, Chief Inspector, computers were his life. No real friends, apart from another computer freak."

"Do you know his name?"

"Dzeko, Anel Dzeko, he works in the Glass Tower for EuPol. Emir has visited him this afternoon."

"Interesting..."

“Don’t get me wrong, Chief Inspector, Anel’s a good friend. I can assure you; he’s nothing to do with the murder.” Pozderac was staring at the smoke he was theatrically blowing out of his nostrils.

“He has worked with Anel all afternoon,” he repeated. “But, uh, we got a strange phone call in the late afternoon. Someone urgently wanted an appointment with him.” Senad was taking notes.

Lazar frowned. “At what time?”

“A little after 3 p.m., I think. The caller wanted to meet Emir, and our receptionist has revealed where he might reach him. But later, she became suspicious and informed me. I advised her to warn Emir, and she did.”

“Why did she suddenly get reservations?”

“The man spoke our language very well, but with a heavy foreign accent. The chill in his voice alerted her.”

“Did he mention his name?”

“No... He contemplated going to make an important purchase. That made our receptionist think.”

“I didn’t know she can think. Are there any other people with whom Emir Besic had frequent contact?”

“I don’t think so,” answered Pozderac slowly. “I only know Anel. Emir has told our receptionist he was going to come back as soon as he’d finished in the Glass Tower. Besides, he was on the night shift, you know.” He pulverised his half-burned cigarette in a metal ashtray and lit a new one. “He was our best man.”

“Can we have a look at his accommodation?”

Pozderac shrugged. “Well,” he said. “I don’t want any trouble, but to be clear, Emir was only staying here when he was on duty. We’re employing two network specialists who, in turn, work a week. They each have their room on the first floor.”

“Do you know where he’s living? Strangely, *Digital Future* is printed on his business cards as his dwelling place.”

“On the heights of Breka, close to the Kosevo Hospital.”

“I know that place. What’s the address?”

“The receptionist will get it for you. Let’s go to Besic’s room now.” Pozderac quenched his cigarette in the heavy ashtray and rose from his chair. They silently left the office. At the reception, Pozderac took a key from a keyboard hanging behind the counter and ordered the blonde vamp to find Emir’s address and give it to the inspectors. They followed the man through a narrow arch portal, reaching a small hall where a wooden spiral staircase led them to a landing with three doors. Pozderac opened the door on the right.

“They each have a room,” he said, pointing to the opposite wall. “But they share a bathroom.”

Lazar entered a brightly lit and soberly furnished room. A high window with curtains and sand-coloured walls without any decoration, a single bed, a bedside table, and a wardrobe. His examination, lasting less than five minutes, yielded nothing. He turned around, facing the manager, and thanked him.

At the reception counter, the blonde gave Senad a card with Emir's address on it.

"We didn't find anything," Lazar conceded, shaking his hand. "Thank you for your cooperation. I don't think a deeper inquiry will be necessary."

"Thank you," said Pozderac with a slight bow.

Senad shoved his notebook in his pocket, and they left the building.

"Weird case," he remarked.

"Indeed, this affair deserves Magas's interest." Lazar was a great fan of Agatha Christie's detective Hercule Poirot. He glanced back over his shoulder, getting behind the wheel.

"What's your opinion?" Senad asked.

Lazar shrugged. "It's too early to conclude. Emir was a well-paid computer freak, a normal young man, I think. An ordinary citizen who got killed by an assassin who's trying to lead us astray. What do you think we shouldn't find out?"

"Do you believe that the drugs we've found should fool us?"

"You're not convinced, yet?" Lazar shook his head. "We're going to take a look at the forensics department. Maybe those guys have already found something."

The National Forensic Institute, with its morgue and laboratories, was located along the Miljacka river, close to Skenderija. A massive metal fence surrounding the building ended with a double gate, a metal fence, and a guardroom bordering on the main building. Lazar parked his duty car on the outside along the wall, next to the guardroom.

A guard beyond a safety glass pane checked their IDs and then electrically opened the gate. They walked in silence to the rear of the building, where they entered the workshop through a small door next to a metal roll-up door. All space was taken up by several workshops giving access to the large parking lot at the rear of the building through metal roll-up doors. The morgue was in the basement, and the laboratories occupied the two upper floors. A special elevator connected all levels. Most of these departments lacked sufficient equipment to be efficient. Lazar feared the promised aid from the West would never come.

He spotted Emir Besic's car on a lowered lubrication bridge in front of a long work table with several toolboxes next to it. Two specialists were taking out the seats.

Ferid Munic emerged from a small office, joining them with a big smile on his face.

"There we have our impatient detective," he said with a broad grin, triumphantly opening his right hand. In the palm of it shimmered a flat cylinder having the size of a six-mark coin. Lazar recognised it immediately.

"Where did you get that?" he asked astonished.

Ferid grinned satisfied. "Under the car."

"Did you clean it?"

"No, we found it like this."

"Fingerprints?"

The specialist frowned.

Lazar understood Ferid hadn't checked for fingerprints.

Lazar let out a sigh. "Never mind, whoever placed it was wearing gloves." He took the disc from Ferid's hand.

"What's that?" asked Senad curiously.

"Transmitter with a battery, magnetic attachment, built-in antenna. Range five kilometres, battery life twenty-four hours." Lazar briefly bit his lower lip, handed the transmitter over to the scientist. "Anything else?"

"Only fingerprints of the deceased. Nothing on the door handles, neither on the backseat and the bodywork. The perpetrator was wearing gloves."

"That electronic transmitter has been made abroad. When will I get your full report?"

"Tomorrow. As far as the results of the laboratory are concerned, you have to be patient," answered Ferid in an apologetic tone.

"Thank you."

When they were outside again, Lazar contemplated finishing the day. Zumra's sad eyes and especially her beautiful body were animating his imagination. However, after a short hesitation, he decided to question another witness first. He glanced at Senad.

"Do you have any idea what Emir might have discovered?" he asked with a frown.

Senad gave him a look of surprise. "You ask me? You're joking, aren't you? We currently know too little to conclude."

"But enough to claim that the case stinks." Lazar got behind the wheel, and as soon as Senad had slammed the door shut, he cleared his throat. "An international scent I don't like it."

Senad frowned. "You should explain."

"After Emir visited the Glass Tower, he was planning to go straight back to *Digital Future*. But when he discovered that a foreigner was looking for him, he changed his mind. He drove to the centre where he got killed."

"How did he know someone was looking for him?"

"Were you dreaming in *Digital Future*?"

"Sorry, you're right: the phone call from a mysterious man."

"The killer has taken Emir's cell phone. Furthermore, the transmitter is an indication that someone was following Emir from a distance. Ordinary criminals don't use these things. So, someone was watching Emir's movements, probably trying to trace his contacts. You don't place tracers if you want to kill someone. Something is not quite clear here!" Lazar loved it to surprise his assistant.

Senad kept quiet.

Lazar let out a sigh of despair, jabbed the key into its ignition.

"Anel Dzeko might have to tell us more," he said aloud. "Try to find out where he lives. But first, we'll stop at the Glass Tower." While driving off, Senad called the switchboard and ordered the officer on duty to look up Anel's address and phone number.

At the moment they were leaving the parking, taking the Sniper Alley, Lazar wondered what Zumra was doing. As long as Besic's murder kept unsolved, he would be an annoying company for a romantic tête-à-tête. Finding what people motivated to kill human beings, tracking down criminals, unravelling mysteries and solving a homicide had become a passion, an inner urge. He was like a pit bull once he got stuck in a case and wouldn't let go until he'd solved it.

At that time of the night, the traffic on the main road Sarajevo-Ilidza artery was pretty fluid, and the ride lasted less than ten minutes. He parked his car on the visitor's parking lot facing the tall tower building. He knew that the natives were providing the guard duty. Much cheaper than engaging internationals.

The Glass Tower counted ten floors constructed in Y-shape with three equal wings. The EU sanctuary, the police force that would soon replace the IPTF. *A cunning way to control our country*. Never before had there been so many foreigners in Bosnia, and he wondered how many foreign intelligence services were active under cover of humanitarian missions. International aid workers were entitled to freedom of movement throughout the country. And almost every stranger was an aid worker. It couldn't be easier.

Lazar released his wry thoughts, almost ashamed he'd been adopting so quickly the American way of life. Though, three years of war had changed his view. Especially the death of all his family members had made him cynical.

"Let's have a chat with the guards," he said with a hint of impatience. They walked side by side toward the glass shed where one of the guards was smoking a cigarette next to the lowered barrier. He looked like a wrestler, two metres in size and weighing at least one hundred and twenty kilos of muscles. Friendly face.

"*Dobar vecer*," the man said. "Good evening."

Lazar smiled, showing his ID card. "*Dobar vecer*, I'm Chief Inspector Magas. Do you mind answering a few questions?"

"Depends," the man started carefully.

"You know I can have you picked up at home if you don't want to talk now?"

The man didn't answer.

"Do you know Emir Besic, a *Digital Future* computer scientist?"

"I do know Emir, what about him?" Hulk's features obscured. *Nobody trusts the police.* Lazar looked around to be sure they were alone.

"He's been here today. Can you tell me when he left?" he asked cautiously.

"Must have been between half-past three and four. Emir was in such a hurry that he didn't even look at us."

"Was he alone?"

"Yes, he was. When he passed by, he was calling. Or no, he was typing a message."

"And no one was following him, or driving away from the parking shortly after he'd left?"

The guard shook his head. "No. But what does all that mean?"

"Emir got killed shortly after he'd left here," said Lazar succinctly.

"Killed?"

"Yes, it's possible someone has been following him from here. Do you know if Anel Dzeko is still in the building?"

The guard shook his head. "He has left around five o'clock."

Lazar reckoned that the Internal Security Department daily gave the guard a list of all personnel with access clearance.

"Don't you happen to know where he's living?" He asked softly, fearing that the guards were not allowed to provide any information to outsiders. When the man started to walk toward the booth, he recalled that he no longer lived in America but Bosnia. Bosnian solidarity, fuck the rules.

"Malik, could you look up Anel Dzeko's address?" asked the Hulk to his colleague inside the booth.

Seconds later, Malik handed a paper to Senad, who slid it in his notebook.

"If you've anything else to say, you can always call me at this number." Lazar gave the man his business card. The guard, visibly affected by the news, stuck the card in his wallet.

On their way back to the parking space, Senad received a message on his cell phone. "Anel's address," he said.

Lazar made a short grunt. "Some pieces of the puzzle are beginning to fall into place, Senad," he continued after an instant of reflection. "When Emir left here, he seemed worried. Do you remember what the manager told us? A caller refusing to reveal his name. That's why the receptionist warned Emir, who left here shortly after. Although he initially wanted to head to *Digital Future*, he made an appointment in town."

"With his killer," returned Senad with a smile.

They got in the car. Lazar didn't start right away, contemplating for a few seconds. "No, no, no," he suddenly yelled. "Emir got informed that a stranger was looking for him and left his friend. According to the guard, he was sending a text message without glancing up. He was sending that message to someone he wanted to meet. But an assassin was watching and following him, making sure he couldn't talk to anyone!"

"If that's the case, the man with whom Emir wanted to speak would have been there as well. Why hadn't he been preventing the murder? Why didn't he call the police?"

"Senad, despite the ban on parking alongside the Miljacka, it's one of the few places where you can easily leave your car. That's why the traffic police usually close eyes. I reckon Emir had arranged that meeting somewhere in the city centre. So, the person he wanted to see wasn't there."

Lazar got the engine started, drove slowly off the parking space, following the gravel road along with the guard booth. He turned his head to the right and saw the guard talking to someone. Both men were engaged in an animated conversation. The guard showed something to the man.

My business card.

Lazar turned onto the paved road while he kept watching the two people in the rear-view mirror.

"What is it?" asked Senad turning around.

Lazar remained silent. The guard was still talking, and the smaller guy had turned his back to the barrier.

"Who is that?" whispered Senad, as if the man outside could hear it.

"When we passed the guard booth, the guy turned his head away. Still, I could swear that's Mycroft Follum. But what's he doing there, and what does he want from the guard?"

"Damn it, Lazar, who is this guy?"

"EuPol Political Advisor."

SIXTEEN

BRAM WAS TREMBLING OF EXCITEMENT. AFTER SHUTTING THE DOOR AND LOCKING again, he looked through the small window beside the door and saw Smith and Jones strolling toward the road. Their fierce discussion, accompanied by hand gestures, worried him. As if they disagreed about something. They stopped a few times, turning around and staring for seconds at the house. But they couldn't see him.

When they'd almost reached the road, he saw Tom handing something to his colleague, but could not recognise what it was. Once the couple was out of sight, Bram hurried to the kitchen, opened the freezer, pulled out the frozen plastic bag and turned on the boiler. He paced from the sink to the refrigerator and back until the water was bubbling. After filling a bowl with the hot water, he dropped the package into it and continued staring impatiently at the slowly melting ice. Eventually, he shook the contents on a tin plate and meticulously checked all the debris.

Button 8 is missing. It might have been lying behind a table leg and was now in Jones's possession. He bit his lower lip, thinking at all the mistakes he'd made. Alleging he'd met Emir only twice by chance was stupid. Furthermore, every sane person would have asked William what he was looking for on his cell phone. No doubt, they'd found the button 8, and they knew that his story about the stolen phone was made up, aware that he'd received a call from Emir shortly before he got killed.

They're wondering what links me to Emir and why I kept it a secret. He desperately sought a way out. Smith and Jones knew he'd seen Emir's body, that he'd called to its cell phone and had spotted them in the BMW.

If they killed Emir, I am now a problematic witness.

He had to take the right measures. For a moment, he was contemplating asking Winston's permission to stay in a shelter for a while. But Winston would ask questions he didn't want to answer. He was on his own. Horrible pictures were flashing through his mind, pushing him to rush toward his bedroom. In the wardrobe, he removed some cardboard boxes and a suitcase. With the help of his Leatherman tool always wearing on his belt, he removed a double bottom plate. From the free space, he took out an anti-shock laptop case, a Glock 17 with corresponding waist holster, a box of 9 mm cartridges, a silencer, and a roll of wipes. After replacing the computer back, Bram marked the storage place with a few transparent strips, took a khaki towel out of a drawer, and paced back to the living room. Once he sat down in an armchair, he spread the sheet open on the coffee table and started to disassemble the weapon. After cleaning all the parts, he reassembled the gun and screwed the silencer on the barrel. Routine. Filling the magazine, magazine in the butt, and loading through inserting a round into the chamber. Security on. After that, he put the weapon in the holster.

After several minutes of reflection, he paced to the bedroom where he changed his clothes for a dark jogging suit, jack and sports shoes. He also took gloves and a balaclava from a drawer, moved back to the lounge, settled down on the couch and threw the jack, gloves and balaclava beside him.

The dusk was increasing, and he felt like a blind pedestrian amid a highway. If his suspicions were correct, a few killers were on their way, though he had no idea why he'd become their target.

What if there were more than two of them?

He wasn't a quick frightened, but unrest was growing. The longer he was thinking about the situation, the more he got convinced that he'd stand no chance against these professional killers. What he'd in mind was madness.

After a long hesitation, he called the man who could help him survive.

SEVENTEEN

LAZAR MAGAS PARKED HIS CAR ALONG THE SIDEWALK AND GOT OUT. THE DUSK WAS almost ready to welcome the night, and on lack of street lighting, the houses seemed obscure grey square blocks with dark rectangular gaps in between. A yellowish gleam was shining from behind several windows. He looked along the barely visible path meandering up toward a few houses.

Senad came standing next to him. "An awful environment," he said.

They climbed the short but steep hill. Anel Dzeko lived in the middle house. Above the front door was a flat roof. Lazar stepped under the shielded lamp and rang the bell. Somewhere inside the house sounded a bell. Seconds later, the door went ajar, and he looked at a man with stinging dark eyes, a crooked nose and a pale face. The young man wore grey cotton trousers with an oversized yellow shirt, and his bare feet stuck in wild leather moccasins. A black headband was keeping the long hair out of his eyes.

"*Dobra vecer, gospodin Dzeko*, I am chief inspector Magas," Lazar said with a loud voice. "That's my assistant Mujdza. Do you mind if we come in for a moment?"

"What's it about?" asked the man in a biting tone, not at all impressed by the two inspectors.

"We have a serious matter to discuss." Lazar gave him his most amiable smile.

Anel did not move.

"And what if I refuse?" he retorted provocatively.

"Maybe you'll get chattier in our office."

The threatening undertone got its effect; the young man made a step sideward, let them pass, and slammed the door shut. "Follow me," he said grumpily.

They walked through a narrow extension.

"You can keep your shoes on," Anel continued.

The lounge contained a table with four chairs, a long couch, and an armchair. On the right side, Lazar saw a narrow counter closing a niche in which was a kitchen housed with just enough space for a cooker, refrigerator and sink. Through a doorway on the left side, Lazar noticed the bathroom. In either of the furthest corners was a door; the right one closed, the left wide open. In the left room, he saw a wooden desk with a computer and screen.

His curiosity obviously irritated Anel, who slammed the door shut and sat down at the table with a grumpy face, beckoning them to have a seat on the long sofa.

Nowadays, the citizen is no longer frightened by the police.

"Mr Dzeko, you're a computer scientist working for EuPol, aren't you?" Lazar began patiently.

“That’s right.”
“And you are befriended by Emir Besic?”
“Yes, I am.”
“I mean you were Emir’s friend.”
“What? I still am.”
“No, you were,” Lazar repeated emphatically, his eyes keeping focused on the young man. “Your friend got murdered this afternoon.”
Anel glanced from one to the other, while all the colour on his face was fading. “Emir is dead?” he asked with a trembling voice.
“Yes, he got strangled.”
Anel shifted in his chair. “Terrible...We’ve been together this afternoon, until half-past three.”
“That’s why we’re here.” Lazar noticed a few tears in Anel’s eye corners.
“Who killed him?”
Lazar shrugged. “Could it be someone from the drug world?”
Anel reacted angrily. “Why might someone from that mafia have killed Emir?”
“Because he used or sold drugs.”
Anel laughed loudly, glancing indignantly from one to the other while rubbing his eyes dry. “You don’t believe that yourself, do you? Emir and drugs? Are you trying to accuse us?”
“We’ve found drugs in his car,” Lazar countered. “That’s calling for clarification, don’t you think?”
“Believe me; Emir hated drugs. He had nothing to do with that.”
The slight hesitation in Anel’s voice hadn’t escaped Lazar’s attention.
“Are you sure about that? Or was he involved in another dubious case? Something involving foreigners.” He thought of the transmitter found under Emir’s car.
The silence filled the room, only disturbed by the hum of the refrigerator in the kitchen. Lazar’s piercing gaze visibly made the young man uncomfortable.
“All right,” answered Anel suddenly. “I don’t know much, but Emir had a business relationship with a Dutchman working for an aid organisation.”
“Do you know that man?”
“I’ve seen him once from a distance. At one of our parties, I reckon. His name is Bram. Bram, uh Ruyter.”
“And what do you mean by business relationship?”
“I have no idea. Emir told me that, for my health, it was better to forget about that Bram as soon as possible. Apparently, it had to do with politics.”
“Politics? A Dutchman in our country?”
“That’s how I’ve understood. That’s all I know. Emir had more than one foreign friend, but I didn’t meet any of them.”
“Now tell me what happened this afternoon.”

"We were working on a project, doing some checks as Emir got a phone call. From that moment on, his thoughts seemed far away. I asked him what was going on. He looked somewhat disturbed. Then he told me hat Safet Begovic was behaving strangely. Minutes later he received another phone call from *Digital Future* which made him very nervous. Suddenly he was in a hurry to leave."

"The project? Could that be the reason?"

"We're checking an application that will simplify network management. Only valuable for IT professionals."

"What time did he get those calls?"

"Between half past three and a half past four...The latter was around half past four. Emir left shortly afterwards."

"You mentioned another name, Safet Begovic. Who's that?"

"A poor nutter who's working for a foreigner."

"Is that all you know? You're Emir's best friend, aren't you?"

"That's right, but we never talked about politics. The war has traumatised Emir, and he hated not only the Serbs but also the British and the French. A sniper killed his youngest brother during the war, and that made him bitter. I think he hated all strangers. Yet he was an excellent man."

"What kind of a man is Safet?"

"I don't know him personally. A war veteran who's decided to make Serb's life difficult."

Lazar was a rational person. In America, his colleagues had admired him for his coolness and objectivity. He'd refused to arrest people without concrete evidence. But after his parents got murdered, the words *right* and *rightfully* got a different meaning for him. During the war, he'd sworn to find those killers and to punish them; the reason why he hadn't returned to America.

"Do you hate the Serbs?" asked Lazar.

Anel shook his head violently. "No. The war brought nothing but misery, and the rich people got wealthier, while the poor lost everything. Surely, the Serbs have done little good to us. However, do you think we were so innocent? Everyone used the name *God* to justify misconduct. What nonsense, the origin of the war certainly was not religious or cultural diversity. The politicians were using that as an argument to maintain or strengthen their influence."

Lazar grinned. "And you don't know what Safet Begovic had said to Emir?"

Anel laughed loudly. "No, but I think a group of nutters is going to kidnap Karadzic. A million dollars may seduce a lot of people."

Lazar exchanging a look with Senad and turned to the young man again. "Mr Dzeko, the idea isn't ridiculous at all. You're right, unlikely that drugs are involved. But Emir was maintaining relationships with foreigners, and I don't rule out an attempt to kidnap Karadzic. You don't happen to know where we can reach this Begovic or Ruyter?"

"No idea, but according to Emir, Ruyter is a good client of *Central Café*."

"Can you tell more about what might help us track down Emir's murderer?"

"No, not at all. I sincerely hope you're going to catch the perpetrator. Emir was an excellent friend."

Lazar grinned. "I am working on it." He stood up to say goodbye as his cell phone rang. He took the call, and while listening, he kept staring at the young man.

"All right," he said after a few seconds, "send the technical team over there. I'm already on my way." He shoved his phone back into a pocket of his jacket, looking straight in Anel's eyes. "Do you live here alone?

"Yes, why?"

"I advise you to be careful from now on. I suggest you keep the door closed for unknown people."

"Why?"

Lazar was hesitating for a few seconds. Then he decided to fuck the police rules.

"They just have just found Safet Begovic's body," he said.

EIGHTEEN

THE GONG REVERBERATED THREE TIMES. BRAM RUYTER RUSHED TO THE VESTIBULE and opened the door, facing a grinning Edhem Hasic. They hugged each other fraternally, and Bram immediately felt better. After having locked the door, he guided his friend into the living room. When Edhem saw the handgun on the tabletop, he raised his eyebrows and looked at him questioningly.

"I think I'm in trouble," said Bram as he sat down opposite his friend. Then he gave a brief account of what had happened to him.

Edhem kept quiet for a few seconds, then grinned. "I brought my artillery," he uttered.

"That's what I've been expecting," replied Bram with a faint smile. He knew that Edhem always was carrying a weapon. That's why he had called him.

Edhem frowned. "Are you convinced that your visitors aren't SFOR soldiers?"

"I reckon they're mercenaries."

"What exactly have you in mind?"

After Bram explained his action plan, Edhem's facial expression hardened.

"Good plan," he said while fetching a gun from behind his back. He checked its functioning, loading a cartridge in the chamber.

Bram nodded approvingly. "Glock 26, an extremely compact and light handgun, mainly made of polymer," he said. "The barrel is sixteen centimetres long. Seven hundred forty grams, including the full magazine with ten rounds of nine millimetres *parabellum*."

"You're an expert," answered Edhem admiringly, screwing a silencer on the barrel. "Your 17 with a modified barrel, however, is a better weapon."

"Where have you parked your car?"

"It's a borrowed car I've parked in the parking lot on the other roadside," answered Edhem with a crooked grin.

Bram understood, without further asking. In this country, it was healthier to avoid indiscreet questions. Not to your best friend either. Edhem was by no means an angel, but a guy he might count on, and that was all that mattered.

They silently enjoyed a final whisky. Both were used to alcohol, drinking now to ease the tension in silence. It was going to be a long night.

At 11p.m. Bram got up. After putting on his waist holster, he checked once more the proper functioning of his pistol. Then he pulled on his dark jacket and the leather gloves, glancing up toward his friend.

Edhem nodded and left the house as they'd previously agreed.

Bram waited a moment, turned off the lights and paced to his bedroom where he rolled the sheets into a thick bundle and shoved it under the woollen blankets, suggesting a sleeping person. *The killers might come looking through the window to verify if I am asleep*. He moved on his toes to the other side of the corridor, checked the guest room and walked back to his observation post next to the window while putting on his balaclava. When he reached the window, he slowly opened the rotating part, causing a faint squealing sound. He stuck his head out and peered over the field from which he had an excellent view. Despite the darkness, an approaching person on the vast meadow would immediately be noticeable. Or he had to crawl over the ground.

Bram also had a large field of vision along the sidewall while in the adjacent bedroom, he could observe almost the entire rear side through its window. Nevertheless, there was a blind spot that an intruder could exploit to unseen approach the guest room next to the hall. *It's unlikely they take that side.* The neighbour might discover the suspects, and those guys certainly didn't want any witnesses.

The long wait began.

Around 1 a.m., he started having doubts. Had he misjudged these guys? Were they part of the regular SFOR troops anyway? He walked on his toes into his bedroom toward the window and scrutinised during minutes the meadows. Reassured, he took up position again on his observation post.

Half an hour had passed. Bram was leaning against the wall, perpetually yawning. His eyelids became heavy, and he slumbered away. Even the shrill cry of an owl who regularly disturbed the nocturnal silence didn't bring him out of his half-sleep. Until a light crackle scared him off. He stuck his head out and gazed over the dark plains, smelling damp grass and seeing hundreds of gleaming lights of male glowworms searching for a willing female. On the left side, he saw nothing but gloomy grassland, descending to the road that wasn't visible from his position.

Then the owl cried again.

The hallway seemed an almost unfathomable black wall. Bram let out a deep sigh, leaning against the wall. After a short time, his eyelids closed again, and he was slumbering.

A squealing sound woke him up. Holding his breath, his eyes wide open, he focused all his attention on the hallway. Due to the nocturnal cooling, the wood was creaking all the time. He turned to the open window, taking deep gulps of air. *Just relax.*

Were they trying to get in through the patio? His eyes were wandering toward the door next to the hall leading to the sitting room. The other entrances were those of the two bedrooms and a bathroom.

Sweat drops were pearling on his forehead. Then he recognised the sound of a badly oiled hinge.

The door at the end of the hallway.

NINETEEN

EDHEM HASIC HELD THE GUN AGAINST HIS THIGH WHILE CAREFULLY LOCKING THE door behind him. The windows of the neighbour's house were all dark, and he assumed the older man was asleep. He paced with rapid steps to the parking lot on the other side of the road and hid behind the first garage, from where he had a view on the two dark forms of the houses through the hollow way. There were neither moon nor stars in the sky. But the city lights in the valley were spreading out enough brightness he could distinguish between surroundings and obstacles.

Bram had given him a good description of the two British mercenaries, which didn't mean that the same guys would do the dirty job. Also, he had to guess their modus operandi. They certainly wouldn't come by car on the main road. Crossing the open meadows behind the house was their only option left. On that side, Bram was keeping an eye. Both had put their cell phone on vibrate. The one who noticed something suspicious must warn the other.

In the first hour, he thought mainly about Bram. Although they were friends, knowing what Bram had experienced in Srebrenica, it was still unclear to him what connected Bram to Emir. MI6 or SAS agents weren't pussies, and this nocturnal adventure could be fatal to both of them. He feared Bram was underestimating the danger. If there were killers after him, they'd got orders from high-level authorities. Even though he hadn't mentioned it to Bram, he knew Emir Besic. Bram was playing a dangerous game. Or didn't he know his opponents? Edhem had been assuming that the relationship between Emir and Bram resulted from an accidental encounter, but Bram's mysterious meeting at *Central Café* and Emir's killing refuted that.

Why hadn't Bram warned the police?

Why had he tried to locate Emir's cell phone?

Why had he run away like a criminal trying to cheat his pursuers?

Why had those Britons visited his dwelling place?

Many questions without answers. Edhem assumed Bram hadn't told him the whole story. Also, he didn't believe British secret services were killing innocent civilians without reason.

Nevertheless, he had a good reason to help Bram. The past.

Srebrenica, 11 July 1995

Edhem had decided to return to the valley earlier than he'd planned. The shelling with grenades and heavy weapons had become a part of his daily life, although he never got used to it. But today they seemed more intense than usual. As he looked through his binoculars toward the valley, he understood, but could hardly believe that the Serbs were invading the city. He beckoned his men to go into cover, wondering how long they could stay unseen. Everywhere running men and women were searching for shelter in the woods. The sounds of shots and cries mixed.

We are too late.

From the heights, hidden among the trees, he witnessed a terrible massacre, helplessly watching thousands of people trying to flee into the hills, getting chased by screaming četniks and paramilitary troops. He discovered countless bloody branches and bushes.

That day his world collapsed. The enclave, which was supposed to be protected by UNPROFOR, got overrun by General Mladic's well-trained soldiers. Three hundred and fifty Dutch soldiers hurried back to their northern camp in Potočari. Their protection had always been an illusion. After all, the Dutch were powerless, facing an arrogant ruthless warlord taking advantage of the International coalition's weakness. Mladic was humiliating UNPROFOR in the eyes of the whole world. Thom Karremans had been defeated in advance, having no chance to enforce favours. He owed this humiliation to the lax foreign policy of his government and the

indecision of a French UN-general.
Edhem and his men were powerless, witnessing one massacre after another they would always remember.
Later he'd heard that the ethnic cleansing lasted three days.
The Serbs shot at everything moving. Paramilitary gangsters with red berets executed cold-blooded men along the road, carelessly pushing the bodies into the ditches. He saw defenceless young men lining up like cattle to get killed one by one, keeping quiet, having only one wish: dying as quickly and painlessly as possible.
But not everyone agreed to get slaughtered. Many men, women, and children were crying, roaring, cursing the četniks, trying to reach the surrounding forests with despairing courage. Hundreds of innocent people fell under the endless rain of bullets. Few could get safely into the woods.
He thought of his family. Would he ever see her again?
Never had he felt so insignificant. There was little he could do for his people. However, after the first shock, he decided to save those who did not surrender. The woods and hills did not have secrets for him, and he was aware that the journey to Tuzla would be long and dangerous.
He'd never forget that escape to Tuzla. Before the refugees reached the Muslim line of defence, they had to cross the Serbian patrols. Hundreds of men, women, and children died in the minefields, while the wounded and the sick pleaded their friends or relatives to be painlessly killed by them; nobody wanted to be caught by the četniks, who were shooting haphazardly toward the forest teeming with refugees. Wounded or exhausted men and women who could not go any further committed suicide.
He succeeded in saving a small part of survivors, leaving Srebrenica as a bitter man. On the 11th of July 1995, he lost all faith in religion and politics. He arrived in Tuzla as a zombie. Looking for family members, he spoke to a Belgian author Bob Van Laerhoven who interviewed refugees, questioned the Red Cross and his military command. But in vain, nowhere did he find any trace of his parents or sisters. Then he made an oath: he was going to dedicate his life to his people, searching for answers and taking revenge.
He was still wondering where Naser Oric had gone. In April, the High Command had ordered him to Sarajevo. But why hadn't he come back? Because of the rumours that someone wanted to kill him? He was still wondering if Naser had been aware of Mladic's operation. Had he betrayed his people?
Why didn't he tell me?
Their friendship dated from 1985, when they had served together in the JNA. After their military service, he had returned to Srebrenica, while Naser became a police officer, committing himself to the Serbian Ministry of the Interior. Later he made it as President Milosevic's bodyguard.
The ABiH had proclaimed Naser as commander-in-chief of the troops in

Srebrenica. There Edhem had met Naser again, and the latter had taken him into his Special Unit. A privilege only for those Naser trusted.

After the war, Edhem headed to Sarajevo, resolved to avenge his family. Most of the women had escaped from hell, but as he hadn't found a trace of his family in Tuzla, he got convinced that they had ended up in a mass grave in Srebrenica.

Sarajevo, 8 October 2002

Edhem took a deep breath. It was dangerous to get distracted by dark thoughts. As time passed, he got more restless, glancing perpetually at his watch. On two occasions, he'd been alarmed by passing cars, but the noisy occupants were drunk young people living miles ahead beyond the hill.

When he spotted a weak gleam of light on the left, he'd been standing there for more than three hours. Some light gleamed behind the hilltop, dancing up and down. Could it be a walking man?

Edhem held his breath. After disappearing for a while, the gleam of light reappeared. This time he gazed across the meadow and then turned to look toward Bram's house. Was there a man? He noticed some dancing slow-moving light dots. After hours of staring into the darkness, you might see the environment coming to life and shadows becoming bizarre monsters, while the slightest sound seems much louder than it is. After three years of war experience, he possessed something like a sixth sense of imminent danger. *Something is going wrong.*

He took a black nylon stocking out of his pocket, pulled it over his head, and left his observation post. For a long time, he kept moving on the road, alternately looking in both directions. There was nothing.

First, he walked on the right side of the road, with the gun at chest level. Then he followed an imaginary curved line to the other side, squatting every four steps while scrutinising the surroundings. Only the sporadic cry of the owl broke the nightly silence.

Reaching the house, he discerned countless little dancing bodies across the meadows. *Glowworms.* He took a deep breath and sneaked like a cat to the sidewall, where the abundant grass cushioned his footsteps. He crouched, pricked his ears, lurking at the neighbour's house where the curtains behind the windows kept motionless. Somewhat reassured he got up as in the distance, the owl screamed again. He walked quickly toward the first window around the corner and stiffened. It was ajar and had a circular opening in the glass. Instinctively he crouched through his knees, pointing his Glock at the dark gap, the finger around the trigger.

Did Bram ignore the noise?

He got up very cautiously, bowed his head closer to the window, staring into the gloomy room. Near the door, he observed a massive silhouette with frightening green eyes. He tried to find out if there were other odd creatures in the bedroom but saw nothing but darkness. His full attention went back to the shadow, and at that moment, he saw a gun. He didn't have time to think; the creature swivelled in his direction. Shuddering, he glanced into a horrible face while his index finger curled around the trigger of his gun. But the monster was faster.

A flash blinded him while the glass was exploding in his face.

TWENTY

ZUMRA'S SILENCE WORRIED LAZAR. ZUMRA DIDN'T ANSWER HIS CALLS NOR TEXT messages. Just the voicemail kept announcing that she would be temporarily absent. He let the phone slide into his pocket, ignoring Senad's curious look and concentrated on the road again.

No one uttered a word. Lazar drove quite carelessly on that narrow winding mountain road in a lousy condition that kept climbing steadily between high conifers. His mind was trying to slide the pieces of a puzzle into place. Emir Besic and Anel Dzeko had been working together when Emir got Safet Begovic's call. Shortly after that call, Emir got strangled, and Safet shot. Anel was a witness against his will, a potential danger because the perpetrator had no idea what Emir might have been telling him. *In the wrong place at the wrong time.*

Barely realising that he'd crossed a village at high speed, he began the dangerous journey through a rugged mountainous landscape on an even narrower road. Although he knew this area well, he had to swerve fiercely from an oncoming car in a hairpin bend, causing him to slow down. The dark, featureless mass of woods passed by on either side and the potholes and cobbles continued in regular succession. Lazar now concentrated on every bend.

"Do you think Anel Dzeko is involved?" asked Senad all of a sudden.

Lazar shook his head. "He's an arrogant computer nerd but has nothing to do with the murder."

"But you've warned him."

"Yeah, I'm worried because what he may have heard makes him a target. Why did Safet call Emir? What am I supposed to deduce from that?"

"You think the killer might be a threat to Anel?"

Lazar remained silent. He knew that the crime scene was nearby and slowed down. Suddenly he saw flashing lights on his right, a hundred metres away from the roadside.

"We've missed a forest path," he grunted, drawing the vehicle to a halt on the narrow strip of grass along the road. *Who's going to live here now?*

He took a flashlight from the glove compartment, turned it on, got out and locked the door. As Senad had joined him, they walked side by side toward the forest path. The sound of vague voices in the distance and creaking branches of the trees on either side, while the light of his lamp set shadows on the road surface in motion, created a creepy atmosphere, accentuated by their footsteps sounding like hollow drums. A few metres before reaching that gloopy path, Lazar pointed the light beam on a dark spot on the other roadside, discovering an off-road vehicle.

"A diplomatic licence plate, an odd place to park," he murmured.

They turned left into the forest path.

"It must be hard for a car to get through here," said Lazar, lightening the soil covered by rotten branches and treacherous potholes. Some twenty metres ahead, the path made a right-hand curve. But the blue flashing lights and his flashlight delivered enough brightness to reach unharmed the clearing. There he noticed two police cars and an old Volkswagen with a shattered rear window. To his relief, there weren't journalists around.

The four smoking cops jumped apart when they discerned the inspectors. Lazar moved the light beam across the clearing until he spotted a black jumbled heap on the ground, about ten metres farther ahead. The body, he reckoned. But arriving next to the hood, he noticed a motionless figure sitting on the ground, bent forward with the head between his legs. Lazar's eyes run from the dead man to the shapeless heap ten yards away and from there toward the house. Nowhere light.

His eyes narrowed, focusing on the Mitsubishi SUV in front of the sidewall. *Strange*, he thought. Then he turned around and addressed the oldest police officer.

"How did you end up here?"

"An anonymous caller has been informing the dispatching that he'd heard shots," answered the patrolman. "However, he refused to identify himself. We found no people here except those two bodies. The owner seems to be absent." Lazar pointed to the car. "That must be the owner's car. What's your name?"

"Salimovic, Sinan Salimovic."

"Did you transmit the licence plate to the control room?"

"I did."

"Well done," praised Lazar, patting the man on his back. Then he put on a pair of thin rubber gloves, crouched in front of the dead man and tried to straighten up the head, but failed. The rigor mortis was complete. He lightened the pale face and held his breath.

"By the beard of the Prophet, this is the shabby-looking guy I've seen passing by *Digital Future*," he called out.

He examined jaws and neck. No doubt, the man was already dead for several hours. Between the scapula, he found the entering point of a bullet. Then he studied the inner pocket of the jacket and pulled out a gun.

"CZ 75B," he said to Senad, shoving the gun into a plastic bag and putting it in his pocket.
"That was of little use to him," replied Senad cynically.
Lazar continued his examination and found a wallet with an identity card in it.
"Safet Begovic," he stated. *The dispatching has checked the licence plate with the registration service and thus established the identity of the victim.*
A loud murmur in the distance got his attention. Glancing up toward the edge of the forest, he noticed several dancing cones of light. A little later, he saluted Milan Delic, Ferid Munic, and his four specialists.
"What a day," Ferid grunted.
Lazar nodded. "Both murders are linked to the previous one."
Ferid looked surprised. "You mean more murders here..."
"Yeah, there's another corpse over there." Lazar shone with his torch toward the dark mass near the trees. Then he grabbed Ferid by his shoulder and pulled him a few metres away.
"Look," he said, waving to the sidewall of the house, "it would be a good idea to demarcate the forest behind the house and look for tracks there."
"Are you thinking of something in particular?"
"Footprints and cartridges. The absence of the owner disturbs me." He gestured to the homeowner's car and took the dead man's gun out of his pocket.
"That's what the victim was carrying. But he never got a chance to use it, and it won't betray much, I guess. The man was shot at the end of the afternoon, twelve hours ago. The rigor mortis is complete." He didn't say that he had seen Safet Begovic shortly before his death.
"I thought someone reported shooting just an hour ago," reacted Ferid.
"Must be the perpetrator," replied Lazar. "Why would an innocent witness wait at least five hours to inform the police? Anonymous that is." He impatiently paced around the car until he stood near the body, while Ferid was giving instructions to his men. In the distance, he saw Milan putting on his plastic work suit.
Lazar bent forward and let the beam of light shine over the left mudguard. As his fingertips slid over a few deep grooves, he growled satisfied. Bowing more forward, he stroked over the short grass with his free hand.
"Ferid..." His shrill voice echoed through the trees.
The forensic investigator approached without rushing.
"Do you have something for me?" he asked undisturbed.
"Take pictures of those footprints."
Lazar aimed the light at the spot where the grass was damaged by a few footprints still recognisable. "Someone with heavy shoes has been lying here," he grunted.
Ferid squeezed his eyes into slits, looking sceptical.

Lazar snorted, crouched and stroked his fingers over the mudguard, gazing toward Ferid. "Do you see these deep grooves? They're recent because the metal is still blank. Take pictures of that before you move the wreckage to the workshop." He lighted the soil. "Heavy shoes made those little holes, causing that compressed grass."

Lazar straightened up himself and tapped Ferid encouraging on his shoulder. "I think that the landlord jumped up abruptly and ran away. Which explains his absence." He gestured Senad and walked fast to the patch of woodland along the main road.

As the light fell on the second body, both halted appalled. A charred human body was no ordinary spectacle. A large hole yawned into the pitch-black skull, and two empty eyelids stared at them ominously.

"Wow," Senad exclaimed.

"He didn't set himself on fire," remarked Lazar laconically, crouching down and moving the light beam across the ground.

"The perpetrator took the handgun," he said after a while.

Senad's features became questioning. "Why a gun?

"Because that's how he killed Safet."

"A gun? It could have been a rifle."

"Then the bullet would have gone straight through the body. This man here had shot Safet before he took a bullet himself." Lazar waved the light toward the trees.

"Sinan, this way," he shouted.

Moments later, the man stood next to him.

"Do you have any ribbon left?" Lazar asked to him.

"Yes, I have."

"The forest along the road must be marked, including a strip of ten metres around the house. Then get me the name of the landlord. That shouldn't be a problem with the licence plate." Sinan nodded and showed his heels.

All of Ferid's technicians were busy, and Milan was preparing to examine the charred corpse. Lazar beckoned Senad for joining him, heading to the house. A few steps from the entrance he abruptly halted, looking in amazement at the door being ajar, what he hadn't noticed when he'd arrived. Lazar beamed at the doorpost and the lock.

"Has been forced," he concluded, thrusting against the door which swung fully open. On the doorstep, he found a piece of wood attached to a metal plate.

"Part of the doorframe." Remaining wary, Lazar stepped into the gloomy room, followed by Senad. In the swinging light beam, they discovered an ample living space.

Lazar flicked on the light switch next to the doorpost. Nothing happened. He aimed the lamp at the ceiling and saw an elementary attached light bulb connected to an electrical conductor disappearing into the wall. He opened the door on the left, and they entered a small room. The cable at the ceiling went to the opposite wall where it penetrated a black metal case.

"A primitive fuse box," explained Lazar, glancing around. In the room stood an electric stove, a sink, and a small square table with a chair on each side.

"There must be a generator somewhere," Lazar murmured. Followed closely by his friend, he opened the second door leading to a hallway that ended with a heavy iron door at the far end. There Lazar pushed two bolts aside, pulled the handle, and the door opened with difficulty. The hinges were making a screeching sound going through marrow and leg. One step farther brought them under a roof supported by two brick sidewalls. Between those lateral walls lined a wooden palisade - with a wooden gate in the middle -, bordering the forest.

Lazar directed the light beam toward a dark opening in the soil, walked to it, and found a steep concrete staircase, which brought him in the basement. He faced a heavy metal door, pushed the latch down, and the door silently turned open. *Well-oiled.*

"What did you find out?" Senad's voice sounded excited.

"A small room, and the generator," Lazar called back. He discovered the exhaust of the generator which was incorporated in a drainpipe. The fresh air got aspired through a square aluminium tube in the sidewall.

A surface area of three to five metres, he estimated. The ceiling was just over two metres high. Against the farthest wall stood an iron workbench with a toolbox on it, and four full jerrycans underneath. He examined the generator in the other corner for a time and noticed four cables bundled in a plastic tube penetrating the ceiling. Full of expectation, he pressed the red start button. The engine started running immediately, and its regular roar broke the evening silence, while a weak light flashed above the door.

"We have light," Senad enthusiastically called out.

Lazar left the basement, spotted two incandescent light bulbs under the roof, turned off his torch, and entered the house.

Senad followed, closing the door behind him.

"You can hardly hear the generator running," he remarked.

Lazar stopped in front of a door and pushed it open. "The reason why they dug a bunker to put it in," he replied, entering a bedroom with a light bulb on the ceiling and a window in the rear wall. Glancing around the chamber, he saw a double bed, two bedside cabinets and a wardrobe against the opposite wall.

"The guy lives a sober life," Senad remarked.

Lazar left the room, checking into the bathroom where he discovered a pile of dirty clothes under the sink. He crouched down, studying the disgusting heap of rags without touching anything, and looked up at his friend after a brief hesitation.

"Ferid has to secure these clothes for laboratory analysis. They are full of earth, clotted blood and human tissue," he proclaimed.

Senad grinned contentedly. "Did we found our killer?"

Lazar shrugged and entered the next room while Senad walked out. In the second bedroom, he found nothing unusual, either. Then Lazar paced to the scantily lit lounge, and his eyebrows rose upon seeing a handgun magazine and a box of cartridges resting on the coffee table. He didn't touch but started to examine the dresser. In it, he found writing utensils, books and dozens of military maps. Four drawers were containing scissors, medicines, office supplies, cigarettes, cheap lighters and a notebook that caught his attention. When he opened it, a photograph swirled to the floor.

At that moment, Senad and Ferid turned up.

Lazar beckoned them toward the coffee table. "Take those things for examination on fingerprints," he ordered.

Ferid muttered something unintelligible, shove the magazine and the cartridge box in a plastic bag, and strode out the room with Senad following him.

Lazar picked up the photograph, studying the man on it with growing interest: a Bosnian soldier with a black beard, a balaclava and Kalashnikov. A terrifying person that Lazar had met several times during the war. He wasn't a choirboy himself, but the stories about this man give him goose bumps: Miralem Lulic, the Black Panther. Lazar lay the picture on top of the cabinet. Then he took maps out of the right compartment. *Sarajevo and surroundings*. One of the drawings showed the house and several red St Andrew's crosses a few hundred metres away.

By the Beard of the Prophet!

"Ferid," he yelled, his voice echoing through the house.

Ferid, closely followed by Senad, came in with a large plastic bag in his hand containing the clothes from the bathroom. "Did you find anything?" he asked calmly.

Lazar waved wildly with his right hand. "No one is allowed to go into the woods behind the house," he yelled. "There are landmines. Possibly one of those things exploded recently, killing a man."

"Okay, I'll call the mine-awareness service and warn my men," acknowledged Ferid, and he walked away.

Senad looked puzzled. "How do you know there's a man killed?"

"The bloody clothes in the bathroom."

"Well, do you already know who lives here?"

"Miralem Lulic." Without looking up, Lazar handed him the photo. Then he started carefully inspecting the map. Especially the area marked with a red dotted line was worrying him. Each Andreas cross equalled a landmine.

"Did he step on one of his landmines?" Senad asked. "Whoever digs a hole for..."

Lazar interrupted his friend. "Then explain to me who put his clothes in the bathroom."

"Maybe he was only slightly injured..."

"If you step on a landmine, you lose at least one foot. How would he have got here with such severe injuries? We would at least have found blood outside, at the front door, in the lounge and the bathroom. No, he wasn't hurt when he entered the house and changed his clothes." He could read disbelief on Senad's face.

"Yes," Lazar grinned, "he changed clothes quickly and then walked back into the forest. Let me think for a moment, will you?"

He tormented his brain, trying to get an idea of what had happened in this desolate place.

"Safet was a war veteran just like this man on that picture. Never heard of the Black Panther?"

Senad's eyes shone with admiration. "He was a war hero," he answered. "Too bad there weren't more such guys in our ranks. Miralem the Black Panther."

"Yes. During the war, I met that guy a few times. A lone wolf, a specialist in delicate assignments, also an expert in woody environments. His reputation exceeded Naser Oric's. The Serbs never discovered his true identity. They gave him nicknames such as *Black Panther* and *Tiha Smrt*, the *Silent Death*, putting a high price on his head. But all the četniks who crossed his path vanished forever. Sometimes their heads were found." It worried Lazar that Miralem seemed to be involved in the murders. The man got trained abroad, called himself a *White Mujahid*, the reason why he'd made his beard grow.

"The more we discover, the less I like it," Lazar growled.

"But where did Miralem go?"

"I'm not a clairvoyant. I think Safet has come over here to ask for help. When he paced toward the house, the murderer shot him from behind, probably sitting in his car on the road. But I don't understand why Safet's killer, in turn, had to die and to be made unrecognisable. What role does Miralem play in this case?"

"Couldn't it be Miralem who killed Safet?"

"No, Safet got a bullet in his back. You have seen the broken rear window of his car, haven't you? Probably several hits. So, the killer shot Safet from the roadside while Safet was driving toward the house. Or the murderer quickly crawled out of his car to have a better shot. He had little time. That's why I immediately ruled out a rifle. After his first shots, he parked his car beside the road. Then he rushed toward the clearing in front of the house from where he intended to finish his work. However, he was shot and set on fire."

"To erase evidence?"

Lazar slapped his friend on his shoulder. "Right," he said, "to make any quick identification impossible. But why burn one corpse and not the other?"

"Because only the identification of the burned man could put us on a trail."

"That might be the explanation. Anel Dzeko told us that there is more than one foreigner involved."

Lazar gathered the maps, glanced around again.

"We're done here," he decided, handing the cards to Senad. "I'm going to turn off the generator. Ferid must seal off all the entrances here."

"And what if Miralem returns?"

"He won't be able to show up very quickly, I guess. I'm going to turn off the generator."

Five minutes later they left the house and walked along the facade to where the Mitsubishi stood. Lazar found all the doors unlocked. He peered inside and discovered four plastic bags in the back seat with the inscription *Mercator*. They contained food and toiletries. To his surprise, the car key was in the ignition. He pulled it out, closed all the doors, and slid the keychain in his pocket. Then he shuffled to the hood, moving the light beam across the ground to the forest.

"By the beard of the Prophet!" He took two steps forward, crouched down and touched the flattened grass.

"Ferid!"

The technician showed up seconds later. "Did you find anything?" asked Ferid with resignation.

"I guess this is blood, which means that Miralem, the landlord, had been hit just before he penetrated the woods. Quite a lot of blood, the injury seems to be severe. Take blood samples, but don't let anyone go into the forest until the mine-awareness service has cleared the place," he snarled. "And Ferid, on the other side of the main road you'll find an ATV with a diplomatic licence plate. Take it to the workshop." He handed him also Lulic's car keys. "The landlord's car also is to be brought to the workshop."

"Can we do that?" Ferid asked in doubt.

"We found both cars at a crime scene, and we ignore where the drivers are. The car on the other side of the road probably belongs to the charred man. I want a full report on the results of the vehicle search. We're going to have a look alongside the road to see if there are any more cars." Lazar chuckled, took the maps from Senad's hands, and gave them to the technician. "The mine-awareness service will be happy to get them."

They walked to the burned corpse where the pathologist was sitting on his knees, examining the skull in the light of the car spotlights while his assistant wrote down what he dictated.

"Milan, have you found anything useful yet?"

"There's not much left," mumbled Milan. "But I can say with certainty that the man was already dead when he got burned. A bullet penetrated the back of his skull. A large part of it has gone, and the man was dead before touching the soil."

"What did the other dead man tell you?"

"Shot in the spine, the bullet is still in the corpus. The victim hasn't lived long after the hit, so it must have happened nearby."

"Hvala, thank you." Lazar waved his lamp backwards because, before leaving the location, he wanted to say a few words to Ferid, who was giving instructions to his men. Lazar rushed toward him.

"Did your men discover something around?" he asked the technician.

Ferid nodded. "We found the place where a sniper had been lying. But we can't find any shells."

"The shooter picked them up," said Lazar sarcastically.

"Or they caught the shells."

"You must be kidding."

"He used something or someone to catch the ejected shells."

"He didn't have time for something like that."

"I don't know how he did it, but we couldn't find any shells. That's a fact. According to the footsteps, there were two guys."

"A sniper and a bullet catcher?"

Safet's killer had acted on assignment. But he also got murdered by order. *Do we have to handle with two rival groups?*

"All right, have pictures taken of those tracks. I'll be waiting impatiently for your report, dobra vecer. Oh yes, seal the house, I might want to come back here later."

Lazar and Senad walked side by side on the main road, along the edge of the forest. As they passed their vehicle, Lazar stopped and looked toward the house.

"The road makes half an arc around the house and then turns to the left," Lazar said, pointing his torch to the trees. They went on another fifty metres and halted. Lazar turned to a heap of branches that sloppily shielded a narrow gap between the trees. However, the vehicle behind it was visible.

"Wow," called out Senad, removing the branches covering the trunk. "An ATV with a diplomatic licence plate."

Lazar let out a faint sigh, stepped along the side and stood up in front of the hood. He swung his flashlight forward over the narrow strip full of rotten branches and pine cones. Then he directed the light beam fifteen metres farther at a jumbled heap.

"Look, there's something that doesn't belong there." He paced slowly to the heap. The crunching branches under their feet made sharp noises. The dark load was a human body lying on its belly with legs pulled together, and hands stretched out forward. As if the man had tried to crawl forwards.

Lazar shone in a pale face.

"Miralem Lulic," he murmured.

He phoned Ferid.

Lazar was already examining the car when the technicians showed up. He pointed out to them the place where they should start, after which he took a look at the car's registration document.

Who is Ahmed Salah?

The police doctor examined the body while Ferid was waiting for Lazar to complete his examination of the car. Ten minutes later, Lazar took off his rubber gloves.

"There's a cell phone in the glove compartment," he told Ferid. "Have all the numbers and conversations checked, and the car examined."

"If it goes on like this, we'll need reinforcements," Ferid replied.

Lazar grinned. "Stop dreaming, Ferid, there is no money. Good luck."

Then he grabbed Senad by his shoulder. "Here enough," he said.

A little later they were in the car, but Lazar didn't start, being in a state of deep contemplation.

Senad stared at him without saying a word.

Minutes of silence.

"Emir Besic, Safet Begovic, Miralem Lulic and a charred body," Lazar suddenly called out in frustration.

"Could the charred man be Ahmed Salah?" asked Senad with a frown.

"No, think carefully. We found two ATVs and identified only one driver. The charred body has been driving the other car. Salah is missing from our inventory; he might be the second driver.

Miralem discovered this car before he returned to the house. That's why, after being shot by a sniper, he came over here."

Lazar paused.

"Yeah," he eventually went on, "his bloody clothes we found in his bathroom with skin tissue, tell me there's still a dead man lying somewhere. Probably Salah. I suppose we're dealing with a clean-up action. It starts with Safet who calls Emir. A little later Emir learns that a foreigner is looking for him. He panics, leaves the Glass Tower and is killed next to the Miljacka in his car. The killer puts two bags of heroin in Emir's car to make us believe it's reckoning in the milieu. At *Digital Future*, I observe Safet passing by. When he gets an eye on me, he drives on toward here and gets shot before he can talk to Miralem. That's murder 2."

"Is it the same perpetrator?"

"Safet has been killed by the man who'd followed him: the charred man. A different perpetrator." Lazar looked thoughtfully at Senad. "And who called the police to report the shooting?"

"A chance passer-by."

Lazar shook his head. "Unlikely. Safet wanted to meet Emir first, which proves that he was not aware of his death. Seeing us, he panicked. That was a chance decision."

His hands were drumming on the wheel.

Senad waited for further explanation. But Lazar started and turned the car over the road.

"Home?" Senad's voice sounded almost begging.

"Not yet, first a visit to the great chief of EuPol."

"What does he have to do with it?"

Lazar didn't answer immediately. He was thinking about Zumra, considering whether he would send her a message.

"How can the Viking be helpful?" Senad asked again.

"Maybe he knows who's behind these murders," he replied.

TWENTY-ONE

BRAM RUYTER HEARD A SQUEAKING NOISE. *MUST BE THE HINGES OF THE HALL DOOR.* He stiffened. *The intruders are coming through the front door!*

During his military career, he'd never found himself in such a situation. His eyes were trying to pierce the darkness so hard that he spotted everywhere hovering coloured flowers. Closing his eyes for seconds, he fought against upcoming dizziness. When he opened his eyelids again, the colour spots were gone. *The flames will blind me, so I have to shoot first.*

As he heard squealing hinges, he raised his weapon with the index finger curled around the trigger. Any hesitation could be fatal. *I'm a good shooter, and it's about my life.*

What followed was totally unexpected, and he didn't have time to think. While he was concentrating on the hall door, the hinges made a screeching sound again. Then three blunt bangs like uncorking champagne bottles frightened him up.

They're coming from the bedroom next to the hall.

He heard the sound of a heavy object falling on the floor and a dark figure with a strange-shaped head and bulging eyes emerged into the hallway. He instinctively crouched down, hearing dull strikes above his head. Slightly blinded, he quickly pulled the trigger twice. He hardly saw the man stumble backward, firing two more times. The intruder went down, pulling the trigger. But the projectile impacted somewhere in the ceiling. The shooting stopped, and the man didn't move any more. Gunpowder made Bram's eyes weep, but he kept pointing his gun toward the vague heap.

Until a dull sound in his back made him freeze.

"Stay calm. We have the situation under control." He recognised Edhem's muffled voice, let out a sigh and turned around, seeing Edhem crawling through the narrow window.

"Another guy was in the bedroom," Edhem said. "He hardly missed me. I doubt if there are more of that kind, let's check anyway."

"Okay, give me a cover." Bram went squatting into the sitting room. His friend, following him like a shadow, positioned next to him. However, no alarming movements or sounds could be detected.

"I make light," murmured Bram, and he flicked on the light switch. After their eyes got used to the lightning again, they paced back into the hallway.

"A military night vision device with a light amplifier. That's why he immediately discovered me," groaned Bram, pulling the mask off the face.

"William Smith."

"Wow," uttered Edhem in astonishment. "Three bullets in the chest." He expertly searched the body, finding a wallet in which he found 20 marks and an SFOR-identity card. "No cell phones."

The man in the bedroom was also dead. He possessed an ID card on the name Tom Jones. The two who'd visited Bram.

"Heckler and Koch with silencers, 9 mm, model USP Tactical," muttered Bram after gathering their weapons. "Assassins."

Edhem nodded. "ID cards to identify themselves as they're checked by police. Too bad we can't keep the guns."

"Better not." Bram couldn't find Emir's cell phone on the bodies, what troubled him. Who possessed Emir's phone? Their employer?

"We have to hurry," insisted Edhem, checking his watch. "In two hours, it will be daylight. We throw the bodies in the trunk of my car. Do you have some large plastic garbage bags? And tape?"

Bram nodded, went to the kitchen and brought the requested bags. Without any hesitation, Edhem got rid of his clothes. Then he took a plastic bag, cut three holes in it, and pulled it over his head and arms. From two other bags, he made a pair of sleeves and pulled them over his arms. Bram stuck them to his torso. Without visible effort, Edhem swung William Smith's body over his shoulder.

Bram rushed to the hall, where he found the front door ajar.

"This is where William slipped in," he murmured. "I'll see if it's safe outside." Without making any noise, he ran to the road. After carefully scanning the surroundings, discovering no suspicious movements behind the neighbour's windows, he gave Edhem the agreed signal. It takes a few minutes to transfer the corpses, guns and plastic bags in the trunk. After that, they cleaned the house. Bram found two bullets in the window frame, telling him he'd been lucky. He extracted the shells, including the one in the ceiling.

"It's a good thing there are no carpets in the bedroom nor the hallway," he said with a sigh. "I'll repair later those holes in the wall and the window frame."

Edhem gathered the empty shells.

After a final inspection, they both took a shower. Bram lent Edhem a jogging suit and put their clothes in the washing machine.

Half an hour later, they pushed Bram's Seat out of the garage onto the road. Then they thrust the Mercedes behind the Seat, and each got behind the wheel.

After unlocking the steering and the handbrake, the cars started rolling down the sloping road with increasing speed. Somewhere in the middle of the descent, Bram fired up the engine. In the rear-view mirror, he saw the Mercedes following.

The ride went past the large cemetery through the north tunnel. Bram respected the traffic codes scrupulously, even though he had a diplomatic passport. But Edhem was driving a stolen car that could have been reported by now. In less than ten minutes, they reached the east intersection, taking the road through the mountains toward Pale. There was no traffic yet. Shortly after crossing the border and entering Republika Srpska, Bram slowed down, spinning around in front of the tunnel entrance and halted at the other roadside, letting run the engine.

Meanwhile, his friend drove the Mercedes to the edge of the ravine. He got out, positioned himself against the trunk and after checking either roadside, he thrust against the metal until the heavy vehicle began to tilt. Then he ran to the Seat and dropped his considerable body into the passenger seat, gazing to the left. The car was gone.

In the distance, headlights appeared. A new day began.

Bram accelerated and drove back to Sarajevo at full speed. Perpetually staring through the windshield with squeezed lips, he was barely aware of Edhem's presence. Numerous questions raged through his mind. When he'd decided to come to Bosnia, he'd known that he might find himself in stressful situations but had never thought of killing people. Uncertainty tormented his conscience. Being convinced that William and Tom had been in contact with Mycroft Follum and Derek Fleming was not concrete evidence that they'd killed Emir. There could be another explanation for their presence at the murder scene. Possession of Emir's cell phone was not evidence of guilt. But if they had nothing to do with Emir's murder, why did they want to liquidate him?

Perhaps they'd been watching Emir, found his body and taken his phone to investigate it. Maybe they'd waited in their car to discover suspicious people, and Bram's peculiar behaviour must have convinced them that he was the perpetrator. Secret services have their own methods of disabling jammers. What if they were indeed working for a British anti-terrorist organisation?

Bram cleared his throat. "Edhem," he said tonelessly, "I've told you I was searching oblivion at *Last Hope*. But that's only partly true."

"You don't owe me an explanation," Edhem replied.

"Given the circumstances, I think..."
"As you wish."
They were approaching the centre.
"Can I stay overnight?" asked Bram without looking at Edhem. "I'm exhausted and need some rest. I can't stay on my guard all the time. Tomorrow I'll tell you what you need to know."
"No problem."
It was already 5 a.m., and daylight came up. The traffic on the ring was increasing.
Ten minutes later, they reached Edhem's dwelling place on the outside edge of the Humska plateau. Bram just wanted to close his eyes and forget about the events. He stopped next to Edhem's car.
He didn't know anything about the two nightly intruders. Possibly that accomplices had seen everything from a distance, waiting for an appropriate moment to strike back. Where had William and Tom left their vehicle? It was hard to believe that they had come on foot.
What would happen when the bodies got discovered?
He got out, just wanted to sleep.

TWENTY-TWO

ZUMRA ABDIC WAS NOT SURE WHAT HAD STARTLED HER AWAKE, WHIPPING HER head back and forth. Numerous shapeless coloured air bubbles hovered behind her closed eyelids. Suddenly she realised that the sounds came from her own mouth and she opened her eyelids. Her dry throat produced another weak hoarse groan, while her head sensed as if someone was using her skull like a drum.
"Stop it," she wanted to yell. Every movement caused needles to pierce her brain. She couldn't arrange her thoughts, fighting nausea. Cautiously she turned her head in either direction. Nothing changed. Total darkness and deadly silence surrounded her. She lifted her arms for a short moment, but they were so heavy that they fell next to her. Her hands began exploring around, slipping over her body down over a soft surface. She couldn't understand, but her fingers sensed enough to create disturbing pictures in her mind. She was lying naked on a mattress without blankets. Then the image of a gloomy, mysterious man flashed through her head, immediately swallowed up by the darkness. Touching her head, she discovered a significant lump behind her ear.
I'm in a hospital. But why is it so dark?
"Timka, where are you?" she murmured.
Moving her head caused a fierce hot pain shot going through her skull.

She started to recall what happened to her. Pictures of loverboy's face, the cemetery, Eurotel, the hotel suite, an unknown young man yelling at her, asking who the hell she was, started to form scenes telling a story, her story.

The mysterious man had slapped her, causing darkness and memory loss.

How long have I been unconscious?

She sat bolt upright, fighting increasing nausea, with her feet touching a rough, cold-stone floor. No matter how hard she tried, she only saw obscurity. Never before had she experienced such silence. Was that the end? Had she entered the *Empire of Demons*? Was she in hell as written in the Qur'an?

Her heart was wildly throbbing against her ribs. Then she sensed a strong, musty smell. *I am alive.*

"Is anybody there?" The soft voice coming out the darkness sounded like a cry of despair. Her legs were shaking, and her heartbeat increased. She straightened herself up, holding her breath and pricking her ears. If nothing happened after seconds, she wondered if the voice had been real.

"Who's there?" shouted Zumra in a trembling voice.

"I'm in the opposite cell," the unknown person answered. "I'm Emma."

Did she say cell? Am I locked up? Despite the stress and bursting headaches, the strange accent hadn't escaped her. The invisible woman was not Bosnian.

"I am Zumra. Where am I?" she called out.

"In hell, you're in hell," the woman squealed.

Zumra tried to ignore rising panic. Her thoughts went to Timka, Azra and Hadar, hoping that Lazar already had started searching for her. But where was he going to begin his inquiry? He didn't even know where she lived or who she was. Then her ears caught a fair movement. What did all this mean? Had she been abducted because she'd pretended to be Timka? Was she a victim of a perverse criminal?

"Where are you from?" asked Emma in tears.

"I live in the city. And you?"

"Romania. They've abducted me."

"Who?"

"I don't know."

"What are you doing in Bosnia?"

"I eh... I've worked in a bar. International police observers took me away from there. I have testified against the bar owner and was on my way home..." The voice got lost in a stuttering wail, and it took Emma a few seconds to continue. "He seemed such a neat guy," she said. "Until he pushed a needle into my arm. When I woke up, I was lying naked in this cell."

"Are we in the hands of women traffickers?" She heard Emma coughing and vomiting.

"Uh, I'm in bad shape," answered Emma in a trembling voice. "He's been beating, torturing and raping me."

"That decent guy?"

"The devil in person."

Zumra staggered forward with outstretched arms. Another step, a third, and a fourth until her fingertips bumped into metal rods. *A trellis door*. She pulled on the bars, shaking like crazy. The rattling of the chains and the squealing sounds of metal on stone sent a cold shiver through her body.

"Save your energy, Zumra, no one can hear us. We are in a basement."

Zumra yelled a horrible scream that echoed through the darkness, and although she realised that it was useless, she kept pulling at the iron rods.

"Stop it, stop it," she heard Emma calling.

Powerless, she lowered her shoulders, slowly calming down. *Will I ever see Azra again?*

"What do they want from us?" she shouted in despair.

"They're searching for a teddy bear that didn't even belong to me. If only I had listened to Daria and given it to someone I trusted. I would be home with my family now. I'll never see them again..."

Hearing fierce snivelling, Zumra wiped the tears out of her eyes.

"Emma, you're all right?"

Emma kept wailing. "We are going to die here. They're animals. It doesn't matter if you give them what they ask, don't believe them. Monsters, all monsters..." Her voice was fading out.

Zumra caught the noise of a screeching door in the distance. She turned her head around and suddenly got struck by a dazzling light. Although she subconsciously closed her eyes, she still could see the brightness through her eyelids while she heard approaching hollow footsteps. She blinked her eyes a few times and then saw her kidnapper standing next to the grille door, unlocking a padlock. The chain made a shrill sound in a grey corridor with a stone arch ceiling vault just above his head. Her eyes roamed from the man to either side of the aisle and the cell on the other side. There, behind bars, sat a naked woman on her knees, head bowed forward. Awful. Zumra heard vaguely her cell door opening while glancing toward Emma. The sight of Emma's body covered with crusted blood and several deep wounds gave her a cold shudder. She also smelled a pungent scent of urine and faeces.

A couple of firm hands grabbed her. "Emma, look at me." Her voice skipped.

"Come on, you," snarled the man.

Emma glanced up to her.

Zumra started screaming. There was nothing human left of that woman. A broken nose, a closed eye and torn cheeks. As if a feline predator had been pulling its claws over her face. The healthy eye stared at her beggingly. She had never before seen so much pain and despair in one person. And Allah was her witness; she had seen infinite suffering in her young life.

She's dying.

Had she not previously said that neither of them would leave this place alive? '*We are in hell,*' had Emma cried out.

"Don't believe what they promise," yelled Emma after her.

Strong hands pulled her away from the place, so roughly that she almost lost balance. Stumbling forward, she found enough strength to take one last look over her shoulder. Emma's bony hands clasped the bars, her face stuck to the metal while thick tears emerged from her undamaged eye.

When the man brutally dragged her, Zumra turned her face away, realising she'd never see Emma again.

TWENTY-THREE

IVAR RAGNARSSON LOOKED LIKE A BODYBUILDER. WITH HIS TWO METRES, ONE hundred and thirty kilos and gloomy aura, he resembled the legendary Norwegian Viking and hero Ragnar Lodbrok. Ragnarsson, son of Ragnar. His enormous body with short grey hair, long face and stinging dark eyes filled the entire doorway.

Lazar knew a lot about that man wearing a grey jogging suit and holding an arm behind his back. However, despite feeling uncomfortable, he grinned his teeth bare.

"Good evening, Commissioner," he said.

"What do you want?" The heavy voice sounded hostile.

"Don't shoot me."

"Did you forget where my office is?" Ivar's English pronunciation was almost without an accent.

"An emergency, Commissioner. I wouldn't disturb you if not important."

"I hope you're right." Ragnarsson freed the doorway, let both of them through, closed the door and led them to a spacious living room where a giant television screen was switched on. After turning it off, he put his gun, which he'd held concealed behind his back, in the bottom drawer. He briefly pointed to a friendly-looking solid matron sitting in an armchair.

"My wife," he said shortly.

The woman nodded and discreetly left the room while Lazar and Senad settled down on the long couch opposite their host.

"My assistant Senad," Lazar said. "He understands English, but doesn't speak it very well."

Ragnarsson nodded to Senad and turned back toward Lazar, looking at him as if he were some weird creature.

Lazar endured the stern gaze. "I've got a busy day, Commissioner," he announced. “Several murders.”

“And what does that have to do with me?”

“You may not be involved, but the EU may.”

Senad made himself as small as possible.

The Viking kept quiet.

Lazar cleared his throat. “Three compatriots, an immigrant we are tracking down, and a fourth, yet unidentified charred person. One of the victims recently visited your headquarters, shortly before he got murdered. We have evidence that both natives worked on a West-European payroll.”

The Commissioner’s features kept emotionless.

“Can I pour you a beer or something?” he asked in a neutral tone.

“No, thank you.

“As you wish.”

Lazar looked the man straight in the eye without blinking. Although they practised the same profession, knew each other well, they were like cats and dogs. Lazar disliked the Viking for his disrespectful behaviour toward the local police. The Swede feigned to be a Messiah of Justice. He would ban the corruption from the Bosnian police, using every opportunity to call the Bosnian police system corrupt and inefficient, doomed to disappear and to get exchanged by a Western European model. Lazar did not deny that the Bosnian police system was outdated and corrupt but considered the authoritarian Western approach as inefficient. The longer the Western institutions remained in his country, the more the population sensed that as an occupation. But Lazar also agreed that his country needed Western support and that its subjugation was the price for the necessary changes.

After the Viking discovered that Lazar had served as an FBI agent in America, he’d tried to engage him as an inside man. Although Lazar still enjoyed American nationality, he remained a proud Bosniak, refusing to become a puppet on a string manipulated by the international community. So Lazar got a powerful enemy after expressing to the arrogant Swede his opinion about the corruption among police observers from Jordan, Pakistan and the Eastern bloc countries. Moreover, Lazar had said at a formal dinner that Ragnarsson must first clean up in his own house before blaming the local police officers. Wounded in his pride, the Swede had openly threatened him. ‘*A mistake and I will have you fired*,’ had the commissioner yelled, forgetting the witnesses all around them. But he was aware that he had to be very careful when planning any action against Lazar. Since that evening, they avoided each other. Yet Lazar respected this colossus, recently appointed as EU Police Commissioner by the EU-Council while still commanding the IPTF until the end of the year.

The Swede raised his bristly eyebrows. “Who are you talking about?” he asked with apparent astonishment.

“Emir Besic worked for *Digital Future* and spent a lot of time at your headquarters," replied Lazar with a sort of amused grin. "Our second victim, his friend Safet Begovic triggered a murder avalanche. Moreover, we assume that there are Europeans involved."

"Do you have any concrete evidence? Is there a link between your murder cases and EuPol?" Ragnarsson glanced at him with a threatening gaze.

"Not directly. However, I fear that this is only the tip of the iceberg, Commissioner. How difficult for me to admit, I think this time, we've got to work together until we know what's going on."

Ivar kept quiet.

After a short pause, Lazar continued. "I'm afraid some planned operation has got out of hand. I think the murders are part of a Cleaning Operation. And that concerns both of us."

The Swede shook his head, ironically smiling. "Do you mean a military operation?"

"Yes, I do. I'm thinking about several executions."

"Executions? You're joking, aren't you?"

"I'm not." Lazar briefly explained what he'd discovered, and under what circumstances Emir got murdered.

The Swede frowned. "Sophisticated transmitters?"

"Yes, ultra-sophisticated transmitters. I fear that the special troops stationed in Camp Butmir use similar equipment to track suspected people. It's not the first time I've seen these miniatures."

"Possibly, but I don't know anything about ongoing operations. I'll consult with SFOR tomorrow."

"I am convinced EuPol is involved. That's why I'm asking for more openness and collaboration because I've got tired of visiting new crime scenes every day." He felt Ivar getting restless.

"Chief Inspector Magas, you once refused my help," he retorted.

Lazar interrupted him by indignantly raising his hand.

"You wanted me as an insider man," he replied, raising his voice. "If you thought I would betray my colleagues, then you failed to learn about our culture. That's why I dismissed those two employees you wanted to infiltrate my office without any further ado. Get started by respecting us before complaining about a partnership, and do not forget that I belong here. You are the intruder, not me, and no UN mandate can change that. For the time being, we still have to live with that, no problem for me. However, if you make it too colourful, I will respond suitably. I still have contact with my former chefs, also with the international press. I'll not hesitate for a moment to hang out your dirty laundry, as you call it, don't you?" Lazar knew that the man despised negative publicity, and when he was about to get up, the Swede gestured him to stay seated.

"Why are you so goddamn sure that we are involved?" he asked in a sharp tone.

"This afternoon, I've seen your Political Advisor talking to the guards after I had spoken to them."

"Do you think that's wrong?"

"A Political Advisor who lowers himself to the security guard level?"

Ivar kept quiet.

"And there's more," Lazar went on. "Someone told me that the murdered natives wanted to kidnap Karadzic!"

"That's absurd," called out Ragnarsson. "Nobody is that crazy."

"I wouldn't swear an oath on that. That's why I ask you again whether you are aware of a military operation in Pale?"

"On every planned raid, I receive a Warning Order 24 hours in advance so I can brief our people in that region. I do not want them involved in such operations because that's outside our mandate. We're not an operational but a consultative police force as you know, and it's up to SFOR to track down war criminals."

"Whoever it is, someone has planned or is planning an operation. Why not that arrogant British bastard?"

"Is your source reliable?"

Lazar shrugged. "Who can be trusted today?" He stood up. "I don't want to take up more of your time than necessary. But I hope you'll let me know if you discover anything. I'll wait for the results of the laboratory before I divulge any conclusions."

Ivar glanced at him. "What do you know about the murder of Cees Visser?"

That question surprised Lazar.

"Cees Visser?" He wanted to save time. Since EuPol had carried out an autopsy on the corpse at the Forensic Institute, he'd heard nothing more about the case. Nobody had questioned him, and the body got transported to the Netherlands in a zinc coffin.

"You've examined the corpse in the hotel," Ivar stated. "What did you find out?"

"My hierarchy took the investigation out of my hands, Commissioner."

"The Dutch government got fed up with this case; we both know what Visser did in his spare time. The younger, the better. Prostitution got prohibited in this country. However, the police allow whores to operate in the best hotels."

"Doesn't prostitution exist in your country?" Lazar reposted.

Ivar kept quiet.

Lazar chuckled. "Prostitution is the oldest profession in the world, and you are not so naive to think EuPol will free our country from this scourge. Aren't the Westerners guilty of that evil? Our people cannot afford whores. But that is a never-ending discussion. The Visser case got closed, I guess?"

"Something like that."

"Let's not beat around the bush. The man got killed. Have you seen the photographic evidence? No extraneous haematomas. No defensive marks. At any rate, no one dies that way naturally. We weren't allowed to do an autopsy, but our pathologist anatomist made a few observations. He found pubic hairs and a condom in one of the waste bins. It won't be difficult to prove that the pubic hair came from the whore with whom he spent an hour. After her performance, the supervisor came to pick her up."

He waited for a reaction.

Ragnarsson frowned. "So, you think that Visser got killed by the woman, or by her supervisor?"

"I'm not able to allege that with certainty until I've seen the intern autopsy report."

"You questioned the hotel staff, as I heard. We did the same but didn't get much information. No one has seen or heard anything."

"If that case had been mine, you probably would know more yet. Why should I leave you in the dark? If Visser died after 1 a.m., the whore and supervisor go free. Do you know how he died?"

"A perforation of the brain through the eardrum," answered Ivar. "The perpetrator knew what he was doing."

"But if the perpetrator is a man who entered Visser's room after that whore left, how could he have killed Visser without any resistance?" Lazar thought to know the answer, but he wanted to find out what the Westerners had discovered.

The Viking hesitated. "The victim got administered a sedative in his drink," he explained. "Our specialists have found a glass in the bathroom, unfortunately, washed out. But it had no place there, so the conclusions are obvious. When Visser was no longer able to defend himself, the killer injected him a crippling product. So, the man was conscious when the killer drove a needle through his ear and brain."

Lazar cursed the forensic technicians because they'd overlooked that glass in the bathroom. Although he had nothing to do with the case, he was still looking for an explanation for that murder. He'd examined the body and found nothing suspicious. Ivar's description made numerous hypotheses possible.

"Where did he get that injection?" Lazar asked.

Ragnarsson chuckled. "Between his toes."

Lazar cursed internally; he had overlooked this possibility assuming it was an Asian way of killing from the Middle Ages or earlier.

"This staging strikes me as a message," Lazar said, suddenly remembering a drawing by Leonardo da Vinci. A religious message? "And the perpetrator wanted the victim to know why he had to die," Lazar added. "His muscles got paralysed, but his senses were still functioning; he was hearing everything the killer said. But why such a staging?"

"Odd, never seen that before."

"The motive is probably revenge or a payoff, and the killer wants us to know. Visser kept in touch with the *Florida Bar*, ordered his young girls there."

Ivar's face became a grim mask.

"I suspect the killer got unnoticed access to his apartment," Lazar said. "He probably walked through the hall among other guests so that neither the receptionist nor the porter could notice him. Thus, there must be a connection between the perpetrator and the victim who opened the door for him."

"Or it's murder on assignment. The whore mixes something in his drink, and after her departure, the killer does his thing," countered Ivar.

"Sounds reliable. Then the girl has, just like her supervisor, an alibi. But, supposing Visser got sedated, he couldn't open the door any more. Then how did the perpetrator get in?" asked Lazar with a smile.

Ivar shrugged but didn't answer.

"No," insisted Lazar with narrowed eyes. "Visser opened the door himself. That woman and her supervisor have nothing to do with the murder. They didn't have a motive."

The Swede stood up. "Okay," he said. "Anyway, the case is closed, Chief Inspector Magas. I was just curious. And, uh, I'll light up at SFOR. One never knows."

Ivar guided his visitors to the front door where they said goodbye with a handshake. After a few steps, Lazar turned to the Swede.

"Commissioner," he said. "The EU may be the target of an attack."

"I'll keep you informed," replied Ragnarsson tonelessly.

Lazar looked him straight in the eyes for a second, nodded briefly and followed Senad to their car. But he was struck by what he thought he'd read in Ragnarsson's eyes.

The Viking is afraid.

Wednesday, 9 October 2002

TWENTY-FOUR

LAZAR HAD SLEPT BADLY. HE TURNED OFF THE ELECTRIC ALARM AND TOOK HIS CELL phone off the tabletop. Not finding what he was looking for, he dropped the phone on the bed.

Zumra, where are you?

When coming home around 1.30 a.m., he'd established that Zumra wasn't there. It bothered him that she hadn't left a message. She'd never failed to do so. *She must be outraged.*

Numerous questions about the murders and the reactions of Commissioner Ivar Ragnarsson and Egzon Subic had kept him awake for hours. He'd just slept a few hours. Without much enthusiasm, he'd got out of bed and taken a cold shower. Then he'd called Zumra again.

The voicemail.

He sent a text message.

Zumra, I'm worried, please give me a call. I love you.

After his morning toilet and two cups of strong coffee without breakfast, he called Ferid. "*Dobar dan*, have you discovered something useful yet?" he asked before Ferid could say anything.

"Oh, it's you," retorted Ferid. "Good morning, Lazar, it's nice to hear you're already awake. I didn't have time to sleep yet."

Lazar ignored Ferid's sarcasm.

"Thank you for warning us about those landmines," went on Ferid. "The MAC specialists have indeed found a zone in the forest with about twenty active landmines. When they finish clearing them, a team will collect the remains of the corpse. I reckon that'll happen in the evening."

"I feared that already. Do you have anything on the victim?"

"We found his wallet. The man's name is Ahmed Salah, a Briton having an SFOR-ID card."

"Okay, so now we know the owner of that SUV parked in the woods. Do you have anything on the other vehicle?"

"The same model registered on Alistair Moon. Both cars are now in our workshop. No sign of Moon unless…" Ferid stopped talking.

"Say it out loud," Lazar said. "The charred corpse. And what do you know about the body we've found in the forest near Ahmed's car?"

"Uh. Miralem Lulic, killed by a rifle bullet calibre 7.62, probably a Dragunov. The high-speed bullet went through his body and caused deadly inner bleeding. A blood trail ran from the side of his house to Ahmed's car. The last few metres he's been crawling, until his last breath."

"Have the clothes we've found in his bathroom analysed as soon as possible. I think you'll find, uh, Ahmed Salah's DNA on it."

"Miralem Lulic survived the explosion because he was lying in a trench, close to where Salah hit the mine. Tomorrow you'll get more details, I haven't closed an eye yet, and I'm going to take a few hours of nap," snarled Ferid.

"Do that, Ferid. Thanks."

Lazar put the cell phone next to him and closed his eyes, trying to build an overall picture of the case in his mind. Later in the morning briefing, Egzon might ask him for a detailed explanation.

Safet had been collaborating with a foreigner, just like Emir. Both were now dead. Lazar considered a talk with Mirsad Pejic. But involving *Sluzbi Drzavne Bezbednosti*, meant its spies might stick their nose more profoundly into the matter. Or did they know more than he suspected?

Lazar decided to take the risk. He called Mirsad. After a few seconds, someone picked up without saying anything.

"You-know-who," Lazar began.

"I-know-who, what's going on?" Lazar recognised Mirsad's voice. They had once agreed to use these short sentences to identify with each other. As someone might be listening, or as they were calling under constraint, they used their names.

"What about a bite to eat at four o'clock?" Lazar asked.

"Do I hear a desperate cry for help? Well, I'll never refuse a good meal." The line went dead. They always kept their phone calls as short as possible, convinced that the Westerners were intercepting all communications.

He sighed. Zumra's nightmares and her mysterious behaviour were making him upset. Like a caged lion, he jumped up, rushed to the hall and grabbed the car keys from the shoe cupboard while his eyes caught the sight of a large brown envelope that had been slid under the door. He picked it up, carefully tore open the flap and pulled out three A4 colour photos.

"What the hell..." he murmured, disbelievingly looking at the entrance of *Hotel Hollandia* that he'd visited two days earlier. He immediately forgot Zumra and quickly watched the second picture: a man with a hockey cap facing the entrance of the hotel. The third picture showed the same man leaving the building. The text at the bottom gave him chills of excitement. The photos were taken with a digital camera printing the date and time on the pictures.

2002/7/10 01.10

He realised that these photos were pieces of evidence in the Cees-Visser murder case. Why did an anonymous informant send him pictures of the presumed perpetrator? Turning the sheets unconsciously, he spotted on one of them a name he'd heard yesterday.

Bram Ruyter
Last Hope

Anel Dzeko had told him that Bram Ruyter had a business relationship with Emir Besic. But he'd concluded that Ruyter, an aid worker, did not have the profile to be involved in the Besic murder case. Initially, he'd been suspecting some war veterans and professional killers, engaged in a dubious case with a link to local and international politics. Now, this Ruyter turned out to be the main suspect in the Visser murder case.

Was there a connection between the murder cases?

Bram leaves the hotel around the time of Cees Visser's death.

According to the printed times on the pictures, Bram stayed in the hotel for one hour. Lazar strolled thoughtfully back to the living room where he fell in an armchair, putting the photos on the coffee table. Leaning back, he tried to remember the events of the last two days. Although these photos were a clear indication, they gave him an unpleasant feeling. He despised anonymous informants. One always had to wonder what their real goal was.

He could understand that an eyewitness did not want to reveal himself, especially in this country. But this informant had made a great effort to take these photographs, being there long before the murder happened. All the pictures got made with a professional camera from the same position. *This cost a lot of money.* Had the informer known of what was going to happen? Or had he guessed what Bram Ruyter was going to do?

What is his motive?

All in all, Lazar counted four individuals who enjoyed diplomatic protection and knew each other. And Bram Ruyter suddenly seemed to be the main actor.

Someone is watching him. Who wanted Ruyter out of the way?

The morning meeting didn't take long because the district commissioner got a call and left without explanation, making Lazar happy. He had little time to lose and rushed immediately to his team meeting room. His gaze focussed on Fadila. He couldn't deny that she was looking gorgeous in her dark blue cotton pants and the tightly stretched yellow sweater that accentuated her full breasts well.

"I urgently need information," he said to her. "About Bram Ruyter, Alistair Moon, Ahmed Salah, Miralem Lulic, Emir Besic and Safet Begovic. Moon and Salah have a visa and a car with a diplomatic licence plate. I want to know with whom they're working and what they've done in the past."

“Will be done, chief,” replied Fadila with sparkling eyes. He knew the rumours that she would go through the fire for him, gossipers claiming she was in love with him. Lazar could only laugh about it; according to him, Fadila was only in love with her work.

“Izet and Nijaz, you’re going to do a house search at Safet Begovic.”

“And what are we looking at?” asked Izet with a smile.

“Everything unusual. If Begovic got involved in some operation, he might have made notes. Look for money, weapons, explosives, agenda.”

Lazar turned to the young woman again. “Fadila, check their bank account, uh, Emir Besic’s too.”

“Aren’t we going to search Emir Besic’s house?” asked Nijaz enthusiastically.

“We’re going to take a look there ourselves.”

As everyone was gone, a grinning Senad turned around and asked, “Do you seriously think we’ll find something in Emir’s apartment?”

Lazar shrugged. “Maybe yes, maybe not.” He looked for a contact, and a little later, the pathologist called in.

“Milan,” Lazar said. “Did you find keys in Emir Besic’s clothes?”

“Yes, I did, but I put all the personal stuff in a large envelope for Ferid. However, I doubt it will help him.”

“Okay, I’ll drop by later to pick up those keys.” Without waiting for a reaction, he broke the connection, turning to Senad. “First to the workshop and from there to Breka.”

At that moment, his cell phone rang, and he picked up the call.

“Did you receive my package?” The voice sounded electronically scrabbled but understandable.

“Yes, what can I do for you?” Lazar asked.

“I have a hint,” replied the voice.

Staring at his friend, Lazar listened to a strange story about Bram Ruyter. As he wanted to ask a question, the stranger broke the connection.

“Who was that?” asked Senad curiously.

Lazar shook his head, wondering what this short conversation meant. The information he’d got wasn’t so valuable because he would’ve found out by himself. Then why the phone call? Does the caller just check if he’d found the envelope?

“Who was that?” asked Senad again.

Lazar shrugged. “Someone who wants to deceive me. I have to leave urgently. In the meantime, you can go pick up Besic’s keys.”

Before Senad could reply, he had already walked out.

TWENTY-FIVE

ZUMRA WAS LYING ON HER BACK, AWAKENING FROM A NASTY DREAM. PULLING UP her eyelids, she discerned complete darkness. Puzzled, she pricked her ears, but it remained ominously quiet. She listened to her breathing and the beating of her heart. *What's going on?*

Hell.

For minutes, Zumra didn't dare to move, feeling like someone who'd rolled down a slope hitting dozens of tree trunks. Her fingers slipped over a rough fabric. *A mattress.* Blurry images flashed through her mind, and all of a sudden, she remembered. *I am lying in a cell.* Emma's warning kept echoing through her head: *this is hell.*

She had gone through hell.

Zumra closed her eyes, and new images started rushing through her mind.

The man thrust her into a gloomy space, and behind her, she heard the massive door getting shut. She stood on a granite floor under a grey vault. In the walls were rings of which a few had chains on it. Farther away, a tall woman was standing next to a wooden high-back chair. She had raven black hair tied in a ponytail. However, her clothes were particularly eye-catching, a leather dress consisting of a short skirt, bra, high boots and gloves. She looked like a warrior from Conan comic strips.

A few steps behind the chair Zumra discerned a large table covered with bizarre tools as curved pliers, knives and awls. The whole decor seemed familiar to her, although she had never been here before. Images emerged from films about the Inquisition and the Middle Ages. No doubt about it, she was in a torture chamber.

The woman beckoned her to come over. Zumra hesitated, realising she was at her mercy. As she approached on the cold floor, she observed an unnatural white painted face, looking like a Venetian Carnival mask. *This must be a dream.* Putting her hands over her belly, she halted in front of the woman who was scrutinising her body. Then the woman slapped her in the face with a gloved hand, pointing to the chair with her other hand.

Zumra opened her eyes, trying to get up. She cringed and fell back with a loud sob. Her breasts and abdomen were on fire. *Why is it so quiet?*

Azra hovered like an angel in front of her eyes, raising her hands beggingly to her. Then the picture evaporated into the air. Reality and imagination mixed up. *She's crying out for help.*

Zumra struggled to get up. She slammed her legs over the edge of the bed, putting her feet on the cold soil. Dizziness threatened to overpower her as thousands of hot needles pierced her skull. She closed and opened her eyelids several times, hoping to stop the hammering in her head.

Azra. Timka. Hadar. Lazar.

Where was Lazar?

What have I been saying to that diabolical woman?

Slowly her memories began to become more evident.

The woman pushed her to the armchair, and she fell backwards before she could react, while iron rings clicked around her wrists. Then the woman pushed an iron band over her forehead and screwed it just as hard against the headrest until her head could hardly move. Then her legs got pulled apart and her ankles attached to the chair legs.

What's going on?

"Your name!" A nasty hollow voice came out of two loudspeakers above her head.

"Your name." This time it sounded ominously loud. The woman was looming in front of her, striking her in the stomach.

Zumra made a painful cry.

"Your name," the woman yelled.

Zumra was still gasping for breath.

"Zumra," she eventually muttered, no longer recognising her own voice.

"Why did you come to the appointment?"

Confusing thoughts were raging through her head.

"My girlfriend is sick," she stammered. *Allah, what am I doing here?* She'd never seen that woman before.

"Where is Timka?"

"At home."

"Does Timka have a sister?"

Zumra shook her head. "I have never met a sister."

The woman slapped her again. She tasted blood, feeling it dripping on her breasts. The gloves were cutting like fine razor blades, and her skin was burning like fire. *Please stop it.*

"Timka has a sister," echoed a strange voice through space.

"Uh, yes, but I've never met her." Her lips were swelling, and the talking got more painful.

"Where's her sister?"

"Uh, Belgium I think," she answered stutteringly. *I should never have been here; they want Timka*. Her daughter was with Timka, may Allah have mercy on her.

"What do you want from me? I have a daughter; I want to go home."

"Why have you been pretending to be Timka?" shouted the woman, nose to nose.

Now she had certainty. When gloved fingers squeezed her nipples, a cry rolled over her lips, and her body started quivering. She screamed it out from unbearable pain. The unreal white face appeared in front of her vision, and she read devilish pleasure in it. *Emma warned me; I am in hell.*

"Does Timka have a son?" Again, that unreal voice from the loudspeakers.

"Yes."

"How old is he?"

"Seven."

"Is that her biological son?"

"He is." The invisible interrogator must have noticed her hesitation. It was a mystery how he communicated with this woman. Immediately she sensed hands gliding over her breasts again, causing new pain. She couldn't move her head, couldn't see what the woman was doing, but it was as if burning coal carved crevices into her skin. She'd spotted glistening dots on the gloves. No matter how she squirmed her body, she couldn't escape the touching and scraped the skin off her wrists and ankles.

"Honey, you'll never enchant a man again," the woman whispered in her ear.

The speakers roared, "Where is the biological mother?"

"Uh, in Belgium..." Two hands crawled over her thighs, and the fingers became bloodthirsty piranhas tearing out pieces of meat.

"Is that son with Timka now?"

"Yes, he is."

"Do you know her son's father?"

"No, she never wanted to reveal his name to me."

The loudspeakers kept silent. Zumra felt the woman's hands squeeze between her thighs, sensing her accelerating breath. She couldn't see what the woman was doing, but she felt a moist tongue running over her breasts.

"Your blood tastes so good," the woman gasped. Was she a vampire?

Piranha-like fingers were approaching her sex. She screamed loud until she got hit on her mouth twice.

"Where do you live?" the speakers shouted.

She thought of Azra, which gave her enough strength to endure these sufferings. If she betrayed her dwelling place, they would find and hurt her. These were animals.

She felt the woman biting roughly into her flesh. *She's nuts*. Her arms had barely five inches of free space, so she couldn't move away.

"Your address, darling, or I'll give you a pain you wouldn't even dream of in your worst nightmares."

"Let me go, please, I want my daughter..."

When the rough fingers started squeezing her most sensitive knob, her body shot up, and fireworks of thousands coloured explosions hovered wild in front of her retina. She screamed like a sheep that got slaughtered, and it seemed as if a hot iron rod was marking her most intimate spot. Her body was trying to free itself, causing the ring around her head, cutting deeper into her skin.

"Stop it," she shouted, whereas her ankles and wrists were pulling on the cuffs. She fell back in the seat, and the woman stuck to her like a snake, sitting down over her upper legs.

Allah, have mercy on me.

She felt a hot breath sweeping over her face, smelling a mixture of garlic and sweat. The cutting glove fingers were roughly seeking a passage between her most intimate skin folds, while sharp teeth on her upper body were leaving a trail of bite marks. At that moment, she understood that the woman was in the highest state of sexual excitement.

Then everything turned black.

Zumra was shivering over her whole body. Although she'd survived this torture, her suffering was certainly not over yet. Why had they stopped? Her memories were still vague. They'd given her an injection to ease her pain. Or had she dreamed that?

She groped her thighs and felt an oil-like substance.

She lay on a bed with clean white sheets, no longer handcuffed, under the spell of whispering sweet words in her ear, while soft hands stroked over her face. A pleasant feeling, a familiar voice. *How tired I am.*

Her eyelids closed. However, she couldn't sleep. A cosy warmth enveloped her body. Softly moving hands were covering her skin with an oily product. First, it hurt a little, but that pain quickly turned into a pleasantly warm feeling.

"How beautiful you are," Timka muttered.

Timka, you here? Zumra felt so relaxed. Everything was going to be all right again.

"I'll take good care of you, Zumra," whispered Timka in her ear.

She had always done that.

"I'll get Azra for you, won't you?" asked Timka with a hint of impatience, softly stroking her cheeks.

Zumra sighed. "How sweet of you. Yes, bring Azra to me."

"Where is she?"

"Azra must be back from school by now." She saw the smiling face hovering over her face. "Bring her to me," she whispered. "She is my life, my treasure, my memory, my everything. Yes, she has to be with me, that's the only way I can protect her. Azra is waiting for me at home."

Timka was massaging her painful pubic area where the burning sensation started fading away.

"You're a darling," whispered Zumra, listening to Timka's hypnotising words with closed eyes. Zumra was glad to have her friend close to her; she could always count on her. *She has saved my life for the second time.*

"Honey, don't worry," Timka said.

"Azra must be at home, Timka."

"I'll bring her to you," Timka whispered. "But do you remember where you live, my dear?"

"Why that question? We live together, don't we?"

"We do sweetheart, but do you remember where? You've been through so much, and maybe you've forgotten."

No, I'm not crazy. My abductors have tortured my body, but my mind remained intact.

"At the Miljacka, my stupid love," she whispered. "Number forty, our nest, don't you remember? You wanted to stay close to your mother. What's wrong with you, Timka? Do you think I'm crazy?" She started laughing without knowing why. She was talking nonsense, and her head was a chaos of thoughts.

Timka's mother? *She still thinks I am a bad woman because* we slept *in the same bed.* But that elderly woman hadn't complained because she didn't want to lose her second daughter either.

"Honey, you live alongside the Obala Kulina Bana, don't you?" Timka's voice was getting impatient.

Zumra hardly felt the sting in her arm.

"Yes," she whispered, "I'm so tired. Let me sleep for a moment."

Then her spirit abandoned her.

Timka had injected her something blurring the reality. No, it wasn't Timka. She'd seen people who weren't there. How could she have mistaken Timka with that evil woman? Deceived, she'd been putting Azra, Timka and her son Hadar in danger. The desperation and the fear of her daughter's well-being were pumping additional adrenaline into her veins. Though, the darkness was her opponent.

Moreover, she was naked and severely injured. Her abductors knew that someone without clothes was helpless and wouldn't think of escaping. Nude people are ashamed and crawl into a corner, making themselves as small as possible.

Yet she was going to risk it, even though she was locked up and didn't know where she was, neither what time it was nor how many people were in the house. How was she going to surprise her guards? Impossible with bare hands and weakened by numerous injuries.

She concentrated her thoughts hard on what she'd observed when that man had brought her in the basement. The front door faced the parking lot. *Start remembering all the details.* Zumra closed her eyes, trying to remember. *Hall. Two doors. Staircase. Hallway. The basement door and another exit in front of it.*

But she'd to get out of the cage, which seemed impossible in the dark and without any tools. Or maybe she could take advantage of the darkness and the lack of light in her cell when a guard visited her. But how? Time was running out. If she ever wanted to see Azra again, she had to quickly figure out something.

She got up, staying dizzy for a while. Then she stretched her arms forward and stumbled cautiously toward the foot end until her hands made contact with a brick-built wall. Her nose picked up the smell of mouldy earth.

That creepy woman had only carved her body and face, letting her hands intact. She began to paw her fingertips across the rough surface. Up, down, to the right, to the left. Then another step to the left. Again, and again repeating the same movements, while searching for a sharp object, without which she couldn't do much. But she felt that the mortar was feeling soft and humid, perhaps ancient clay loam. She picked up some pieces and pulverised them easily between her thumb and index finger. Yet she couldn't get enough earth out of the joints to loosen a stone.

The longer she worked, the more desperate she became, conscious that she wouldn't last long on her heavy feeling legs. Unexpectedly she bumped into the bars. Her fingers slid along the metal rods and made contact with the wall hinges. But not a single loose brick. Disappointed, she started to shift sideways along the bars toward the other wall. The distance seemed endless. Every time she wanted to give up, she thought of her daughter, which gave her new energy to move on. Ignoring the fatigue, she fought the pain and proceeded. Reaching the other side, she found out that the trellis door was locked with a chain and a padlock. She sighed loudly and began to grope desperately along the wall. The more desperate the situation, the harder she rubbed the stones. Sweat was running on her forehead, her heart beating fast. Then she felt something moving. She took a deep breath, relaxed her arms and groped up again. It wasn't imagination: there was a loose brick.

She started pulling and dragging. As if moving back and forth a loosened tooth until it came out. For a few minutes, she fiercely went on. Two centimetres, three, and suddenly the brick got free. Despite the moderate temperature, the sweat was dripping into her eyes. Ignoring it, she pulled the stone toward herself, holding a whole brick between her shaking hands whereas she heard earth falling on the floor. She kept immobilised, normalising her breath. Then, after putting the stone carefully in the middle of the mattress, she headed back to the trellis door, crouched on her knees, groped at the bottom along the wall and dispersed the spoiled earth along the wall with her hands. She was relying on the darkness in the cell, hoping that whoever came to get her, in the gleam of the corridor lights, would not notice the missing brick and gravel.

Back on the edge of the bench, she realised that the hardest part was yet to come. Now she needed luck. Or a miracle. Her plan seemed like madness, but it was her only chance to leave this cage alive. Throughout her life, she had hated violence. Yet she had been beaten, humiliated and tortured, even though she had never done anyone any harm. She was tired of calling on

Allah in every challenge. Whenever she needed Him, He wasn't there.

"That's His will," a believer would say.

But Zumra was not going to accept fatality. She needed room to move. And courage. With cunning and patience, it might work. *Don't expose yourself too quickly.* She tried out several positions and held the stone in various ways. It seemed too heavy to grab it tightly. Then, after minutes of trying, she discovered how to handle the brick correctly.

After half an hour, she stretched out. Resting, but not sleeping. Turning her back to the gloomy corridor, she put her right arm along her abdomen, the stone in the palm of her hand.

The long waiting began. Fear started to increase. *Stay awake.* Pretty difficult after what she'd experienced, enveloped in total darkness. She continuously repeated in her head every movement she thought she ought to make. Maybe she would get one chance, and when that failed, she probably wouldn't survive, condemning Azra, Timka and Hadar to death as well.

The monotonous sound of the ticking clock in her head brought her a few times into a slumbering state. Waking up after a more prolonged blackout, she realised that this short sleep was the herald of a deeper sleep, which prompted her to make all kinds of movements. Twice she sat upright, rubbing the sleep out of her eyes, whereas insecurity and doubts crept up on her.

What if no one comes to watch me?

She thought of the woman in the other cell.

"Emma, are you still there?" she shouted with a muffled voice.

There was no answer.

She lay down again.

A heavy door opened and closed. The lights turned on, but Zumra was ready. A big shot of adrenaline flashed through her body. Frantic footsteps got louder and louder. *No boots*, she thought. Her heart started to beat faster. That monstrous woman was much more dangerous than a man.

'Take it easy, stay calm,' screamed a voice in her head.

The footsteps stopped in front of the cell door. For a moment, nothing happened. Zumra held her breath, remaining motionless in her foetal holding thing.

"Are you awake yet?" The voice sounded hypocritically sweet.

Zumra kept her breathing as quiet as possible while getting her eyes used to dusk. She had a small advantage. The woman was standing in the full light of the illuminated passageway, and when she entered the cage, she would be almost blind in the gloomy cell. Or did she just come to bring some food that she would shove under the bars?

Zumra kept motionless. *Provoke a reaction by remaining passive.*

"Zumra, no bullshit. I know you're awake."

Did she really know? Was her plan going to fail? But even though her heart rate accelerated, she didn't move.

"I don't like such games, do you want me to hurt you again?"

Zumra heard shaking bars.

Patience, a spider kills much larger prey by showing patience. It remained quiet for a while. Perhaps that demon began to doubt. For some reason, the abductors wanted to keep her alive. That woman wasn't in charge. Why did she come to visit her or bring her food? Unaccompanied?

"When I enter, and you're awake, I won't have mercy." The horrible voice gave her chills. The chains rattled, a lock jumped open, and rusty hinges squealed as the door swung open. Zumra's heartbeat accelerated. *Don't show any reaction.* That woman was a suspicious predator.

The hard blow against her spine came utterly unexpected. She had almost jumped upright. But she bit her teeth hard.

"Impossible," she heard the woman mumbling. Was that woman panicking?

"Zumra," the voice sounded in her ear.

A pause.

"Do you hear me, it's me, Timka?" whispered the woman, while she grabbed her shoulder, shaking lightly at first, then harder.

But Zumra didn't move, entirely concentrated on that precious moment to come.

"My God, don't do that to me, you can't die yet, sweetheart." It sounded stunned. Zumra sensed a sour breath stroke along her cheek, while a hand groped her forehead. Her body heat and sweat would betray her at any moment. She swivelled on her back in a quick movement, glancing at a surprised face above her. The brick hit the woman just above her left temple. Blood splashed into her face. But in a reflex, the woman had turned away. Zumra realised that the blow hadn't hit the woman hard enough. She straightened herself up and get off the bench, looking furious at her tormentor who sat dazed on her knees, trying to scribble up. But Zumra was out of her mind and smacked the brick in the woman's face. She heard a crashing noise of bone and the woman fell on her back. By the force of the blow, Zumra had dropped the stone, which she quickly picked up again. Screaming out of control, she threw herself on her agitated tormentor, sat down on her with her thighs spread and raised the stone between both hands. Ignoring the pleading gaze of a dying human, she smashed the brick with all the power left in her. She hit her several times until the hated face between her naked legs had become an unrecognisable bloody knit.

Zumra was trembling violently, and it took her a few minutes to regain her senses. As if in a trance, she looked at the lifeless body beneath her.

She let go of the stone that fell on the floor.

Dazed, Zumra scrambled up and stumbled into the passage. The cell door on the other side was open. She wondered what had happened to Emma. In the corridor light, she checked her body and started to shudder at the sight of clotted blood and countless cuts. Her thighs were also ugly. She didn't expect to find suitable clothes in the house. Anyway, she did not have enough time to search, not knowing if there were other people in the house.

I have to get out of here.

When she reached the far end of the awful corridor, all her limbs hurt like hell, but she immediately began to climb the stairs opposite the door of the torture chamber, ending up in a wide hallway. There she stood for minutes panting fiercely with pricked ears.

Nowhere did she hear voices.

Was that woman alone in the house? Was that why she'd been approaching her so carefully? Zumra remembered that she hadn't seen any food. What had got that woman in mind? Making fun with her?

At the far end of the hallway, the door was open. Zumra rushed to it, and immediately felt more comfortable. In the hall, she spotted a cloth stand with a brown lady's coat hanging on it, which she eagerly dragged off the stick. She pulled the garment around her shoulders, tied the buttons and put the belt around her waist. In the shoe cabinet, she found sneakers, all at least one size too big, but that wasn't so bad when she pulled the laces together very tight.

Get away from here.

She pulled open the front door, blinked several times with her eyes against the bright daylight and froze. Instinctively she stepped back and slammed the door shut. Rising panic disrupted her breathing rhythm.

A car was driving through the gate into the parking lot.

TWENTY-SIX

Apeldoorn, 2001

IT WAS THEIR LAST NIGHT. BRAM WAS LYING ON HIS BACK, MAYKE TURNED TOWARD him with her right leg over his thighs and one arm over his chest, kissing him softly on his mouth. But his anger didn't subside. He wanted to erase Bosnia from his memory. Since they were married, they'd never been separated for more than a day, and he had an inexplicable hunch.

"Do you think it's wise to snoop around over there?" His voice sounded angry and reproachful.

"It's going to be a scoop, dear. I finally want to reveal the truth."

"Risking your life for that?"

"After years of investigation, this will be the culmination of my work. I have always wanted to know who's responsible for the mass murder in

Srebrenica. During my research, I've met Suada Omarovic, an admirable young woman who has escaped hell and found her happiness in Belgium. Suada's story is so unbelievable, so heartbreaking that it must be true. And she will never return to Bosnia."

"Let the past rest, Mayke."

"Honey, don't you want to know who's responsible for Srebrenica's downfall?" She kissed him on his nose. "There you've lost either your career and girlfriend. Do you think Karremans is the only person responsible? What if the downfall of Srebrenica and the other two enclaves were part of a conspiracy?"

He laughed involuntarily. "Do you believe that conspiracy theory? Mayke, I thought you were..."

"I've got the evidence," she interrupted him. "The Europeans, especially the British and the French, the Americans, uh, all agreed to give up the eastern enclaves, Gorazde, Zepa and Srebrenica, in exchange for Sarajevo. Apparently, the generals were able to convince the Bosnian high command that these were the only way to save the maximum."

He'd heard that story over and over again.

"Bollocks," he said. "I think the Serbs took these enclaves because Karadzic knew that Milosevic, Tudjman and Izetbegovic were going to confer with each other, that a peace agreement was in the making. The plan foresaw dividing Bosnia according to the ethnic occupation at that moment. Karadzic wanted to save Srebrenica because of the silver mines and the strategic location of the city. Thus, before the treaty ought to be signed, Mladic launched an offensive and occupied the three enclaves."

"Honey, do you think that Mladic would have launched an offensive without the guarantee that there would be no air raids to disturb his invasion? Do you agree with me that the Serbs meticulously planned this attack and the subsequent evacuation? No doubt that Mladic well prepared for the transportation of women and children, the execution of the men and burying of their corpses. As an ex-military, you know what logistical resources such an operation requires. Mladic mastered the job in just three days. That requires meticulous planning and preparation."

"Possibly," Bram murmured, not entirely convinced. His hands provocatively began to stroke Mayke, hoping that she would abandon the issue.

But Mayke was a stubborn woman; she blocked his pushy hand by squeezing her thighs together.

"Suada Omarovic has observed several UNPROFOR officers on the Jahorina," she continued. "They regularly gathered with Karadzic and Mladic. And after each meeting, they raped imprisoned Muslim women."

"Women who didn't resist."

At the beginning of 2000, he'd read a complete report, published in a book by *'Centar za istrazivanje I documentacija, Centre for Research and Documentation.'* He remembered the title, *'Begged to Get Kille*d. *Crimes against women in Bosnia-Herzegovina.'* It was a report about UNPROFOR authorities having sex with imprisoned Muslim women. Several victims accused a Canadian and a British general. The Canadian general would even have got eyewitnesses killed. Rumours and assumptions. Nevertheless, it was a fact that both officers had rejected the invitation for a confrontation with the witnesses. Guilty or not, that certainly did not speak in their favour.

"Suada possesses evidence," she insisted with a bright smile. That was the first time Mayke mentioned evidence.

He gazed at her intently. "What evidence? In such cases, there is rarely any evidence." He could read triumph in her eyes.

"After being abused, Suada has stolen something from the general," she said. "If someone finds that incriminating piece of evidence on the Jahorina, I wonder what explanation General Flower will give."

He listened with half an ear because Mayke's hand has started doing naughty things.

"Every time there were high visitors, the prominent guests were assigned a small chalet where a friendly Serbian major provided them with muslin girls. The guests were even allowed to abuse them. After the orgy, the same major brought the girls back to the *Women's House*. That's what Suada called the lugubrious building. In the meantime, the prominent guests could take a shower, making themselves presentable again before leaving the Jahorina in their armoured vehicles. Of course, the soldiers were not allowed to know what their chiefs had done. That the girls freely could move around, doesn't mean they're free. Everywhere in the surrounding forest lay landmines, so it was almost impossible to run away."

Bram let out a sigh. "Every lawyer will find a sensible explanation for all the evidence you are going to reveal. Has nothing to do with rape, they'll say. Those women cooperated, not opposed."

"Honey, those women had no choice; they were prisoners." Her voice was getting louder. "Well, I agree with you on one point: what Suada was able to gather, is in itself not decisive proof."

He frowned. "But you still have a trump card up your sleeve."

She nodded, making a mysterious face.

"Believe me," she said, "if I publish my evidence, Flower won't be able to deny".

Sarajevo, 9 October 2002

Bram stared dreamily at the ceiling. Mayke's voice had sounded so confident, and by now, he'd become convinced that what she'd discovered, might have resulted in her death. Tormented by nightmares, he hadn't had much sleep. The same nasty dream almost every night.

Terrifying shadows armed with sickles chase him through the most complex landscapes. He zigzags between tall trees, past dilapidated houses and across burnt fields until he's too exhausted to run any farther, while dark, faceless figures with hoods are approaching him dangerously close. Just before the leader is going to drill his flaming sword through his body, he wakes up.

There was no question of sleeping any more. For hours, Bram had been tossing and turning, thinking of Mayke, and their last night.

Holy shit, what did she discover?

He got up, heard Edhem showering and strolled to the window. With mixed feelings, he watched the result of ethnic cleansing: the high number of ruins among untouched buildings. A clear warning to the Bosnian Serbs that their repatriation there was undesirable.

Bram had seen hundreds of ruins near Sarajevo, and the most striking was the *Oslobodenje*, five hundred metres beyond the Stup traffic junction in the direction of Sarajevo, a few hundred metres behind the *Glass Tower* in which EuPol housed.

His thoughts were with Emir Besic, the two Britons they had thrown into the ravine, and Derek Fleming. There was also Anel, Emir's friend who was working for Greg Stone in the *Glass Tower*.

Greg Stone? He vaguely remembered this Belgian IT he met during a party at the European Union Monitoring Mission. A short meeting.

"You can take a shower," he heard Edhem shouting from the kitchen.

He desperately needed a shower.

Fifteen minutes later, Bram was sitting in the kitchen facing Edhem. On the table was a round serving tray containing a beautiful coffee pot, two porcelain cups, a ditto sugar bowl and two long, elegant spoons. A basket of bread with butter and various kinds of cheese completed the whole.

No one uttered a word.

Bram knew that Edhem was not troubled by conscientious objections. Whoever had experienced Srebrenica could never be the same again. He too had changed since 11 July 1995. He would always remember the frightened faces of the citizens of Srebrenica. However, he couldn't forget the armed Muslim Bosnians killing Serbs in the surrounding villages at night, then hiding behind the Dutch soldiers, hoping that the Serbs would shoot at them so the Blue Helmets would eventually fight on their side. But the Serbs didn't walk into the trap. Every night the same ghosts appeared in his nightmares. Sometimes he saw Jasmina turn up to accuse him of cowardice. But hadn't he desperately tried to save her and her family? In vain, the politicians had decided who could live and who not; they had been playing God. He had resisted, and they'd locked him up for misconduct. In the eyes of his colleagues, he was a traitor. In interviews, they were claiming that Dutchbat 3 had done everything possible, and they got celebrated as heroes.

Furthermore, they called it a shame that Bram Ruyter had sent an *incorrect story* out into the world. That hurt, but he'd built a shield around him. Nothing could touch him any more.

Edhem seemed to understand his inner anger. They had both played a role in the same tragedy. *Luckily Edhem is my friend.* Without his help, he would never have got out of this situation in one piece. That's why he felt guilty for telling his friend only a part of his past. Besides, he'd concealed the fact that finding Emir Besic's corpse hadn't been a coincidence. Yet Edhem had helped him without asking questions.

Bram squeezed his lips together. The ease with which he'd killed a man was terrifying him. No, he'd been enjoying it. If those two arseholes hadn't underestimated his warrior skills, his remnants would now be rotting somewhere. But their arrogance had made them careless, overlooking his violent past. *Fuck the rules.* At last, Bram understood the mentality of this population. Eye-to-eye.

Edhem poured two cups.

Bram sipped of the syrupy nectar, knowing that he would get sour burps afterwards. He glanced up at Edhem.

"I already knew the place where we dumped those two Britons," he announced with emotion.

Edhem's features remained impassive.

"Where we've dumped those boys," continued Bram whispering, "is the place where my wife Mayke got murdered."

TWENTY-SEVEN

"IMMEDIATELY INTO MY OFFICE." GREG STONE RECOGNISED THE VOICE OF THE deputy commissioner.

"What's the matter?" he asked.

The connection went dead. For the first time, the French deputy commissioner Normand Montpetit summoned him to his office. His voice had sounded sharp, although Greg couldn't guess what the reason might be. Half an hour earlier during the coffee break, he'd observed Montpetit sitting with Mycroft Follum, who'd been staring at him repeatedly.

Thoughtfully he put the receiver down, feeling increasing anxiety. He left his office and walked with fast pace toward Norman's office. The door was open, and he saw Normand sitting behind his desk. The Frenchman glanced up and waved him in. Stone had always got along well with him, and when they were alone, they usually spoke French.

"Shut the door." Montpetit's voice sounded like that of an eighteenth-century soprano castrato. Stone considered the voice was shriller than usual. Moreover, he spoke in English.

Greg halted in front of the desk, glancing around. In the right corner, invisible from the corridor, he discerned Margaret, Head of Internal Affairs, a big bossy woman with male facial features looking at him with hostility. Among friends, he called her an evil bitch.

"You can sit down," Normand snarled.

Stone didn't like the tone of his voice. "Thank you," he said with a loud voice, sending a short unfriendly glance at Margaret.

The Frenchman cleared his throat. "Greg, I hope you don't mind Margaret being there."

"Do I have a choice?"

"Margaret is here as an observer; you don't have to worry."

"Why should I worry? Is something going on?"

Montpetit let out a theatrical sigh. "A delicate subject. I was told you've got a girlfriend." He turned his chair a quarter away from his desk and bent forward, studying his shoes as a schoolchild who'd done something wrong.

Stone reacted ironically. "Wow, I didn't think I needed a permit." All of a sudden, Margaret's presence was disturbing him tremendously. He glanced in her direction and saw her taking notes. Without waiting for an answer, he turned toward the deputy.

"It's really none of your business," he hissed. Anger and annoyance flared up in him. Once he'd behaved nicely to interrogators, and that had cost him three months in prison. And this interview began to turn out as an interrogation. He was a free citizen, not accountable for his private life, and he didn't think he'd violated the rules of his contract. Daria Badora was not a criminal. He could hardly control his anger.

Montpetit's face turned red. "I just want to help you."

"*Tu as raison*," snarled Stone. "*J'ai une copine, mais cela ne te regarde pas*. She moved in with me, and I suppose that English bitch told you about her." He gestured briefly to Margaret. "She'd better look in the mirror before she starts to interfere with others. Doesn't she have an affair with Linda, her closest employee?"

Suddenly Margaret sat upright, staring at the deputy commissioner with flaming eyes. *She understands French.*

Bonaparte's face became a grim mask. According to the rules in the gendarmerie, subordinates didn't have to speak like that to him. Greg assumed Montpetit was aware of facing a civilian technician, not a submissive French police officer. Moreover, it was about a private matter.

"Margaret is here as a member of the ...", Montpetit began.

"Internal Affairs," Stone interrupted him. "You've already said that. But I don't belong to the police, neither the French nor the EU." He refused to speak English. "If people gossip about me, and you think that's important enough to tackle me about it, be aware that several police officers, being part of your boys, have alarming secrets."

"You're right." Napoleon's face turned even redder. "As long as you respect your contract, I shouldn't blame you. I don't want to interfere with your private life. But your girlfriend is apparently staying in the country illegally."

Greg Stone thought the time had come to adopt a formal tone. He looked the deputy straight in the eyes.

"Mr Montpetit, is this an official interrogation here?"

"No, certainly not." Norman hesitated. "You know I appreciate your work. That's why I warn you before you commit a serious mistake."

Hypocrite.

Stone leaned in. "*Écoutez bien, Monsieur Montpetit,*" he said. "I own a copy of my friend's passport and her residence permit."

Normand frowned. "Get me that copy," he snarled.

Stone smiled nastily. "I am not a police observer," he riposted much more vehemently than he'd wanted. "So, I repeat my question: is there an investigation ongoing against me or not?"

Normand shook his head. "No, this is an informal conversation. I don't want you to jeopardise your career and reputation for a hooker. We all know that those girls from Moldova are cheap sluts."

Stone closed his eyes for a moment, taking a deep breath.

"For the sake of clarity, Monsieur Montpetit," he scowled, "as there's no investigation going on, I don't have to prove anything either, but I'll show you my goodwill and show you a copy this afternoon."

"I'm counting on it."

"I don't need to tell you anything else." Stone straightened from his chair and walked away. But in the doorway, he turned around.

"As I know, is it your mission in Bosnia to fight the trafficking in women. How can you call all Moldavian girls being whores? You are prejudiced and racist. When my girlfriend begged IPTF for help, the duty officer refused. I've saved her from the criminal claws, although that's supposed to be your job. Did you forget about the 2000 murder?" Greg Stone suggested the murder of a girl who'd requested IPTF help in 2000. After signing her statement, the police observers sent her back on the street. She got abducted, and the criminals settled a bloody example. They dumped her tortured body in the neighbouring forests, with a bullet in her head. The perpetrator had never been arrested.

Norman's features became strangely agitated.

"Watch your tongue," he groaned like a wounded predator. He'd also reached the limit of his English-speaking knowledge.

Stone took a deep breath. "I don't have to accept your discriminating bollocks," he reacted with a grimace.

"Well, you asked for it," exploded Montpetit. He grabbed a bundle of papers lying in front of him and held out his hand.

"Take it," he shouted.

Stone took the bundle.

Normand grinned triumphantly. "You got fired," he yelled.

It was as if Stone got a blow to the stomach. He glanced astonished on the document, recognising a resignation letter already signed by the commissioner. The meeting with the deputy had been a pitfall. They needed confirmation that he lived with Daria under the same roof.

And he'd walked into the trap as a rookie.

TWENTY-EIGHT

ALTHOUGH BRAM RUYTER TRUSTED HIS FRIEND EDHEM HASIC, HE HADN'T REVEALED him everything yet. Mayke's death had been his real motivation, not revenge. Furthermore, he was still fighting ghosts from the past, which had pushed him to write a book to get rid of his nightmares. But he hadn't yet found the necessary concentration to write much.

He drew a deep breath. "As I have already told you after I left Bosnia in 1995, I returned to Apeldoorn, where I had to manage a dark period. I hated the whole world, and according to psychiatrists, I was suffering PTSD. Those fools tried to convince me that what I'd been through was part of my job. '*The assignment is over*,' they said, '*so it's a good idea to get everything out of your mind.*' They insisted that Visser had done the right thing. I'd crossed the line when I attacked him. Those bureaucrats feigned to understand my behaviour, alleging they didn't prosecute me because of my presumed disturbed mental state. All I had to do was turn the knob, and everything would be sunny again.

"To hell with those fools who'd never been into a war zone. The Intelligence Service and members of a Committee of Inquiry were under political pressure, searching for answers to what had happened in Srebrenica. They've questioned me countless times, looking for a scapegoat. At first, they wanted me to testify in court. But they wisely declined when I refused to accept their version. Those acorns feared the truth because my story differed from the story Thom Karremans and his staff sent into the world. The Ministry of Defence didn't take any chances and sent me to a couple of shrinks who diagnosed me as mentally unstable. That was enough to expel me from the army. Ex-colleagues came threatening me at home. I had to keep my mouth shut. Those fucking arseholes were looking for excuses for their cowardly behaviour and let themselves be celebrated as heroes."

Bram paused a moment, took a sip of coffee and went on. "I'd been again a civilian for several months when a reporter approached me. She showed great interest in what had happened in Srebrenica on the 11th of July 1995 and the following three days. First, I got the door shut in her face. But she was determined, and a beautiful woman as well. At her third attempt, I let her in."

He laughed sadly. "Mayke was very understanding when I told her why I was feeling so bad. '*It has nothing to do with PTSD*,' she said, and she patiently listened to what I had to say about Srebrenica. The government kept quiet, still concealing the truth. The people involved also tried to justify their failure, out of fear or out of shame, who knows? '*We did what we could*,' claimed the politicians. That's what Pontius Pilate said when he'd got Jesus crucified.

"Mayke believed me. After several visits, I proposed her to have dinner at a well-known restaurant. That was the turning point in my life. That night we made love. The next morning, I decided to put Bosnia out of my mind for good, convinced that I had done everything possible to save Jasmina. Going on to hurt myself wouldn't change the facts. I would never see Jasmina again, so I thought it better to close this chapter and starts to live a new life with Mayke."

Edhem smiled. "That was a wise decision."

"That's what I thought, too."

"You don't have to apologise." Edhem leaned in. "I don't blame you. You're the only one among those who don't want to apologise. You admit the battalion could have done more to prevent genocide. The world was looking at the Blue Helmets, and Mladic would never have attacked them. The war was not over yet, and he had a lot to lose as NATO would turn against him. But every history has it's *what if*."

Bram nodded. "As Mayke and I moved in together, I could call out my happiness across the rooftops. Srebrenica had been a nightmare, and I didn't want to hear or read about it any more. But Mayke encouraged me to write about my experiences, convinced I got talent. Writing had been a child's dream, and at her insistence, I tried to write a novel. What else did I have to do? I'd been an infantryman, and in civilian life, there are no comparable jobs. The writing was also a way to get rid of my accumulated anger and to regain my inner peace.

"My first novel *The Lie* wasn't exactly a bestseller, but it sold well, uh, under the table. Nobody liked to admit to having bought or read the book. No one wanted to believe what *The Lie* revealed. Srebrenica had become a taboo theme. '*That can't be true,*' yelled depraved patriots. The Ministry of Defence didn't like what I'd written. They knew it wasn't fiction and they threatened me with a trial. But when Mayke got involved, they quickly dropped off, afraid that their attempts to intimidate me might have the wrong effect on public opinion. So, they spread the rumour that I was a sick man who'd lost his mind. A shame for the nation that I was pulling through the mud honest officers and soldiers who had bravely defended their country. What a joke."

Bram sipped some coffee and continued. "Mayke was a wonderful woman. We were a happy couple until March 2001." A haze came over his eyes, and he grabbed his cup, lifted it to his lips, but put it down again without drinking.

He gave Edhem a short look. "I will never forget that horrible day when someone from the press agency *De Goede Morgen* came along and pragmatically told me that Mayke was dead. A dramatic car accident. The messenger didn't know the details. Later I discovered that her car had crashed into a ravine with the whole team."

Bram saw that Edhem was listening with interest. "I didn't want to believe it, and I didn't accept fate until Mayke's body arrived in Apeldoorn. I hardly remember anything about the funeral ceremony, and all the worries linked to it. I got consumed by sorrow, but could not express it. Events in Srebrenica had already emptied me once, and I'd given the small amount of remaining emotion to Mayke. Now she had passed away, I felt empty. My nightmares came back. The phantoms drove me through the most awful environments, and strangely enough, Jasmina was part of it. After a month or so, I understood I had to go back to Bosnia. Here Jasmina and Mayke disappeared from my life, so here I had to get rid of my nightmares. Cees Visser is part of that, too."

Edhem sat up straight, his eyes narrowing to slits. "Cees Visser is dead," he said curtly.

"*To je šala, zar ne?* It's a joke, isn't it?"

Edhem shook his head thoughtfully. "You don't know?"

"Shit, you're kidding. How do you know that Cees Visser is dead?"

"It was on the news yesterday. With all the excitement, I've forgotten to tell you. A room maid has found Visser naked in his hotel room. Cause of death is unknown, but a hooker visited him. Might be a heart attack."

"I would have liked to have had a word with him," replied Bram without looking at his friend for fear of betraying himself.

Why am I hiding the truth?

Edhem got up and strolled to the small window. "How did you end up with *Last Hope*?" he asked.

"A coincidence. I was looking for a job that could take me to Sarajevo. I attempted it as a security officer at UNHCR, but I was already too old for that. Then I searched among non-governmental organisations and found *Last Hope*, a small organisation with limited resources. It mainly supports other organisations, such as the IOM. After an interview with the director of

Apeldoorn, I got immediately employed. I hadn't expected that given my past at Dutchbat 3."

"A Dutch NGO. But, isn't your boss British?"

"Indeed. I think that the British government gave a large donation so that Winston could become office commander. And *Last Hope* can use donations, although it receives a contribution for every assignment carrying out for a UN organisation."

Edhem's features hardened. "The British want to be in charge everywhere. But how did you get in touch with Emir Besic?"

Edhem's sudden curiosity surprised Bram. "EUMM party." He told about his coincidental meeting with the young Muslim. "After Besic had revealed that he was Derek Fleming's neighbour, I asked him if he would dare to spy on that guy if I paid him. At first, Besic was suspicious but agreed when I told him that Fleming probably had something to do with my wife's death. He wasn't interested in money. His brother had got shot by a sniper, you know, and in his eyes, the British were Serb friends he hated like the plague. I asked him to pay particular attention to Fleming's visitors. He promised to take pictures for me and to hack Fleming's computer if he got an opportunity."

Edhem frowned. "And why do you think Fleming has something to do with Mayke's death? You said it was an accident."

"According to the official version, was it an accident. But on the eve of her visit to Pale, Mayke has sent me an e-mail with several attachments. I wonder if she got a presentiment because she also sent a kind of testimony from a raped woman. Besides, she briefly informed me about her plans. During some EUMM party, she had a long talk with Derek Fleming. He seemed to be concerned about the reason for her visit to Sarajevo, especially when she'd talked about the bad behaviour of UNPROFOR commanders and their secret meetings with Karadzic and Mladic on the Jahorina. Fleming had tried to dissuade her from visiting Pale, alleging it was life-threatening to start asking questions about Karadzic there. He had also asked where she hoped to find that evidence, but she'd given him an evasive answer."

"So, you're convinced that she's got murdered?"

"Yes, I have seen pictures of the accident site. There were no skid marks. According to the official version, the car suddenly crossed the road, crashing into the ravine. The subsequent explosion left few traces. Independent experts appointed by Mayke's parents found evidence of C4 and a bullet in one of the bodies. But the official investigators rejected that report, confirming the accident. I've spoken to one of the experts who excluded an accident. According to him, the EU was preparing a new mission in which its cooperation with the Serbian entity was of the utmost importance, and the government wanted to avoid that this incident might compromise the relationship between the European negotiators and the Serbian Republic.

"And what role did Fleming play in all this?"

"It's no secret that Fleming and Political Advisor Follum are on good terms with the Pale politicians. The place where Mayke's car crashed into the ravine is at the exit of the last tunnel in Serbian territory, just before the long turn behind the federation border where we dropped the two Britons. An ideal place for an ambush. Mayke's driver was a famous ex-rally driver. No doubt about it, Mayke has been ambushed. Which means that the killers were aware of her arrival. Someone tipped them off, and I think it's Fleming."

Edhem drew a stern face. "So, you think Fleming found out you hired Emir Besic to keep an eye on him, and then ordered those two Britons to get rid of you?"

Bram poured coffee and took a long sip. "I don't know what to think. When Emir sent me a message, he'd been at EuPol the whole day. He parked in the parking lot along the Miljacka. The park lends itself to discrete encounters, and we used to gather there."

He cleared his throat. "I've seen the two Britons over there. How did they know where Besic was going and with whom he wanted to talk? Perhaps Emir has seen or heard something, but that doesn't explain why the Britons got there so quickly."

Edhem shrugged, then paced back to the table and emptied his cup. "I'm going to get a newspaper," he said.

Ten minutes later, he was back with the *Dnevni Avaz* under his arm. He sat down across from Bram and browsed the newspaper.

"Listen," he said.

On Monday evening, a 23-year-old young man has been discovered dead in his car, parked alongside the right bank of the Miljacka, close to the *Princip Bridge*. The victim got killed by strangulation with a metal rope. An autopsy will be performed at night.
According to the spokesman of the Sarajevo police, it concerns a solitary young man who was working for a well-known IT company. The man is unknown to the police, which doesn't rule out the possibility of a settlement in the milieu. (JK)

He slammed the paper and sighed relieved. "There's nothing in it about those two... but it will be too soon for that."

Bram got up. "Edhem, I got the case wrong. Time to sort a few things out, and that's why I've got to go to my place."

"What are you up to?"

"I should have paid more attention to what Mayke told me."

"Something important?"

"Possibly, now Emir is dead, I'm going to handle things differently. I was too proud and furious to check Mayke's sources of information. That was a mistake."

"Do you want me to come with you?"

"No. I'm going to pick up my notebook. It still contains the e-mails Mayke sent me in 2001 from Sarajevo."

After picking up his Glock in the sleeping room, he glanced over at Edhem. "I'll call you later."

Bram left the house with an odd feeling. Why did he conceal that Mayke had given the name and address of a young woman she'd visited?

Suada Omarovic's sister.

TWENTY-NINE

LAZAR MAGAS DROVE UNDER THE RAILWAY BRIDGE AND SLOWED DOWN. TO HIS left lay a vast forest, to his right flowed the Miljacka. The road continued for another fifty metres before making a long turn to the left. As he noticed a rectangular concrete strip, he turned it up and discerned on the far end a two-storey building in an inverted L-shape. While driving along the tall lined up close-knit trees, his gaze wandered over the vegetation on the left. At the end of the concrete and the trees, he parked next to three cars.

The entrance was a heavy door in the angled wing looking out across the parking lot. He rang the doorbell, waved to the camera and got briefly surprised by a crackling loudspeaker.

"*Dobar dan*, with whom have I the honour?" a digitally distorted voice asked.

Lazar showed his ID card to the camera. "Chief Inspector Lazar Magas of the Homicide Department."

The speaker remained silent for a time before crackling, "Push the door until you hear a click."

Lazar nodded and stepped through the doorway into a rectangular hall where a heavyset man behind a counter glanced at him questioningly. Lazar took a brief look at the six monitors aligned in the wall, showing a 360-degree vision around the building.

"Whom do you want to meet?" asked the replica of Conan the barbarian.

"The office commander and Bram Ruyter."

Last Hope seems to take security very seriously. Many NGOs were all too careless and often deplored burglaries. The athletic receptionist picked up a phone and reported the visitor, waiting for an answer. Then he put down the handset.

"Mr Chambers will see you in a moment, please take a seat." He waved to the four chairs next to the door.

Lazar hesitated. As he finally decided to sit down, he heard a metallic click, and a bald man with a grey beard appeared between the doorposts. Lazar walked past him into the gangway and halted. They shook hands, while the door got closed by itself.

"I am Winston Chambers, *Last Hope's* office commander."

"Chief Inspector Lazar Magas, Homicide Department."

Chambers led him to the far end of the corridor where they entered a soberly furnished office. Lazar noticed two large windows, a desk with two chairs in front of it and a cheap cupboard with six shelves. Through the doorway of the adjoining room, he saw a man with a rugged hairdo and thick glasses sitting behind a computer, glancing up at him. Lazar nodded briefly and turned toward his host.

Winston gestured to the chair across the desk. "How can I help you? Your English is amazing."

"I've lived in the United States for years," Lazar replied as he sat down. "My compliment, you've turned this building into a fortress."

"Not an excessive luxury when you're thwarting women traffickers," replied Chambers with a faint smile. "Two days ago, we lost one of our guests while driving her to the airport."

"I heard about it. Colleagues from the Immigration Police are dealing with the case." The incident got mentioned in the morning meeting.

"I don't think they will be very successful," said Winston.

"You're right. Those nightclubs which are employing illegal girls from the East have become a scourge, Mr Winston, and I wonder if the international presence isn't largely responsible for it."

"Quite possibly, everywhere you deploy soldiers or international communities, you'll find brothels. Is the reason for your visit that abducted girl?"

Lazar shook his head. "No, I would like to have an interview with Mr Bram Ruyter."

Chambers features froze. "He took a week's vacation."

Lazar couldn't interrogate an aid worker without his permission. Theoretically, a first-degree crime cancelled out diplomatic protection. Still, the international aid workers were entitled to the intervention of their embassy, which, if desired, informed its national authorities. However, the federal government could decide whether to entrust the case to the Bosnian legal system or to bring the accused to justice in his own country. Usually, a local preliminary investigation was carried out by competent inspectors in cooperation with investigators sent by the national authority. Now the EU was represented, international police observers could assist the local police. But these International Police Workers did not have any police authority. They were unarmed, gave advice and reported to the EU council. Yet it was practically impossible for the Bosnian justice to bring an international aid worker to a Bosnian court.

Lazar let out a faint sigh. “Mr Chambers, I’ve got in charge with a murder investigation in which one of the victims turns out to be a good acquaintance of Mr Ruyter.”

“Is Mr Ruyter involved?”

Lazar shook his head. “Ruyter is just a witness. Coincidentally, he knows one of the victims. He might give me important information about that person. Why do you think he could be involved?”

Winston’s features hardened. “You know that you cannot interrogate us without the presence of our advisor.”

“Oh, Mr Winston, this is not an interrogation, and I’ve no intention of accusing anyone. Do you know Emir Besic?”

Winston didn’t answer.

“An excellent computer specialist,” Lazar continued. “We found him strangled in his car.”

“And what has Mr Ruyter got to do with it...”

Lazar interrupted him with a single hand movement. “Mr Ruyter has met the man several times. I try to find out about what they have been talking. Besic worked for a well-known IT company doing business with EuPol. I think he could be a member of a terrorist organisation. You understand that we want to clarify matters as soon as possible.”

“I understand.” Winston’s face brightened up. “On Monday evening, all of a sudden Bram asked for a week’s leave for personal reasons. He felt responsible for the kidnapping of his protégée, and he needed a break, he said.”

“What do you mean by a break? Was he overworked?”

“He looked very concerned. The young woman had trusted him.”

“An emotional man, or was there more going on between him and that woman?”

Winston shook his head. “Emma Badora was very young. He was protecting her as a daughter. Bram is a good guy, Chief Inspector. In 1995 he was in Srebrenica, and that leaves scars.”

“Did he belong to Dutchbat 3?”

“He did. After his return home, he suffered PTSD. As he kept accusing some of his superiors, he got expelled from the army. Shortly after that, he married a reporter, and it went uphill again. But what I tell you, has nothing to do with your investigation,” Chambers uttered in an apologetic tone.

Lazar felt overwhelmed by an extreme sense of excitement. Bram Ruyter seemed to be an odd bird which he ought to catch as soon as possible.

“All information about Mr Ruyter might help me further,” he stated. “You’ve mentioned he’d married a reporter. Is his wife in the country?” He feigned ignorance, knowing that those talking a lot, sometimes reveal what they want to keep quiet.

Chambers sighed. "The misfortune continues to haunt Bram. His wife was investigating Karadzic, I guess. She came to Sarajevo, went with her team to Pale in the hope of collecting testimonies about Karadzic, and she perished on her way back to Sarajevo with her whole team. Her death was a terrible shock to Bram. That might be the reason why he has become an aid worker."

"Mr Chambers, do you mean Mr Ruyter is here to do penance for what happened in Srebrenica?"

"Possibly, but he's doing an excellent job."

"If I understand correctly, on Monday he asked for a leave. Did he work that day?"

"He did until he heard Emma Badora got abducted. I advised him to take the case as it is, but he left furiously."

"I don't call that normal behaviour," Lazar said thoughtfully. "Was he nervous, irritable?"

"What are you after?"

"Just routine. Mr Ruyter seems to me as a very explosive person. Do you know Cees Visser?"

"I know that name." Chambers's face set off in an almost hostile grimace. "That's the military attaché found dead in his room. It was in the paper."

"Did Mr Ruyter know him too?"

"I suppose so because they were both in Srebrenica. But what do you want to hear, Chief Inspector? If you want to know more about his assignment in Srebrenica, I suggest you talk to him. What I've told you is no secret; everyone here is aware. But we never talk about it. A sensitive theme for a Dutchman."

Lazar nodded. "I understand you, Mr Chambers. Can you give me his address?"

"No problem. Let Bram know right away that he also owes me some explanation." Winston quickly wrote something on a Post-it and handed it to the chief inspector.

"I will do that. If Mr Ruyter does show up here, can you give him my business card and ask him to call me immediately?" Lazar took a card out of his wallet and put it in front of the man.

"You can count on me, Chief Inspector."

Lazar left the building with a satisfying feeling.

THIRTY

ZUMRA ABDIC RUSHED TO THE FAR END OF THE HALLWAY WITH PRICKED EARS listening to the approaching car. The sound of the engine faded away, followed by the noise of slamming doors. Voices were getting closer.

They didn't notice anything.

The squealing front door drove her heartbeat upwards, as she stepped through the doorway in front of the basement door. Her eyes wandered through the room. *A kitchen and two doors*. The door on her left hand probably led to the living room, and the heavy wooden door in the farthest corner should lead outside. She hurried toward it and pushed the latch down. The men's voices in the corridor were getting louder. She turned the key around and opened the door carefully. After gently shutting the door behind her, she turned around, facing a green wall of tall deciduous trees. Panic was rising in her, her heart pounding. Hesitating could be mortal. Then she noticed a small track winding through the trees, but couldn't see where it led to. Taking a deep breath, she moved toward it and started to run, hoping that her assailants would need time to find out about her escape. Not having heard any children's voices, gave her hope.

I have to get home.

The narrow path snaked between the close-knit trees, and when she glanced over her shoulder, the house had gone. It went down until it ended up in ferns and thickets. On her left, she discovered a small trail of flattened leaves. She walked toward it and ventured between the tall plants, following the path that had been made not so long ago by a human being.

Then someone yelled in the distance.

They have found the woman. From several directions, she heard men screaming, although she couldn't catch the noise of approaching steps. She felt like a hunted animal and continued her way between the long leaves. Voices echoed through the forest. The chase had begun, and the hunters would undoubtedly find this trail. She accelerated her pace, ignoring the pain, whereas the thicket, thistles and thorns scarred the skin of her naked legs. The panic caused adrenaline shooting through her veins. She turned to the right, stumbled between two thick trees, walking over an unevenly hard soil. All of a sudden, the ground started to slide, and her feet lost grip on the steeply sloping earth. After hovering a second, her body hit the ground, made a few tumbles and lay motionless. A miracle she hadn't collided with a tree trunk. Dazed, she laughed toward the clear blue sky peeking through the crowns. Then she closed her eyes. *I have to get out of here.*

Zumra crawled up, taking deep gulps of air and let her eyes roaming around. But she couldn't discover immediate danger. Listening to the chirping of birds, she started to move again, going downhill. She feared that the hunters would unexpectedly emerge from the leaves in front of her. Her whole body was aching, crying out for a break. But she accelerated her pace, heavily panting and fighting the pain.

She needed a rest. As she discovered a group of trees, she stumbled toward it and fell gasping for breath behind a thick tree trunk. When she could breathe normally again, she briefly checked her body. Her lower legs were full of scabs of clotted blood and blisters, but she could not identify any severe injuries. *I have to leave this forest and find the main road to find help.*

She had lost any sense of time, having no clue where she was.

After a short rest, Zumra started to move again. The journey went on along a dried-out riverbed. Sometimes, swarms of birds flew away from the crowns, or crows with big red eyes were gazing angrily at her. Twice she frightened a deer that ran off in a panic.

Occasionally she stopped, listening with pricked ears. Only birds hidden in the tree crops were making various sounds. After a short rest, she dragged herself laboriously over a bumpy bottom full of holes and tree roots. Her overheated feet in the oversized shoes were hurting, and she suspected she was walking on bloody blisters. Hope was fading until she encountered a slightly descending narrow path. Brambles on one side, trees on the other. After walking for more than an hour, it went gradually up again while the vegetation was changing. Grey tribes and conifers. She smelled a penetrating glue odour. Young trees grew between tall, dark giants whose tops formed an almost impenetrable canopy against the sunray. Thus, it became darker and darker, whereas a strong, musty smell arose from the soil profusely covered with damp leaves.

The path narrowed to barely a metre width. On the left, it went down steeply. A wrong step might have serious consequences. That's why Zumra stayed close to the ascending side.

The constant scrubbing of the raw fabric over her wounds made her skin burning. Despite the pain and thirst, she progressed in despair, hoping things would soon be more comfortable.

Where there are paths, there are people, probably farmers. Somewhere in front of her was the inhabited world. Hope. She continued walking and panting heavily. Once in a while, she yelled desperately for help. Calling for Allah didn't help either.

At some instant, she wished to be dead. But the thought of Azra pushed her forward. Every time she thought of giving up, she made another step. Her lips and throat were cork dry, while the song of the river sounded like the voice of a thousand sirens calling her. *'Come for a break and water.'*

But her mind opposed. *Forget this steep, dangerous descent. Although you manage to reach the river unharmed, you'll have to climb up the slope again.*

Zumra didn't have enough energy or willpower to do that. She stumbled on and tried to think of more pleasant things, to forget her misfortune. Ghostly images flashed through her mind. She slowed down her pace, stopped, took two more steps and fell against a large tree trunk, time for another little break. Her tired gaze wandered in all directions. Trees, trees, trees.

After barely five minutes driven by unrest, she straightened herself up and started moving again. The path swung alternately between shrubs and one and a half metre thick trees. Clambering at a snail's pace and pulling up on each tree, she mastered the steepest parts of the stairs carved out by nature, consisting of earth, rocks and roots. She moved from tree to tree, and it was getting harder and harder. Every time she stopped, made the next step even more complicated than the previous one. There seemed to be no end to it.

'*You have to stop,*' her body yelled. Her eyes only followed the movement of her feet, in the hope they would encounter concrete at the next step. As her resistance approached the zero-level, she suddenly saw green crops appear under her feet. She had already made several steps before realising what that meant.

I am leaving the forest. Tears started rolling across her cheeks. The gravel path beneath was a sign she was entering the inhabited world again. She tottered down over a slightly sloping piece of grass. *I made it.* In front of her lay a green meadow surrounded by several ruins. The area seemed familiar to her, but she couldn't remember where she was.

Sarajevo must be somewhere in the south. Her legs were shaking. She fought against the temptation to lay down on the grass. A lovely day greeted her, but when she glanced to the right, her gaze focused bewildered at the approaching black car in the distance. The car was like one of those modern 4x4 SUV monsters she'd noticed at the torture house. Without hesitating, she turned around and ran up the grass strip. As she reached the forest, she heard a car passing by. *They didn't see me.* She glanced back over her shoulder, tripping over a carrot and hitting a tree trunk with her head.

Then she felt in an endless hole.

THIRTY-ONE

EVERYTHING LOOKED EXACTLY AS HE'D LEFT IT. NO FURNITURE HAD MOVED, AND the bed seemed untouched. He had a good memory for such details. During his military missions, Bram had learned to trust no one, neither the landlord nor the cleaning lady. That's why he always placed ultra-thinly adhesive marking strips that were almost invisible to the eye.

As he checked the wardrobe door with his penlight, he cursed out loud. To his astonishment, he discovered two torn marks. No doubt, someone had searched his wardrobe. But the lid of the hollow bottom seemed untouched. Bram took the laptop out, replaced the cover and paced to the living room, where he checked the cupboards. Despite the broken strips on the doors and drawers, nothing seemed missing. Since he lived there, was it the first time he noticed an intrusion.

Any thief would have taken everything valuable. He examined the drawers of his desk and first thought everything was still there. However, three photos in the bottom drawer, computer out prints from Mayke in conversation with Derek Fleming, were missing. Had he put those pictures in a different place? He tried to remember when he last had been watching them. No tragedy, he had those images on his laptop. He didn't think about it any further, connected his computer to the modem and started it up. Once connected, he opened his Hotmail account and scrolled back to the beginning of 2001. His face brightened as he found Mayke's message he'd been searching for, and he downloaded its attachments. On his computer, he just had the photos Mayke had sent to him. Suada's story hadn't interested him.

On the contrary, it had bothered him that the woman had been influencing Mayke's life that much. Everything about Bosnia had made him resentful. He would have preferred to cancel Bosnia from his memory.

He carefully read the document, a copy of Suada's diary. The more he progressed, the more he understood why Mayke had accorded so much importance to Suada's story.

From the Journal of Suada

If I ought to die, then as a woman. My boyfriend was all too willing to accept my request. I didn't know if I was in love with him. Yet I gave him what an honourable woman usually keeps for her future husband.

But death was lurking around every corner, and I didn't want to die like a virgin. A bad idea, because I gave myself to a bad guy. After having deflowered me, he was at first sweet and attentive, and I began to believe in a shared future. Then he took me to a special place to offer me a surprise. And a surprise it was. I'll never forget. He sold me for a ridiculous amount of money to the Serbs, who took me to the Jahorina.

The months went by, and life was not as bad as I had feared. I lived with fellow prisoners in the Women's House, where I was the youngest. '*Being only fifteen make you unique,*' everyone said. '*The Serbs saved you for a special occasion.*' According to the rumours, I was the girl reserved for a foreign general who preferred young virgins being innocent and clean. My friend had sold me as a virgin! He had deceived not only me but also the Serbs.

Sometimes, at night in bed, I was crying for hours, thinking of my parents. They didn't know where I was and were probably very worried.

And now the time has come to meet a foreign general.

I stood in the middle of a scantily furnished room with intertwined fingers on my stomach, trembling like an aspen leaf in the autumn wind. Curiously, I let my eyes wander through the room, but there was little to see. Sink, a wardrobe and a wooden bed with a mattress. Neither chairs nor table.

I was in one of those chalets close to the top of *The Mountain*. Before the war, I had skied here several times with my parents and sister. That seemed so far away. I now knew that the rumours about imprisoned Muslim women as sex slaves for the Četniks and their guests were true.

Special troops got trained on *The Mountain* where the Montenegrin leader of the Bosnian Serbs had deployed his command post. Here he met his commanders and high-ranking UNPROFOR authorities, playing the generous host and entertaining the Blue Helmets whereas his heavy artillery was firing at Sarajevo. His guests got everything they were missing in their proper camps, including entertainment of carnal pleasures. Violating helpless prisoners.

Until now, I'd been spared because I was so precious.

I shuddered. The soldier who had brought me to this room had ordered me to freshen up and put on other clothes. '*A foreign general wants a charming company*,' he'd explained with a filthy smile.

The young man was waiting outside, and I wondered how long he would be patient. What could I do? I was at the mercy of my enemies. So, let's follow the advice of the older women: *'don't resist, that only causes pain.'* Hopefully, I didn't get pregnant because the baby of a četnik would be the summit of humiliation.

'Allah, help me.' But like all the gods involved in this war, mine also chose to remain silent.

I hesitantly shuffled to the wardrobe, pulled open the two doors and stared with big eyes at dresses, skirts, shoes, shoulder bag and sexy underwear. I had imagined life as an adult woman differently.

Two towels hung over a metal rod next to the porcelain sink. On it, I found a piece of soap and a washcloth. As I looked in the mirror, I glanced toward an unhealthy pale face with slightly sunken cheeks bordered by dirty, tangled strings of dark hair. The elderly had taught me how to make myself as unattractive as possible to keep the men at bay.

As in a trance, I let my clothes slip off and shoved them with my right foot under the sink. I opened the faucet, stared at the hypnotic water jet until the tub was almost filled up, and turned off the valve again. When I lifted my head, I glanced at the reflection of my body. Skinny, small breasts, thin arms and legs. Clear signs of malnutrition.

'Get started washing,' shouted an internal voice. This time it was my turn to be humiliated.

I grabbed the washcloth.

Fifteen minutes had passed. I sat down on the edge of the bed, brushing my wet hair with a plastic brush I had found in the purse. By the lack of better, I had put on a far too short blood-red skirt with a thin top, then putting my feet in light sandals. I felt so sluggish.

Time was passing by. My tiny hands lay intertwined on my thighs. Pictures from the past flashed through my mind. Another five minutes had passed as the soldier entered the room. Struck by my fragile beauty in an ultra-short skirt, he held his breath for a moment. Fortunately, I was a precious gift for a general. Otherwise, he might have raped me there. Now he had to control himself, and he cleared his throat. "Slijedite me," he said. "Come on."

He took me to the backdoor where we went outside. We silently walked side-by-side along a narrow path. On both sides were chalets, holiday lodgings for tourists before the war. Nowadays they served as brothels where Serbian leaders and their guests satisfied their lust.

We entered one of those chalets, and the soldier took me to the major's office. The man was sitting in an armchair reading a book. He had an imposing belly, a round face and a red nose as a result of excessive Slivovitz use. He stood up with a smile on his face, examined me from top to bottom, nodded approvingly and turned to the soldier.

"You can leave, I'll take her to our guest," he said with a chuckle.

The soldier greeted and walked out.

The major turned to me. "What's your name?"

"Suada...Omarovic," I stammered.

"Listen carefully, Suada," he began in a paternal tone. "None of us is to blame for this war, but we have to make the best of it. You're lucky to be alive. If you do your best here, they'll release you soon, and you'll be able to join one of those aid organisations."

He walked up to me, put his right palm under my chin and forced me to glance up at him.

"It could be worse," he said with a sigh. "Believe me. I understand your feelings because I have a daughter who's from your age."

'Do you do that to your daughter?' I wanted to ask. But of course, I kept quiet.

"Be nice and kind to our guest, and you'll be out of here in no time. General Flower desires a Turkish virgin, and he wants to smell a different scent," he said.

Let bring this behind us as soon as possible, I thought.

"Follow me," the major said when he realised that he was talking to deaf ears.

I blindly walked behind him through a narrow corridor with a door on either side. The major halted before the right door and knocked softly.

"Come in." I heard a masculine voice. The major opened the door and pushed me into the room.

I stood in a small space with wooden walls and lowered blinds letting in narrow dazzling stripes of sunlight. My eyes went swiftly around and caught sight of a wooden bed, a wardrobe and a table with two chairs. There was also a toilet and shower behind a curtain. These chalets all looked alike.

I faced a foreign soldier sitting on the edge of the bed. He had a V-shaped face and light-brown hair with thin silver stripes through it. An attractive guy, I ought to admit. In reality, he was the Evil Wolf who wanted to eat the Red Riding Hood.

He smiled friendly. "Hello, my child, do you speak English?"

With all that international presence in Sarajevo, I had been learning that language fast, hoping to leave the country after the war. I stood stiffly, showing a fool's face, which didn't temper his enthusiasm at all. He had already partially undressed, sitting there in khaki shorts and ditto T-shirt. He had his camouflage suit, and gear neatly pleated on the table with a gun belt on top. His combat shoes were on the carpet next to the door. All of a sudden, I was aware of having seen this guy on television several times.

The major chuckled before turning around and leaving the room.

The general tried again. "They told me that you speak English."

"Just fairly," I replied with an exaggerated accent.

"That's enough." He got up and approached like a creeping cat, whereas the hump in front of his boxer shorts was betraying his state of mind.

It's going to be quick, I thought.

He grabbed my hand with an almost paternal smile, pressing a kiss on it. The gesture of the gentlemen who felt most comfortable at mundane parties, while in reality, he was a hypocrite who violated imprisoned women. A despicable pervert.

You're a monster.

"Calm down, I won't hurt you," he whispered.

How reassuring.

"Take off your clothes, my dear Turkish girl." His voice suddenly sounded hoarse.

I took off my few clothes, putting them on the table over his belt. He grabbed my hand, pulled me to the bed, smiled broadly and thrust me backwards. I fell on my back and kept motionless, staring at the ceiling.

"How beautiful you are," he gasped in ecstasy. He no longer seemed in a hurry, and I waited in vain for his frontal attack. After a moment, I raised my head and saw him bent over my belly, sniffing my female scent. He was naked, and his stiff cock hit my knees, whereas his eyes were feasting on my shaven sex. His imagination must have run wild because he drooled like a bulldog, while his hands trembled over my legs and slowly but compellingly shoved them apart. He brutally pushed his thing forward, missing in his haste the supposedly untouched paradise. With a deep growl, he grabbed me by the shoulders. "Let you go, you filthy Turkish bitch."

Think of something else and just let it happen.

His next attempt succeeded, and as a horny dog, he started to move his loins forward and backwards. The paternal figure turned into a growling animal with madly sparkling eyes. His breath was smelling of garlic, and when he tried to kiss me on my mouth, I turned my head away. He didn't insist long. While he rode me, I was gazing past him at the low ceiling, counting sheep. But that didn't help neutralise the part of my brain registering pain. He wanted to humiliate and hurt me, to punish me because of his weakness. His big hands were clawing roughly in my breasts. Yet this pain was nothing compared to the fierce burning in my vagina. *He must have a horse dick*.

At first, I started to cry softly, then panicking, I began to resist.

"Stop it, you're hurting me," I exclaimed.

But he wouldn't listen. His movements were getting more intense, furiously clasping my slender shoulders and grunting like a wild boar searching for truffles. I was wailing.

Shaitan had got possession of me.

"Shut up, you, filthy Turkish slut," he growled furiously, enclosing my throat with his big hands. He was strangling me, while underneath, it felt as if he was tearing me open. I tried to gasp for air, silently calling out for Allah's help.

My struggling did not make any difference but only stirred up his animal frenzy. When he finally exploded into me, he growled as a horny wolf. My sight got blurred. Eventually, his curved fingers opened. I could breathe again.

"Wow. That was good," murmured the general, getting up. The rapist looked down on me with contempt, like a ruler holding a dangling sceptre. "Too bad, I had asked for a virgin. Get dressed and disappear."

He didn't wait for my reaction, took a bath towel from the bedside table and rushed into the shower. He might have been thinking that deflowering innocent girls were safer, making the use of a condom unnecessary. But he had discovered that I wasn't a virgin, considering me now as a potential danger to his health. *He feels deceived and will probably have a few restless nights*.

I moved toward my clothes, reached for a fleece in my purse, stroked it between my legs and then dropped it to the ground. Then I put on the skirt. As I picked up my panties, my gaze focussed on the flap of the General's trouser pocket, which was open. Without thinking, I grabbed in the pocket, my fingers clamping round a wallet that I quickly slipped into my purse.

"You're still here?" The curtain was sliding open, and I met his eyes wandering distrustfully from his clothes to me. I quickly pulled on my panties and rushed to the door, hearing he was back under the water, probably thoroughly scrubbing his sceptre.

After I'd changed clothes, the major took me back to the Women's House. Fortunately, there were only two older women, briefly glancing at me before continuing with their activities. So, I could put General Flower's wallet in an empty-chip bag and bury it outside at the edge of the forest, using a tablespoon. All of this lasted no longer than ten minutes.

On his way back toward Sarajevo, the General had noticed his loss and headed back to the Major, accusing me of theft. Thus, one hour later, I faced the angry major and the general. But I denied without blushing. Nevertheless, I had to accompany them to the chalet, where they searched the room in question. When they didn't find anything, the major returned to the Women's House and checked the possessions of all the girls.

I felt happy about my vengeance. Flower had to understand that he would never get his wallet back. However, I hid my joy, whereas the general was screaming and raving. In the end, he left. But his eyes on me were telling enough. He wouldn't forget me. He might have been thinking I had handed over his property to my masters Mladic or Karadzic who would keep it, using it later to threaten him, if necessary.

After he'd left, I heard that the general had taken part in an ultra-secret meeting. From conversations among soldiers, I discovered that Mladic, Karadzic, an English, a Dutch and a French general had conferred for signing an agreement. The war was almost over.

All the women on *The Mountain* got hope again. Soon we'll go back home.

How naive I was.

Bram pulled the cable out of the laptop and closed the lid of the anti-shock case. He went into the bedroom to put up new strips, grabbed his computer and left the lodge. While glancing at the neighbour's house, Bram wondered why the curious neighbour hadn't shown up yet. For a moment he thought the curtain had been moving, but he was not sure. *I urgently need to catch up with Timka.*

Suddenly he believed he knew who had killed Mayke.

THIRTY-TWO

LAZAR PARKED THE CAR IN FRONT OF THE FIRST APARTMENT BUILDING. ON THE right side of the cul-de-sac, ten metres next to the sidewalk, he watched three seven-storey buildings with concrete slab garages across the road.

Senad waited on the sidewalk. "A sad place," he said as Lazar joined him.

"A lot of international aid workers live here," remarked Lazar starting to move toward the entrance. They entered the building through a double door, and a corridor led them toward the stairwell, where they halted in front of the elevator. Scrutinising the damaged elevator door, Lazar lost all faith in the local technology, but he didn't feel like taking the spiral staircase either.

"Old and rusty," he said.

Senad chuckled, pressing the green button. "Do you think there's a risk?"

Lazar kept silent, looking up and listening with mixed feelings to the crackling sound of the moving cage. His eyes examined the desolate walls in the stairwell, which initially had been painted yellow. Indefinable stains and blatant inscriptions formed a disgusting large mosaic.

The doors slid open with an ominous squeal, offering them an interior that wasn't looking very inviting. As Bram stepped inside, he thought of the film classic, *The Elevator*. He didn't feel comfortable with it. When the cage opened its doors again, he got out first, ignoring Senad's amused grin. Their footsteps in the gloomy corridor sounded hollow and creepy. Most entries in various colour variations had got reinforced with iron bars. Others had security locks. All windows were barred.

He stopped in front of a wooden door without any security lock. 615.

Senad raised his eyebrows. "Apparently, Emir didn't fear burglars."

"Criminals prefer foreigner lodgings."

"Logically, there's a lot more to get."

Lazar unlocked the door with the key that the pathologist had found in Emir's clothes. They faced a wide corridor containing a built-in shoe cupboard leading to a hall where four doors provided access to the bathroom, bedroom, workroom and the lounge.

"You start in the bathroom," Lazar said to his friend, whereas he entered the workroom. He examined a large closet, a desk and a metal rack with eight 19-inch drawers. Next to the window stood a coffee table with three bamboo chairs. For an instant, Lazar contemplated calling Fadila. Finally, he decided to wait somewhat longer and started to inspect the three drawers of the wooden desk. They contained writing utensils, but no notes. Then he moved toward the big bookcase with a lot of technical books in it. At the bottom were six drawers divided into two rows by three. But they didn't contain anything valuable.

"I'm in the bedroom now," he heard Senad calling out while entering a soberly furnished room divided into living and dining room with a small open kitchen. He found some scrapbooks in a television cabinet which he stacked on the coffee table. Then he sat down and started to browse these albums.

Leafing through the last collection, he suddenly whistled between his teeth. The pictures assembled in thin packets were loose between white cardboard sheets. The first photo showed Mycroft Follum. Lazar got up and walked to the window that looked out on the street. He compared the picture to what he saw, and returned satisfied to his place, studying the remaining snapshots. He'd seen Follum's driver before, but he couldn't place him. Another photo showed Follum walking to the next block, as his driver was moving toward the entrance of this building. A further picture showed Follum, his driver, a young woman and a big guy with Slavic features he didn't know.

Senad entered the room and sat down next to him. "I didn't find anything."

Lazar jabbed a finger on the photographs. "I think we have something. Emir has photographed EuPol's Political Advisor Follum and his driver."

"Both seem to live in this apartment," Senad noted, studying the photographs.

"I wouldn't be surprised if the driver lives on this floor, probably next door," answered Lazar pensively, raising from the armchair. "I'll check."

He walked out.

A minute later, he was back.

"The man in the picture lives next door," he said. "Derek Fleming."

Senad frowned. "So, Emir was spying on his neighbour."

"Yes, but for whom did he do that?"

THIRTY-THREE

BRAM SWITCHED OFF THE ENGINE AND SCRATCHED THROUGH HIS BEARD. HE'D parked alongside the right bank of the Miljacka, close to the metal bridge spanning the river. He gazed out of the windscreen, his eyes focussing on the five-storey building painted in yellow, giving it the look of a prison rather than an apartment.

He got out, grabbed his pale green shock-absorbing laptop case, locked the door and watched in the direction where he'd found Emir's corpse. There was not a single car, but he saw many flowers. He blew his nose and let his eyes wander across the park. Then he moved toward the pharmacy and walked along the sidewall through the narrow passage that led him to a courtyard surrounded by the large Parrot Building. On the left side was a small tunnel connection to the road, on the right side, narrow passage to the unpaved path along the bank of the river. Each floor counted two footbridges spanning the courtyard and connecting both wings, with along the street side a staircase and a lift. Alongside the apartments passed an aisle bordered with a metal railing, from where people could gaze down to the courtyard. Bram ascended the external concrete staircase to the third floor and stepped onto the footbridge. Then, believing he'd heard footsteps downstairs, he stopped, leaning over the railing. There were neither footsteps nor living creatures around. Since he got the feeling that someone was watching him, his nerves were on edge. A few days ago, in *Central Café*, he'd noticed a guy he'd seen earlier. Maybe it had nothing to mean because the *Central Café* was a busy place. *I'm getting paranoid.*

Bram's eyes roamed the facades of the building, seeing everywhere reinforced doors and small barred windows. He stopped at number 312. That was the address he'd found in one of Mayke's e-mails whom words were engraved in his memory forever.

'But there's something else that makes me so sure I can nail that British bastard on the cross.' Timka was the key to the puzzle. Now he understood why Mayke had been so convinced that she could publicly execute a general.

'I have irrefutable evidence,' she'd said.

But he hadn't paid enough attention to it.

After having picked up his laptop at his lodging, he'd got only one thought: talk to Timka as soon as possible. Mayke had visited her, and he blamed himself that after her death, he'd only viewed and printed photos of the EUMM party.

Having read Suada's diary, he knew he'd wronged Mayke. He let his thoughts go back to his last night with her. She'd been talking like an Oracle, while he only had been thinking about sex. As if he'd unconsciously sensed that it would be the last time.

Apeldoorn, 2001

The morning was coming up, and the farewell made Bram desperate. They had been alternating talking and making love. Not one eye shut. Now they were lying stretched out on their backs, and he didn't look at her. Stubbornly she insisted that her assignment be essential to the newspaper.

"It will change our lives, dear," she alleged mischievously.

"I am satisfied with how it's now," he pouted. He had no interest at all in Suada's life story, desperately trying getting Bosnia out of his mind. Although the war had been part of history for already six years, his psychological scars had still not healed. He just wanted to hold Mayke in his arms and to convince her how much he loved her. He turned over to face her and let out a deep sigh. "Forget that nonsense, Mayke, I have a peculiar premonition."

She smiled and gave him a quick kiss on his mouth. "Are you a clairvoyant now?" Her enthusiasm was undeniable. "Ten days, fourteen at the most."

"I recently read that those accusations against the Canadian general are unjustified. Anyway, the victorious write history. It's not from me, it's from Napoleon. Other rumours say that Bosniaks bombed their people to blame for the Serbs to get Western military support. I am thinking of the 68 dead, and 144 injured in the market attack in Sarajevo on the 5th of February 1994. In Srebrenica, too, Bosniaks have been guilty of war crimes. Oric and mates did hit-and-run raids in Serbian villages, killing a lot of innocent people. I also recall of Van Renssen, one of our soldiers who died when a Bosniak threw a grenade at his vehicle."

Bram paused a moment before asking, "How Suada did she finally got away?"

"She received the help of a Serbian major, having a daughter of her age. He thought she was too young to die."

"Wow, a Bosnian Serb helping a Muslim woman? Well, there are probably good Serbs too," he admitted reluctantly.

"Why are you so sarcastic? Not all Serbs are arseholes." Her voice sounded reproachful. "Two days after that secret meeting on the Jahorina, the major has helped Suada to leave with the Red Cross because apparently, she was seriously ill. He was afraid that General Flower wanted her dead and that Mladic would be happy to fulfil his wish."

Mayke had told him several times about Suada's suffering, and he knew that she'd been living in Sarajevo with her older sister until shortly after the war. At the end of the nineties, she'd moved to Belgium where she finally married a Belgian guy. Meanwhile, she got a permanent residence permit. Why, of all people, did Mayke have to meet that woman?

"Honey," Mayke said in a sultry voice. "I am interested in the agreement that the Europeans have made with Karadzic and Izetbegovic. I may discover explosive information there, which is good for a TV broadcast, and I'll give you enough material to write a heartbreaking novel about Suada's adventures, the Women's House on the Jahorina, the involvement of UN officials, and all the irregularities that happened there."

His last novel in which he revealed his truth about Srebrenica was a flop because the higher authority had been boycotting its publication. It had got sold only privately. But a story about Suada seemed like a great idea to him.

"You don't have to go to Sarajevo for that." His voice sounded hoarse.

She smiled, stroking him with great sophistication which caused his penis reacting violently. She wanted to distract him from the tricky theme. And he was too happy to let her, enjoying her sexual excitement. She nibbled softly on his earlobe.

"But there's something else that makes me so sure I can nail that British bastard to the cross." Her voice was shaking.

"We'll talk about that later," he said.

She smiled, and her fingers were challenging his proud lord. "I can prove that Flower raped Suada. If I get that evidence, the general won't be able to deny it. And it will cost him a fortune to avoid a trial."

She released his pylon.

"No!" he cried out, frustrated.

"Yes, yes," she whispered with shining eyes. She finally realised that Bram was only interested in her sweet torments and fantastic curves.

It ultimately pushed Suada into the background.

Sarajevo, 9 October 2002

An older woman appeared in the doorway. She had long white hair and a worriedly wrinkled face.

"*Dobar dan*. Are you Mrs Omarovic?"

The woman stood slightly bent, wearing a grey dress that reached to her ankles, grey woollen socks and self-knitted slippers. Her face, crooked nose and broken teeth reminded him of a Walt Disney movie witch. Her eyes turned to his suitcase.

"*Dobar dan,* who are you?" It didn't sound very kind.

"I'm looking for Timka."

"She doesn't live here any more, what do you want from her?"

"*Oprostiti, moye ime je Bram. Sam muz od Mayke. Novinar koji te posjetio*. My name is Bram, Mayke's husband. You know, the reporter who has visited you."

The elderly woman glanced at him from head to toe, and the suspicious look faded away."*Sam mama, Dana*, I am mama Dana. Come in."

Bram stepped past her and came in a hall where three doors provided access to other rooms. Near the door was a built-in wall cupboard. He took off his shoes and got a pair of knitted slippers. Then she took him into the living room where she beckoned him to take a seat on a long worn-out sofa. As he sat down and put his suitcase next to him, she shuffled without saying a word to the small adjoining kitchen where she started to set coffee.

He let his eyes wander across the poorly furnished room.

After she'd made a cup of syrupy coffee for both of them, she pinched her eyes. "Why didn't Mayke come with you?"

"Mayke has been killed in an accident shortly after she visited you," he said. "She fell into a ravine on her way back from Pale."

Bram was surprised that she didn't know.

"My condolences, mister," she said softly. "Mayke was such a sweet woman."

Has Mayke been talking to Timka? To his surprise, he saw tears in Dana's eye corners rolling slowly over her wrinkled cheeks.

"She gave me a hundred marks when she left," she said.

That didn't surprise him, Mayke would have given her last penny if she could help someone out of misery.

Dana dropped her arms powerlessly along her body. "My cute Timka no longer lives here. These are hard times, mister. The war was cruel. I lost my *muž*, my husband, just like Timka. And there was that child to take care of."

"Timka has a child?"

"No. Yes. Suada has a child."

Mayke had spoken of irrefutable proof. And that didn't mean the wallet, neither Suada's testimony. Dana Omarovic sat down facing him. She slurped from her coffee, and there was a short silence.

After some time, she glanced up with a sad face. "Suada was still a child when she got a prisoner by the četniks on the Jahorina, and later on handed over to the Red Cross. So young and pregnant. She was barely sixteen when she gave birth to her son." She paused for a moment.

Bram kept silent.

"My dear Timka had miscarried a few days earlier," she continued. "Fate wanted it that way: Timka wished a child, but had a miscarriage, whereas Suada refused to acknowledge her baby. She called it a bastard, the result of a rape, Shaitan's child. If it hadn't been for us, she would have killed it."

The woman was constantly nodding. After a short pause, she continued with a monotonous voice. "The doctor claimed that my little angel would not give birth to any more children. Without hesitation, she has registered Suada's child as her own. Nobody needed to know, so we have avoided the shame. That miscarriage and Timka's desire to have a child made everything all right. Allah thinks of everything, and He is great and merciful. If Timka's husband would've come back, we would've told him he had a son." She slurped from her coffee. "But he didn't return. Suada refused to live in poverty, and we couldn't convince her to stay. She left for the West. Timka stayed with me until her sweet little son Hadar walked alone. Although I have enough space here, we had nothing left to eat. Fortunately, my husband had bought the apartment. Otherwise, I would have been out on the street. We lived off the alms and the help of our neighbours. My only remaining child thought it was a disgrace and left."

Her voice broke, while tears were rolling down her cheeks.

Bram felt helpless. "Sorry, Mrs Omarovic, I can later..."

"No," she interrupted him, resolutely wiping her face dry. "That's our life here, Mr Bram. The war has been over for seven years, and yet we still live in poverty." The bitterness in her voice hit him hard.

"What chance do have single young mothers to survive?" she groaned. "There are hardly any men left to marry. And who marries a woman with a child?"

No one uttered a word for a long moment.

"There are few jobs," she eventually continued. "But my little angel found one in a bakery. But she was too handsome; the owner wanted her in his bed. Everyone wanted to give her a job if she was willing to pamper her benefactor. My little angel didn't want that." Her hands were shaking. "Then, my dear girl met a strolling cat who also had a child. Shaitan can get her. First, they came to live here with the kids. Without shame about their feelings, they slept together, doing things with each other that Allah will never forgive them. But they took care of me, and I kept quiet. I begged Allah to forgive my little angel. He can punish me because I let them do it. I pray to Allah that He may give my little angel access to Paradise.

"Gospodin Bram, if you have nothing, you cannot be selective." Her shoulders were shaking, her eyes expressing a mixture of disgust and sadness. She looked at him, beggingly as if she was apologising for her daughter's behaviour. He'd never seen so much pain in someone's eyes.

Dana shook her head. "That's how it went until they found an apartment. They have also made out a plan; one is going to work, while the other is looking after the kids. They alternate and succeed to survive."

Her face expressed disgust.

Bram nodded, keeping silent.

"My angel is a good child, Gospodin," Dana continued. "Once a week she comes to clean, bringing food for the whole week. She also does my laundry. No, she won't let her mother down." Her crooked fingers were holding her mug of coffee while fresh tears fell on her bony hands.

Bram got a crop in his throat, remembering the tears he'd seen in Srebrenica. He let her talk.

"Yes, yes, life is so hard," Dana went on. "You can't always control it. My little girl is under the influence of Shaitan, but how else can she survive? Hadar, my grandson is doing well now, and he'll have a better life than mine. My little angel makes great sacrifices. Allah, I beg You, be merciful to her."

Bram wondered what she was trying to tell him. Now that he knew the truth, he'd got to see Timka. "Mrs Omarovic, do you know where I can find Timka?"

She shook her head. "Don't judge too harshly. She's not a bad woman, Gospodin Bram. And she's a good mother." She slurped the now lukewarm coffee.

"Can you tell me where she lives, Mrs Omarovic? It's essential."

Her shoulders were shaking. "She lives nearby. Yes, she's well now, my Timka. But she's ashamed of her mother. Yes, that's it. She's ashamed of her sins."

He felt uncomfortable. When Dana was in control again, he emptied his mug, knowing he would have acid burps for the rest of the day.

"Where exactly in the city does Timka live?" he asked.

"Across the Miljacka. There's a wide driveway to the entrance of the white building."

"Does she have a job?"

Dana nodded sadly. "Yes, Gospodin Bram, she has a job, and that's the most important thing, isn't it? The government does nothing for us. Nobody helps us. We've got to take care of ourselves. How good we were under Tito. Did you know Tito?"

He smiled politely. "I've heard about him, ma'am. A charismatic man. Died in 80."

She gave a long sigh. "Yes, yes. How well we were doing then. No one was hungry, and there were no wars."

"Mrs Omarovic, do you have a picture of Timka?"

The older woman glanced up at him, thoughtfully. "*Moj mladiću*, I think I have a picture of her somewhere, made right after the war before her sister left. Do you know anything about Suada?"

Bram shook his head. "She's happily married. Mayke interviewed her a few times. But I never met her."

"Yes, Mayke was a sweet woman." She got up and shuffled off to the old buffet. After fumbling around in a couple of drawers, she came back with a pile of photos. Older pictures. There were three women and a child on three of them: Suada, Timka and her son Hadar.

Timka was a handsome woman. According to his estimation, she had to be twenty-seven and Hadar seven. His heart began to beat faster. For the first time since Mayke's death, he felt an intense desire to continue her work. She'd wanted to expose a rapist, and now he thought he'd found proof that she'd been right. He could now call Mayke's editorial team and sell the story. But Bram hated the media. After Srebrenica, they had written dirty things about his friendship with a Bosnian interpreter, influenced by the statements of some colleagues. He'd been threatening the media with contempt, now realising that he'd made a mistake. Media have power and can destroy people. He decided to get to the bottom of the matter and write about it later, for Mayke.

"Can I borrow one of these photos?" he asked.

"Take what you want, *moj mladiću*. I hope you can change my little girl's mind. Tell her to take that creepy woman out." Mother Omarovic rocked her head back and forth, murmuring inaudible words. She seemed absorbed in thoughts.

Bram put a picture into a pocket, packed his suitcase and stood up. "Thank you very much, Mrs Omarovic."

The woman, however, remained seated and babbled on; she no longer seemed to belong to this world. He walked out.

As Bram walked over the footbridge minutes later, his ears caught the noise of running footsteps beneath the stairs. He looked over the railing, waiting a few minutes whereas his eyes were roaming the clearing. But there was nothing to see.

He thoughtfully descended the stairs. Yet this environment gave him goose bumps. Everything seemed so unfriendly and grey, and every sound was metallic and hollow. The plants in the middle of the green courtyard didn't change that much either.

For the first time since he arrived in Sarajevo, he thought about what had happened on the Jahorina. A general had raped Suada, a juvenile. Not only was this young girl intelligent, but also relentless. She had proved this by the way she'd stolen the rapist's wallet and hidden it.

Now he must talk to Timka urgently.

Just before the narrow passage to the outside world, he halted abruptly and looked back. From where he stood, he could oversee the clearing and both footbridges. The man on the furthest footbridge wasn't gazing in his direction and walked on at a fast pace. Bram remained motionless for a time, listening to the squeaking hinges of an opened and closed door. The corners of his mouth curled up.

I'm an idiot, he thought, and he hurried out.

Sitting in his car at the wheel, he started thinking about his next steps. Timka lived on the other side of the Miljacka, alongside the Obala Kulina Bana. Suddenly he decided to have first a chat with the Belgian who'd taken the pictures at that EUMM party. Perhaps more pictures could give him additional clues helping him further.

Suada left her family without knowing in what danger she put them.

Mayke had found some evidence, but in her enthusiasm, she'd been careless in trusting the wrong people.

I'll avenge you, Mayke

THIRTY-FOUR

LAZAR WAS STUDYING THE PICTURES FOR THE THIRD TIME, LOOKING FOR indications he finally couldn't find.

"Emir has worked for Ruyter," he said to Senad, who was sitting next to him. "If we believe his friend Anel. Ruyter is also involved in the murder of the Dutch attaché, but that case is officially closed. I'm still intrigued by the way the corpse got exposed. Looks like the perpetrator's trying to send us a message. Maybe a warning. Goddamn it. I need a clue to link Emir Besic to Ruyter." He shoved the last series of images toward Senad, rose from the couch and started to inspect once again the TV cabinet and the workroom.

He didn't get wiser. Back in the living room, he slowly looked around. "Did you notice anything odd?"

"Are you thinking of something in particular?"

"Where do you think those pictures come from?"

"Where do they come from?"

"By the beard of the Prophet, where is the camera?" Lazar wasn't waiting for an answer, rushing toward the adjoining kitchen. He inspected all the cupboards and drawers; however, he couldn't find what he searched. Shaking his head, he stepped to the window and looked down.

"It wasn't in his room at *Digital Future* either," he uttered. "Damned, where's Fadila?"

"Give her some time to collect her equipment. You got called her just ten minutes ago."

"It's all right, and take that mean grin off your face," snarled Lazar. He was thinking of his visit to Ivar Ragnarsson, and later the scene in which

Mycroft Follum was interrogating a guard at the EuPol building gate. He didn't know this little guy, although he had seen him several times at official receptions. A sneaky dwarf. But Follum was one of the EuPol-high-ranking people enjoying diplomatic immunity, just like any foreign official. Although, according to the Bosnian Intelligence Service, Follum was a spook.

"Who could be interested in what Follum does, apart from our Intelligence Service? Definitely, Besic was Ruyter's informer."

Senad dropped a packet of pictures on the table and leaned back.

"Do you think Ruyter is involved in Emir's death?" he asked with a puzzled look.

"He didn't kill Emir himself, but I wonder if he belongs whether to Moon or to Salah. Maybe he is the master brain?" Lazar said thoughtfully, his fingers fidgeting with his hair locks. *Why is Egzon making everyone to believe that the killings are part of a trivial drug case?* He was anxious because it could take some time before he would get the results of the autopsy and a report from the forensic service. The time factor was playing against him. Anyway, he was convinced there was a link between all these murders.

The bell rang, and he shot up.

Senad winked. "That must be Fadila."

Lazar hurried to the front door and let Fadila in. She was carrying an aluminium suitcase, and her eyes were sparkling. The young woman looked elegant in her blue pants, suit and grey blouse with the two upper buttons lose, revealing the onset of her breasts. He thought she'd been wearing a yellow sweater in the office. All of a sudden, he was wondering what she would look like in a nightdress. *Calm down.* He guided her to the living room and glanced hopefully at her whereas she grabbed a notebook from her suitcase and started to leaf through it.

"I have some information," she said.

"Go ahead," he grunted.

"Peculiar case, chief. Moon belongs to SAS. In 1992 he infiltrated Arkan's troops. Salah is known as a mercenary who fought for the mujahidin during the Bosnian war, although we have no concrete proof of that nor that he has beheaded civilians. But our intelligence thinks he was an MI6 infiltrator. Ruyter is a Dutchman who works for *Last Hope*. Before he came over here, he served in the army. However, he got expelled from it in 1996. Since then, he's devoted himself to fighting the women traffickers."

Lazar hadn't yet informed his team members about his visit to *Last Hope*.

"Ruyter's girlfriend probably has been murdered by Pale extremists," he interrupted her. "Do you remember that case with that reporter's team from Holland?"

"Yes, I do," replied Fadila, looking him right in the eye. "We were kept at bay in that case." The corners of her mouth curled upwards, and she immediately looked less rigorous.

"Strange coincidence that Ruyter turns up in Sarajevo. Do you have any more?"

"Ruyter is a regular visitor of *Central café*. He sits there almost every night."

"Alone?"

"Most of the time with a staff member."

"Do you know the name?"

"No, but that's not hard to figure out."

"Anything else?"

"Since Moon and Salah officially belonged to an SFOR elite group, their corpses have been transferred to SFOR. Case closed."

Fadila gave him a sweet smile, making him feel uncomfortable.

"Safet Begovic was a war veteran," she continued. "He lived on what he earned on the black market. But he also did business with a well-known arms dealer named Trifko Petrovic."

"That's getting crazier and crazier," replied Lazar with pinched eyes. He turned away from her and submerged in thought, his gaze upon the window.

"Did you know Miralem Lulic personally?" asked Fadila after a while.

"Yes, a fundamentalist. Did bad things during the war."

"Who didn't?" Her voice sounded bitter.

"You're right, there are no rules on the battlefield and in each man hides a monster." He glanced at her. "You must be tough if you want to survive. As for Miralem, he was a killer machine fighting among mujahidin."

"You're not going to win a war with kindness," she acknowledged. The tender glow in her eyes was fading away.

Lazar knew what she'd been through, and he didn't want to hurt her.

"Where did you get all this data?" he asked.

"The State Security Service is keeping records of all the foreigners working in Bosnia. We've limited access to their database."

Lazar smiled. "I've arranged a meeting with Pejic for this afternoon. I wish you success with Emir's computers. They're on the left." He accompanied her to the adjoining room.

"Our technicians don't have the means to read the hard drives," he said with an apologetic gesture. "You'll have to make a backup here."

She took a quick look at the installation, smiled and walked hip-swaying to the computer rack. "No problem, but I'll need some time."

Lazar was in a bad mood. Although he knew the modus operandi, the investigation stagnated in the absence of a motive. *Maybe Mirsad can help me further*. He beckoned to Senad that he was leaving, and they left the building.

"Sorry, Senad," Lazar said, "I've got a meeting with Mirsad Pejic alone,

I'll take you to headquarters first."

"No problem, I'll do some investigating."

"And Senad, tomorrow I'll be late. I need some sleep."

Senad smiled. "Do you mean Zumra? Have fun. I'll be fine."

Lazar didn't react and got behind the wheel.

Zumra, where are you?

THIRTY-FIVE

BRAM WAS ABOUT TO RING FOR THE THIRD TIME WHEN THE DOOR SWUNG OPEN. THE small and chubby man in his fifties appearing in the doorway was wearing a black jogging suit. Both his egg-shaped head with close-knit eyes and his bald skull and narrow mouth with a thick grey moustache on the upper lip gave him the look of an old Chinese monk. He seemed confused and irritated, frowning on seeing Bram's laptop case.

"I don't need anything," he said, ready to go back inside.

"How are you?" asked Bram in a jovial tone.

Seconds passed before Greg Stone's features brightened up. "Hey, we know each other..." he exclaimed surprised.

Bram stretched out his hand. "Yes, we've met at an EU party."

Greg shook his hand. "That evening, we had a beer at the bar together."

Bram nodded, sharply scrutinising the man who'd photographed Mayke. He recalled that at that party, their gathering had barely lasted a few minutes, too short of asking him about Mayke. The Belgian had observed too many young stallions around his beautiful girlfriend, and he'd preferred to join her.

"I've something urgent to discuss with you," Bram said in a pressing tone.

Stone narrowed his eyes. "Actually, it's not the right moment. But it's okay, cheer me up a bit." He stood aside and waved him in. After Bram passed by, he slammed the door shut. "Follow me."

Bram walked with him to the far end of the wide hallway and climbed the three steps to the landing where the stairs continued up. He glanced shortly to the table with a telephone on it in the left corner and entered on the right side a large room divided into a living and a dining part. A large window door in the rear wall offered a beautiful sight on the Humska mountain where his friend Edhem lived.

Bram's eyes caught a woman sitting on the couch, recognising her as Stone's girlfriend at that EUMM party. *Very handsome*. She was wearing a white jogging suit, closing tightly around her slim body. Over her beautiful face, wreathed by long, pitch-black hair, appeared a vague sad smile as she gazed up from her magazine.

"*Dobar vecer,*" she had a soft, hoarse voice.
"*Dobar vecer,*" he replied.
"My girlfriend," intervened Stone. "She doesn't speak English. Please, sit down. Can I offer you something to drink? Beer?"
"That's okay for me," answered Bram with a smile.
As Stone walked to the kitchen, he let himself fall down into an armchair, put his case on the table in front of him and observed the young woman who'd turned back to her reading in a magazine, probably feigning not to notice his thoughtful gaze.
He slightly swelled eyes puzzled him, wondering why she'd been crying recently. What did a Moldavian woman in Greg Stone's lodging? Was Stone one of those old perverts who unscrupulously rented a sex slave? Emma Badora's face flashed through his mind, and anger began to flare up in him.
Stone reappeared. After having put up a can of beer for each, he sat down next to the young woman. It hadn't escaped his attention that Greg had given her a reassuring slap on the thigh, before gazing in his direction.
He cleared his throat. "I've just got fired." His voice sounded tense.
Bram got straight. "Fired? Why?"
Stone grabbed a document from the table and handed it over to him.
After reading, which took him a few minutes, he turned toward the Belgian. "Can you explain?"
Stone shrugged. "Bullshit, she has a visa."
Bram turned to the woman. "*Imate li putovnicu* - Do you have a passport?"
"*Da* - Yes."
"*Svibanj li ga vidjeti* - can I see it?"
"*Nema problema, evo ga* - no problem, please." She took her passport from the purse and gave it to him.
Stone glanced up in amazement. "Wow, you speak the language too."
Bram didn't react, checking the passport. Then he scowled at the woman. "The visa is no longer valid."
"I have a residence permit." She searched her purse again and gave him a folded sheet of paper.
Bram watched the stamp of the Ministry of Home Affairs in the top left corner, read the document carefully and returned it to the woman.
"*Hvala* - thank you," he said thoughtfully. Although everything seemed fine, Bram knew that such documents weren't entirely trustful. They might be real, but corrupt officials could have provided them. He turned to face Stone.
"These papers look all right to me," he affirmed. "Then why have you been fired?"
The Belgian laughed sadly. "I don't think it matters any more whether Daria is living with me legally or not. Some Britons have set up a conspiracy to fire me. I already have submitted a complaint to the Commissioner's

secretary. But I don't believe the Viking will honour my legal right to be heard."

"You have rights, Greg. Your Commissioner should at least listen to your version of the story. If you don't get a satisfying response, you've got to contest the decision on the court. But how are the British involved?"

After Stone had told about his final interview with Normand Montpetit, Bram cautiously scratched his beard. Stone's problems weren't his concern. However, he wasn't going to divulge the reason for his visit too quickly, being afraid Greg might send him away. He seemed tremendously affected by his dismissal, just as the young woman. He could understand her sadness; if Stone had to return home, what about her? She couldn't just follow him.

"Greg, sorry for my unannounced visit, but I have an urgent request. You took some pictures of my wife last year during that EUMM party, you remember?"

Stone raised an eyebrow. "Do you mean the St Patrick's Day party?"

"Yes, that's the party I'm talking about," Bram answered with impatience.

"And what was your wife doing at that party?"

"She was a reporter."

Stone nodded. "Yes, yes, I've been talking with a beautiful reporter that night. She was planning to visit Pale with her team. I had a few drinks with her and shot some pictures. She asked me to send those pictures to her, giving me her e-mail address. What I did the next day."

Bram smiled wide. "I know. She sent me those pictures." He opened the case lid, turned his laptop on, clicked on an image, and swivelled the laptop screen toward Stone.

"Yes, my pictures," Stone affirmed.

"Did you take more photos at that party?"

"About thirty, I think."

"Do you still have them?"

"I think so."

"Could I have a look at them?"

"What do you want to know?" Stone fixed him suspiciously.

"Shortly after that party, my wife got an accident."

"That reporter team that crashed was that..." Stone hit his forehead. "I should have known, my sincere condolences. I was working for the EUMM then, living exclusively for my work. I've picked up rumours in the cafeteria, but I didn't pay any attention to it. I will look up all the photos and send them to your e-mail address. Is that all right for you?"

"It's urgent, Greg, when can I expect them?"

Greg Stone bit on his lower lip for a moment, gazed at him tightly and gave a deep sigh. "Well, I'll do that right away. What's your e-mail address? Or do you want them on diskettes?"

"Send them to my e-mail address," Bram said. "Thank you." He pulled a card from his wallet and handed it over.

"My laptop is in my room," Greg said. "I'll do it right away." He got up and hurried to the trap hall.

Bram closed his suitcase, looking across at the woman.

"Are you happy here?" He had muffled his voice.

A melancholy smile appeared on her face. "Greg is a wonderful guy. Without him, I'd be in a bad state. I like him. We're both single, and there's a real future for us."

"Well, what if Greg must return to Belgium?"

"We've talked about it," she said tenderly smiling. "Greg is willing to come to Chisinau as a tourist. He can stay there for three months, enough to get married. Then I can go to Belgium with him."

Bram nodded, knowing that it wouldn't be as easy as she imagined it would be.

Stone reappeared and sat down next to his girlfriend. "I have sent all the photos. Hopefully, they'll help you further." He grinned and, apologetically, shrugged. "I don't want to take you out, but I still have something urgent to discuss with Daria."

Daria?

Bram shot up, fixating the young woman like a sphinx.

"Your name is Daria," he called out. He had seen her passport, but the name had not crossed his mind because he didn't have any interest in her. He caught her puzzled look, realising he'd spoken English. "*Daria... Jeste li radili u Floridi*? Did you work in the *Florida Bar*?"

"*Da.*" She was frowning.

"*Znate li Emma Badora?* Do you know Emma Badora?"

She hesitated and glanced at Stone. "*Kako to mislis?* What do you mean?"

"Emma is no longer in the *Florida Bar*, *Emma je napustio Floridi*. Emma has left the *Florida Bar*. She had to be home by Monday. But she probably got abducted."

"What?" Daria now clearly seemed to be shocked. Bram also met Stone's surprised look. He recalled Emma's voice during her interview in his office, every word flashing through his mind. '*An older woman named Daria has been protecting me. Before her departure, she advised me to flee at the first opportunity, telling me to wait for an IPTF raid and ask those agents to get repatriated. Then I would have to testify facing a judge. Daria knew something about a commander, and she gave me something to put pressure on EuPol in case it didn't keep its promise.*'

Bram had never been asking himself what that secret could have been. But now Emma had vanished, he suddenly considered Stone and Daria as witnesses in a mysterious affair. Could there be a link between Stone's resignation and Emma's abduction?

He read fear in Daria's eyes.

"*Sto se dogodilo?* What happened?" she asked.

"One of our security guys had to take her to the airport, but they fell in an ambush. At least two cars were involved. Our man was knocked down and needed medical treatment. We don't know what the perpetrators have done to Emma. She vanished."

"*Koji je tvoj udio u svim ovim?* What is your role in all this?"

"*Ona me je vjerovati, s*he trusted me."

Daria shifted to her seat. *She would like to ask me something but is wondering if she can trust me.*

"I help the victims of women's trafficking," he explained softly. "In cooperation with the IOM. I'm not corrupt. I've handled Emma's file, making sure she was safe."

"Apparently not safe enough."

He nodded, embarrassed. "We have done what we could, and I admit that this is not an acceptable excuse. We've learned from it."

Stone intervened with a hand gesture. "There is a Frenchman in Sarajevo who wants to kill Daria. Someone from Mitrovica."

Bram's stomach contracted. Emma's abduction was more than the revenge of a brothel owner whom she'd betrayed. He probably had nothing to do with it. He glared at Daria with piercing eyes. "Do you know why Emma got abducted?"

Her shoulders were shaking. She hesitated, probably afraid of making the wrong decision. Obviously, she hadn't told Greg everything.

Stone remained silent.

Daria's face was expressing desperation, but she remained silent.

"Daria, I need to know why Emma got kidnapped," Bram insisted. "I'm afraid your life in Sarajevo is no longer secure. Greg's resignation is no coincidence." He looked at her severely. "I'm afraid you didn't tell him everything."

She closed her eyes for a while until she finally decided to talk, clearing her throat. "Has Emma been telling you what I've given her?"

Bram nodded. "She claimed to own something that would help her if EuPol made her life difficult. Her roommate gave her something, alleging that it was a kind of life insurance. But I haven't paid much attention to it. I thought she was exaggerating, thinking she could blackmail us. She'd heard a lot of negative stories about the IPTF."

"Which are true," replied Daria fiercely. "Numerous police officers are collaborating with the mafia. Why do you think I've chosen to get out of that environment in my way? I was taken several times to the regional IPTF office in Ilidza. They promised me all sorts of things. But no girl with a bit of common sense would betray or testify against those bar owners. In 2000, a girl who'd testified against an owner got murdered and left in a forest. I've warned Emma. However, I owned something precious. When Greg got me out of the *Florida Bar*, I've handed my life insurance to Emma. It was her only way to get safely out of Sarajevo." Her eyes were getting damp.

"But what the hell was it?" Bram snarled.

"They abducted Emma for a cuddly bear, my cuddly bear."

"You're kidding, aren't you?"

She shook her head.

"No," she said. "That Frenchman is looking for what I've hidden in that little bear."

THIRTY-SIX

LAZAR FELT MISERABLE, ASKING HIMSELF WHY HE WAS SO DEPENDENT ON A woman. Zumra meant everything to him. However, he didn't know anything about her, neither where she lived, nor where she was. That made him upset and let his heart beat faster. He desperately glanced at his phone, but only her voicemail was available. *Zumra, where are you?* He slid the phone into his pocket, turning his gaze toward the facade with the tall windows.

Dalmacija Kucé, a medium-sized restaurant with a porch in front of it, was mainly known for its fish dishes. But Lazar had chosen this place not only for its seafood. While entering the hall, he glanced through the open archway giving access to the dining room. No single customer was sitting there. He chuckled to the approaching man, the bar owner Samir Trpkova, a large, solidly built fifties with an angular wrinkled face radiating serenity and tranquillity. His greying hair was cut short.

"What a pleasure to see you again," Samir called out warmly, while they hugged each other like brothers.

Lazar smiled. "The pleasure is mine."

They stood in a long narrow lobby, with on his left hand the dining room and on the right side a sizeable brown walnut bar, enhanced by four red leather bar chairs with backrest.

"Today I need my corner," Lazar said in a muted tone.

Samir chuckled. "No problem, what do you like to drink?"

"As usual."

Samir practised Islam, living according to the Qur'an and Hadith laws. However, he kept alleging that the Qur'an didn't prohibit Rakija, and he wasn't afraid of having a good drink like most Bosniaks.

'*How could that be prohibited*?' he asked all the conservative religious brothers or imams trying to lecture him. "When angel Djibriel dictated Allah's word to the Prophet, there was no Rakija yet." Usually, he shot in a roaring laugh and solemnly proclaimed that his interpretation of the Qur'an was the correct one. '*The Mullahs are claiming that every translation of the*

Qur'an is an incorrect interpretation so that the text might no longer correspond to the original revelations the Prophet got from Angel Djibriel,' he called out convincingly. '*But there are verses allowing alcohol, and all verses are correct, even if he later changed his mind in other verses. Allah doesn't make mistakes.*'

He put two glasses of white liquid on the bar. "Here's my homemade slivovitz, pure and strong. Živjeli," he said in a solemn tone, picking up his glass and raising it.

"Živjeli." Following Samir's example, Lazar abruptly swallowed the liquid and then made an ugly grimace. Samir replenished the glasses.

"You have planned a confidential meeting," he whispered.

"Yes, with Mirsad Pejic."

It was Samir's job keeping other guests as far away from Lazar as possible. Lazar knew everything about Mirsad, head of Department D. This letter stood for *Duh*, meaning ghosts. A section that officially didn't exist. After the war, several politicians and generals gathered together to debate Bosnian's future, which resulted in Department D of the State Security Service.

Samir was a proud Bosniak, not a fundamentalist. The war had taught him that neutrality wasn't a warranty for a peaceful society, which made him become an informer for the State Security Service. In exchange, he got its protection.

Ne dirajte kuce Dalmacija - Don't touch the Dalmatian house. Even the mafia was fearing the State Security, and in particular, Section D. Although, he was a loyal Bosniak, Lazar did not belong to this exclusive group of loyal Bosniaks, but he collaborated with Section D unofficially.

"Will you eat?" Samir asked.

"Yes, some cod, but first a mixed cheese dish."

Lazar was just swallowing his second slivovitz as the door opened, and a small, stocky man with hard features made his appearance. Round face with deep gleaming eyes, a somewhat flat nose, full mouth and double chin. He wore a grey jacket, white shirt and grey tie, while his black shoes reflected the light from the coloured ceiling lamps. Always neatly dressed and perfumed. Mirsad Pejic.

"*Dobar vecer,*" hummed Pejic, stopping next to Lazar. During the war, Mirsad had provided him with useful information more than once. A suspicious, dangerous man.

Lazar smiled modestly. "*Hi Mirsad, kako si* - how are you?"

"Have you been putting your fingers in burning oil?"

"I don't know. That's why you're here." Lazar nodded at Samir as he and his guest walked ahead to their usual spot beyond a curtain. Mirsad chose the corner against the partition wall, while Lazar took place across from him, from where he could see the corridor through the gap alongside the curtain.

"I have ordered fish," he said to Mirsad.
"I didn't expect anything else."
As soon as Samir was gone, Lazar immediately came to the point.
"Is there an operation going on against our Pale-friends?" He meant the Karadzic clan.
"We're not always aware of what SFOR is planning, especially since they got a new intervention group called the *White Wolves*, under the command of Arthur Brubaker, a lunatic."
"Never heard of that group, neither of Brubaker."
"He's been in Butmir for half a year, I guess. His group is part of DynCorp, a private army including the American police observers. But their seat is in England."
"What do the other countries have to say about this?"
"Officially the *White Wolves* are part of SFOR, but we have doubts about that. Nobody knows the details of its mission. Its members are even worse than the SAS soldiers. Brubaker leads all the operations himself, informing the authorities once the action is over. He's got two helicopters and thirty well-trained killers at his disposal." The bitterness in Mirsad's voice hadn't escaped Lazar. He knew Mirsad didn't have any empathy for the British.
"Do you know what they're up to?" he asked.
Department D was a feared subsection of the *Sluzbi Drzavne Bezbednost BiH*, Canton 9, and Lazar did not doubt for a second that the State Security Service was aware of all SFOR's movements.
"The High Command informed my department about the murders. You are in charge of that investigation," began Mirsad, but he went silent when the owner showed up.
Samir put a bowl of mixed cheese, a basket of bread and two glasses of slivovitz on the table. "The main dish will arrive within an hour," he said.
"*Hvala*." Lazar waited until Samir had left the corridor and then gestured Mirsad to continue.
Mirsad shifted in his chair. "As long as those *White Wolves* take action against war criminals, we are not going to intervene. Let them kill that scum." He emptied his glass.
Lazar was drumming his fingers on the tabletop. "What do you know about Alistair Moon, Ahmed Salah and Bram Ruyter?"
The vague smile on Mirsad's face disappeared.
"Moon and Salah are mercenaries," he retorted. "In 1994 Salah and Osama bin Laden met Izetbegovic after which Salah started to train mujahidin of the seventh brigade in Zenica, carrying out assignments with them for al-Qaeda. During the war Moon has joined Arkan. However, Salah and Moon were SAS or MI6 infiltrators. Lunatics, but we can't adhere to them because they belong to the *White Wolves*. The fact they're working for different parties during the war is meaningless because both men provided the British

government with information. These mercenaries are enjoying diplomatic immunity."

Good to know that Salah and Moon are dead. Lazar knew a lot about the cruelties of mujahidin for whom he felt little sympathy. Of all the war crimes attributed to the Bosniaks, a great deal was the work of those fighters dressed in white tunics and headscarves who'd been brought into the country by the fundamentalist Muslim president to deal with the Catholic Croats and the Orthodox Serbs. However, their atrocities were not inferior to those of the Arkan Tigers.

"Well, and what do you know about Bram Ruyter?"

Mirsad grabbed some cheese and a piece of dark bread.

"A special case," he answered carefully.

"Indeed, his wife has been killed in a car accident on her way back from Pale last year."

Mirsad shrugged. "Well, I'll tell you what I know about him, but it's just between us."

Lazar nodded.

"Bram Ruyter," Mirsad continued, "is working for *Last Hope*, an NGO dealing with victims of trafficking in women."

Lazar made a disappointed face. "Hopefully, you've got more."

"Be patient, my friend. Shortly after Ruyter showed up in Sarajevo, he met Emir Besic. Suddenly Moon and Salah were showing some interest in him. And finally, they met. Considering their reputation, we were suspicious. You know, we had been watching those two for a while."

"Have they been doing business with Ruyter? Anything to do with Emir Besic?"

Mirsad chuckled. "That short encounter was a coincidence or a checkout. *Central Café* is an attraction for foreigners, and Ruyter is a regular customer. So, it's normal he talks to other foreigners. He probably came here to find out who's been killing his wife."

"Wasn't that an accident?" Lazar had never considered it an accident, and he recalled what the anonymous informant had told him on the phone.

"It was murder," replied Mirsad emphatically, "committed by Karadzic's supporters with the Pale police complicity. In order not to disturb the good relationship with our European friends, the lady died officially by accident."

Both said nothing for a while.

Lazar stretched out and leaned in. "Salah and Moon are dead, and I'm wondering why you're not aware."

Mirsad stopped chewing and turned toward Lazar. "We don't watch them twenty-four hours a day. We don't have the means to do that." He paused for a few seconds. "Are you certain that both are dead?"

Lazar hadn't yet received the autopsy reports, suspecting Subic not having forwarded any information to different police or state departments.

"Both foreigners were enjoying diplomatic immunity, so SFOR has claimed their corpses, as I learned about an hour ago," confirmed Lazar. He grinned darkly. "Salah stepped on a landmine. We were able to identify him through identity papers and car documents. As far as Alistair Moon is concerned, DNA testing is going on. We got his car and a charred corpse." Lazar studied Mirsad's face features.

The little pulled on his nose, shaking his head. "So both mercenaries are dead."

"You seem to be worried about their death."

"We hoped they were going to take us to the mastermind behind the scenes," Mirsad growled.

"The guy who's calling the killings?"

"Men like Moon and Salah always work for a master."

"And what about Bram Ruyter? Do you have an opinion about him?"

Mirsad chuckled. "He was in Srebrenica, from 1994 to 1995 while a hitman was operating in the enclave, killing important Bosnian military chiefs. The High Command called him *Cleaner*."

"He was one of us, I've heard," Lazar interrupted. "Reliable witnesses have told me that the Army Command called the duo Naser Oric and his subcommander Ejub Golic *unguided missiles* and that they wanted to get rid of them. There were strong indications that Golic was involved in these murders."

Mirsad shook his head. "Rumours are not always true."

"The same source claimed that Oric has murdered at least thirty significant people. He might have killed them to obtain and maintain the status of a warlord and commander of the 28th division. In any case, he has worked his way up to become the sole commander in and around Srebrenica."

Mirsad shrugged. "Oric is our hero, don't forget that."

"Possibly. If you call the killing of 600 to 3000 innocent civilians, a heroic deed, then, of course, I've no objections to that."

Mirsad's face got tightened, and he laid down his fork. "On which side, are you?"

"I am a Bosniak as you are, but I disagree with unnecessary violence and the killing of innocent people. Oric would have done a better job fighting the VRS. Maybe he could have prevented Mladic from crushing the enclave."

"Listen to what I'm going to say, and judge afterwards," Mirsad growled.

"I'm curious," murmured Lazar.

"Lazar, I'm a realist. From 1994 to 1995, bizarre things happened in Srebrenica. Numerous military chiefs got mysteriously murdered there. These are facts."

"I know those stories, and Naser Oric might be the culprit. Or an accomplice."

"The enclave was overcrowded, making it difficult to approach someone unnoticed, slitting his throat, or killing him in any other way. On the other hand, it was easy to hide among the masses."

Lazar chuckled. "If *Cleaner* existed, he must have been incredibly lucky."

"Probably, because he never got arrested. Did you know that Oric feared for his life? After being called to Sarajevo in April 1995, he never returned to Srebrenica, choosing to stay in Tuzla."

Lazar smiled, amused. "Or he was ordered to stay there."

"The official version might not match with reality. The helicopter that ought to bring Oric to Zepa got shot down. Coincidentally, at the last moment, Oric had decided to stay in Tuzla for another day because he wanted to discuss something with the commander. After the helicopter incident, rumours were saying that a mole in Srebrenica was passing on information to the Serbs. Whatsoever, Oric believed the *Cleaner* story. There was a high price put on his head. The Serbs had given him the nickname *Muslim Beast*, and his death had become their priority. It's a fact; a Serbian killer was operating in the enclave. An infiltrated Bosnian spy in Karadzic's headquarters had confirmed to the Bosnian authorities that *Cleaner* was not a myth. We were looking for someone who could move unobtrusively in the enclave."

Mirsad paused briefly. "That's why we kept a close eye on Bram Ruyter when he showed up here," he concluded.

"Because he's a Dutchman?" Lazar gave him a cynical smile.

Mirsad shook his head. "No, because he stayed in Srebrenica during that period."

Lazar recalled what Winston had told him. Moreover, there were the photographs he'd received anonymously, proving Ruyter was at the crime scene at the time Visser got murdered. Motives and opportunity. But were these pictures authentic? Or had someone tampered with them?

Lazar leaned in. "Do you know Cees Visser?"

"The Dutch attaché who got murdered."

"That guy was in Srebrenica in the same period."

Lazar informed him of the three photographs he'd received from an anonymous informant, about the anonymous phone call and of what Winston Chambers had told him.

Mirsad stopped chewing but said nothing.

Lazar hesitated a moment and said, "I think Ruyter is the prime suspect in the Visser case. How many officers were murdered in Srebrenica?"

"Twenty or so, I've heard. I was not there. After the Četniks had invaded the enclave, they started to clean up the territory, killing all witnesses."

Lazar grinned triumphantly. "So, you don't have any concrete evidence that Bram Ruyter might be that *Cleaner* or the man who provided information to the Serbs."

Mirsad grinned wolfishly. "I've never alleged Ruyter is *Cleaner*. A few months ago, we got a phone call from a man saying he'd seen *Cleaner* in Sarajevo. He also admitted being a survivor of Srebrenica, a former soldier of Oric's troops. Imprisoned by Serb paramilitaries, he got questioned by *Cleaner*. After that, they drove him with fifty other prisoners into a shed, where a dozen paramilitaries fired on anything moving. He was hit on his head and lost consciousness. They must have thought he was dead, throwing him with other corpses on a truck. After being dumped into a mass grave, he awaked buried under corpses, convinced he would suffocate. But Allah seemed merciful to him, and he survived. The Serbs had to wait the next morning for a bulldozer to close up the grave. That night he was able to flee. After two weeks of walking through the woods, he reached Tuzla, more dead than alive. When, after all those years, he spotted *Cleaner* in Sarajevo, he panicked. And I can't blame him for demanding a hefty reward for his information." Mirsad went silent for a moment. "The poor bastard was living in a small hut outside Sarajevo, and he thought having won the jackpot. If only he'd trusted us and given us the name of the perpetrator..."

"What happened?"

"Well, we advised him to visit one of our safe houses. However, he didn't show up, and we concluded that he was an impostor. Until the next day, a man walking on the market place next to the cemetery at the Kosevo stadium found the poor wretch with a slit throat."

"How did you know it's the man who'd called you?"

"The police found in his pockets a piece of paper with our phone number and the address we'd given him. The inspector in charge of the investigation contacted us."

Lazar had heard about the murder of a beggar, recalling that the police had classified the case as unsolved robbery.

"I've heard about that murder," he said softly. He'd hoped that Mirsad would give him a useful hint, no new riddles.

Mirsad nodded. "The man got killed shortly after Ruyter had shown up in Sarajevo. That's why we wanted to know more about him. Many Dutchmen in Srebrenica were pro-Serbian, so it's only natural that we started an investigation."

Lazar burst out laughing. "Bram Ruyter as *Cleaner*?"

"Why not? But you're right. When we discovered his relationship with that reporter, we immediately removed him from our suspect list. Our *Cleaner* is a Serbian or a Serbian fanatic. Ruyter hates the Serbs."

"However, he's my prime suspect in the Cees Visser case."

Mirsad grinned. "But there's nothing you can do because there's no case. Don't be fooled and ask yourself why someone put you on Ruyter's trail."

"I do."

"I don't believe in Ruyter's involvement with those murders."

Lazar became impatient. "You haven't said anything about the others yet. What do you know about Emir Besic?"
Mirsad shrugged. "A computer freak who's hating the četniks."
"Does the name Safet Begovic mean anything to you?"
"A poor wretch who's trying to survive."
"I assume you know Miralem Lulic?"
Mirsad's eyebrows went up. "Which Bosniak doesn't know him?" he barked. "A bloodthirsty White Mujahid. Can't believe he's dead, too."
"These three men have got a common business with Salah and Moon," explained Lazar.
Mirsad seemed surprised. "Are you sure about that?"
"Yes, and Salah and Moon have tried to get rid of Safet, Emir and Miralem. I think something turned wrong." Lazar told Mirsad what he'd discovered at Bogusevac.
Mirsad shook his head violently. "*Cleaner.*"
"I thought he'd specialised in slitting throats," retorted Lazar.
"He was also a good sniper, and that's what makes the Srebrenica murders so mysterious. Several troopers got shot by a sniper, others got killed inside the enclave, apparently by the same person."
"But how do you know it was the same perpetrator?"
"The victims received a warning. Shortly afterwards they died either from a bullet or with a slit throat. The killer used whether a Dragunov special version or a razor-sharp knife."
"Most snipers in this country use Dragunov. How did the victims receive their threat?"
"A 7.62 calibre shell with their initials engraved on it, I recall. The victim found it in his clothes or between his equipment. So, they knew what to expect, but not how they were going to die, nor when. In this way, *Cleaner* created a fear psychosis..."
Lazar shook his head. "And how could he move out and back in without being noticed?"
"Mystery," Mirsad admitted. "Whether he was a Dutch soldier in civilian clothes or a Serb soldier getting help from a Dutch trooper at one of their observation posts."
"A Dutchman would never have been able to get that close to the victims. Moreover, cutting someone's throat is not immediately part of Western culture." Lazar still refused to believe that *Cleaner* story. There had to be another explanation. Ferid had revealed to him that the shooter caught the cartridges.
"So, do you think the Srebrenica *Cleaner* is involved in my murder case? But what the hell is his motive?" Lazar asked sceptically.
"How should I know?"
"And I keep turning in a circle."

After a short break, Lazar took a pile of photos from his inner pocket and threw them on the table.

"Do you know these men?" he asked, frustrated.

Mirsad studied them carefully. "British diplomats at EuPol," he growled. "One is a Political Advisor, and the other is his permanent shadow. They're inseparable. Furthermore, Fleming is a British MI6 agent. The third is a Serb, eh, Milan Garasanin, a loyal Karadzic supporter and a senior police officer in Pale. Where are those pictures taken?"

"Emir's apartment."

Mirsad sat up straight. "Damn, what is this Četnik doing in Sarajevo?"

Lazar grinned. "A proof that the Britons keep in touch with Karadzic. During the war, they were friends with the Serbs. The same is true for the French. And the Americans. Do you remember the American diplomat Richard Holbrooke?"

Mirsad nodded.

"He promised Karadzic that he would not be prosecuted if he voluntarily withdrew from politics," Lazar said.

Mirsad sighed. "What does that change?"

There was a moment of silence, only disturbed by Mirsad's loud tapping on the tabletop.

Lazar ate a large piece of bread with cheese, then leaned back.

"There was more than a friendly relationship between Emir and Ruyter."

"Do you think?"

Lazar got an inspiration and leaned in. "You're a smooth eel," he snarled. "You've put a man on one of these people."

Mirsad looked him straight in the eye. "What brings you to that idea?"

"You know what Ruyter is up to in Sarajevo, and also that Emir has been working with him. Have you installed electronic listening devices in Emir's apartment?"

Mirsad laughed faintly but did not comment.

"That's it," continued Lazar. "You had Emir watched, but why? Damn it. You know more than you want to admit. Your interest, your presence here, is proof that something is going on. Are you afraid of terrorists? An attack?"

"Actually, nothing's indicating that an attack has got planned somewhere. Salah and Moon are or were mercenaries. Murderers, yes, but not terrorists who are seeking public interest. Safet, Emir and Miralem hated the Serbs who had slain their relatives. Possible that they were working with Salah, but he was a Muslim who'd trained mujahidin. Then what does an ex-Arkan tiger do among those Islam fundamentalists?"

"Moon's religion is *money*, and he isn't cheap. That group probably believed they could kidnap Karadzic."

"A million dollars is tempting, but Miralem had enough common sense to understand he'd never be able to spend a single dollar of it, provided that their action was successful. The Karadzic clan would mercilessly chase them no matter where they were hiding. Miralem is a fearless soldier, not an idiot. He also fought alongside mujahidin. I even heard he'd got trained in Iran. A lunatic, not interested in wealth. The same applies to Emir Besic. Two lone fundamentalist wolves. That Salah and these three gathered might be an indication that a group of fundamentalist Muslims was active. But Moon doesn't fit into that picture.

"Could Ruyter be interested in a similar operation?"

That remark made Mirsad burst out laughing. "I thought you were more realistic."

At that moment Samir appeared with the main dish. Rich in fish and rice. Mirsad's face brightened up. His favourite meal knew Lazar, and he ordered a carafe of white wine.

During the meal, there was hardly any talk and only about everyday things, which gave Lazar time to think about the events of the last two days.

After the meal, they drank Bosnian coffee.

Lazar was excited because he was still groping around in the dark, feeling that Mirsad knew more than he revealed.

"What do you think about Ragnarsson?" asked Mirsad unexpectedly.

Lazar shrugged. "Excellent commander with a fantastic curriculum vitae. He deserved his international recognition in Kosovo, but in my opinion, he's a naive idealist who doesn't accept that our mentality is different from that of the Westerners. He hasn't learned much about our history, ignoring the fact that we've lived under the Communist yoke for almost fifty years. '*I will nip the crime in the bud*,' he shouts in any of his interviews or speeches. Well, a true Viking, a nickname that suits him.

"He believes it's sufficient to invite high-ranking international police officers here to reorganise our police system completely. EuPol will do no better than IPTF did. Whereas he talks about democracy, he's behaving like a despot trying to subjugate everyone. Furthermore, he thinks that three years will be enough to carry out all the reforms successfully. I bet that in ten years, EuPol will still be here. Don't forget that all these high-ranking civil employees got very well paid. At some point, they're only searching arguments to justify an extension of their presence."

"Aren't you western minded?" Mirsad asked stiffly.

Lazar nodded. "Don't get me wrong, a United Europe appeals to me, but I doubt whether it will succeed the way they're proceeding."

"What a pessimistic jerk you are."

"No, a realistic one. Cultural diversity will create tensions in the long run. Soon, the impoverished Eastern bloc countries will join the EU. Why do you think they get attached so quickly?"

Mirsad shrugged.

"So far," continued Lazar loudly, "all the wealthy industrialised countries in Europe have been producing where they could get cheap labour, including child labour, such as in South America, India, China. Amnesty International and UNICEF are impotent against multinationals. They are making a lot of noise, but nothing changes. Raising energy prices and its related transport cost is determining the end price of the product. Nowadays, industrialised countries also have to start ecologically thinking.

"After the fall of communism, poor Eastern bloc countries became new production areas. Cheap labour and low transport costs are decisive arguments in favour of integrating these developing countries into the EU. Without being noticed, many companies are already moving to those regions. One day, however, somebody will have to pay the price for this. For the West, I predict increasing unemployment. In which area do you think the multinationals will invest? These weak new Member States will become slaves to the EU, which, thanks to these cheap labours, will make its products more competitive and remove all obstacles about the supply of logistical resources and the subsequent export of the end product. These companies are operating within the framework of European rules. In many Western European countries, companies are already closing, moving to these new Industrial Eldorados. Yes, I see a bleak future for the Westerners. The rich will become more prosperous, the poor, even more miserable. Dissatisfaction will be growing, leading to political changes by which extremism will flourish again. Well, who am I? Politics has never been my strong suit."

Lazar laughed apologetically and sipped his coffee. "Ragnarsson knows something. I think he's scared." He secretly glanced at Mirsad, who eagerly enjoyed his piece of Baklava.

"So you've become good friends again?" remarked Mirsad with a smile.

"No. But I have visited the Viking. He was very nervous."

"Don't play with fire, my dear, this guy has the support of the EU Council. His word is the law, and he depends directly on SGSg Jacques Klein, who can have you dropped off! Having good cards aren't making you immune. With your big mouth, you're a thorn in their side. Your constant criticism hinders their reform. Moreover, they're looking with a crooked eye at your great influence with the politicians. Your first mistake could be the last."

Mirsad sat bolt upright and wiped his mouth with the paper napkin.

"Lazar," he said, "as long as those mercenaries are after Pale guys, we're closing our eyes. I'd prefer to deal with the two war criminals myself, but my hands are tied. I can only applaud the fact that others are doing the job. We've nothing to do with it." He grinned demonically.

"I understand, but I'm afraid that this case will explode in our faces."

"Well, I'll call in my informants at SFOR. At first, I thought, the murders were related to fundamentalist Muslims. Lately, we see appearing a lot of mosques, and nobody knows exactly wherefrom all that money comes.

Certainly not from the West. After the war, a large number of mujahidin have stayed here. Fundamentalism is growing by the day, but nobody pays attention to it. The Americans even deny that about seven thousand mujahidin fought at our side, that one of the terrorists of 11/9 served with the seventh Muslim brigade in Zenica. Miralem and Besic were fundamentalists. Salah is known for his radical ideas, but that can be an illusion, especially when you consider that he and Moon worked together. Safet is a poor bastard who tried to make money, trading with one of the most radical arms dealers I know. So, I guess he has chosen the wrong trading partners. Emir's death might be a coincidence. You said yourself that Safet called him, so it could be that the killer didn't want to take any chances."

"Possibly, but unlikely. The death of those two foreigners worries me. They are indeed proof that the case has an international dimension. It senses like a conspiracy. I have a peculiar premonition which rarely deceives me."

Mirsad nodded. "Well, I know you don't make a fuss for any reason. That's why I'll look into the matter. Wait and see and stay alert. As soon as I've spoken to my informants, we can gather again to decide what to do. Okay?"

"I'm counting on you."

"There's another thing you need to know about Cees Visser. He was a paedophile."

"I know."

"Did the name Loverboy come up in your investigation?"

Lazar kept quiet.

Mirsad gave him a look of concern. "Loverboy is an American, an international police observer we know by the name of Tommy Branson. But that must be a fake name. He's CIA and active among the highest circles, arranging girls for the most prominent people. In America, you call those whores escort girls. We know that he rents a suite in Eurotel where well-known politicians, high-ranking UN and EU officials can enjoy themselves in all discretion with the girls that they order from him. Not the usual foreign whores, but selected Bosnian women without a family, or are living alone. Besides, he employs liaison people in the *Florida Bar* where he rents underage girls if there is a demand for it. The suite contains hidden microphones and cameras, so he's collecting data on all people using his services."

Lazar leaned in. "How do you know that?"

"Secret services are working in a gloomy world. But nothing remains secret for long, certainly not in Sarajevo. In the past, we would have been indignant, but now we let the CIA go their way as long we benefit from their work. The CIA might think we're foolish, or that our intelligence services are worthless. How else could they've overlooked the fact that the hotel manager is a family member of mine?" Mirsad's face showed a happy grin.

Lazar shot him a glance of suspicion. "Why are you telling me all that?"

Mirsad shrugged. "Why? Lazar, today I've seen a copy of yesterday's video. Given its nature, I've done further research. Zumra is your girlfriend, isn't she?"

It was as if Lazar got a blow to the stomach. Suddenly he sat bolt straight, holding his breath for a moment. He felt as facing a tsunami which was going to kill him in a few seconds.

"How do you know?"

"We know all about the people who are playing a role in our vulnerable community. You are a policeman with a bright future in the prospect. We secure our future, hoping that we will not be threatened by war for a second time. However, I've only known for a week you're living with a girlfriend. Or should I say, a girlfriend who occasionally comes to stay with you?"

"Zumra is my private life. She's the best thing that ever happened to me. We will marry..."

Mirsad shook his head. "Loverboy brought Zumra to Eurotel and the client, or the guest with whom she had to share the suite, knocked her down and abducted her."

Lazar rose from his chair. "What?" he yelled appalled.

Mirsad took a pen from his inside pocket and wrote an address on a paper napkin. "That's the address where she lives with a girlfriend. Take it easy. Loverboy is a dangerous guy who gets powerful protection. I wouldn't like fishing your corpse out of the Miljacka."

Lazar was shaking all over his body. Why hadn't he seen the truth? The name she muttered in her sleep, her sudden absences, her mysterious fuss about her dwelling place should have prompted him to take action.

"What do you suggest I do?" He almost whispered.

"I'll send you a CD with the video tomorrow. Perhaps you can recognise the actors on it. It's not Loverboy, he just took her to the suite and left her alone. So far nobody knows that we're aware of her disappearance. Keep it discreet, because there are a lot of high-ranking people involved in the Eurotel case. Don't go there, because we'll lose a good source of information. I have the feeling that Zumra's disappearance is related to the murders of the last forty-eight hours." Mirsad got up and shook his hand. "You're a good policeman, Lazar, that's why I inform you. But I ask for discretion. I didn't tell you anything."

Mirsad turned around and stepped between the curtains.

Lazar felt confused while dark thoughts raged through his mind. Then Mirsad's head reappeared alongside the curtain.

"And another thing," Mirsad said in a muted tone. "Zumra has a daughter." He walked away without waiting for a reaction.

Lazar paid the bill and strolled to his car, absorbed in his thoughts. He got behind the wheel and grabbed his cell phone. A few seconds later, he got Senad.

"Senad, have a search warrant issued against Bram Ruyter by tomorrow morning. And I need an intervention team. We'll leave at eight o'clock."

THIRTY-SEVEN

A GHOST. BRAM JUST KEPT STARING AT HER. SHE HAD RADIANT BLUE EYES, AND HER long dark hair fell on her shoulders. A friendly, sweet-looking girl in a floral dress, white socks and brown slippers, not older than eight, anxiously held the door ajar. Her eyes betrayed a mixture of curiosity and distrust. *Who's that girl?*

"Hello, I'm looking for Timka," he said aloud to be heard inside, his brain working at full speed.

He heard a woman's voice beyond the front door. "Who's there?"

The door swung open, and he faced a handsome young woman he recognised immediately from the photo her mother had given him.

Bram smiled. "Timka, I've met your mother."

She looked puzzled. "And who are you?"

My accent. "I'm Mayke's husband," he answered.

"Mayke? Oh, I understand. Come inside," she exclaimed. Her face started to shine. Meantime, the young girl had moved into another room, and he heard two children's voices. His head was spinning. Confusing thoughts were raging through his head while he took off his shoes, slipping his feet into a pair of slippers for visitors. What he'd discovered with Greg Stone kept worrying him. Especially Emma's fate. Before he came there, he had called Edhem. But only got his voice mail, on which he'd left a message.

Timka led him to a sparsely furnished living room and beckoned him to take a seat in a worn-out armchair.

"Coffee or tea?" she asked.

He settled down. "You tell me."

"What about coffee?"

He nodded, and she walked to the adjacent kitchen. Barely a few minutes later, a strong smell of coffee reached his nostrils and Timka reappeared, putting a bowl on the tabletop with a jug and cups.

"That's a nice surprise," she opened the conversation. "And you speak our language very well."

"Thank you. I'm doing my best. I've taken special courses before coming to this country."

"Did Mayke comes along?"

Bram frowned. "You don't know?"

She raised her eyebrows and shook her head. Then he told her about Mayke's accident.

She looked affected. "My condolences, I wasn't aware of it. Mayke was so..." Her voice stopped.

They drank tea in silence.

After a moment, Bram shifted in his chair and cleared his throat. "Mayke told me a lot about you and your sister," he said, looking her straight in the eye. "Probably the reason why she went to Pale to sniff around."

Timka let out a sigh. "During her visit, Mayke told me that she'd met my sister Suada who seemed to be happy in her new homeland. She'd married a loving man. Too bad, she doesn't want to see her family any more."

"You have a son?"

"Yes, Hadar, a beautiful boy. He doesn't know anything about the whole drama..."

"I understand. I've experienced things here that I also want to forget."

"Have you been here before?"

He nodded. *Mayke hasn't told her*. "Srebrenica, I had a Bosnian girlfriend, but she didn't make it."

"What a tragedy, losing two beloved women in a foreign country."

"Violence seems to haunt me."

She looked a bit confused. "But what do I have to do with that?"

"Today, I know what Mayke was after. I think you're no longer safe here. Particularly your son isn't."

"What do you mean?" She glanced up toward the hallway, and he heard whispering kids who were approaching.

"The biological father wants to destroy the only concrete evidence of his behaviour during the war," explained Bram with a low voice. "Your son is in grave danger."

Timka glanced at the two children entering the living room.

"Mum, where is Aunt Zumra?" asked the boy.

"I don't know," Timka replied. "But she'll be home soon." The concern on her face didn't escape him. His eyes focused on the young girl who was standing in front of him. The resemblance was remarkable.

He smiled toward her. "What's your name?"

"Azra," replied the child radiantly.

"And where is your mother?"

"She's coming home later."

Bram watched Timka fidgeting with a cup of coffee. After hesitating for a while, she turned to the children and gestured to the corridor.

"To your room," she ordered. "There's something else I need to discuss with this gentleman."

Bram frowned. "Timka, what's Azra's mother's name?"

"Zumra. Why that question?"

He felt embarrassed. "Strange coincidence, Azra looks like two drops of water to the woman I've known in Srebrenica. Jasmina could be her mother."

"Jasmina? Your girlfriend in Srebrenica?"

He nodded. "Jasmina was twenty-two. Now she'd be twenty-nine."

Bram scratched his beard. "Are you two forming a pair? I mean, uh, Zumra and you?" He recalled her mother's ambiguous statements.

"Is Mommy alleging that?" Her features turned into a melancholy smile. "Zumra and I are excellent friends, have always been helping each other. It wasn't easy to survive with a child each. We're alone, and we sought comfort from each other. But that doesn't make us lesbians."

"How did you meet with Zumra?"

"She was very much in need, begging in the streets with her three-year-old daughter, who touched my heart. I couldn't resist and invited Zumra to my dwell. After hours of talking, I suggested she moves in with me. We became friends, promising our children a better future. My mother gave us shelter until we found a suitable place of our own."

"Do you have a picture of Zumra?"

"A group photo was taken in the city, somewhere on a terrace. A polaroid. I have to check." Timka got up and hurried to the buffet, rumbling in a few drawers. Then he saw her features change and she came back, triumphantly waving with a photo which she handed over, probably hoping he was wrong.

"Zumra, myself, and the children between us," she said.

"That's Jasmina," he whispered, glancing up to her.

"I assure you, that's Zumra," she countered, coming around the table. All of a sudden, she stopped and grimaced. "What's your name again?" she asked, almost inaudibly.

"Bram," he answered, looking at the picture again. There was no doubt, that was his Jasmina. She was slightly fuller, looking very handsome. She held Azra's hand.

"Bram, you said," Timka repeated. "Bram...oh no…"

He looked up at her with slightly pinched eyes.

"Bram," Timka called out, "that's the name she sometimes shouts in her nightmares. Bram. Allah, be merciful to me."

Bram looked again at the picture and then carefully laid it on the table. Had Mayke met that woman? Unbelievable coincidence. But why was Jasmina now calling herself Zumra?

Timka had settled down in an armchair, gazing at him inquisitively. She seemed confused, uncertain, remaining suspicious.

"Zumra is Jasmina," stated Bram with conviction. "How old is Azra? When was she born?"

"April 16, 1996," replied Timka, probably realising that she didn't know anything about her friend.

Bram made a quick calculation and then nodded. "Azra is my daughter."
His cell phone rang.
Edhem.
"You'll never believe me, Edhem..." Bram said.
"Where are you? I'll come over to you." The voice sounded anxious.
"What? Did a fire break out somewhere?" Bram tried to be light-hearted.
"Where are you?" yelled Edhem.
Bram gave him the address.
"Stay where you are! You're wanted for murder!"

THIRTY-EIGHT

NORMAND MONTPETIT GAZED SUSPICIOUSLY AT IVAR RAGNARSSON, GETTING AN unpleasant tickle in his belly. He found the Viking's urgent invitation extremely unusual. The Swede poured two glasses of whisky, put the bottle and drinks on the tabletop and sat in front of him. His features looked tense.

"My wife's gone to see a friend," he said tonelessly. "Now we shall talk undisturbed."

That doesn't sound good. Normand reacted with a forced grin, "You sound so... formal. Is there something I'm ignoring?"

Ivar sighed. "How long do we know each other? Two years, isn't it? Since Mitrovica. Cheers." He raised his glass and waited for Normand to do the same. "As in the good old days."

Normand's shoulders pulled together. Ivar's toast was an allusion to a period he wanted to banish from his memory. Since his appointment in Sarajevo, it was the first time the Swede reminded him of what had happened in Mitrovica. A theme that both had been avoiding anxiously. He wondered what the Viking had in mind, took a sip and carefully placed the glass on the table.

Ivar gazed toward him for a long moment. "I signed Stone's letter of resignation because Stone has violated EuPol principles," he said slowly. "I trust your judgement and agree with your arguments. But you've disappointed me again, Normand." His massive, dull voice expressed dissatisfaction. Normand felt a chill going through his body. *What have I done?*

"The resignation letter is a masterpiece. But as in Mitrovica, you've underestimated a subordinate. Stone decided to resist. He has already submitted a written objection."

"So what?" replied Normand scornfully. "He's guilty of the charges against him. He lives with a Moldavian whore he has bought. Thus, he's supporting the women trafficking, and he's transgressing our rules of ethics." His voice started to rise in tone. "What insolence to object and deny the facts."

The Swede growled. "He doesn't deny the facts, alleging that he has saved the woman. And if he can prove it, legally he cannot be dismissed. But there's more: he's accusing you of having falsified elements in your resignation letter, and he'll prove it with a copy of that woman's residence permit. After you accused him, he allegedly showed you that document, he says. Your letter of resignation is a lie you've let sign me without investigating his arguments. Can you explain?" Although his pitch did not have changed, his eyes were embers.

Normand recalled how disrespectful Stone had behaved toward him, the excuse he'd needed to hand him his resignation letter. Anyway, Follum had left him little choice. Suddenly this Stone seemed even more dangerous than he'd thought possible.

"I can't recall that he has shown me this permit. I've got a witness," responded Normand indignantly.

Ivar grinned coldly. "I've spoken to Margaret. Stone didn't have a copy of that woman's permit when you called him in your office, but he alleged he would show it to you, not to her. That woman understands more French than you English. Assumptions are not evidence, as you know. Anyway, I'm not a Stone fan. According to his contract, he did not commit any offence; nonetheless, his behaviour is in contradiction with our ethics. So, his resignation remains in force, no matter what he threatens to do."

Normand could hardly hide his relief. "Thank you."

Ivar shook his head. "When he brings the issue to the media, we'll get a lot of fuss, but who'll believe him? An elderly guy living with a whore? As far as EuPol is concerned, he poses no danger. But Stone seems to know more about you than I could have imagined. He found out Kouchner put you aside in Mitrovica. His tenacity suggests that he won't let himself be fired so easily." Ivar got up, paced across the dining room, took a briefcase from a chair and sat back down. With a short movement, he swallowed the rest of his whisky.

"Normand," he said sternly, "I'm tired of your antics. Since Monday, odd things are happening in Sarajevo, and I don't believe in coincidence. First the murder of the Dutch military attaché who had apparently paid sex with underage girls. Then three natives got murdered. I reckon they belong to a group of Western Europeans employed by a private organisation, but carrying out assignments for SFOR. Those men are driving around with a diplomatic plate doing all but humanitarian work. I've also learned that native gangsters have abducted a young Romanian woman on her way to the airport after they'd knocked out her presumed protector who can't remember what happened. That girl had testified in court against a brothel owner, so I suppose that her corpse will turn up soon. An informer has told me that Emma, the concerned girl, had a good friend named Daria Bazila." He chuckled as a predator. "And that Daria happens to be Stone's girlfriend you mention in the resignation letter. The same woman who has worked in Mitrovica and is wanted for homicide, accused by a French policeman."

Normand swallowed, but his face remained unaffected.

"Coincidence," he retorted.

"Do you also call it a coincidence that the British delegation is avid for Stone's post? Stone gave me a few interesting clues in his defence letter. Did Derek Fleming whisper in your ear that you had to fire Stone? Do the Britons know anything about your heroic deeds in Mitrovica?"

Normand rose from his seat. "These accusations are unfounded. I don't have to accept them."

"Sit down," yelled Ivar furiously.

Normand stiffened. Nobody knew he was visiting the Swede, and he wasn't a match for this colossus. He sat down.

"I've been watching you for some time," Ivar said. "And what I've discovered gives me the creeps. I was always wondering what happened in Mitrovica. How stupid I've been to believe your story. The alternative was too monstrous; even dare to consider it. Moreover, you got appreciated by your government. Everyone I talked to about you said with a full conviction that a great future is awaiting you." He shook his head violently as if he blamed himself for being so gullible and unprofessional. "But I'm not an idiot, my dear. As the EU Council appointed you as my deputy, I ordered a confidential Interpol investigation into your two killed colleagues in Mitrovica. I wanted to ease my conscience. I'd got you out of trouble before, and I wanted to know if I could rely on you."

Normand shook his head. "It was an accident. The bartender tried to trap me. That whore clung to me! Damned, I just jabbed her away. She lost balance and fell downstairs, breaking her neck. A regrettable accident."

Ivar's dark gaze gave him chills.

"Yes, several witnesses have confirmed your story." Ivar chuckled like a hyena. "Two colleagues, the bar owner and you are linked by that bar incident. And strangely, those witnesses got killed: two police officers got shot during the riots, while the bar owner and his girlfriend got murdered by Daria Bazila. Coincidence?"

"*Merde*, there are many witnesses to this."

"I agree. Everything seems to have happened as you've reported. The captains Dumont and Leduc undeniably died through a sniper's bullet. I believed this version until recently, probably because I didn't want to know the truth. Nothing is more horrible than police officers having colleagues killed." Ivar gave him a long disdainful look.

Normand held his breath while his face was turning sallow. "Have you lost your mind?" he stammered when the silence became uneasy.

"I blame myself also for what happened after Mitrovica. Had I made the right decision, we wouldn't be sitting here today. This morning I've received from Interpol the investigation results." Heavily breathing, Ivar opened the case and took out a large brown cover. "Here's the proof that you're a fucking bastard."

Normand frowned and got up. "I hope you take these words back because I'll introduce a complaint."

"Sit tight, or by God, I'll beat you to a pulp." Ivar's voice echoed across the room. His face had turned red, and Normand was afraid that he would turn his words into deeds. His heart was pounding wildly, and he wondered what was on the cover.

Ivar did not leave him in limbo for long, opened the flap, and took three photos out of a brown envelope, which he, with a despicable gesture, threw on the table.

"Do you remember these faces?" he asked with raised eyebrows.

Normand's breath stopped for a moment when he recognised Marcel Dumont, Claude Leduc and Julien Cartier. He shoved the photos away.

"The Three Musketeers, as they called themselves," uttered Montpetit.

"Right. It wasn't enough to have Dumont and Leduc killed. Also, their relatives and this Cartier had to die as well. Was your crime so terrible that you had to kill another eight people?"

Normand's mouth became cork dry. He didn't quite understand what the Swede meant. No doubt, he had Marcel and Claude on his conscience, but that was their fault. They'd blackmailed him, wanted to accuse him of murder if he didn't pay. People playing with fire can burn themselves ugly.

The Swede raised his eyebrows and hesitated for a few seconds. "You don't know what happened to their family members, do you?" He was visible confused.

"No, and stop your childish riddles," Normand replied.

The Swede is bluffing!

Ivar grinned demonically, took a bunch of pictures out of the cover and threw them furiously across the table. Two images fell to the ground, and Normand hurried to pick them up.

That's not possible. Charred corpses?

A woman in a bathtub seemed to be dead. A dead man stretched out next to a motorcycle in the middle of a wide road. The bartender and his girlfriend, almost unrecognisable mutilated.

The Viking leaned in and jabbed a finger on the images. "Denise Dumont died in her bathtub," he yelled furiously. "Officially she stepped into her full bathtub, slipped out, bumped the back of her skull against the edge, lost consciousness and drowned. An accident, but the suspicion of murder persist."

Ivar poured his glass half full, hesitated for a moment and did the same with Normand's glass.

"Linda Leduc," he continued, "Captain Leduc's wife, is said to have set fire to her house after she'd administered a narcotic drug to her three children. Murder and suicide. But here, too, doubts arise." He paused briefly, gazing angrily at his deputy. Then he uttered a snorting laugh and continued. "The man on the road, Julien Cartier, the common friend of Marcel Dumont and Claude Leduc, kept boasting that a colleague had murdered Dumont and Leduc because they knew too much. The doctors diagnosed PTSD. Cartier got murdered. And of course, the barkeeper and his girlfriend, witnesses of that incident in Mitrovica. Do you believe seriously that Daria Bazila killed those two men?"

Normand shuddered. "Awful, why are you so sure their deaths weren't accidents?"

Ivar jabbed his fist on the tabletop, and the glasses shifted a few centimetres.

"Even in the absence of concrete evidence, there is sufficient indication to conclude that the accidents have been staged."

Normand was afraid of reacting wrongly. The very astute Swede was trying to gather evidence against him. Involving Interpol proved that. *That Ivar has invited me, means that he has not succeeded in establishing his hypothesis. Otherwise, he would have arrested me already.*

"No hard evidence to formulate a credible murder theory has been found in the three accident sites," continued the Viking, "But a witness, a neighbour, has seen Julien Cartier visiting Denise Dumont the day before her death. Cartier was with her for an hour or so and then rushed off with his bike. The same witness noticed a car parked twenty metres behind Cartier's motorbike, chasing the car straight away. I admit it's a hypothesis because the police couldn't identify the car driver." He sighed. "By witnesses, we know that Julien Cartier first visited Denise Dumont and later Linda Leduc. The next day they were all dead. We think that those accidents might be linked to the two killed men in Mitrovica. So, don't sell me out for an idiot."

Norman slid the photos toward Ivar, cursing internally and fearing for his future in Sarajevo. Glancing down under Ivar's murderous gaze, he had never imagined that the Mitrovica case would take on such proportions. Where was Dragon? Since his visit, he'd evaporated. Norman desperately needed him.

"Normand, you understand I cannot prove my allegations. Unfortunately, clues are not proof. But I do know what happened in Mitrovica. We also know that Kouchner replaced you for professional misconduct, even though it's been removed from your file. So, I'm giving you a chance to leave your post honourably. Don't be afraid, I won't officially fire you, because that would take too much time and cause a mess with the media, which would be detrimental to our reputation. You resign, and you'll receive all possible credentials. I'll give you a fortnight to fix that. If you refuse, your name will go through the media, and that might be the end of your career. Probably your protectors will drop you, or you'll have an accident, just like Cartier." His voice sounded bitter.

Norman swallowed; his dismissal was the last thing he'd expected.

"Ivar, I understand you," he reacted appalled. "You're exaggerating, I've nothing to do with what you've described. I'm outraged! Damned, you're accusing me of serious crimes without any proof. But I'm willing to attribute that to the stress..."

"Don't try me, Normand." Ivar's eyes sparkled. He stood up and paced to the window while twisting his hands as if he wanted to strangle someone.

Then he turned around. "Do you know where Dragon Borjan is?" With three paces, he stood beside him.

Normand shrugged. "I haven't seen him since Monday."

"Captain Borjan? That guy doesn't exist in the French gendarmerie. How did he get here? Who provided him with a security card? What game are you playing?" His voice echoed throughout the room.

"Really, I've nothing to do with him. He showed me governmental documents, and I had to tolerate him. He's here awaiting his transfer."

"What was he doing in Mitrovica? I've done research there, too. He was a member of the International Police, but no one knew what he was doing. They thought he'd infiltrated the Bridge watchers, but that seems absurd. He speaks the local language, just as he speaks several other languages. But he's not a French citizen. Yet he has a valid French passport."

"He's probably an agent of the French Intelligence Service, DSGE."

"I didn't accept this post to become the puppet of some superpower. When I got the IPTF command, I thought I'd bring a bit of order. But a large part of IPTF gets controlled by a private organisation under a contract of the United States Department of State. Damn it, they're setting up operations I don't know about, even though I'm in charge. Since Monday, I've been counting six deaths and one disappearance. Three foreigners whose authorities keep silent and make it impossible to investigate. There is a clear link between all those killings, and I don't like it." He furiously raised his hand when Normand opened his mouth to protest.

"I'll find out the truth. But you won't witness that any more, Normand. You've got two weeks to disappear. Then I'll come and pull you out of your chair. And now, get out of my sight." Ivar was standing threateningly next to him.

Normand swallowed, stood up and hurried to the exit. He drew a deep breath, rushed to his car, took his cell phone, dialled an emergency number

and pressed the green button.
Seconds later, he heard his correspondent's voice.
"Ragnarsson wants me out," he said.

THIRTY-NINE

BRAM WONDERED HOW GENERAL FLOWER'S MEN HAD TRACKED HIM DOWN. A mystery, because until Emir's death he'd shown no interest in Suada or Timka. His only purpose had been to find out the people Mayke had met. It was only after Besic's murder he began to wonder if there was a link between Suada's story, Mayke's death and Timka. He stood up.

"We don't have much time, you'll have to trust me," he said. "Where is Jasmina or Zumra?"

Timka didn't answer.

"DNA testing shall confirm that General Flower has raped your sister," he explained. "He's aware, wants to kill your son and make his corpse disappear."

"Is this general really in Sarajevo?" asked the young woman appalled.

He shrugged. "I don't have the slightest idea. He employs professionals, staying himself underground, but he's not far away. A hitman might already be on your trail, although I ignore how they've found out. I've no doubt Mayke got murdered for discovering the truth about the general. I've read Suada's diary. No doubt, Flower has raped her. She managed to steal and hide his wallet, which doesn't prove Flower's guilt. But any DNA test will prove that Hadar is his son. Your sister also wrote that Flower attended a secret meeting about Srebrenica's fate. If we can condemn him for rape, many will wonder what other crimes he's committed. Thus, what your sister has written about Srebrenica will not be considered a figment. Mayke has trusted the wrong people and got murdered because she discovered Flower's secret. It's just a matter of time before a hitman finds you and your son. Please, trust me, come with me before it's too late. I'll take you to a safe place where we can discuss quietly what to do."

Timka still hesitated, gazing at him with a doubtful and frightened look. "But what are you doing here in Sarajevo?"

"I repatriate victims of women traffickers for *Last Hope*, a non-governmental organisation," he declared.

She was wringing her hands and dancing on her legs.

"A friend is on his way over here, Timka," he continued. "A Bosniak. Get prepared for a few days absences. Take what's essential and tell your children we are going to visit Zumra. But hurry up." He omitted to say that the police were looking for him, fearing that she wouldn't trust him if he told her. He was hoping Edhem would be more convincing.

Much to his relief, she rushed toward the hallway and talked to the children. During an instant, he considered calling Winston to ask permission to occupy the unused shelter. But he rejected that idea. His boss would need a justification.

The bell rang. He groped for his waist holster, seeing Timka appear in the doorway of the nursery and he gestured her to stay there while he leaned against the left wall.

The bell rang again.

"Who's there?" he yelled.

"Edhem."

Bram sighed, let in an excited Edhem, and guided him to the living room. He turned around, facing his friend. "What's happening?"

"The police want to arrest you!"

"What have I done?"

"Murder!"

"Who would I have killed?"

"The police think you're involved in the Emir Besic and the Bogusevac murder cases."

"Bogusevac? Where's that?"

"It doesn't matter. You've got to getaway. Who's this woman?" he asked, pointing a finger to Timka who stood in the doorway.

"Suada's sister Timka, I've told you about a general who raped a woman on the Jahorina during the war. Well, that girl later gave birth to his son. Timka has adopted that child as her son." At that moment, the two children walked into the living room and stopped next to Timka.

At that moment, Bram saw Edhem's features change.

"Where is she?" Edhem yelled, looking wildly around.

"You mean Zumra?" asked Timka.

Edhem looked questioningly at Bram. *Does he know Jasmina?* Edhem had never said that he knew Jasmina when he'd told about his girlfriend in Srebrenica.

"Where's Jasmina?" Edhem shouted, and without waiting for an answer, he rushed to the hallway. Nobody was moving. Azra held Hadar's hand, both staying close to Timka. They heard Edhem running through the house, shouting Jasmina's name. When he reappeared in the living room, he seemed desperate. He turned to face Bram. "Where is she?"

"She's not here," Bram replied.

Edhem glanced up at Timka. "Do you live here together?"

Timka nodded.

"Damned, where is she now?"

"She hasn't come home yet." Timka cringed when the big man brought his face close to hers.

"Edhem," Bram interrupted, "I'll tell you everything you need to know later. I've just found out. The boy is in mortal danger, and probably Azra and Timka also. But tell me why the police are after me. There's little time left. I'm going to take you to a safe house where no one is going to look for us."

Edhem's eyes were pacing from the girl to Bram and back all the time. *Something is disturbing him*. Bram could guess what it was. He waved to the picture on the table, and Edhem picked it up. Then his face went pale.

"By Allah, Jasmina's alive," he called out, gazing at Bram in astonishment. "The world is small, mate. How glad I am not having killed you." His face radiated determination. Suddenly Bram realised how much Edhem must have been hating the Dutch, realising that Jasmina was the cause they had become friends. She had saved his life. If he wouldn't have mentioned her, he'd be dead by now.

Edhem kills Dutch people who were in Srebrenica.

Was Edhem an ex-boyfriend? No, Jasmina wasn't like that. She did not have a boyfriend when he fell in love with her. But she had a family. He looked in Edhem's eyes and suddenly understood everything.

Edhem seemed to have noticed.

"Yes," he retorted, "Jasmina's my sister."

The safe house was on the main road past the village of Bojnik, hidden among the trees, fifty metres away from the road. A narrow bumpy, barely passable path led into a clearing behind the house. It was a tough challenge for Bram's Seat and Edhem's vintage car. When they all faced the house, Bram turned around, making a waving move toward the forest.

"There's a barely practicable narrow path," he explained, "winds dangerously between the trees toward a second shelter three hundred metres lower. That lodging is rarely unoccupied, and there's always a security guard. That's the place where we had accommodated Emma Badora." Bram was wondering if Tim Watson had already returned to that other house.

He had chosen this remote place because it had several escape roads. Safe houses of other organisations had been robbed several times, and each time the security guards had been beaten up. To get their girls back, the traffickers were capable of the worst. Besides, the house where they were standing was only to be used in case of an emergency. Few people in the organisation knew about it.

The brick house had a heavy iron front door in the middle of the front wall, which had to be operated electrically from inside by a security guard. The outside cameras covered the whole perimeter around the house. According to local law, a guard wasn't allowed to carry a weapon, but beautiful words didn't stop violent criminals. So, all the guards were discretely carrying a gun, including Bram. Anyway, nobody checked men with diplomatic ID cards and vehicles.

The rectangular brick building had a faintly sloping roof with two chimneys and a satellite antenna mounted on the sidewall. Twenty metres away from the house, between the trees at the edge of the forest, stood a concrete build garage with a massive double gate, electrically controlled by a hidden button.

Edhem started walking around the house, while Bram explained the children and Timka how safe that house was. Nobody knew they would be inside.

After a few minutes, Edhem reappeared on the other side.

"My compliment, Bram," he said with a chuckle. "Easy to defend. Small, high-positioned windows with bars, a small fortress."

The two children remained next to Timka, staring curiously toward the forest. They were attracted by the woods, and the excitement was written in their eyes.

Bram walked to an unusually thick tree next to the edge of the forest, stepped behind the trunk facing the woods and took a bunch of keys out of a small cavity at shoulder height. Then he returned to the others and opened the three locks from the rear door. By then, Timka had got her suitcase from the car.

Bram guided them into a small room. "This kitchen is in the centre of the house," he explained. "On either side, you've got a sitting room, with two adjoining bedrooms. This setting and the adapted furniture offer our guests a minimum of comfort and privacy. As long as we ignore who's looking for you, you'll stay here." He guided them across the house, showing the hallway and front door, the command room and the two sitting-living rooms, each room equipped with fitted furniture. The bathroom toilet and the command post, equipped with four monitors, were only accessible from the kitchen.

"This space is for you," he said to Timka. "You can use both bedrooms. Food is in the kitchen, but until tomorrow you've got to be satisfied with the little reserves. There is also a percolator."

The kids went to a bedroom, excitedly talking to each other. Bram had been watching Azra the whole time, wondering how the reunion with Jasmina would turn out. Then he left Timka in the living room and headed with Edhem to the other wing. On his way, Bram took a bottle of Rakija and two glasses from the kitchen, and paced back to the lounge, settling down across his friend. He filled two glasses, gazing at Edhem.

"I think you owe me an explanation," he said with a serious face.

Edhem smiled amusedly. "You didn't tell me everything either. We're friends, aren't we? But you omitted to tell me that you were going to visit this woman."

Bram nodded thoughtfully. "In her apartment, you said something that keeps haunting me since. *You were glad you didn't kill me*."

Edhem quickly threw the Rakija down his throat.

He shrugged."I'll be honest. When I heard that you'd been in Srebrenica with Dutchbat 3, which I consider responsible for the death of my whole family, I started to think about killing you. But your story confused me. At first, I doubted you were talking about my sister until you described family details. You've been trying to save my family, that's why you're still alive, and we're friends now. It's as simple as that. In my country, you're a friend or an enemy."

Bram chuckled, thought about these words while filling the glasses again.

He looked in Edhem's eyes. "Where were you when Mladic invaded Srebrenica?" He remembered that Edhem had told him to have witnessed the invasion from the surrounding hills.

"I've told you the truth," Edhem growled. "I've seen what happened, but there was nothing I could do. Our remaining warriors gathered and run toward Tuzla. But I stayed behind with my small group, helping the citizens who got out of the city. I couldn't have imagined that the situation would be so disastrous."

"You were Naser Oric's confidant."

"Not quite. I worked under Rasim Delic's orders. Delic was the Commander of the Bosnian Government Army, and he didn't trust Naser. I had to report to him about all the incidents in Srebrenica. He didn't like the fact that good fighters and potential commanders regularly got murdered in the enclave. According to rumours, Naser had all his potential competitors killed. Some soldiers claimed that his deputy commander Ejub Golic did the dirty work. But others said that a Serbian killer had infiltrated."

Bram narrowed his eyes. "I've read in official documents that Naser, compared to his equals, was living in relative luxury and that nobody dared to dispute that. Were they afraid of him?"

"His friends and acquaintances called him *Sheriff of Srebrenica*." Edhem showed a wry smile and continued. "Naser had grown his beard, considering himself a White Mujahid. He wanted to be like the bloodthirsty warriors of the *Dzamijsky Golubovi*. Naser once showed his confidants, but also the International press, photographs of burned houses, mutilated, beheaded and burned corpses. *'My work,'* he was claiming proudly. But Naser sometimes exaggerated. You know, at the beginning of the war he made sure that the people in Srebrenica didn't starve to death. Then no one asks where he got the food, which villages he'd burned down or how many Serbs he'd killed. War is never fun. There are neither good guys nor bad guys. Everyone's convinced he's fighting for the right cause. And of course, there are criminals making war as an opportunity to get money, girls, or everything that they desire. But you have that kind on all sides."

Bram poured the rest of his glass down his throat. "How do you know that the police is suspecting me of murder?"

"I've friends everywhere, even within the police. One of them tipped me off that a chief inspector thinks you've killed Cees Visser. He showed pictures of you at the hotel."

"Photo's?"

"He has shown three pictures of you. You're wearing a cap or something. On one of them, you're entering the hotel, on the other picture you're coming out later. You know, in the same period, the military attaché got killed. A third picture shows a close-up of your face."

Bram jumped up, paced around, getting furious. Why had someone taken pictures of him and handed over to the police?

When he turned around, he saw Timka standing in the doorway.

"May I the children let playing outside?" she asked softly.

Bram tried to smile reassuringly. "Too dangerous. There are treacherous gullies. You also quickly get lost. Today I'd advise you to keep them inside. They can watch TV. But sit down, Timka, we've got a lot to talk about."

Timka hesitantly sat down next to Edhem.

"Tell us the truth," asked Bram, sitting down again. "You now know that Zumra and Jasmina are one person and that Edhem is her brother, and I am her ex-lover. Until now, none of us did know Jasmina is alive. There might be an explanation of why Jasmina calls herself Zumra."

Timka shook her head, apparently still not convinced. "She owns identity documents stating that she's born in Potocari as Zumra Abdic," she insisted.

Edhem cleared his throat. "I've got papers identifying myself as Edhem Hasic, but my real name is Kamal Buhic. I've changed my identity for security reasons. That's all you need to know." He took a quick look at Bram.

"Where's Jasmina, uh, Zumra?" he asked fiercely.

Timka fidgeted with her fingers in her lap, gazing worried from one to the other. "She's at an appointment," she whispered.

"With whom?"

"A foreigner, but I don't know his name. An important person."

"What do you mean by important?"

She moved back and forth in the armchair. "Well, you'll find out anyway. Zumra and I are escort girls, keeping high-ranking gentlemen company. That's well paid, and we have two kids to raise."

Bram sighed deeply. "You don't have to apologise, Timka. We want to find Jasmina. Do you know where she went?"

"Yes, but she won't be there any more. Usually, the assignments are of short duration. Only on weekends or holidays, we might do this for a longer period. A guy comes to pick up one of us. He usually takes us to the suite or the party room. Rarely does he take us to a private place, and only when he's convinced it's safe," she babbled.

"One of us, did you say?"
"Yes, we made a deal with that man. We're alternating, and only one of us is active while the other one stays with the kids. So, we don't have to see what the other one is doing. We try to keep this part of our life away from our kids, doing this work only to give them a better life. Yesterday it was my turn, but Jasmina has taken my place because I have my period."
Bram exchanged a short look at Edhem. Then his eyes went back to Timka. "Why are you worried about Jasmina?"
She hesitated. "We've agreed to send each other a message every time we're finished."
"Didn't Jasmina keep to the agreement?"
"She went to the appointment yesterday afternoon, maybe for a few hours. But I haven't heard from her since. I tried to call her, but her cell phone is off. Very strange, indeed."
"I don't understand, she lives with you, doesn't she?"
"Yes, but, uh, she has a boyfriend with whom she spends a lot of time."
"And who is this boyfriend?"
"A chief inspector. Lazar Magas, a well-known person in Sarajevo."
"Have you called him yet?"
"No, Jasmina never revealed him where she lives. She was waiting for the right moment to do so."
Bram and Edhem exchanged a glance.
"Aren't you free?" Edhem asked.
"Our pimp is a dangerous guy; we think he's working for IPTF. He has tricked us. My fault, I succumbed under his charms. When I realised the danger, it was too late. He forced us to work for him. Not only would we earn good money, but we would also do something positive for our country, he said. He threatened to have our children taken away if we turned down his offer."
Suddenly Edhem got furious. "And who is that man?"
"He calls himself Tommy Branson, Loverboy."
Bram had noticed that since Timka had mentioned Lazar, Edhem seemed extremely nervous. But also, when he'd heard Loverboy, his shoulders had tightened.
Bram leaned in. "Who is Loverboy?"
"Timka is right, Loverboy is a dangerous guy," Edhem replied. "He has a special status at IPTF, especially with the Americans. Everyone knows him. He comes to *Central Café* and in the Irish Pubs, and has connections with the *Florida Bar*. He fulfils the most perverse desires of senior officials and humanitarian workers." He showed a skewed smile, but Bram saw that something was disturbing him.
Bram turned to Timka again. "Do you know where he has taken Jasmina?"
"Eurotel. It's a gathering place for high society. Regularly they organise

special parties."

Edhem stood up and gazed at Bram. "I urgently need to meet a friend who might help me to trace Jasmina. You stay here. Now that you've found Timka's son, I'm afraid it's not just the police that's looking for you. The pictures which the police have received prove that someone is watching your movements." He left the house through the back door.

Timka stood up hesitantly. "So, you are Azra's father?"

Bram nodded. "That's what it seems to be. Only Jasmina can confirm this, but everything is matching, and I don't believe that Jasmina was dating with other men at the time."

She nodded and headed back to the children.

What a week: an acquaintance is murdered, my dead girlfriend is still alive, suddenly I'm a father, the police are looking for me for murder, and I've got two Britons on my conscience. That was too much for a man alone. Besides, he was occupying a shelter without Winston's permission.

Suddenly he thought of his car. He headed toward the guardroom, where he operated the keyboard and started a program on the middle monitor. He clicked on "*garage*" and typed the 8-digit code. After pressing enter, a message appeared: *Door open.* He finished the program and hurried out. After having moved his car in the garage, he closed the anti-theft gate and pushed the hidden button above the doorpost to lock the door. Back into the living room, he saw Azra coming up to him. She hesitated, fidgeting nervously with her hands.

"You speak our language very well," she said with a soft, melodious voice. Despite her timidity, she seemed to be a curious child.

"Yes, your mother taught me that when you weren't born yet." He sat down on the long couch, wondering what she wanted from him. To his surprise, she settled down next to him. From the corner of his eye, he saw Timka's head sticking through the doorway.

"You used to know Mum?" the girl asked.

He nodded and saw her eyes fixed on him as if she was trying to enchant him. But he kept silent.

Azra continued. "Were you good friends?"

"Yes, we were fairly more than friends."

"Ah, then it's true. Where have you been all the time?"

"Why? I'd got to return to my country."

"And you left Mum alone?"

"I had no choice, Azra. They locked me up because I'd defended your mum." He wondered what Jasmina had told her daughter.

"I've good ears." There was a mischievous smile on her lovely face.

"You're a good girl," he replied, stroking over her hair. "Your mum raised you well."

"Yes, Mum is the best in the world. Are you my dad?"

Bram stared at her with a smile on his face but didn't answer.
"Edhem is my uncle, and you're my dad, aren't you? It was as if she was expecting confirmation. He didn't know what to say, certainly didn't want to disappoint her. He turned to face Timka.
"She heard," she said. "I couldn't stop her; she wanted to ask you."
Bram nodded, completely confused by a mixture of contradictory feelings. How much he would have liked to take Azra in his arms, but what would Jasmina think of it when she showed up again? He glanced up at Timka, searching for help, but she shrugged.
He moved closer to Azra. "How old are you now?"
"Six and a half."
"You're a big girl for your age. How are you doing at school?"
"I'm the best in the class." Quite naturally. "And I also speak English. Mum says I have to learn English to become rich later on."
He burst out in a laugh. "Your mother is right," he admitted. "Did she also teach you that you must sleep a lot when you're little? That's good for your mind, and then you become an intelligent woman."
Timka's corners of her mouth curled up.
"Yes, we always go to sleep early," she answered with a serious face. "Do we must go to school tomorrow?"
Bram shook his head. "No," he said hesitantly. "We'll stay here for a few days."
"Is Mum coming here?" she yelled enthusiastically.
"Yes, but now you have to go to bed."
The girl made a disappointed face, but he kept nodding gravely. "All right, I'll go to sleep. Can I use the bathroom?"
"Of course, feel at home here. Tomorrow we'll have a lot to tell each other."
She jumped off the couch and ran dancing into the kitchen.
Bram sighed deeply.
"You'll be a good father," Timka said.
He didn't know if she meant it.
"A sweet child," he replied. "And she speaks like a ten-year-old."
"Zumra, uh, Jasmina will be surprised. I've just tried to call her, but she still doesn't reply."
"Don't worry, Edhem has relations. He's in all states now he discovered his sister alive. He'll do anything to find her." He didn't want to give Timka and Azra false hope. Fortunately, Azra's mother was sometimes staying away for a more extended period. So the girl wasn't worried. He didn't need a crying child now.
Five minutes later, Azra emerged from the kitchen and jumped on the couch, putting her arms around his neck and giving him a big kiss on the cheek. She was gone again before he could react.

"I'm going to sleep in Azra's room," Timka said. "I wish you a good night." She turned around and walked to the other room.

Bram remained seated for a few minutes, then went to the command post where he turned on the monitors. After checking the surroundings, he walked satisfied toward a bedroom, took off his shoes, put his holster on the bedside table and lowered his outer garment to the ground.

Bram left the door to the sitting room ajar. Then he stretched out on top of the blankets.

His last thought before sleep was overwhelming him went to Azra.

FORTY

Srebrenica, 11 July 1995.

IT WAS A MATTER OF LIFE AND DEATH. ZUMRA WANTED DESPERATELY TO SAVE HER parents and sister. She'd put all her faith in Bram, but they'd taken him away from her. She stood alone inside the secure compound, contemplating what she would do. After all, she didn't have much time to find a way out. Her parents and younger sister were gazing desperately toward her. How naïve she had been to believe that the Dutch army would help the population. If their family members didn't get access to the camp soon, the Serbs would pick them up. *I have disappointed them.* She saw the tall man who had Bram let taken away, come over to her. Through Bram, she knew that Cees Visser was taking orders from the deputy commander. He was a behind-the-scene man, doing the dirty jobs, a sneaky arsehole belonging to the military intelligence she couldn't trust.

"We are going to find a solution together," said Visser, joining her with a broad smile. "It's up to you to decide what's going to happen to your family." His words gave her goose bumps. She glanced toward the gate where four Blue Helmets made sure no one slipped in. Thousands were shouting outside the fence, begging for access, still convinced that the Blue Helmets would protect them, as once the French General Philippe Morillon had promised them in March 1993.

"Where's Bram?" she asked vehemently.

He set an apologetic face. "He can't handle the stress any more. Did you see how he behaved? I've sent him to the nursing block where they'll take care of him."

Zumra hadn't heard their conversation, but the body language had convinced her that Bram's words hadn't pleased Visser. Bram was not crazy at all.

"You need me, my dear," Visser said softly, bowing to her. "Do you want me to bring in your parents or not?"

"Of course," she whispered, although she guessed what Visser was up to.

"We don't have much time," he continued. "Mladic has been requesting a list of all the natives working for us. According to the rules of engagement, we're not allowed taking up family members."

She smelled a stinking breath close to her face.

"But I might make an exception," he whispered in her ear.

The screams outside the fence faded away, and she focussed her mind on that creepy guy. Although she wanted to save her family, she refused to face reality.

"What do you mean?" she stammered, barely getting the words out of her throat.

He put his hands on her shoulders, showing her his yellow teeth. "You follow me to a place where we can quietly catch up," he said bluntly.

She felt dirty and filthy, but she didn't resist. Visser pushed her to the barn, and she walked along meekly, as if in a trance.

Our love nest. He knew.

When she halted, he gave her a cheeky push in the back. "Come on, there's not much time left." His features hardened. "Do you want to save your family?"

She was in despair, thinking of running away. Yet she headed toward the stacked boxes, convincing herself that her youngest sister got the right to live. Then she faced the pile of emergency rations, watching the Dutch officer pushing away the empty boxes.

"Get inside," he ordered.

She hesitated, being in an impossible dilemma of whether choosing her honour or her family. He grabbed her arm and tried to pull her in. But the idea of what was going to happen caused her conscience to revolt. Propelled by all of her fuelled up anger, she yelled an elongated scream and violently stabbed her hands against his chest. Surprised by that violent outburst, he stumbled backwards, losing his balance while she ran away, realising that the consequences would be disastrous for her family. However, she continued running until she almost reached the exit. Behind her, the sound of heavy military boots was amplifying. Then two claws grabbed her shoulder, stopping her abruptly and turning her around. A shriek of pain and frustration escaped her throat.

"Not so fast, you dirty slut," grunted the creepy man, panting like a locomotive. She wasn't afraid any more, but angry, starting to fight off.

"Is there anything I can do for you?" The harsh voice came from behind her back. Visser let her go.

She turned her head toward a tall man approaching with great strides, recognising Bram's friend who'd always ensured that they could have some undisturbed happy moments in their personalised paradise. He didn't look at her, gazed sternly toward the major, in whose eyes she could read immense anger.

" What's going on here, Major?"

"Get out of here, or you'll regret it," shouted Cees Visser furiously to the non-commissioned officer, who didn't seem intimidated.

"I know the lady, Major, and I'm afraid I've got witnessed a rape attempt. I am wrong, I hope."

The major started to calm down already. "Attempted rape?" He reacted astonished. "How dare you? This woman is just upset because we can't save her family, which I've tried to make clear to her as carefully as possible. But she's got hysterical. God knows what's going through her mind."

They were talking in Dutch, ignoring she'd been an interpreter for the three Dutch battalions, learning the language as well, although Bram had taught her the most of it.

"No problem, gentlemen," she interrupted in English. "I'm going to join my parents. I've done here."

The major grinned widely. "Well, I'll gladly take you to the gate."

Zumra nodded at Bram's friend and rushed toward the gate. What else could she do? Visser said something to the soldiers, on which one of them opened the gate ajar. But while she was joining her parents, thinking she got rid of that jerk, she saw him heading toward a group of uniformed Serbs. While she was explaining the situation to her family, she saw the Major come over accompanied by two grim-looking Serbs. They halted in front of them.

"Follow us," the tallest soldier said.

When they didn't react immediately, the soldier slapped her father in his back. He started to move, and to her surprise, Major Visser followed. She had always known that some Blue Helmets were Serbian-minded, admiring the great warrior Mladic. Now she got proof of it.

One Serbian soldier walked in front, the other at the rear, next to the major. They marched along the fence toward a large white house three hundred metres ahead. Reaching the house, she observed countless men hanging out of the window on the first floor. Furthermore, she saw several Serbs in uniform, among them a lot of paramilitaries.

They went inside.

Men of all ages occupied the chambers downstairs, but no women. The Serbs lead them into a small room simply furnished with a table and a couple of chairs. Her eyes caught numerous dark spots on the floor and on the walls. As she got closer to the table, she discovered the same faint traces of it, sensing the smell of clotted blood, urine and faeces, although she didn't detect them anywhere.

The major forcibly dragged her sister to the table, and she tried to follow her. But the two Serbs stopped her.

The major grinned dirty.

"Are you still a virgin, little whore?" he shouted.

When he ripped Azra's clothes off the body, Zumra made an elongated cry.

Sarajevo, 9 October 2002

Zumra opened her eyes, but it remained dark. She couldn't hear anything either, but she was lying on a rough, slippery surface.

Leaves and branches.

Her head was dizzy, and she was shivering from the cold. She had no idea where she could be, nor what had happened. Moving her head in all directions, she noticed grey shadows and small lights high above her head. Unconsciously she touched her forehead and felt a thick bump.

Why am I lying among the trees? She recalled the cellar, the forest.

Her escaping. The oncoming car. She ran away. That's all her memory had to tell her. She struggled to get up, stretched her arms forward, touched a tree trunk and hugged it with both arms. For a long time, she kept standing, heavily panting and remembering she was almost naked. Her whole body was burning. She pulled the cloak straight and knocked the dirt off it.

I have to get out of here.

Looking around, she discovered a gap between the trees.

There's the road.

Stretching her arms forward, she started to move carefully with short steps, heading toward the edge of the forest. Too late she remembered that the narrow strip of grass ran downhill until the road. She struggled to stay on her feet and to halt, while two blinding cones of light were approaching. Was that the same car?

She had underestimated the slope. Her legs kept moving, and she couldn't stop, stumbling onto the road.

Squeaking brakes and slipping tyres.

Zumra's eyes got blinded. The collision was unavoidable.

I am dead.

All the memories got dark.

FORTY-ONE

GREG STONE HAD A CROSS-EYED HEADACHE. HIS EYELIDS ROSE SLOWLY, AND A milky haze replaced the darkness with a white surface. It took him some time to understand that he was staring at the ceiling. As he moved his head, the surroundings changed into a colourful carousel of images. His mind was still clouded. When finally realising he was lying on the floor next to the couch, he tried to scribble up, fighting nausea. But he fell backwards while the darkness threatened to swallow him up again. He drew a few deep breaths, opening his eyelids. But nausea remained, and his head felt as if a Japanese restaurant chef chopped onions into it.

Grabbing the couch, he crawled into a sitting position, took another deep breath and pulled himself up. Standing unsteady for a while, his hand went unconsciously to his head, where he felt a sticky bump on the left temple. He felt confused, looking dazed at the door of the landing, while memories came back in short flashes.

Where has that guy gone? Or did I have a dream?

Daria?

The gloomy fog that had enveloped his memories began to vaporise. His gaze wandered over his legs and hands, and his brain registered crusts of blood on his shoes, trousers and shirt. With such an amount of blood loss, he had to be fucking dead.

His eyes roamed across the room, and he froze. Daria lay naked outstretched on the couch with her sweatpants around her ankles. Discovering her breasts were gone, leaving a bloody mass, caused him a moment to gasp for breath. "Daria, Daria," he yelled, stumbling forward. He fell on his knees next to the couch, looking in bewilderment at a wide dark gaping wound on her neck. Tears filled his eyes as he hesitantly laid his hands on her face.

Cold skin.

The killer had almost beheaded her. Two large, glassy eyes stared at the ceiling, and her mouth gawked wide open in a last desperate cry for help before a knife cut her throat. The odour of blood was nauseating. Infinite sorrow overpowered him. His shoulders trembled as tears flowed down his cheeks. Then he saw a bloodstained butcher's knife on the rectangular coffee table. He tried to regain control over himself, think clearly. *Call the police!* His legs started moving, but on the way to the landing, he held himself back. A feeling of déjà vu made his body shiver, whereas an alarm bell sounded through his head. *Bloody hands and clothes*, he thought. *It can't be my blood, so it's hers.*

He headed back to the couch, looking around nervously. On the floor behind the sofa lay a wrench. His breath accelerated as his mind began to build up a murder pattern. *What the hell has happened?*

A whirlwind of images flashed through his mind.

Daria's voice, screaming, *'No, don't.'*

He sees a wrench in a raised hand, and everything gets foggy again.

Have I hit her? Impossible, I loved her. Damn, I have to get out of here. Perhaps the neighbours had heard something and called the police. *Damned, with all that blood on me, they'll immediately consider me as the prime suspect.*

Time was running out. He stripped himself, headed downstairs to the bathroom and took a shower. Daria's blood mingled with the gushing water, vanishing forever in the drain. After a few minutes, he rubbed himself dry, looking in the mirror above the sink. He noticed that the wound on his head was bleeding again. The cupboard contained bandages, and after making a compress, he fixed it over the deep cut. Then he took two aspirins, flushing them with water.

I must leave the country as soon as possible.

Stone headed back to his suite, where he pulled on dark sweatpants with a shirt, a cotton sweater and a coat while considering a clean-up of the living room. *The body must disappear*. He took his wallet from the bedside table, put it in his chest pocket, gazed across the room and rushed to the living room. When he stepped through the doorposts, he halted abruptly.

In front of him stood two police officers pointing a gun at him.

FORTY-TWO

LAZAR SENSED LIKE A TICKING BOMB READY TO EXPLODE. THE UNCERTAINTY MADE him angry and caused a raging headache. His head was full of swirling thoughts, bringing his mood below the freezing point.

After his conversation with Mirsad, he'd driven to Zumra's house, but neither the woman nor the children were at home. Back to his accommodation, he'd showered and slept for an hour, troubled by recurrent nightmares.

Two heads with bulging eyes roll over the bottom, trying to bite him. They have giant mouths with long sharp teeth that always open and close at a fast pace. No matter how fast he runs, the wrinkled, pale heads are rolling like bowling balls close behind him. Until he can't go any further, stopped by a tall, gloomy wall. The skulls started to transform into two bloody faces he recognised. They are laughing loud and hollow, shooting up to his throat. Sharp teeth pierce his soft flesh.

He woke up, sweat-soaked. He knew that stress could provoke nightmares but also traumatic experiences. Those ugly faces belonged to the past. But then the ringing of his phone brought him back into the present world. He picked up the call. It was the dispatching duty officer announcing him for the murder of a hooker by a foreigner. Lazar had forgotten he was also on duty that night.

Barely one hour later, leaning against the mudguard of his car, he peered toward the house where two policemen at the open front door were smoking a cigarette.

Senad came to stand near him, looking weary.

"According to the first indications, a Westerner has killed a hooker," explained Lazar curtly.

"We're short of space in the morgue," Senad answered in an ironic tone.

Lazar squeezed his lips together and made his way toward the house, chuckling on seeing the police officers extinguish their cigarettes quickly.

"Has the forensic team arrived yet?" he snarled.

The tallest nodded. "It has, and the suspect is still in the house."

Lazar climbed the five steps and went in. The hallway brought him to the lounge at the far end of the corridor. His eyes scrutinised in a few seconds the crime scene, and what he observed made him angry. The body sprawled on the couch was not yet examined by Milan Delic, while Ferid Munic and his men in protective clothing were marking all traces and items linked to the crime. The forensic photographer's camera regularly flashed. However, Lazar's attention went to the other side, where he spotted a chubby guy sitting next to a police officer. He rushed toward them with long steps.

"What does this mean?" he yelled.

The policeman looked puzzled. "Chief Inspector, this is a Belgian citizen who works for EuPol. We found him here, next to the body. I think he was about to flee."

"Fine, and what's he doing here? Do you show him all the evidence we are collecting?" replied Lazar, staring grimly at the Belgian suspect.

The policeman didn't answer.

Lazar studied the tired facial expression of the Belgian. *Fifty,* he thought.

"Who are you?" he asked in English, while Senad joined him.

"Greg Stone. Who's asking?" His voice was shaking and aggressively.

"I am Chief inspector Lazar Magas, and this is Inspector Senad Mujdza, Homicide Department. Who's this woman on the couch?"

"Daria Bazila, my girlfriend."

"Why did you kill her?"

Stone's eyes opened wide in astonishment. *Surprise or fear*?

"I didn't," he retorted. "Someone has knocked me down, killing Daria after that."

"Who?"

"I haven't got a good look at him..."

Lazar nodded and turned to face the policeman.

"Take the suspect to the main building and lock him up," he said coldly. "Give him water and food if he asks for it, and have a doctor examining his head injury. I shall interrogate him myself later on. No one else has to be allowed to speak him. Am I clear enough?"

The man nodded, grabbing the Belgian rather harshly at his shoulder and made his way out. Lazar headed back to his friend, who'd started making sketches of the crime scene. He told him he was going to take a look around, pulling on his medical gloves and blue paper booties.

First, he examined the kitchen. Then he started a search through the house, beginning with the attic. After that, he entered the small suite underneath which was uninhabited. He descended to the ground-level suite, where the Belgian and his girlfriend had lived, inspected the place, checking all the cupboards. However, he couldn't find anything relevant.

Reaching the lowest level in the basement, he paused in the dark corridor, gazing at the back door ten metres ahead. The house counted two basement levels, which together made up the difference in height between the front and the rear of the building. He walked toward the door, pulled the handle, and the door swung open. It wasn't locked. He stepped outside and stood on a landing from where a concrete staircase descended until the road beneath.

His anger started to percolate. Hoping to resolve that case in the next few hours, he was looking for additional elements. They had the perpetrator in custody, the victim and probably also the murder weapon. The perpetrator worked in the Glass Tower and would get international protection, which meant he would be deported to his country. But all of a sudden, he hesitated. The open basement door might be a problem and a way out for a good lawyer. Or the case was not evident at all.

Nevertheless, the police officers had caught the perpetrator of the crime scene. As long as Stone's embassy and EuPol did not intervene, he would be in charge of the investigation, especially since the victim was a foreign woman, whether or not illegally in the country.

A noise on his right side made him look up, and behind the neighbour's window, he discerned light. He rushed into the house, ran up the stairs, hurried outside and knocked on the neighbour's front door.

Seconds later, the door opened, and he stood in front of a tall man with a black beard and not too friendly features.

"Chief inspector Lazar. I've seen the lights on, so I thought you wouldn't mind answering a few questions," he said, showing his most charming smile.

"Yes, it's a bit late," the man answered. "But if I can help... What do you want to know?" The bearded man didn't let him in.

Lazar waved to the left. "Do you know these neighbours?"

"Of course, it's hard to overlook such a handsome girl."

"Do you know that handsome man, too?"

"Greg and Daria, nice people, chief inspector."

"Did you hear anything unusual tonight?"

The man hesitated. Citizens don't tell much to the police. Hearing, seeing and shutting up. But those neighbours were foreigners.

The man nodded thoughtfully. "Yes, I've heard her scream. Two, three times and then it was quiet again."

"What time was it?"

"I didn't pay attention to it. It was so short, nothing to worry about. Might have been between nine and ten p.m. Did something happen?"

Lazar ignored the question. "Do they fight a lot?"

"They don't. Sometimes Greg and Daria sit on the terrace just like two love birds. At first, I believed that he paid her for sex. But they are in love. Daria has talked to my wife a few times. She said she would be married soon. Did something happen to?"

Lazar interrupted him, making a waving gesture. "I can't say anything, but Daria has got an accident. Have you seen visitors here around 10 p.m. or earlier? Or any suspicious people walking behind the house?"

"Yes, around 6 p.m. I saw someone coming out of the house. I'd never seen that guy before."

"Can you describe him?"

The man paused. "Pretty great, sporty look. Long black hairs in a tail and a circle beard."

Lazar got interrupted by his cell phone ringing.

"Thanks for the information," Lazar said. "That will be all for now." He headed away from the house and checked his phone: Marco Kebo, a friend who practised as a doctor in the City Hospital, Emergency Department.

He picked the call. "Marco, what a surprise, are you all right?"

There was a pause that didn't predict any good.

"Lazar, are you still with Zumra?" Marco asked.

Marco Kebo was one of the few acquaintances he'd introduced to Zumra.

"Yes, what a question," Lazar returned.

"Uh, do you know where she's hanging around?"

"What do you mean?" Lazar began to get impatient.

"Zumra has been brought in here."

"What? What happened?"

"She has been hit by a car."

"Where?"

"In the north of town, somewhere near Vogosca."

"Her condition?" His voice was shaking.

"She's in a terrible state."

"I'll be right there."

Lazar put the phone in his pocket and paced with significant steps into the house to get Senad.

Three minutes later both left the crime scene.

The staccato of their footsteps echoed through the long, wide corridor. Lazar was glad that his curious friend hadn't been asking any questions. Hesitantly he faced for seconds the door number 111, took a deep breath, opened it and entered an ether-smelling room. With fear in his heart, Lazar glanced toward the bed alongside the window and got shocked, seeing the mummy on it. With a few significant steps, he reached the bed.

Her head was wrapped in bandages, letting only her eyes, nose and mouth free. In her arm was a small tube connected to a plastic bag hanging from a metal L-shaped stand. The upper body had several electrical wires connected to an irregular squeaking cardiograph.

He swallowed.

"Zumra," he whispered, leaning over her. His eyes moistened. "What happened to you?" He carefully touched her arm, which was lying alongside her body.

Senad kept staying at the door, while an older man in a white dress entered the room. "Lazar," the man said softly, "there's nothing you can do here. She's in bad shape as you can see, you cannot question her."

Lazar nodded, wordless moving out of the room, followed by Senad and the doctor. Then he halted, turned toward Marco and asked about her general condition.

"She has a severe concussion, so we'll have to wait for the night. A car has hit her, and fortunately, the driver has brought her here immediately. If he had called the police or the emergency service, waiting on the place, she probably would be dead by now."

Lazar looked at him with almost glassy eyes. "Where's the driver?"

"He's sitting with a nurse in the nurse's coffee shop. He's very impressed. Don't be too hard on him, Lazar, he saved her life."

Lazar started to move when Marco Kebo cleared his throat. "Lazar, there's more."

Lazar turned around, narrowing his eyes. "What do you mean, Marco?"

"Uh, concussion and the bruises on her legs were caused by accident. But she has also been tortured."

"What, who, where exactly did the accident happen?"

"Somewhere in the vicinity of Vogosca, that's all I know."

"Damned, what was she doing there?"

"She was only wearing a cloak with nothing underneath. Her genitals are in an ugly state. I think she fled."

"Thank you, Marco, do your best with her. I'll talk to the driver now." Lazar was familiar with the city hospital and headed toward the nurse's coffee room. He walked to the middle of the corridor, knocked on a door and entered in a scantily furnished space. There were four chairs, two worn-out fauteuils, a long couch and a small fridge on which stood a coffee-cycling machine. A nurse sat on the couch next to an older, unshaven man wearing worn pants and a thick sweater.

"Stay seated," Lazar said. "I'm chief inspector Magas, and that's my assistant Mujdza." He sat down at the table and looked at the man who seemed upset. "You've found the woman?"

"Chief Inspector," he reacted nervously. "I swear to you, I am not to blame. She unexpectedly appeared in front of my car, and I couldn't stop. I brought her here immediately."

"You have done the right thing." Lazar gave him a jovial smile.

"According to the doctor, you've saved her life. What's your name, and where do you live?"

"Muhammad Filipovic, I am a farmer, and I live with my wife and two sons just outside Vogosca. I was on my way home when the woman suddenly came from between the trees, running down the hill. I thought she was going to stop, but she ran right in front of me. I barely touched her, but her head was smashed on a stone. She was heavily bleeding, and I put her in my car. I drove here as fast as I could."

"Have you seen other people around? Other cars or pedestrians?"

"No, it was dark, I really..."

Lazar made a waving gesture.

"All right, Mr Filipovic," he said. "The woman came running out of the woods, I understand. Do other people live there?"

The man shook his head, his hands fidgeting in his lap.

But Lazar wasn't interested in him. He knew the Vogosca region. The further north, the denser the forests and the worse the roads. Somewhere there was a house where somebody had taken Zumra.

Loverboy took Zumra to the hotel room, Mirsad Pejic had told him.

But who was the man who'd hit her, taking her to that hidden house?

Thursday, 10 October 2002

FORTY-THREE

ALWAYS BE PREPARED FOR THE UNEXPECTED. THAT'S HOW MEN LIKE HIM SURVIVED. He woke up at the slightest noise and only needed a few seconds to respond to any threat. Again, the light buzzing of his mobile phone had awakened him. No danger, this time. Months of survival exercises in hostile environments had sharpened his senses to a level that ordinary people thought impossible. Only a few managed to survive a year in inaccessible areas full of natural hazards, hunted down by assassins. He was the only one in his group who'd survived the hard tests, having had to eliminate three hunters in the process. The brotherhood gave him the name Brother Lynx because he was able to approach his target and kill it before it even sensed his presence. Since last year he was enjoying the full confidence of the Council that assigned him with the most challenging tasks. Precisely because he had the art of staying unnoticed.

After his last assignment, he should have left the country for a compulsory training period to refresh the acquired qualities weakened by a quiet life in civilisation. But the Council had decided otherwise. After the execution, he'd been tasked to take up his position again. All that went through his head before he picked up his mobile phone from the bedside table.

Lodbrok and Aslaug's son must fly to Odin immediately. Return to the protected issue afterwards.

Although he knew the meaning of those words, he typed quickly:

Request ACK.

This new task surprised him. It was the first time he received an assignment in the middle of the night. *It must be an emergency. What about my replacement?* The Dragon had stopped spitting fire, and the situation was back to normal. After a killer mission, an executioner usually had to leave the country. But after this second cleanup mission, he had to stay. Yet he didn't leave traces, and there were no witnesses. Unlikely that his current identity had been compromised. But a second execution increased the chances of being discovered.

He'd never thought that Lodbrok's son would cause instability. *Don't ask any questions*. He belonged to the elite, and would never challenge an order.

The New World Order was not a fabrication, as some YouTube movies suggested. President Bush had introduced it in several speeches. Unfortunately, the world wasn't ready for that.

Ordinary people saw *Evil* as something abstract, a political fabrication to justify war against America's enemies. At the same time, the colleagues continued to worry about their positions of power. Society was not yet ready for the consequences of all these necessary measures, while human rights organisations were too naive to face the truth. You fight terrorism neither with words nor dialogue, the novices were taught; no slogans, but action. The war against *Evil* was real and did not only take place on the battlefield.

The revelations in social media that the Fifth Column existed disrupted European politicians who voted repressive laws in some countries making such proclamations punishable. And the enemy was cunning. The leaders of the Free Islamic State were aware that powerful men had seen through their plans and launched a counter-offensive. The Secret War was no fairy tale. Yet multinationals, billionaires and the media kept repeating that the Fifth Column was another racist slogan of right-wing extremist parties and their militants. Moreover, they furiously denied the growing influence of Islam in the West.

Brother Lynx knew that 9/11 was not a coincidence, but the beginning of a new era and he was proud to belong to the elite that fought *Evil*. Nemesis Brotherhood provided balance, even though it had to use extreme methods to fight extremism. Multicultural society had only a chance when extremism disappeared.

The display lit up, and he read the confirmation. Lodbrok's son could have been allied, but he'd become an obstacle. A high priority task.

It made him sad that he had to sacrifice this man to maintain stability. The Dragon had been a bad man, giving him a pleasure to kill him. A simple task.

But his new target was difficult to approach.

For a short time, he would need a new identity, which would also have to change his appearance.

Soon, a good man would die.

FORTY-FOUR

BRAM WOKE UP. DESPITE THE CLOSED CURTAINS, THE STARS AND THE MOON provided enough light to vaguely distinguish the surroundings. He recognised walls, a door, cupboards and a coffee table. *Safe house*. At first, he thought he'd been dreaming until he heard another grinding sound coming from outside. *An animal?* But wild animals are afraid of people.

Rarely do they approach inhabited places so close. He listened, pricked up his ears to catch the slightest noise outside. It hadn't been his imagination, muffled voices along the rear façade alarmed him. He crawled up, got dressed, took his gun holster from the bedside table, fastened it to his waist belt and paced to the command post. On one of the monitors, he saw two dark figures walking along the back façade, observing the barred windows. He hoped that Timka or one of the children wouldn't wake up and switch on the light. If the men outside were common burglars, maybe he could scare them. But if they belonged to General Flower's gang, it might cause problems.

Both men wore balaclavas and seemed to know the house inhabited. One of them studied the camera. Bram cursed; The front and rear doors contained a particular bank vault system employing three twenty centimetres long rods entering the wall, while all windows got fenced off with iron bars, sufficient robust against ordinary burglar tools. But if those guys were after Timka's son, they could use explosives, grenades or worse. But they weren't there just to kill the boy, they also wanted to make his body disappear.

Arson to smoke them out? *If only Edhem were here*. Five o'clock. What to do? Should he call the other house and ask for backup? Meanwhile, Tim Watson had to be back. There were two more girls in that house, sent by the International Organisation for Migration, under protection by Tim Watson and Louis Lejeune, a retired Belgian paratrooper who lived in Sarajevo.

The men at the back door moved around the house. He zoomed in and discovered that they were holding a gun with a silencer. These were not ordinary burglars. They paced to the garage, examined the iron gate, consulted briefly, turned around, walked along the sidewall and eventually stopped at the front door. After staring some time at the camera's, they finally walked to the road where they took off their balaclavas. However, the distance was too great to recognise their faces. Shortly after that, they evaporated in the morning twilight.

Bram sighed, swivelled his chair and jumped up. His hand stopped halfway down his waist as he started laughing. Timka stood in shorts and a nightdress between the doorposts.

"Oh, sorry," she said, frightened. "I've got heard a noise and... I really couldn't sleep." Her eyes wandered to the monitors.

"Here you are safe," Bram said reassuringly.

"Is Hadar really in danger?"

"He is, but we'll do everything we can to catch these guys. I owe Mayke that. Flower's men have probably found you because of me."

It was already six o'clock, too late to go to sleep. Anyway, this nocturnal visit had disturbed Bram more than he was willing to admit.

"Would you like a coffee?" he asked.

"Yes, please."

They strolled to the kitchen where Timka settled in a chair, while Bram started to make coffee.

"I've heard men talking outside," Timka remarked.

"Probably burglars. Don't worry, I promise that I'll do everything I can to protect the kids. Azra is my daughter, you know."

The conversation silenced. It had been a long time since Bram had found a woman so handsome. He watched her face. She looked at him for a moment before she averted her gaze. What did his future look like now? Jasmina had a boyfriend. He didn't know how he would react to her or how she would respond to him. Maybe she didn't want to see him any more. If she denied his fatherhood, it would complicate the situation.

Timka glanced at him again.

Bram had poured coffee and sat down across from her. He gave her a comforting smile. "Have you ever thought about living an ordinary life?"

She snorted with indignation. "Do you think I didn't try that? I've done every possible job. As soon as an employer realises that I am a single mother, he wants me in his bed. I got raped twice. When I met Tommy Branson, I thought I'd found my dream prince. He played with my son, brought presents, took me out to dinner. Since long I hadn't visited a restaurant. I introduced him to Zumra, uh Jasmina and he continued playing the kind benefactor until he'd collected our weaknesses. Then he forced us to become escorts. At the same time, he became the intermediary, paying well. Now he sends us a message to make an appointment. Then he comes picking up one of us at the cemetery next to the football stadium. If we wish, he'll take us back there too. But most of the time we take a taxi."

Bram laid his hand on hers. "I'm not judging you, Timka, I know the situation here. Not at all favourable for a young single mother, since there are more women than men. I'm convinced that you've done the best for the kids. I can tell by their behaviour." He felt her hand slightly shaken, but she didn't pull it away.

"When we've earned enough, we might leave the country, visiting Suada." Her eyes became moist. "No, that would be a bad idea."

"Everything will be fine. You can count on me."

He stood up, poured coffee and went to look at the screens. After convincing himself that everything was quiet, he grabbed his phone and called Edhem. This time his friend answered.

"Are you all right?" asked Edhem worried.

Bram gave a short account of the men he'd observed around the shelter.

"Ordinary burglars," assumed Edhem. "Anyway, I've got a few urgent matters to deal with, and then I'll come to you. It might be late. That's how long you have to survive."

"Very funny, I'll try."

"I'll take you to my dwell. Besides, I've picked up Loverboy's trail."

"Be careful."

"He may give me answers. Don't let visitors in."

The connection went dead.

Bram paced back to the kitchen.

"We'll stay here until Edhem is back," he said. "Something tells me that Loverboy won't bother you any more, Edhem found his track."

Timka raised her eyebrows but said nothing.

"There's nothing else to do here," he said. "You could use some rest. I'll stay awake." Bram emptied his coffee and glanced at his watch.

She gave him a grateful smile, got up and strolled back to her room.

Bram rejected the idea of getting his laptop out of the car. There was no internet, nor telephone in the house. Everyone at *Last Hope* used cell phones. If necessary, he could always walk to the other shelter, where he could get on the internet.

A barely audible buzz tone came from the other room. Bram rushed to the observation post, fearing the worse. On one of the monitors, he recognised Tim Watson. *Holy shit, what's he doing here?* How could Tim know? Not even Winston knew he was here. Why did Tim come to visit the house?

He must have taken the keys from my desk.

Watson was already managing the second lock. He didn't once look up at the camera.

Bram rushed to Timka's bedroom where he found her awake. She flew up, startled. Next to her, Azra was still sleeping with a blissful smile on her face.

"Someone's coming," he murmured. "Stay in the room and don't make any noise." Without waiting for an answer, he shut the door. Hearing a slight scratching sound, he ran on his toes to the kitchen where Watson already was inside, closing the back door very carefully.

"Hey, what are you doing here?" asked Bram vehemently.

Tim turned around. He was a friendly-looking man with cut short dark blond hair and blue eyes.

Tim seemed astonished. "Bram, you here?"

"What do you want here?" Bram looked him straight in the eye.

Tim's features changed. "Oh, you're not aware. We need to bring in a new protégée. There's no place downhill any more." He meant the other safe house. "I've come to check that everything is okay here."

They shook hands, and Tim settled down on the large couch. "I didn't know you were here."

"Temporarily, my house is no longer safe. Have a drink?"

"A beer, please."

Tim was wearing khaki pants, desert shoes, khaki sweater and a water-repellent fleece jacket with Sherpa lining. *He has come through the wood.* Bram went to get two cans of beer in the kitchen. After handing Tim a tin, he sat down across to him.

"Does Winston know you're here?" asked Tim with a straight smile.

Bram scratched through his beard and took a sip of beer.

"I didn't have time to inform him yet," he said. "What about Emma's kidnapping?"

Gathering his thoughts, he sipped his beer. *After entering the kitchen, he closed the door very carefully. Holy shit, he knew I was here.*

Winston had told him that Tim had been injured on the head. But he couldn't see a single injury. Besides, Tim's voice sounded unusually high. Was he prejudiced because Tim hadn't protected Emma? No, he sensed something was wrong, and his features must have betrayed him. Angry at himself, he stared into the dark barrel of a gun with a silencer.

"Don't do anything stupid, Bram," Tim said. "I know you're carrying a weapon. Put it carefully on the table."

The words sounded icy, and Bram realised that this man, despite the stunning resemblance, was not Tim Watson.

FORTY-FIVE

LAZAR HAD GATHERED AND BRIEFED THE INTERVENTION TEAM IN THE PARKING LOT behind the police building. "Surround the house, but Senad and I will politely knock on the door first," he'd emphasised. "You'll only use firearms when the suspect opens fire."

Lazar wanted to do it peacefully. But it would be irresponsible to underestimate the suspect. Too many people already died in this case. Bram Ruyter was a trained infantryman, who'd been in Srebrenica during the big killing. That made him a dangerous suspect.

An hour later, ten armed men in blue uniforms, bulletproof vests with helmet and heavy shoes surrounded the house. After everyone got in position, Lazar nodded to Senad. They climbed the stairs, stepped on the platform and halted in front of the door. Lazar contemplated for a brief moment grabbing his gun, but in the end, he dropped the idea and knocked on the door.

It remained silent inside.

He knocked again.

No reaction.

Ten automatic rifles were aimed at the doors and windows. But no one tried to leave the house.

Lazar glanced at his partner. "Let's do it."

Senad's features were getting tense.

They grabbed their guns, while Senad made a big step back. His right foot shot forward and hit the wood under the door handle. The door swung open, and Lazar entered the hall where he perceived two doors. He gestured Senad to the right door as he stopped in front of the left. They opened at the same time, gun at shoulder height and lurching forward.

Nothing happened.

"Safe," yelled Lazar.

"Safe," shouted Senad.

Lazar stood inside the lounge and watched to another door in the middle of the right wall, assuming it led to the hallway. He headed back to the hall and joined his friend in the corridor.

Senad glanced up, kicked open the first door on the right and jumped into the room. "Empty," he shouted. Then he checked the bathroom and the second bedroom while Lazar was covering him.

The house was empty.

Lazar felt disappointed and angry. "Nobody slept in the beds," he said.

"Our bird has flown," replied Senad, checking the wardrobe.

"Without carrying luggage? No. I think he's gone into hiding with someone, whether deliberately or not. Maybe he's taking a week's vacation with a girl somewhere on the coast."

They searched the whole house but found nothing suspicious. When Lazar slammed the fridge, his phone buzzed. He read Egzon on display and picked up the call.

"A murder at the *Princip Bridge*," groaned Egzon without introduction.

"I'm too busy," Lazar growled. "We now know the man behind the Besic murder, but he's on the run. Why don't you give the new case to Ejub?"

"The new victim is Anel Dzeko, Emir Besic's best friend. Your case."

Lazar froze, holding his breath for a moment. *How does Egzon know that name?* Had anyone in his team talked too much?

"Is the body at the place where we found Emir Besic?" he asked.

"Close. The victim is an IT specialist employed by EuPol. The case stinks, Lazar, I must insist on a detailed report this time."

Did the Chief want him to inform that he was aware of what he hadn't written in his report? A warning? A threat?

"All right, I'm on my way," he said. Egzon hung up.

He felt gloomy because he hadn't given Anel Dzeko protection.

But the fact that Egzon Subic knew where Dzeko had worked, gave him goose bumps.

FORTY-SIX

IVAR RAGNARSSON SAT BOLT STRAIGHT, SORTING OUT HIS THOUGHTS. HE wondered if he shouldn't have fired his deputy immediately. That Belgian

IT guy made him worry; Stone wasn't going to capitulate. On the contrary, he had already launched a counteroffensive. The Swede let out a faint sigh and scratched through his short hair. What did the French ambassador's representative have in store for him? His secretary had announced the man via the intercom. Earlier, someone from that embassy had informed him that a member of the ambassador's staff urgently wished to catch up with him on a sensitive subject. Normand?

A young man with a briefcase stepped into his office. He was wearing an anthracite-coloured suit. Very elegant.

Ivar didn't know what to think of his visitor. Strange that the French ambassador had insisted on this meeting. An attempt to rehabilitate Montpetit?

"Louis Grandjean," the man introduced himself nearly inaudible.

Ivar came from behind his desk, and they shook hands. "Have a seat." He walked back to his comfortable leather office chair, which colleagues mockingly called *The Iron Throne*. Scrutinising his visitor, he started to get uncomfortable. He glanced at a friendly face with short black hair, bright blue eyes, strikingly long black eyelashes and thin eyebrows. Friendly features. But those icy blue eyes were disturbing him. They seemed so unreal, numb.

Had Montpetit introduced a complaint to his ambassador? Ivar was already sorry for having agreed to this meeting. He was the highest police authority in Bosnia to whom the EU Council had given carte blanche, and no one could have forced him to meet that man. He distrusted politicians and remained vigilant, especially since his government had informed him that someone was trying to get his post. The French?

"I have a busy schedule," Ivar said reluctantly.

The Frenchman kept smiling. "I'll be as succinct as possible, sir." His voice sounded like that of a chain-smoker. But Ivar's sharp gaze had already noticed that Grandjean's fingers showed no traces of nicotine. And his handshake had been particularly firm.

"I'm coming to discuss the Deputy Commissioner issue," said Grandjean.

Ivar narrowed his eyes. "You are a direct employee of the ambassador, aren't you?"

"I'm a legal advisor, sir. We are worried about a very delicate matter, sir. EuPol's future is at stake." His English was impeccable.

"So important that Deputy Commissioner Montpetit should not be part of this meeting?"

"We'd appreciate it if the deputy commissioner wouldn't hear about this meeting."

"Did Montpetit complain to the ambassador?"

"Not at all. My visit concerns Dragon Borjan."

Ivar shivered. The image of the vanished Borjan flashed through his head.

That man who wasn't registered anywhere made him nervous. He didn't want any spies in his organisation.

"Dragon is Montpetit's direct employee," he retorted.

"Not quite correct, sir. The French authorities have called him back."

"I didn't know that."

"Disciplinary measure." Louis paused a moment. "Unfortunately, we can't find him. Also strange that we've found all his gear in his lodging whereas his car is missing. We don't want Montpetit's reputation got tarnished, because our government has big plans for him."

Big plans? Ivar wondered which influential circles were protecting Montpetit. The man was undoubtedly intelligent, but also a lousy commander. He stood out with ill-considered decisions that he usually had to rectify later on. Grandjean did not seem to know that he'd given Montpetit an ultimatum.

Ivar chuckled. "Are we talking about the same person?"

Grandjean ignored the irony. "What problems does Monsieur Montpetit have with our English allies? I've heard that a certain Mycroft Follum doesn't make it easy for him."

"I am not aware of any problems. I thought we're going to talk about Dragon Borjan."

Grandjean leaned in. "That's right. Did you know that Borjan killed several Serbs in Mitrovica?"

The emphasis on Mitrovica hadn't escaped Ragnarsson's attention. He withheld his breath for a second. Montpetit had dishonourably discharged Greg Stone based on slander, without proof, and Ivar had relied on Montpetit's judgement until Stone's letter had opened his eyes. Ivar could have withdrawn his decision, but Montpetit already had informed Special Envoy of the Secretary-General Klein who wanted the Belgian IT to disappear from Sarajevo as soon as possible. Nobody refuted this American cowboy. It was also clear to him why Montpetit feared the British: they knew about the Mitrovica-affair.

"I still don't see any connection," parried Ivar in a grumpy tone. That slimy smile on Grandjean's face irritated him, especially those icy eyes which were contradicting the friendly mask. Suddenly he wondered what position Louis held in the embassy.

"Montpetit knew Dragon's victims," Louis continued softly.

This bastard knows it and is waiting for my reaction.

Grandjean took his suitcase.

"I'm going to show you several objects. Please, examine them. Then I'll ask you a few questions." He got up and prepared to step around the desk. "May I?"

Ivar moved his chair back, and although he wanted to get rid of Louis, he got curious.

Louis put the briefcase on the tabletop, opened the locks and raised the lid. On the bottom lay photographs and an unusually large pen.

Grandjean sat down again. "Look carefully at the pictures. Then examine that extraordinary pen. Maybe you've seen it before. Take your time."

Ivar remained motionless for seconds as he stared at the contents of the suitcase. Then he bowed forward and grabbed the five photos format A4. He immediately recognised the two young men in the police uniform. There was also a photograph showing the barkeeper, his bodyguard and a young woman.

What game is he playing? "Where did you get these photos?"

"Found in Dragon's house."

"Who's this woman?" Ivar knew who she was; she also figured in the photos Interpol had sent him.

"A whore who slept with the bar owner. They all are dead, except the bodyguard."

Then Ivar's eye focused on the writing pen, raising his eyebrows. "What does this thing have to do with the case?"

"Found in Dragon's apartment. It has something special, but maybe you know what it is. You're a policeman, aren't you?" It sounded challenging.

Ivar hesitated, mistrusted riddles and mysteries.

"Are you playing the game of *who's the smartest*?" he asked.

The Frenchman smiled triumphantly. "I resolved the mystery in ten seconds. But I'm not a policeman."

Ivar laid the pictures back, grabbed the glass cylinder and carefully turned it between his fingers as if he handled a poisonous snake. Except for the shape, he discovered nothing unusual. Transparent with a continuous tube in the centre. He squeezed his lips together and pressed the end. A bright blue flash made him squeeze his eyes, while an electric shock flashed through his immense body. He let out a short cry, dropping the pen in the case.

"An electric discharge," he shouted with horror. "You son of a bitch." He looked furiously at his thumb where the current had penetrated his body in search of a grounding. There was a red lump.

"You could have warned me, damn it." He sounded outraged.

The Frenchman laughed modestly. "Then you wouldn't have pushed. Did you see what happened?"

Ivar looked into the briefcase and nodded. "A needle instead of a writing tip."

"Correct, a syringe to be correct. But don't panic, our forensic guy has removed the poison." Grandjean stood up, slammed the briefcase and sat down again, pulling.

"I wanted to convince myself that you didn't know this object." He gave Ivar a guilty smile. "Dragon used such a pen to kill his victims. The electric shock mechanism should keep curious people at bay. To deactivate the needle, you must turn the upper part of the shaft."

"You don't buy such a thing in a department store, I suppose."

"No. We are suspecting Dragon to have been working for some multinational agency. That's why we called him back. We fear that he was preparing to kill someone in the headquarters."

"Here? But he's gone, you said."

"We discovered that the bodyguard on one of those photos has been visiting Sarajevo. We think he might have avenged his friend the barkeeper in Mitrovica. If so, we'll probably never see Dragon again."

"And who was Dragon's target?"

Louis shrugged.

Ivar Ragnarsson still couldn't understand. An unbelievable story, but who would believe what happened in Mitrovica?

"Am I the target?"

"No. We believe it's a politician."

"What's the real reason for your visit here?" Ivar raised his voice.

Louis kept glancing at him with an engaging smile. "As I've said, it's an internal French affair. Our ambassador wanted to know whether you're involved or not. You aren't, and that's reassuring. But I have a warning, sir. You do not know your subordinates as well as you think. Think about Montpetit; you're aware of what happened to him in Mitrovica. But you only see the tip of the iceberg. Well, we would hate it to question your integrity publicly. I hope we can count on your discretion, sir. Mr Klein wouldn't like to see diplomatic complications arising between two major European nations just before EuPol takes over IPTF's role."

The voice of the slimy Frenchman had a threatening undertone. Ivar didn't like it. Although he was the autocrat of all international police observers, he depended on Mr Klein. Kicking him on the toes could be dangerous for his career. He thought about what had happened to Kathryn Bolkovac.

"All right, if that's all, I'm busy here..."

"Sir, it's been a pleasure. I will indeed praise your cooperation when I report to my ambassador and Mr Klein."

Was this guy sent by the French Embassy or by Klein? This ill-mannered Texas diplomat was his immediate superior, but he distrusted him just as he distrusted all politicians.

Both men stood up and shook hands. Grandjean took his suitcase and turned to face Ivar. "I know the way," he said. "Your secretary will take me safely at the guardhouse."

Ivar sat down again, looking at the door.

Why this staging? The whole performance had seemed so unrealistic to him. In Sweden, they called him the Scandinavian Sherlock Holmes because he'd solved all his cases before he started an international career.

Did he get what he searched? Grandjean kept intriguing him. He'd behaved like a magician. Damned, that was it. To create an illusion, you must create a distraction. But what trick had Grandjean been showing him?

Get everything straight. Ivar had known everything Louis had told him. He hadn't provided any useful information to that man either. But the self-satisfied grin on Louis's effeminate face had suggested the opposite.

What did I give him?

What has been the purpose of the photographs? He knew the depicted people, and Louis knew that; he hadn't asked any questions about the actors. So why had he shown those pictures?

The photos are unimportant.

The pen? No, he'd never seen it before.

Why did Louis want to know?

Damned, that's what he wanted me to believe.

Photos and writing pen, the magic trick, and he had fallen for it.

To arouse my curiosity.

He shivered as he began to understand the trick. Sweat started to pearl on his forehead. *The pictures had to distract me.* The pen was the trick.

An innocent but painful electric shock that caused him to release the pen. The lump on his thumb had already got his attention, whereas Louis left his office almost unnoticed. He had been happy to get rid of this arrogant Frenchman.

His breathing became heavier.

I must recall that guy. Call security.

The lump had not been caused by the discharge, but by a tiny needle. Ivar felt his heart beating in his neck. A haze appeared over his eyes. His brain sent his hands to his eyes, but his muscles refused to obey. Everything in the room became blurred.

That son of a bitch had got what he searched.

At that moment, he stopped thinking.

FORTY-SEVEN

LAZAR SLALOMED BETWEEN POLICE CARS AND STOPPED WHERE HE'D PARKED LAST Tuesday. As surveillance vehicles were blocking all roads to the *Princip Bridge*, the crime scene got cordoned with plastic ribbons by two police officers. Two other patrolmen hold the growing mob and journalists outside the securitised perimeter.

They got out and silently moved side by side toward the bridge. While walking, Lazar scrutinised the growing mob that the police authoritatively was keeping outside the demarcated perimeter. *There's an improvement.*

Near the bridge, two foreign police officers were observing the forensic guys working on the grass strip along the bank where a torn plastic bag contained a dark mass.

The corpus.

Lazar saw Senad grabbing his notebook, and he rushed to Milan Delic, glancing at the noisy mob on the other side of the ribbon.

"Have you found anything of interest? I suppose you've identified the body," he asked.

The crouched man next to the body didn't even gaze up as he said, "According to his identity papers, his name is Anel Dzeko. The bullet entered the skull from behind."

At that moment, a woman and a man, wearing the British flag on the sleeves of their light-blue uniform, approached. Lazar recognised the two foreign observers he'd never met before.

"Superintendent Brice and Harington," snarled the man in English.

Lazar ignored the outstretched hand. "Chief Inspector Magas," he retorted in his language, knowing that numerous International Police observers mastered the local language. "What can I do for you?"

Harington lifted an eyebrow. "The Commissioner has instructed us to assist your Homicide Department in its investigations." Harington, proving he understood the local language well, was tall and lean with typical British features. His partner was a woman with pronounced male features, short-cut hair, crooked nose, whiskers and missing breasts. Both wore their national uniforms in combination with the blue EuPol police hat.

Lazar gave him a stern look. "Your commissioner's not my boss, guys. My assistants are as capable as the EU's. Anyway, as long as you don't get in my way, you can observe from a safe distance." Without given the arrogant Harington time to counter, he headed to the dead body.

"Do you have an idea about the time of death?" he asked Milan.

"Between midnight and two o'clock. The *rigor mortis* is almost complete," replied Milan.

"Got he killed here?"

"No. The perpetrators wrapped the corps in these plastic bags and dumped it somewhere upstream in the river. The current carried the parcel to the bridge where it got stuck on a pile of stones."

"Who found the body?"

"An old man walking his dog; the animal made the discovery."

"Are there any other witnesses?"

"Ask Ferid, he arrived first."

"Thank you."

Lazar trudged toward Ferid, who was giving instructions to the forensic photographer.

"Do you have anything special?" asked he, looking around.

The technician shook his head. “The victim’s pockets are empty.” He coughed in his hand. “Not exactly, just a wallet with some money and his identity papers in it.”

“No keys?”

“No.”

“Odd.”

Farther on, the British were still watching the scene. Lazar grinned, knowing they had to avoid provocation. He turned to Senad.

“Isn’t it strange that the victim neither has his house nor car keys?”

Senad raised his eyebrows. “Maybe he got murdered at home.”

“I doubt. Please call the registration office and ask for Anel’s car licence plate number.”

“I’ve got the results of the Bogusevac murders brought to your office,” Ferid said without glancing up.

Lazar thanked, turned around and walked back to the pathologist, still examining the corps. He cleared his throat and asked, “When will I get the results of the autopsies in the other case?”

“I’ve sent already my first results,” answered Milan gruffly.

“Hi Lazar, I’ve got the licence plate,” called Senad out from the bridge.

Lazar automatically raised his hand, but his thoughts were elsewhere. He had a bad gut feeling, fearing more killings. His eyes went across the river, roaming the house blocks. *Anel died around midnight. At home?* The crime scene wouldn't reveal any further secrets. He turned around, beckoned Senad and walked to his car.

They didn’t say a word during the ride. The traffic on the road toward the Crni Vrh precinct was light, and ten minutes later, Lazar halted alongside the pavement beneath the hill. He knew that besides Anel, a lot of international aid workers lived in this quiet environment.

They got out. Waiting on the sidewalk, Lazar let his eyes explore the narrow road and the parked cars on either side.

“I don’t see his car anywhere,” he said. “What’s his licence plate?”

Senad handed him a piece of paper.

Lazar memorised the licence plate and returned the paper. One after the other they climbed the steep path until the porch, where they found the front door ajar.

“What now?” asked Senad astonished.

“Stay behind me.” Lazar grabbed his gun, entered the house and halted abruptly between the doorposts of the lounge.

“Wow,” he exclaimed. The whole room was in disorder. The chairs, table and cupboards were violently thrown up down all over the place and partly damaged. Lazar stepped over a broken frame, picked it up, pulled out the picture, glided it into a pocket and entered the small kitchen where utensils lay scattered across the floor. In the bedroom, they found a mattress cut into pieces with the padding scattered across the floor.

"No blood anywhere," Lazar observed. "Anel got killed elsewhere."

"What were they looking for?"

"I'd like to know." The contents of the drawers were also spread out across the floor. Lazar's eyes focused on the computer in the office, surprised it had survived the vandalism. He stepped toward it, eyed the unscrewed side, bringing his face next to the frame. At first, he thought that everything was still in place until he discerned a flat grey plug hanging loose.

"The hard drive is missing," he exclaimed.

Everyone was present at the team meeting room. Lazar asked Fadila to make coffee. As the young woman had left the room, he paced to the window and immobilised, gazing at the Unis Towers. He felt listless and frustrated due to lack of sleep. But Zumra's physical condition also made him deeply unhappy and desperate. He didn't know what to do. *An escort girl.* Why hadn't she stopped when they started their relationship? Many questions, but he had to concentrate on this case. And the murder of a foreign prostitute. At first sight, this case had nothing to do with his murder case. But he couldn't ignore that his prime suspect Greg Stone met Bram Ruyter and had known at least two victims. The description of the perpetrator given to him by Greg's neighbour could not be more explicit. Moreover, Bram Ruyter had vanished. Lazar did not believe in coincidences. The number of deaths was multiplying. Cees Visser. Safet Begovic. Emir Besic. Miralem Lulic. Anel Dzeko. Daria Bazila. The Westerners Ahmed Salah and Alistair Moon. *Why Anel?*

Lazar turned around. All the team members were sitting in their usual places. As he paced back to his seat, Fadila came in and poured coffee. He sat across her, sipped some hot brew, glancing up toward her.

"Political shit," he called out, considering politicians as the *Evil.*

She frowned. "What do you mean?"

"Safet, Emir and Miralem were involved in something that went wrong. According to Anel, Emir had a business relationship with Safet and a few foreigners. I assume he meant Bram Ruyter, Ahmed Salah and Alistair Moon. Salah and Moon got murdered in Bogusevac. And now Anel is also dead. That can't be a coincidence."

"The police commissioner stubbornly continues to inform the media that it's all about drugs," Nijaz said. He wasn't the smartest of the team. However, fortunately for him, he was an excellent tracker, which had convinced Lazar to engage him.

Lazar looked at him with raised eyebrows. "Did you find anything in Safet's house?"

"Nothing remarkable, otherwise, we would have reported it: just a forced door and a hidden shelter where Safet stored his gun. But no weapon, only oil-soaked rags. The poor wretch lived in extreme poverty. Nowhere money, no pictures, few clothes, no notes and no food. Cans of beer, though."

"But the front door had got forced?"

"Yes, someone entered by force. The window in the bedroom was open, and on the sill, we found traces of earth. A man has jumped out of the window. Beneath the window on the ground were footprints, leading to the forest."

"You see," grunted Lazar dissatisfied. "That's fucking important. And you Fadila, did you succeed in hacking Emir's computer?"

"I've made a full copy of the hard drive," she confirmed.

"All right, that'll be for later." Lazar didn't believe that the hard drive content would help him. But he wouldn't have wanted to take any chances.

Fadila hesitated for a moment and said, "Maybe it has nothing to do with it, but it did attract my attention. When I left there and walked down the corridor, a strange sniffer came out of the elevator. As he walked by, he bowed his head down. Before I got in the elevator, I saw him glancing over his shoulder. Especially his skittish look struck me. I think he was scared."

Senad winked at her. "You're a dangerous woman."

She rewarded him with a murderous look.

Lazar leaned in. "What did he look like?"

"Tall, thin, long black hair."

"Age?"

"Not even thirty, I guess."

Lazar stood up and rushed out of the room. But less than a minute later he was back, holding a picture. He shoved it under Fadila's nose, and her facial features faded into a wild expression of astonishment.

"That's him," she stammered, glancing up.

"Anel, our last victim," said Lazar. He let her keep the photo he'd taken out of a broken frame in Anel's house.

Senad straightened. "Shouldn't we go and have a closer look at Emir's apartment?"

"We'll do that later if necessary." Lazar strolled to the window again. Every time he studied the Unis Towers, his thoughts went to the 11th of September 2001 tragedy, but this time he was thinking about the Bogusevac murders. Behind him, it got silent, and he smiled. The team he'd put together was special. Fadila, a computer freak, spoke several languages. Nijaz was an excellent tracker who found clues being invisible for the others. Izet, nicknamed chameleon, was an artist who fused with his environment with few things, able to stay unseen watching the most suspicious people. Lazar was demanding and quickly annoyed when he had to repeat something. Incomplete information made him resentful.

All of a sudden, he turned around, studying his team members for a while.

"Every killer has a motive," he started emphasising every word. "He leaves traces, whereas potential witnesses usually don't understand the importance of what they see." He paused, fidgeting with his right earlobe.

"Nijaz and Izet," he continued, "you're going to do neighbourhood investigation around Anel's house."

The two men nodded.

Senad looked confused. "What's the motive in this last case?"

Lazar shrugged. "I agree Anel doesn't fit the picture of the Bogusevac murders. He loved peace and tranquillity. Many would call him a coward." He paused for a time before continuing. "Anel was Emir's partner, and he could have told him something. Unintentionally a potential danger."

Nobody moved.

"Maybe Anel and Emir are the main actors," tried Senad.

Lazar shook his head. "Or someone wants us to believe that. It wasn't a secret that both were working on a program. That's why Emir regularly visited Anel in the Glass Tower, a public secret."

"That program could be the motive," insisted Senad.

"According to Anel, not important enough to kill for it."

Lazar sat down again.

Fadila leaned in. "Emir was with Anel when Safet called him."

"Right," admitted Lazar smiling. "But there is more. When you were going to leave Emir's apartment, you spotted Anel in that building. What time was it?" His creative mind started to resolve a puzzle, desperately searching for the missing pieces.

"Must have been around 9 p.m."

"According to the pathologist, Anel died around midnight. So at least three hours after you've seen him. The killers confiscated all he was carrying on him, including his house keys. But not his wallet. Then the perpetrators rushed to Anel's house, where they turned everything upside down, but in the end, they only took the hard drive of his computer."

Senad's eyes started shining. "Thus, they wanted Emir's program."

Lazar nodded. "That's what it seems. But they deliberately left that wallet behind. So, why did the perpetrators let us identify the body?"

Fadila intervened, "You don't believe the murders were after software?"

"No," replied Lazar. "The disorder in Anel's house was exaggerated, staged to make us believe they were looking for the hard drives." He contemplated for a moment. "I urgently need to speak to Trifko Petrovic."

Fadila frowned. "Chief, he's plunged in illegality, and no one knows where he's hiding." Her voice shook lightly.

"I'm aware. But Petrovic is often in Sarajevo. Time to check those rumours. There's a restaurant called Prijatelji."

She coughed slightly. "Yes, but that's private, an attraction for politicians and prominent businessmen."

Lazar chuckled. "Do you mean mafia? Petrovic is a businessman. But even though his arms trade is illegal, he maintains relations with the highest political circles. I know the owner of that restaurant." Their faces betrayed amazement. "Safet worked for Petrovic. Perhaps Petrovic can make me wiser. Together with Ruyter, he's the only living link with Emir and mates."

Lazar turned to face Izet. "You should go to Bogusevac and thoroughly search the house and its surroundings. Nijaz, you go with him. But the priority remains the neighbourhood investigation around Anel's house."

"It's all right, chief," answered Izet with a grin. This kind of work suited him better than studying crime theories.

"Fadila, give me the key to Emir's apartment."

Fadila took the keychain out of her purse and handed it to him. "What do I do with the copy of the hard drives?"

"Don't waste time, for now. If Anel's killers had looked for the hard drives, they wouldn't have destroyed the kitchen and the bedroom. I insist the drives are a diversionary tactic."

Fadila stood up. "Okay, chief, is there anything else?"

"Go ahead. Guys, I want your updates by the end of the day."

Senad followed him down the hall.

"We're going to Emir's apartment," Lazar said.

Fifteen minutes later, they entered Emir's apartment. The interior looked the way Lazar remembered it. The scrapbooks lay untouched on the table. Nothing had moved, nor been touched, although he reckoned that Anel had visited the apartment after Fadila's departure. He examined the furniture, grinned self-confidently and paced to the kitchen where he leaned over the glass on the sink. He sniffed deeply and smiled. *Rakija*. Satisfied, he took a plastic bag from his pocket, turned it inside out, grabbed the glass, pulled the plastic over it and closed the bag with the particular pressure closure. Silently he handed it Senad, who casually glided it into his jacket pocket.

"No traces of a burglary," Lazar concluded. "Anel sat here for hours, drinking rakija."

Senad frowned. "How can you be so sure?"

"That glass and Fadila seeing him in the hallway. Emir was his friend, and I guess he had a key to this apartment. He came to get the program code. I mistakenly assumed that he had it on his proper computer."

"Emir had the code."

Lazar headed to the study room. One glance and his eyes started to glisten when they focused on the computer rack.

"All the hard drives are gone," he said to Senad, who had joined him. "Taken by Anel. Later the killer took it from him."

Lazar stepped up the corridor and waited until Senad had locked the door.

So it was the computer program after all. But Lazar's gut feeling said something else. Following a sudden inspiration, he returned to his steps and knocked on Derek Fleming's door. Nothing happened. He shrugged and walked to the apartment on the other side.

A bossy young woman opened. No, she had seen nothing and heard nothing.

The residents of the next three apartments didn't help him either. Eventually, he stopped at the last door next to the stairwell. Although he no longer expected useful information, he did not want to leave anything to chance. He knocked.

Ten seconds later, the door opened ajar, and a wrinkled face appeared. A 70-year-old lady wrapped in a dark headscarf glanced at them with suspicion.

"What do you want?" She had sparkling eyes and a shrill voice.

"I'm chief inspector Magas." Lazar showed his badge. "And that's my colleague Mujdza."

A woman with a curved back pushed the door further open. "What can I do for you?"

"Did you hear or see anything between nine and midnight last night?"

The woman opened the door completely. Then, with a skittish glance, she looked from left to right and bowed toward Lazar. "Last night there was a lot of people walking around, Inspector," she said. "First, you were here. Then a woman arrived and stayed for hours." She leaned a little farther forward and whispered, almost incomprehensibly, "Is there something wrong with that young man?"

Lazar smiled amusedly, realising that the lady spied on her neighbours. "No, ma'am, that young man had an accident. Did you see or hear anything?"

She checked on both sides again. "It was rather late, around 11 p.m. because I was getting ready to go to bed. Then I heard footsteps, and I looked through the little spy. I couldn't see anything because of the darkness in the corridor. However, I heard a soft knock on a door. Those guys stayed there for about five minutes before they switched on the light. When they left, I saw two shapes passing by. I would have sworn one of them was a woman. They took the stairs."

Lazar bowed his head toward her. "I guess you've seen their faces?"

Her eyes twinkled enthusiastically. "I was getting ready to go to bed, inspectors. And I didn't have my spectacles on. Were these people dangerous?"

"No, ma'am. And what happened after that?"

"I went to sleep, Inspector. I always go to sleep at that hour. You know, regular habits..."

Lazar interrupted her with his most charming smile. "Thank you,

Madame. You've helped us a lot."

Back downstairs, Lazar rushed to the rear door leading to the courtyard with the rear wall of the building on one side, and a row garages on the other side. Lazar marched toward the exit and stopped along the sidewalk. There blew a fresh breeze despite the dry weather and wearing summer clothes, he was already shivering. He bowed forward and started strolling in the middle of the road while gazing at the soil.

Senad followed on the sidewalk. Troubled after a few steps, he asked, "What are you searching?"

"Blood," Lazar replied, staring at the bottom until he reached the end of the alley where he counted four garbage containers. He checked the ground along the edge of the forest, turned around and started pacing back, scrutinising the road and the garages to his right.

Senad continued to follow.

All of a sudden Lazar halted at the sight of a dark spot on a garage door. He walked to the middle of the road, squatted, examined the soil for a few seconds and paced back to the garage. Leaning forward, he inspected the rough surface with his nose almost pressed against the metal. *That's it*, he thought. He beckoned Senad to approach.

"Look, leftovers of tissue and bone," he said. He examined every centimetre of the surface, turned to face the garbage containers across the street. Behind it was just forest.

"We've found the crime scene," he exclaimed.

"What?"

"Call Ferid. He has to come here with his team. Anel has been shot here," said Lazar excitedly.

Moments later Senad confirmed the team was on its way.

"Without enthusiasm," Senad added.

"I can understand that, but at last, we have a useful track."

"Tell me."

"In the garage door, I found a bullet and human tissue. Most probably from Anel. See that stain?" Lazar pointed to a big dark stain on the road. "That's where he died. The two guys who had knocked on his door earlier emerged from the woods and passed the containers. One of them shot Anel in his head. They knew he was in the apartment and they waited for him. Anel stayed in Emir's apartment until midnight, thinking it was safe then to leave. He snuck out of the courtyard to explore the area. Careful, but not careful enough."

Hearing loud voices, Lazar looked past Senad, noticing several men leaving the last block and coming in their direction. A shiver ran through his body, and he moved toward the mob, raising his badge. But he had a lot of trouble convincing them.

He pointed to the garage.

"There are stains on the gate," he explained. "So be patient until our specialists have finished their work. We won't harm anything."

The mob was increasing fast.

"Last night, something terrible happened here," he called out. "So I ask you to keep your distance." He felt vulnerable among these screaming guys, some of whom had already drunk too much rakija. They overwhelmed him with questions, which he answered evasively to save time. Some were shouting insults. Fortunately, Senad attracted attention when he recognised a guy and started talking to him. Most of the curious gathered around him, hoping to get more information.

Less than thirty minutes had passed when two neutral vehicles of the forensic team and a surveillance car arrived. While two police officers kept the mob at bay, the technicians secured the crime scene.

The situation was under control again.

Lazar explained to Ferid what he needed to know. Then he took Senad aside. "Something's still missing," he whispered in his ear.

"You mean Anel's car which the killers may have found, causing they knew that Anel was in the neighbourhood."

"Probably that vehicle is around the corner or in front of the entrance. I think there are a few parking places along the main road."

Fifteen minutes later, Senad was back, confirming he'd found the car.

Lazar gave Ferid a brief account of what he had discovered, while Senad gave him the glass he'd taken from the apartment.

Then they drove back to headquarters.

Back in his office, Lazar found several folders on his desktop. *The forensic team has done an excellent job.* Surprised, he looked at a picture of Bram Ruyter next to the folders and wondered where Fadila had got it. Better quality than the photos he'd received from the anonymous informant.

The first folder contained the result of the forensic investigation in connection with the Besic murder. The autopsy report began with a description of the individual.

Lazar confined himself to the understandable data.

Subject: Emir Besic murder case
Cause of death: strangulation.
The victim has been identified as Emir Besic. He has received a blow to the head, probably from the flask of a gun; however, it's not the cause of death. Strangulation with a metal cord has cut off the oxygen supply for a long time until death occurs.
Time of death: between 3.30 p.m. and 4.30 p.m.

That was the confirmation of what he'd established at the crime scene himself.

Car licence: Emir Besic.
On the steering wheel: 5 usable fingerprints of Emir Besic.
In the back seat: fingerprints of three strangers. But not a single fingerprint of the suspected perpetrator Ahmed Salah.
Under the back seat: two five-gram bags of heroin each. Poor quality heroin.
The door handles on the back: wiped clean.
On bags of heroin: no fingerprints.
Car chassis at the bottom: a miniature transmitter.
Front bumper slightly dented.

Another page described the murder weapon.

The murder weapon is a metal wire, an ordinary bicycle brake cable with a six-millimetre diameter round bullet pressed onto it at both ends. The killer probably uses two handles in which the extremities of the wire got attached to a particular clamping system. Detachable by merely pressing a lever or button. Own production. The cable is stretched and has caused a deep cut in the neck.

He looked at the snapshots of the murder site. On the grass floor in front of Emir's car, tyre tracks were visible, but not a word about it in the report.

In the photos displaying the mob, he could not identify any known or suspected individuals.

The second folder contained information about the Bogusevac murders. Three corpses, three autopsy reports. But few details about the charred body.

Subject: Charred body
Identification is impossible, DNA examination necessary.
Cause of death: a bullet has entered the back of the head, causing immediate death. The body has been burned postmortem.
Skin tissue has been found at about three metres from the place where the body lies. Evidence has been sent to the lab for analysis.
The perpetrators have been using kerosene to burn the corpse. The high heat has been erasing most of the traces within the immediate vicinity of the body.
Pictures in the appendix illustrate all these data.
Note: The administration has been transferring the corpse to SFOR.

The autopsy report on Safet Begovic confirmed what he'd established.

Subject: Safet Begovic.
Cause of death: a bullet has entered the back, going through the lung and sticking in the body. The victim has suffocated in his blood. Death has occurred shortly after the impact.

Time of the murder: between 18.30 and 19.30.
Weapon: pistol calibre 9 mm.

Lazar remembered that, when he'd moved the body, the rigor mortis was already advanced. So the anonymous call happened hours after the murder.

The expertise of Safet's car revealed few additional elements for the investigation.

Brand: Volkswagen
Owner: Safet Begovic.
General condition: shattered rear windows, two bullets in the passenger seat. The shots have been fired by the weapon, one of the killing Safet. On the left mudguard are grooves derived from bullet hits. The metal is still blank.

The murder weapon: pistol, calibre nine millimetres Parabellum.
Gun not found.

The house. Owner: Miralem Lulic.
On the right window frame: found a bullet hole, calibre 7.62x54 mm R, presumably fired by an SVD, better known as Dragunov.
Remark: the grooves on the mudguard of the Volkswagen probably caused by the same kind of ammunition.

Lazar immediately thought of what Mirsad had told him about the mythical *Cleaner* and hoped that this guy would remain a myth.

Then he read the autopsy report about Ahmed Salah.

The crime scene: in the woods, two hundred metres north of the house, corpse torn in several parts.
Corpus. Identity: Ahmed Salah, ID established based on the identity documents found.
Description of the crime scene: the victim has stepped on a landmine with his right foot, and the explosion has torn off the entire leg and the other leg just above the knee.
Cause of death: internal bleeding. Loss of blood. A shard of metal has pierced through a coronary artery.
Contents of vest pockets: a cell phone, a spare magazine, two metal cylinders, wallet.
Portfolio contents. Passport with visas, SFOR ID card, 200 Convertible Marka
Close to the body is an H&K 9 mm pistol with a silencer.
The body has got transferred to SFOR.

Lazar assumed that these cylinders were the handles in which the strangling cable could be clicked.

He found no report from the mine awareness service. There was, however, an expert's report of the car registered in Ahmed's name.

The car is 4x4.
Found fingerprints: Ahmed Salah.
Glove compartment contents: Car papers. Cell phone.
Trunk contents: spare wheel, ten bicycle brake cables and ten bags of heroin.

The car that hit Emir's car bumper, Lazar thought. He should talk to Ferid because they could compare the tyre tracks of Ahmed's vehicle with those of Emir Besic's car found at the crime scene.

As far as Alistair Moon's car was concerned, there were only fingerprints and car documents.

The last sheet contained the analysis of Miralem Lulic's clothes. Much gibberish to explain that the human tissue and blood on the clothes found in Miralem's bathroom were from Ahmed Salah.

He picked up his phone and dialled a number. Ferid Munic picked up.

"Thank you for your quick work," Lazar said. "I have an urgent request. We found a cell phone on Salah's body and one in his car. The phone found in that car might be from one of the other victims." He thought of Emir.

"Okay, those phones are now in the Communications Department. I'll ask them to check," Ferid said.

"Thanks, wait a second. I have something else. The bicycle brake cables in Salah's car and the two cylinders in his pockets are probably the murder weapon in the Emir Besic case. Can you also check if the tyre marks of Salah's car match those found at the Besic crime scene?"

"No problem."

"Have a nice afternoon," Lazar said,

He looked at his watch.

Time to interrogate the Belgian.

FORTY-EIGHT

GREG STONE KEPT SLAMMING HIS FISTS AGAINST THE COLD METAL, AND THE BLOWS were sounding like drumming on an empty oil barrel. After the doctor had examined him, he'd spent several hours sitting on the bench like a beaten dog, overwhelmed by grief and guilt, while terrible images kept haunting through his head, driving him mad. Tears had been flowing abundantly until his pain began to give way to incomprehension, anger, and despair. Who could do such a horrible thing? And why? Who was that naked man he'd seen before darkness had embraced him? What had happened afterwards?

After hours of contemplating, fear had begun to dominate his thoughts. He'd started roaming through his cell. Despair had been producing more and more adrenaline, and the urge for self-preservation had been growing. Suddenly he'd started shouting and crying. He knew that pounding his fists against the door was pointless, but he couldn't think of anything else to express his frustration and draw attention to himself. What was awaiting him was probably nothing compared to what he already had experienced at home. History repeated itself.

After being yelling for hours, *I didn't kill her* with a skipping voice that finally got hoarse, he calmed down. He'd lost any sense of time as he heard approaching footsteps. An officer entered, bringing water and bread. He left without saying a word, refusing to answer questions.

They kept him waiting, not respecting his legal rights. After 48 hours, either they had to accuse him or to release. Probably the EuPol presence in the country didn't seem to change their attitude and methods, because they kept declining his requests to make a phone call. Meantime, twenty-four hours had passed. Greg got convinced that the chief inspector was hostile to him. Strangely, this guy spoke English so well. Did he belong to the State Security? Were the stories about ex-Yugoslavia true?

He looked around. *Four by four*, he estimated. A metal bed anchored in the ground, with a hard mattress and a pale green blanket on it, stood in front of the door.

By experience, he knew that interrogators would give him some time to think about everything, making him insecure and frightened. The increasing waiting time had to exhaust his mental strength, breaking his resistance by tiredness so that he would not be able to reason. They were hoping that he would confuse himself with contradictions, starting to feel guilty, eventually confessing everything they suggested to him.

He recalled what had happened back home two years ago. Accused of murdering his wife, he'd suffered an endless interrogation. Reaching the breaking point, they'd granted him a break. Fortunately, the lab had provided enough evidence to incriminate him.

He cursed loudly.

The door flew open, and a big uniformed guy with a torso to make Conan the barbarian jealous emerged into the cell. The Slavic face with a hook nose and thick eyebrows did not betray any emotion. To Greg's surprise, the man did not touch him. Could everything he'd heard during his military career, about Yugoslavian prison sentences, have been invented?

The giant guided him through a long, bald corridor. Their footsteps on the granite floor sounded hollow. At the end of it, they stepped through a connecting door. The police officer ordered him to stand next to a brownish door which he pushed open. The screeching of the rusty hinges went through marrow and bone. The man waved him in.

Stone entered a square loft that didn't look much friendlier than his cell. In the middle stood a metal table anchored on the floor, with on either side two chairs fastened to hooks in the soil. The guard pointed to a chair, and when he'd settled down, the man spun around and left the room, shutting the door behind him. Stone let his eyes wander through the room. There was a smell of bleach or a similar cleaning agent. But the purity did not alter the fact that he was sitting in a gloomy interrogation room. Grey walls, high ceiling with a ventilation system, neon lighting and a metal door. A soundproof room from an era of radical interrogation methods that convinced the most persistent suspects to confess.

He planted his elbows on the cold metal and supported his face with both palms. Fatigue was overpowering him, but instinctively he felt that he wouldn't see a bed so quickly. He was not allowed to be overwhelmed by his grief. He had to mentally strengthen himself against what was in store for him. Daria was dead, and there was nothing he could do about it. He was alive, and it would be unjustified to spend the rest of his life in a cell after all that he had gone through. Shuddering, he thought of an event that had changed his life, bringing him to this cursed land.

Belgium, 2000

He'd promised Lea to drive her to the hospital that afternoon, where she had an appointment with her cardiologist. However, he first was going to repair a friend's computer, which wouldn't take long. Barely two hours later, he finished the job. But when he got in his car, his phone buzzed. Another friend, having trouble with his car, asked him if he could tow his vehicle to a garage. Being still on schedule, Stone accepted and headed to assist this friend. But in the end, he was late for the appointment with his wife, Murphy's law. *Lea must have taken the bus*, he thought.

The trip back home brought him past a supermarket where he realised that he'd been looking for Dan Browns '*The Delta deception*' for days. He parked among hundreds of cars and walked into the supermarket, heading toward the bookstore. But the book wasn't there.

When he got home, he found the house empty. The children organised their own lives, and he didn't know when they would be back, assuming that Lea was still in the hospital.

He started his computer and surfed the internet.

By the evening, the bell rang. When he opened the door showing a most kindly smile, it wasn't his angry wife he'd expected to face, but two sullen-looking police officers.

"Has something happened to my children or my wife?" he asked puzzled.

The most unfriendly looking guy reassured him. "We've come for you."

Suddenly everything went very fast. Without empathy, the tallest told Stone that a jogger in a nearby forest almost had tripped over his wife's naked body. He'd to come along to identify her body. He couldn't believe it. Impossible, what would his wife have done in the forest? She had an appointment with her cardiologist.

At the police station, they took him to a small room with a table and two chairs. An officer put a Polaroid picture under his nose. Large glassy eyes in a bloody face stared at him accusingly. The world around him exploded. At that moment he realised he would never hold his Lea again.

After identification, they kept him as a witness. That's what they were pretending. They hardly give him time to wail and put him in a cell for hours, without shoelaces, belt and watch. *Peculiar treatment of witnesses*, he thought. But he'd no experience with such things. Grief made it impossible for him to think clearly.

The awaiting had lasted forever, and he'd lost all sense of time. Then two unfriendly looking inspectors took him out of the cell and brought him to the interrogation room. A merciless interrogation began. First kindly informing, then blaming and finally accusing.

"Where have you been this afternoon?"

His answer elicited a pitying grin on their stern faces. No doubt, they didn't believe him, and he was their prime suspect.

Sometime in the late evening, they took him into custody. When he asked about his children, an inspector casually noted that they would interrogate them first. For the sake of the investigation, he was not allowed to see them.

Eventually, they brought him to the investigating magistrate who was remanding him in pre-trial detention.

For two days, inspectors and uniformed men were searching for incriminating evidence. Overzealous inspectors misled his friends, family and children with veiled allusions, and hypotheses. Brainwashing.

Stone's lawyer told him that they had gathered enough evidence to prove his guilt. That's what got written in the newspapers. That's what inspectors told his children. Even his lawyer started to doubt his innocence and advised him to tell the truth. *Confessing*, he meant.

All those rumours caused neighbours, family, and friends confessing imagined stories to the cops about his odd behaviour. Or what they thought had been weird. '*Their gossip is necessary to avoid that he might evade his rightful punishment*,' they told them. Those who knew him very well suddenly started to doubt.

What goddamn motive would he have?

But the investigators quickly found an answer to that question. They constructed a motive of the statements made by his friends, acquaintances and family members, supported by a fake report of two psychiatrists pretending they just wanted to help him. They twisted small marital quarrels into verbal and physiological violence. Biased people took events related to his relationship with Lea out of their real context. Once the motive established, they started searching for the opportunity to commit the crime.

Too bad for him that he didn't have an alibi. Not a single witness had seen him in the supermarket where he'd been walking around for an hour. And odd enough, there were several examples of *'The Delta deception'* available. Nobody believed that he'd overseen that book. And when, why hadn't he asked the saleswoman?

Who'd put that book there later?

Lea was in the wrong place at the wrong time. Just like Stone. But the pedantic investigating magistrate didn't hesitate to accuse him. Meantime, the investigators were only searching for incriminating circumstances. His profile got updated: all of a sudden, he was a screaming husband who regularly brutalised his wife.

The reports were very cleverly drawn up, leaving room for the most imaginative interpretations. One psychiatrist, blaming him for his lack of cooperation, declared he was a narcissistic psychopath. *Lea didn't want to be dominated by him any more and wished to leave him.*

The motive.

Moreover, he'd got the opportunity to murder because he didn't have an alibi. He strangled her with her scarf and then staged a rape.

Bad luck for him, the perpetrator had used a condom. For the investigators, this was further proof that he did it deliberately, thus a premeditated murder.

Where have you thrown that condom? They repeated that question countless times. No one wondered why there weren't condoms in his house. They didn't try to find out whether or not he'd bought condoms.

The council chamber confirmed the pre-trial detention. Meantime, Stone's wife got buried while he'd to stay in the cell.

He stayed for three months in jail, awaiting trial. Wailing didn't help. Although each individual is supposed to be innocent until a conviction is pronounced, the media described him as a monster.

Sometimes he yelled out his innocence until his throat got hoarse and almost no sound came out. His hands got bloody from hitting the door. When he tried to do the same thing at night, the guards gave him a rattle that left no trace, and they called for a doctor who injected him a sedative.

The interrogators were numb and cruel. They didn't allow him to sleep but tried to break him up. For a watertight file, he'd got to confess. So later on, no one could blame them.

His grief gave way to despair and anger. After all, he was no longer capable of emotions, overwhelmed by feelings of hatred. *One day I'll make them pay*, he promised himself. He was not guilty, and that strengthened his resolve. He'd got to persevere because confessing things he had not done would justify their wrong behaviour. *'Why confess while innocent?'* they'd say. *'Your fault.'*

The longer these guys mistreated him, the more his faith in righteousness subsided. He began to doubt, gradually becoming convinced that his case was hopeless. Eventually, he was about to give up.

Fortunately, the inspectors needed a break, not noticing that he'd reached the breaking point. The miracle happened during this coffee break when the investigators got the results of the DNA examination. *Why did it take three months?*

Consternation. The skin particles they've found under Lea's fingernails didn't match with his DNA, but with that of a man who was sentenced twice for rape. That man confessed during his first interrogation. Finally, the picture of the murder was complete.

When Stone didn't show up, his wife, who didn't want to miss her appointment in the hospital, walked to the bus stop across the exit of the chalet village where she lived. A friendly neighbour offered her a ride. Hundreds of metres farther ahead, that generous man drove into a forest path, turning into a monster. He dragged Lea between the trees, raped and strangled her.

Stone was free. Suddenly the media wanted his point of view, but he showed them his middle finger. The next day, the investigators handed him the confiscated computer after he'd signed a delivery receipt. They behaved friendly, while he noticed uneasiness on their faces. They reluctantly apologised.

But he was no longer the friendly guy from three months ago. They'd destroyed him, and he would never forget. As they stood in front of him with a stupid grin on their faces, he felt like a wounded bull ready to trample them. But he held back, giving those cunts a disdainful smirk. They didn't react, and he left the office, the computer under his arm.

Then a new agony began.

Greg's children kept blaming him for their mother's death. Their mother would be alive if only he'd come home that afternoon, as he'd promised to Lea. They abandoned him. He assumed they're ashamed because they had believed the gossip even though he'd never been violent at home. He forgave them because the inspectors had used psychological manipulation. '*We know your father did it, but with a good lawyer, he will be free soon. You don't want that. Help us. Explain that he regularly hit you when you were minors. He also brutalised your mother, as we know, from witnesses,*' an inspector had whispered in their ears. But that man didn't mention those suggestive statements in his official report.

They'd made his life a mess. He sold his house to pay for his lawyer's fees and the inheritance of his kids. Out of shame, Lea's family chose to ignore him. Blinded by grief, they'd believed he was the perpetrator, and Lea's murderer had to pay. Why would the police have arrested the wrong person? Now that they knew the truth, they still considered him guilty because he wasn't home when Lea needed him.

But his colleagues and chiefs couldn't ignore him. After they'd presumed him guilty without waiting for the verdict, they feared the confrontation with him. Like the media, they'd spread false stories about him during his three months in prison.

As Stone occupied his office again, they hardly dared to look him in the eye. Their body language betrayed their discomfort. He feigned forgiveness, but whenever the opportunity arose, he made them feel how much he despised them through vicious, hateful remarks. During social diners, he enjoyed casually revealing the secret sins of one or other guests. Even in the twenty-first century, the '*Count of Monte-Cristo's vengeance*' still worked. Very quickly, they understood. They feared his revenge, his ironic remarks and allusions. He managed to strand two marriages. But he never crossed the forbidden line, respecting the military rules.

He knew a lot of small and big secrets, and the concerned hoped that he would spare them if they showed compassion. Those hypocrites got friendly hole scrapers, looking for an opportunity to get rid of him.

Although he could bring them to the court, he refused to do so because he didn't trust the system any more. Why pay lawyers to have justice done? Giving forgiveness is suitable for a believer. *God forgives, Greg does not.*

The most courageous of them openly suggested he should consult a psychiatrist before doing bad things. But there was no law to force him. One of those shrinks had put him in jail with his biased diagnosis. Why should he trust those soul seekers? Such a shrink had without evidence written down his scientific opinion why he'd kicked Lea. And the magistrate considered his allegation as biblical truth, charging Greg Stone for murder.

Although he'd become a volcano on the brink of an eruption, he was not crazy, but aware of his problem, knowing it would be better to make peace with what happened. Nothing could change this tragedy. All those hypocrites were repeating: '*Respect the rules that society impose on us.*' But in his case, the system had betrayed its own rules when it wanted him to lock up for the rest of his life, without evidence… just because a magistrate wished a quick success or harvesting fame. Case closed.

But not for Stone.

He didn't accept that a few arrogant representatives of the law had destroyed his life without ever having to account for it. He'd lost everything.

Months were passing. Gradually, Stone could no longer derive satisfaction from his revenge. Tolerating those hypocrites in his presence got unbearable. He feared what he could do to them. He started to look out for a solution.

Unexpectedly, he received a proposal. No psychiatrist, knowing what he'd experienced, would have given him the green light for it.

Nevertheless, he got a task in Bosnia.

Sarajevo, 10 October 2002

The screeching hinges frightened him. He opened his eyes and saw two civilian men coming in, slamming the door shut. He straightened up.

Stone had seen those two at the crime scene. He even remembered their names, so his memory was still functioning. *Inspector Senad Mujdza and Chief Inspector Lazar Magas of the Homicide Department or something alike*, he recalled. Magas didn't look Slavic at all. Immediately he recognised who would play what role. Lazar the gentle, understanding interrogator. Senad Mujdza the evil one who would occasionally roar him in his ear, perhaps using violence to get him confessing.

Mujdza stood in the furthest corner, somewhere behind his back. Despite his precarious situation, Stone couldn't resist smiling.

Lazar raised his eyebrows. "You find this amusing?" he asked fiercely.

Stone shivered unconsciously, feeling a breath along his neck.

"Why did you kill that woman?" The evil one roared in his ear.

"I didn't kill her," he snarled at the Chief Inspector, crossing his arms over his chest, determined to resist. Daria's death was his fault. After she'd revealed to him that someone wanted her to kill, he hadn't taken her words seriously enough. Being innocent, he wasn't going to make it easy for these inspectors.

The blond-haired looked at him in amazement. Subconsciously, Stone thought of Eric the Norseman, a cartoon character from his childhood. He contemplated whether or not telling the whole story.

They'll never believe it.

"My name is Greg Stone," he said. "I'm a Belgian citizen, and I worked for EuPol. If you wish my cooperation, start by recognising that I didn't kill that woman!" The tone of his voice rose up slightly, but he made an effort to control himself.

Lazar smiled kindly, not looking upset at all. "I haven't accused you of anything. Not yet. First, I try to understand the situation. You no longer work for EuPol, so you are an immigrant without diplomatic protection, suspected of a serious crime. You have the right to inform your embassy or to ask for legal assistance. But if you're innocent, as you claim, we can first look at the case calmly. Convince me of your innocence, and you don't need a lawyer."

Stone sat up straight. "Can I have a cigarette?"

"No problem, Mr Stone. Would you like some coffee, too?"

Stone nodded.

Lazar gestured his colleague, who left the room. Then he started to leaf through his brown folder.

Five minutes later Senad put a bowl on the table with a coffee pot, three cups, a pitcher of milk and a packet of Marlboro with a disposable lighter.

Stone bent forward.

Lazar poured in coffee for each and shoved the Marlboro package toward him.

"Hvala." Stone lit a cigarette, inhaled deeply and blew the smoke toward the ceiling. "I'm ready," he said.

Lazar laughed friendly. "Where did you meet Daria for the first time?"

Stone closed his eyes for a moment. After Daria had moved in with him, he'd asked her how she'd ended up with the women traffickers. He'd engraved every word of her story in his memory.

He let out a deep sighed and briefly told about Daria's journey from Chisinau to Belgrade, Mitrovica and Sarajevo. Without going into details, he explained how Daria had ended up with him. His voice was trembling while he hardly could withhold his tears. When he kept silent, glancing at Lazar, he saw a thoughtful face.

"A nice, romantic story," Lazar said with a touch of irony. "But what does Mitrovica have to do with her murder?"

"She got threatened because a girlfriend had given her something in Mitrovica." Stone made a pause. Images flashed through his mind. Daria was a handsome woman who, like him, had been through a lot of trouble. Each of them had felt attracted to the other. Their love hadn't been a sudden explosion of emotions, born of physical attraction, but a slow smouldering tender love, arising out of appreciation for the character and inner beauty.

After she'd told him, with a trembling voice and wet eyes, what she'd experienced in Mitrovica, he'd believed every word of her story. He still did.

He shivered as he started to tell the story.

Mitrovica, 2001

As Daria crossed the threshold of the *Miami Nightclub* followed by two fellow sufferers, it became clear to her that she wouldn't practise an honourable profession, and she was already regretting having left Moldova. But there was no way out. Daria and her friends didn't have the money to pay for the return journey.

The same day, her two travelling companions got raped by the bar owner. She could escape that treatment. But what difference did it make? Technically, the work she did was a permanent raping, because it happened against her will. That night she met the bar owner's bodyguard who had the reputation of being a rapist, an animal. There was also a French officer of the United Nations Interim Administration Mission in Kosovo, UNMIK, who visited them regularly, accompanied by Bridge watchers and the Kosovo Police Service, KPS. He played under a hat with the landlord who'd made Anna, a compatriot, dependent on drugs.

Daria got quickly aware of it and was waiting for an opportunity to get out of there. One evening Anna came into her room with an envelope containing several photos and a voice recording on a memory chip. Anna hoped that Daria one day would escape. She thought it was too late for her because she seemed convinced having been HIV infected. Above all, Anna had a drug addict. That's why she revealed a terrible secret to Daria.

At the beginning of 2000, there was a UNMIK-Commissioner who had sworn that he would stop organised crime. An authoritarian prick who despicably called the girls '*whores*'. One day, after a raid, he asked Anna to testify against the bar owner. She refused. From that moment on, the commissioner regularly carried out checks in the bar. She knew that the man would continue to do so until she gave in, and she informed her friend Drako. A few days later, obeying Drako, another girl tried to lure the commissioner into a trap: she asked him to speak in private on the pretext that she had valuable information. The commissioner followed her upstairs, but smelled danger. Anna ignored what happened between the two of them, but there was a scuffle upstairs, and the Commissioner pushed that girl in her back; she fell down the stairs, breaking her neck.

Drako promised to keep silent as the Commissioner stopped his raids. The two police officers who'd accompanied the commissioner also vowed to shut up. Everyone signed the accident report. Besides, the bar owner took pictures from the commissioner at the bottom of the stairs next to the victim. To protect himself, he alleged.

Everything went according to plan, and the raids stopped.

But the case got a tail. A few days after that event, the two UNMIK officers who'd accompanied the commissioner requested money for their silence. The commissioner paid but secretly forged a plan to get rid of them. He feared that once back in France, those men would always request more and more money, to end up revealing the secret. They were a danger to his career, and he made a pact with Drako. The killing of these blackmailers had to resemble an accident.

A few days later, Drako summoned the Commissioner and revealed his plan. In that part of Mitrovica, there was a place called *Little Bosnia*, where hundreds of Albanian Kosovars lived. The Serbian Kosovars wanted to chase them away, and when the Bridge watchers organised a riot, UNMIK police had to intervene; the Commissioner made sure that the two blackmailers were among the police force that had to disperse the mob. He handed Drako pictures of both blackmailers. Drako's accomplices did the rest: the two men got shot by unknown snipers during the riots in February 2000.

The French, facing an angry crowd, were powerless. Dozens of men and women, primarily Albanians, lost their lives as a result. The Albanian community publicly accused the French of allowing the Serbian Kosovars to commit their crimes. The next day a French general closed the headquarters of the Bridge watchers, the *Dolce Vita.* He had to deploy twelve tanks to succeed. Riots broke out everywhere. Snipers from both ethnic groups shot at KFOR soldiers.

The French commissioner got replaced.

Anna gave Daria pictures of the two French officers and a voice recording of what she'd told her.

"You have to put it away, Daria. You know, Dragon Borjan is looking for that evidence," she said.

Everywhere Daria went, her childhood's teddy bear accompanied her. Mother's gift shortly before she died. The bear reminded Daria of her mum. She hid everything in the belly amid the straw and sewed the animal up again. There was nothing to feel about it.

That night Daria got proof Anna had been telling the truth. Dragon Borjan raided and abducted Anna and the owner. Early in the morning, Daria left with a friend and her brother, who wanted to take them to Bosnia. The bar owner's friend found later the bodies of Anna and the lover. Dragon Borjan immediately accused Daria of murder. He knew she possessed the evidence, and he'd come to Sarajevo to kill her.

Sarajevo,10 October 2002

As Stone finished his story, he lit a new cigarette. "After Daria had told that story," he added, "I was convinced her story was real. Why would she have made it up?"

Lazar nodded thoughtfully. "Yes, why?"

"She was terrified, and I discovered this Dragon Borjan standing in front of my house last Thursday. He tried to hide his face."

"So Daria got killed for that teddy bear?"

"That's the way it is."

Lazar shook his head, leaned in.

"All crap, I don't believe a word of it. That's enough, tell us why you have killed Daria!"

FORTY-NINE

LAZAR DIDN'T LIKE THE SUSPECT, CONTEMPLATING HIM AS ARROGANT AND provocative, despite all the evidence against him. Greg Stone had warned neither the emergency services nor the police. And his story about Daria seemed to come from a Ludlum-thriller. The procedure required him to charge the suspect and to conduct him to the Public Prosecutor.

Innocents do not run.

Lazar scrutinised Stone's unshaven face. The dark walls under his bloodshot eyes and his restlessly moving hands on the tabletop helped make him look like a cornered predator. *An odd bird*, Lazar thought. But despite his fatigue, Stone gazed fearlessly, challenging. *He's the perfect prime suspect.*

Lazar gave his opponent time to relax and sipped coffee. His thin folder contained a few trump cards.

Egzon Subic had insisted on hand over the case to another chief inspector, but Lazar had convinced him of Stone's involvement in the Sebic case: Stone was the last person Sebic had seen alive.

"Mr Stone, when the police penetrated your house, were you about to run?"

"What do you think?" retorted Stone fiercely.

"And you were going to get rid of all the incriminating evidence?"

"I admit."

Lazar hadn't expected a spontaneous confession. *Too easy.*

"You must understand that's not the typical behaviour of innocent people," he said frowning.

"What is the typical reaction of innocent trapped people?" countered Stone with a sigh. "I had no other choice."

"What about calling the police?"

Stone chuckled. "You're serious?"

"You got caught red-handed!"

"Calling the police meant killing myself. Running was the only option."

"Explain yourself."

"I know your methods." Stone took a deep breath. "As soon as you get an incriminating clue, you no longer look for exonerating circumstances. All odds are against me, chief inspector. Do you agree? The forensic truth designates me as the prime suspect. You've found enough evidence to have me convicted whether I make a statement or not. All you need is my confession to conclude your case, the sherry on the cake. That's how it works. You've found my clothes covered with blood. You also have the bloody wrench, and the butcher's knife with which Daria was killed."

Lazar raised an eyebrow. "How do you know all those details?"

"I've got plenty of time to examine the crime scene, and I'm not blind, neither stupid. You've concluded yourself, haven't you? All you have to do is waiting for the lab results. I assume they'll confirm everything I've said about evidence."

Lazar began to lose his temper. "Only the perpetrator can know those details."

"You've seen the crime scene, and I reckon you're a bright detective. In short, the murder weapon is visible. Daria hasn't stabbed herself, so if you find fingerprints on the weapon, they belong to the perpetrator. Or the perpetrator probably wore gloves. However, I bet that my prints are on it. Shouldn't you ask me why I didn't wipe them?"

Lazar wanted to say something but chose to listen.

Let him talk and kill himself.

Stone looked weary, but a hellish fire burned in his eyes. He looked like an angry, wounded bull, ready for the frontal attack. Then he began talking.

"I am sitting next to Daria on the couch, watching television. All of a sudden, a naked man appears on the landing. We are both scared. The man doesn't speak a word and keeps standing between the doorposts with his hands on his back. Why should I be afraid of a disturbed naked man? A madman or an exhibitionist who's just laughing like an idiot. I get up, walk toward him and see him make a sudden movement. At that moment I hear Daria yelling, probably to warn me. But I am not fast enough to avoid the blow. My head explodes, and memory stops.

"When I open my eyes again, I lie alongside the couch. It takes a while before I am entirely up to my senses and finally can get up. That's the moment I discover Daria, lying naked on the couch. I crouch, touch her face and realise she's dead. I think I'm going crazy. My world collapses. Hard to describe how I feel. At some point, my mind tells me to call the police. But just before I pick up the receiver, another voice tells me to examine the crime scene first. I move back into the lounge, scan the room, see the wrench and the knife. I also see the blood on my clothes and hands. My bleeding head injury is far too small to explain all that blood over the couch and the floor. The stench of it makes me sick.

"That wrench looks like the one I have in the trunk of my car. I realise that it's probably the same. I have to run and let the evidence disappear."

Stone's voice stalled. He closed his eyes for a second, deeply breathing, rocking in his chair. Mujdza got closer to him to be able to intervene if he tried something idiotic.

"That knife was covered in blood," Stone continued. "I assumed that my fingerprints were on the handle, that the man who knocked me down was the murderer and that he'd staged everything in such a way that all the evidence pointed to me. Thus, the blood on my clothes will be Daria's."

Lazar leaned back, his gaze fixed on his intriguing suspect; what Stone had said matched with his conclusions after he'd investigated the crime scene. And the abundant evidence had bothered him. Throughout his career, he hadn't seen a single crime where the incriminating evidence was so convincing. He wondered why Stone if he were the perpetrator, would enumerate details that only the perpetrator could know? Whether Stone was innocent, a scapegoat or an idiot.

"Your attempt to make all that evidence disappear and run may or may not support your hypothesis. Perhaps you panicked, choosing to escape as quickly as possible. Admit you made that naked man up." Despite emerging doubts, he'd got to put pressure on Stone, to make sure.

Stone shook his head, energetically. "Do you think I knocked myself unconsciously?" He shouted desperately with raised arms. "Can you provide a rational explanation for my presence at the crime scene when the police appeared although I had enough time to disappear?"

Lazar smiled. "Murderers make mistakes. Maybe you haven't thought of everything. I also had a hypothesis when I came in here, the most likely: you had a fierce argument with Daria, she defended herself and hit you on the head with that wrench. You may have lost consciousness for a moment, but then you went out of the line; you raped her, then killed her with that knife. That you've slit her throat may indicate you were out of control. Frenzy. Hate. A passionate crime. After your terrible act, you came down and began to think again. You had no choice but to make all incriminating clues disappear and to run. If you got arrested, you could declare that you were absent when the murder took place."

Stone shook his head wildly, bit his bottom lip, staring at him. Lazar thought he could recognise emerging panic in his eyes.

Now he will confess.

Stone thought otherwise.

"So, in your opinion, a wrench belongs to the kitchen utensils," he said dryly. "Or do you think Daria headed to the car, took the wrench, rushed back and quietly punched me?"

Lazar cursed inside. *What was this massive tool doing in the house?*

Stone went on. "And how did the police suddenly get access to the house without me noticing? I didn't hear a doorbell. The cops came in very secretly, so they weren't there by chance." He drummed his fingers on the tabletop. "I reckon you received an anonymous phone call."

Lazar nodded but said nothing.

"That's what I thought," retorted Stone. "That confirms *my* hypothesis. How did the police get into the house without I could hear anything? Without having to kick the door in?"

Lazar hesitated for a short moment. "The front door was unlocked."

"Do you finally understand?" Stone straightened his back. "The murderer came through the front door, knocked me down, raped and killed Daria. He pulled me to the couch where he almost beheaded Daria, so I got drained with her blood. He also cut her breasts. Probably you'll find the skin in my belongings."

"That must also have drained the guy," returned Lazar, annoyed. Stone's arrogant behaviour was destabilising him. He would have expected a man like a beaten trembling dog, fearing but not lecturing him.

Greg Stone slammed his fist on the tabletop. "Think about it. The killer has prepared everything very carefully." He bowed forward. "The perpetrator takes the wrench out of my trunk, forces the door lock and enters the bathroom. The television is playing loud, which may explain why we didn't hear anything. Quickly he undresses because he doesn't want any blood on his clothes, knowing that he'll have to shower after his crime. He stands between the doorposts, doesn't say a word and looks at us. A harmless lunatic, I think. That's his intention. I walk toward him, and he knocks me down with that wrench. I recall he's wearing transparent gloves. His plan works. What he does afterwards is what I've told you. Or better, after his horrible deed, he waits until I'm starting to move again. He calls the police and runs out of the house. Or do you think I've called the police? I suppose the phone number of the anonymous caller is registered. Anyway, you can forget about that number. He probably used my phone."

Lazar was speechless. The whole story sounded so plausible. Yet Stone's reconstruction of the murder was not entirely correct. Lazar thought of the unlocked basement door. Someone had come and gone along it. By using the front door, the chance someone could see him would have been too high. The killer had unbolted the front door after he'd murdered the woman, to give the police easy access to the house. So Stone would have less time to run.

Lazar straightened, and his features became agitated.

"And the motive might be a teddy bear." He recalled the whole story Stone had told him earlier. He was guessing what Stone would declare next. The presumed killer was Drago Borjan, a French Police Officer. Suddenly he recalled that Stone had spent a night and a morning in the cell. If he had been the perpetrator, he'd have had enough time to invent a plausible story.

Lazar got doubts again. "Mr Stone, your story sounds like an Agatha Christie novel. You allege that the content of Daria's little bear is the motive. But if that's true, I guess Dragon Borjan must be the killer."

Stone's gave him a disapproving grin. "You're wrong again, chief inspector, it wasn't Borjan, the man I saw was young, almost effeminate."

"Isn't that odd? You give me a motive and a possible perpetrator. But now, you produce another mysterious murderer, an unknown man you hardly can describe. That's convenient for you. Everything went so damn fast that you're not able to give an excellent description of him." Lazar's voice rose in tone.

"I can only say what I know, and that's enough to reconstruct the case. If you think I did it, explain to me why I'd have killed the woman I love. What's my motive? And don't tell me that this massacre is supposed to be a passionate murder. Too much contradicts that."

Lazar took a quick look at his colleague, who shrugged. Knowing that he would write down the interrogation in an official report, he felt lucky to have such a fantastic memory. He leafed through the folder to give himself time to think. This Belgian had taken the wind out of his sails, having an answer to everything. He cooperated without being forced to do so. A good lawyer would undoubtedly use that in court as possible proof of innocence. Mixed feelings tormented Lazar. In any case, Stone was a logical-minded guy with an astute mind. Difficult to trap.

If he made up this story, why was Stone so stupid to get caught so easily?

He sighed, opened his notebook, tore out a leaf and wrote:

Verify what number has called the police.

He beckoned Senad, who came to pick up the note and left the interrogation room without saying a word.

"Is the cell phone we've found on the coffee table yours?"

Stone nodded but said nothing.

"What's the number?"

Stone gave the number, and Lazar wrote it down in his notebook.

"Why have you been fired from EuPol?" he asked:

"Several Britons claimed that Daria was staying illegally in the country. But Daria had been granted a stay extension by the Ministry of Home Affairs that's valid until a second court reaches a verdict in her case. My dismissal is unlawful and based on gossip. I suspect someone wanted my position. I've filed a statement of defence with the Commissioner, and I'll file a complaint with the EU Council."

"Do you know Emir Sebic?"

Stone nodded. "Sure, but what does it have to do with this case?"

"It's up to you to tell me. Sebic regularly visited one of your team members."

"Yes, Anel Dzeko."

"Do you know that both got murdered?"

The surprise on Stone's face seemed real. All kinds of loose thoughts flashed through Lazar's mind. A good memory was a blessing, but that gift also included disadvantages. A vast reservoir, full of pieces of information. Comparable to a massive box in which you throw the pieces of dozens of puzzles and then have to take out a fully fledged one. Not easy. Now he tried to discover whether the parts of the Daria case fitted the Sebic case as well. Stone had known two victims in the Sebic case. He got fired, his lover murdered. Was there a link between the two cases? Could he be innocent?

Senad came in, gave Lazar a piece of paper and moved to the corner again.

Lazar took a quick look at the note.

"Mr Stone, as you predicted, or knew, the anonymous caller used your cell phone."

Stone chuckled. "It doesn't surprise me, and I suppose you have a good explanation for this."

"Well, I want the real perpetrator in the cell. So right now I'm your best friend and your hope of ever being released if you're innocent. Do you know

Bram Ruyter?"

"Yes, I do. But what has Ruyter to do with it?"

Lazar interrupted him. "Have you met him recently?"

"Yes, last night."

"Was it a friendship visit?"

"Not really. We know each other from a short meeting at a party. But I met Bram's wife last year when I was still working at the EUMM; she'd come over to write an article. She went to the party, and I photographed her several times. The next day, I sent her those pictures. A few days after that party, she went to Pale, and her car crashed on her way back. Bram had received the photos I sent to his wife, and he wanted to know if I had more pictures of that party." Stone hesitated for a moment. "He wanted all the photos I took during that party."

"Wow, did he say why?"

"He said something about the accident. I guess he wanted to know with whom his wife had been talking. There's nothing unusual about that either. I sent those pictures to his e-mail address."

"Was that the only reason for his visit?"

"Yes, but as I mentioned the name Daria, he reacted very excitedly. He asked if Daria knew Emma. She told him that she'd given a teddy bear to Emma. They also talked about the Frenchman who wanted to kill her."

"As I understand, you've never seen that little bear?"

Stone shook his head. "I've never said I have."

"And what did Bram tell you about Emma?"

"He hadn't attached much value to her story. These women use more fictional means of persuasion, hoping it will suffice to obtain something. Bram seemed confused when he left my house."

Lazar heard bells ringing. The pieces of the puzzle rushed through his head, and some of them fell into place.

"Mr Stone, you told me that you've sent photos to Bram's address. What was in those pictures?"

"I didn't look at it."

"They're on your laptop?"

"Yes."

"And where's that laptop?"

"In the suite of my accommodation, in the bottom drawer of my desk. You must have found it."

Lazar was trembling of excitement. The laptop could have helped him further. Now he thought he knew why Daria had got murdered and why the Belgian had to be the scapegoat. Lazar had thoroughly searched his suite and hadn't found a laptop. So, the killer had taken it with him.

Stone didn't have time to make his laptop disappear.

The case progressed. The killer knew what was on Stone's notebook.

Therefore Daria had to die, with Greg Stone as the killer.
Bram had received those pictures.
He was in mortal danger.

FIFTY

"IT COULD ALL HAVE BEEN SO DIFFERENT," MURMURED ZUMRA ABDIC, GAZING AT the ceiling. "If I'd accepted Visser's proposal, I could have saved my family, and I wouldn't be lying here."

Lazar sat next to her in a chair, holding her hand. Despite Dr Kebo's protest, she'd insisted on speaking to him.

"Lazar, listen to what I have to say. Please, don't interrupt me. I am in an awful state, and I don't know if I'll survive this. That's why I want you to hear the truth from me."

Lazar nodded.

She started to speak with a lot of emotion about Srebrenica, the Dutch camp, Cees Visser and Bram.

"Cees Visser had Bram Ruyter locked up to have a free way to rape me. The only way to save my family, I thought first. But finally, I refused and run away. One of Bram's friends has prevented the worse for me, so I headed to the other side of the fence with my parents and sister. Visser followed me and called out a few Serbs who took us to a white house."

Lazar's rough fingers were still stroking over her hand. A shiver ran through her body, and she closed her eyes.

Then she told her story.

Srebrenica,11 July 1995

She yelled, trying to tear herself away from the two shouting men who were enjoying her fear.

"Don't be so impatient, honey, it will be your turn later," a man whispered in her ear.

A terrible scream echoed across the room. Azra, her younger sister, lay stretched out on the table, arms and legs being immobilised by four men, while Major Cees had let his pants down, trying to penetrate her.

Zumra bit a hand and got free. However, an instant later, she got a massive blow to her belly and slammed double, losing balance and rolling over the ground, screaming like a pig getting killed.

Her sister's crying went through the marrow and leg, taking her father out of his lethargic state. He glanced at his wife, nodded shortly and raced to the table like a madman. A loud bang sounded and made her deaf. Her father abruptly stopped his heroic intervention and fell forward on the floor. With the courage of despair, she tried to get up, got on her knees and saw her father lying in a growing blood mare. Little of his face was left, his blood flowing over her mother, who was sitting next to him, crying. The world went mad; a new bang sounded. She vaguely heard her sister yelling. Still sitting on her knees, she stared like a junkie at her mother's body lying over her father's. Blood everywhere.

She stood up and wanted to walk away, her eyes recording the wildly moving beast upon her sister. Then her head exploded.

The surroundings went black.

When she opened her eyelids again, the stars and a crescent-shaped moon giving a ghostly light were staring at her. She could barely breathe. Something was pressing on her chest. Painful stabs shoot through her head she barely could move. When she finally succeeded in bowing her head, she watched into a pair of glassy eyes. Her hands seemed to be stuck as she tried to touch her head. After minutes of pushing and pulling, with last forces she got the heavy load moving, rolling it over next to her.

A stiff cold mass. A corpse.

Why am I still alive?

Her ears were ringing, and her head was dizzying. The grey shadows around her frightened her. *You don't have to be afraid of the dead*, whispered an inner voice. But amid the dozens of mutilated corpses, she felt as if they were looking at her, wondering why she was still alive. This was madness. At any moment, she expected one of them to jump up and drag her into his eternal realm. The buzz of flies and the smell of death turned on her stomach. She started to gag, pulling and pushing, trying to crawl out of the pile of stiff corpses. Eventually, she succeeded to crawl out of a decomposing collection of meat. But no matter how much she strained her eyes, she only perceived formless grey shadows. Then her hands touched a low wall of soft earth. *I am standing in a well, a deep excavation*, she thought. The ground was at shoulder level. In the distance, she heard screams and saw moving lights. *Where am I?*

Terrible images flashed through her mind. *My parents and my sister are dead.* They must be buried somewhere under the corpses. Too dark to look for them. She'd to get out, the sooner, the better.

Thinking of Azra brought tears in her eyes. *I hope death has put her out of her misery.* She laid her arms over the edge and pulled her body upward. It took her several minutes to get out. For minutes, she kept lying stretched out to catch her breath. *I have risen from the realm of the dead.* She touched her head and moaned lightly, feeling a deep cut and a lot of blood. *That's why they thought I'm dead, throwing me amid the corpses.* Had Allah then heard her cry?

She crawled on her hands and knees, felt earth and stones. After a few metres, she stood upright and faced a gloomy wall. The woods were her only chance. She began stumbling toward it.

"Who's there?" sounded a muffled voice. At night sounds carry far away, and the calling guy was pretty far away. She'd been careless, making too much noise. There had to be guards somewhere.

"Someone is trying to escape," someone yelled.

That made her run. In a few steps, she got absorbed by the wood. She didn't see much and branches swayed over her face, tearing her skin open. But terror gave her wings.

"Come back, we won't hurt you." The noise of yelling people came closer. Branches broke, heavy footsteps approached.

"Show yourself, and we'll treat you well." The hunters were laughing like crazy, convinced they would catch her soon.

She stretched her arms forward, running even faster, gasping like a locomotive. *One mistake and they catch up with me*. Then she bumped into a thin tree trunk. A little bit dizzy, she took a deep breath and proceeded, stumbling uphill. Reaching the top of the hill, she was running out of breath. The screaming in the distance got louder.

They won't get me.

Fear was unleashing adrenaline through her severely weakened body. The noise behind weakened. Imagination? All of a sudden sounds came from a different direction. She needed a short rest, unconsciously slowing down her pace. Suddenly, her feet lost their grip, and she floated forward. Finally, free. Her arms made wild movements in the air as a young bird does when falling out of its nest. *A ravine*. Death would ultimately save her from the Chetniks. The faces of her mother, father and sister were flashing through her mind. Shortly they would gather again, just a matter of seconds. Branches were lashing every spot of her body. When her face hit something hard, she waved her arms faster to slow down her fall. Breaking branches and scourged leaves hit her mercilessly in the face.

The fall seemed to last forever.

Regaining consciousness, she found out she wasn't yet in the Kingdom of the Angels. She felt broken, heard relieved voices, and glanced at surprised faces leaning over her. She was lying on the ground, surrounded by a small group of people. They were in a narrow trench beneath a steep cliff, the gathering place of a group of refugees that had escaped from the town. An older woman, whose daughter and younger sister had got murdered by the Serbs, took care of her. She told her that she was a miracle child. She'd survived a fall of about thirty metres. The vegetation and the tops of the tall trees had muffled her fall, resulting in many bruises but no breakage.

The group was on their way to Tuzla, a dangerous journey that could take weeks. She was still too weak for the trip, and the group left her behind, fearing she'd slow down their progress. But the woman without family stayed, taking care of her. They managed to survive with healthy plants, eating carrots, leaves and mushrooms, drinking plant juice or water from mountain rivers.

But she'd forgotten who she was. She could only guess that she'd fled from Srebrenica, which explained her fall from the cliff.

The woman helped her to survive on the long journey to Tuzla. The Serbs shot haphazardly through the trees. Fortunately, they were afraid of the armed Muslim soldiers in the woods and didn't chase the refugees.

After three weeks they reached Tuzla.

During registration with UNHCR, the woman testified she was her sister Zumra, confirmed by two other refugees.

That was enough to get new identity papers from the Red Cross. For her, the ideal solution. With that new identity, she could start a new life, her past being a dark gap.

FIFTY-ONE

LAZAR SWALLOWED. NEVER COULD HE HAVE THOUGHT ZUMRA'S PAST HAD BEEN SO dramatic. And the worst had yet to come. Suddenly he realised that he'd paid too little attention to her daily life outside of their relationship. He should have insisted.

Zumra had closed her eyes. *Her brain has suffered a lot,* Kebo had warned him. It could be dangerous to make her remember things which were still hidden in a dark corner of her memory.

She was crying. Lazar let his eyes wander from her muffled head to her face, caressing her hand. The sight of the numerous brown spots, made by antiseptic products for treating multiple fine cuts, made him shudder. Kebo had told him that the wounds were already infected as she'd been brought in. Zumra had suffered severe traumas, and he understood that these ravages would leave permanent marks. Both physically and mentally.

She went through hell.

Urgent questions shot through his mind. Above all, he wanted to know who his girlfriend really was. Despite the disconcerting information he'd collected about her, he still loved her. *She must have got her reasons*. The more he examined her tortured body, the more significant became his anger. Holding her hand, he couldn't think of anything to express his empathy.

"Do you want a drink?" he whispered, concerned.

She didn't seem to hear him. Tears were rolling down her cheeks.

Lazar got a lump in his throat, keeping caressing the back of her hand.

"You were dreaming," he said after a short pause.

"Yes, yet I know what those dreams mean. Sometimes I dreamt of my sister, Azra, or I was on the run from those men. Each time I could escape by jumping down. In reality, the ground beneath my feet was falling away, and I accidentally fell into the abyss."

Lazar bowed to her. "What happened to the woman who'd taken care of you?"

"We travelled to Sarajevo together. Shortly afterwards she got ill and died of pneumonia. I was suddenly alone, even after I gave birth to my daughter."

Her voice stopped.

"Where is Azra?" she asked after a short break.

The truth came closer. Lazar hesitated to question her, thinking of Kebo's advice. She was in lousy shape, had to rest and to avoid any excitement. Regarding Kebo, Zumra had suffered amnesia caused by a cranial trauma. Her memory could come back, but it was uncertain. However, despite her amnesia, she'd named her daughter Azra, the name of her sister. Subconsciously?

"I don't know where Azra is now," he said. "But I promise you that I'll check out." Mirsad had given him her address. "Where do you live?"

"I live with Timka, Azra and Hadar." Her voice was barely audible.

"Are you married?"

"No. Azra is all I have left of my hopeless love in Srebrenica. And my name is Jasmina."

"Jasmina is a beautiful name." After a short hesitation, he said, "And your lover's name was Bram, I guess."

"How do you know?" she asked after seconds of silence.

"You mentioned his name in your dreams." Everything got clear. Would she know that this Bram lived in Sarajevo? He doubted.

She coughed a couple of times, with her head coming off the head pillow for a moment.

"Bram has tried to save my family and me," she said. "But that scary Major Visser wanted me, and he let Bram lock up." Her words came in a hurry as if she was afraid to lose the memory of her secrets and not to get enough time to confess everything.

Without realising it, she'd given him a motive for Visser's murder. He was now firmly convinced that Bram Ruyter had killed the military attaché out of revenge. *It's about time I meet that Bram Ruyter*. And there was also the man who'd brought Zumra to Eurotel. He'd always wanted to put that out of his head, but he'd to face it. After all, Zumra was a prostitute.

"Zumra," he murmured. He knew her under that name and refused to rename her. Jasmina belonged to another world. "What happened after you got abducted in that hotel?"

She cramped, pulled back her hand and turned her head toward him. The pain he read in her eyes frightened him.

"You know it," she stammered.

He nodded.

"You're a good man, Lazar, and I don't deserve you. I wish you never got involved. I was afraid to tell you everything because I didn't want to lose you." He'd to bow over the bed to understand her.

"What you want is no longer relevant, Zumra. I'll find the bastards who did this to you. But what happened? Where did they take you, and who?"

He was shocked by the hardness in his voice and saw fresh tears in her eyes. He would need time to process all this. "First, we must deal with the current affair, find the man who'd done this to you."

"I've only seen the man in the hotel, and also very briefly. He was young, difficult to estimate his age. He hit me, and I lost consciousness."

He recalled what Mirsad had said.

"You'd never seen that man before?"

"No."

"Why did he hit you?"

"He was expecting another woman, uh... my friend Timka. She'd got her period and asked me to go in her place. The man was furious when he saw me, or better when he realised I wasn't Timka. When I regained consciousness, I was lying in a cell in the basement, completely naked."

"Do you know where that house is?"

"No, I fled through a vast forest."

"Can you describe the house?"

She wiped her tears. "A big house, amid huge conifers and invisible from the road. I tried to escape from the front side," she said. "But a vehicle arrived on a large parking lot in front of the house. Then I rushed toward the rear. There was a door that led outside through the kitchen. I found a narrow path, and I ran." That matched with what the driver, who'd run her over, had told him. The North of Vogosca was mountainous with lots of forests.

"What did they request?"

"They wanted to know everything about Timka, her sister and son. But the woman who tortured me enjoyed it."

He frowned. "A woman has tortured you?"

Zumra nodded. In fits and starts, she described the woman.

"But there was also a man who remained hidden. However, he could see what that woman was doing to me. He questioned me about Timka, through loudspeakers settled in the ceiling.

"After they'd interrogated me, I got an injection. That reduced the hellish pain but put me in a kind of twilight situation. I suddenly thought of seeing Timka, saying everything that woman asked me. Too late I realised that it wasn't Timka, but that horrible woman."

"What did she do to you?" he snorted, annoyed.

While she was telling her story, he got freezing. He'd seen a lot of horrible things and had done them himself. But what she told him touched him deeply.

"How did you get out of there?"

"Back to consciousness, I discovered I was lying in my cell. Then I realised that my daughter was in danger. Those evil people would seek and kill Timka and her son. There's no reason why they should spare my daughter. What that other imprisoned woman had told me, assured me that the abductor was going to kill us all."

"The other woman? You mean..."

"Yes," she interrupted him. "There was another woman. She lay in a cell across the corridor. When they came to get me and turned on the light in the passage, I've seen Emma for a moment. Awful, she no longer looked human. Her face got mutilated beyond recognition, and her body was full of wounds. That's the last time I saw her. When I got back, she was gone."

"Emma? Did she say her name?"

"Yes, Emma Badora. She'd worked in a bar and was on her way to Romania when they abducted her. She told me that she'd trusted the aid worker."

Lazar held his breath for a moment. Emma Badora, the woman who got abducted on the way to the airport. He contemplated what Stone had said about a teddy bear his girlfriend had handed her roommate. Emma Badora. Without knowing, his Zumra got involved in the murder cases he was investigating.

"You don't know where they took Emma?" he asked.

"No idea, but given her condition, she'll not have survived for long.

"How could you get out?"

Her voice was shaking when she told how she got free, and he didn't interrupt her once. *I can't believe how she attacked and killed her female executioner*. It was his duty to register her statement, but he refused to do that to her. What she'd been through justified her action. It's an act of legitimate self-defence. He decided to investigate the case himself, as there was a link to the Badora murder.

When she got silent, arrived at the point where she'd opened her eyes in a hospital room, he asked out loud, "Do you know why they are looking for Timka?"

"They're looking for her son to make him disappear."

Suddenly he was in a great hurry to visit Timka.

Friday, 11 October 2002

FIFTY-TWO

LAZAR FELT EXHAUSTED, WORN AND DRAINED, HIS MUSCLES AND HIS MIND WERE taut. He needed rest. After a few sleepless nights, a day off would be welcome. Zumra's confession was still occupying his thoughts, and he required calm to figure it all out. He closed the door, didn't even bother to turn on the lights and stepped into the lounge. After leaving the hospital, he'd visited Timka's lodging, but hadn't found anyone home. Why bother about her friend and kids? She'd cheated on him. Might he ever forgive her?

He turned on the lights and stiffened. Then his hand flew to his hip.

"Freeze, Chief Inspector Magas, I don't want to hurt you," snarled the intruder, an athletic-looking man sitting in an armchair which was turned toward the hall door. The intruder had an angular face with green eyes, thick eyebrows and firm chin. Lazar ignored who he was. For sure, not a burglar; the man had been waiting for him.

Lazar's eyes focused on the gun that the man was pointing at him. A high dose of adrenaline shot through his veins, and his muscles trembled, ready for action. *Three steps. Not insurmountable.*

"What do you want me to do?" he asked with feigned resignation,

"Stay calm. I'm here to prevent you from wasting your time." The man waved to the other armchair, and Lazar sat down hesitantly, weighing up his chances. The intruder across to him was not far away. Under normal circumstances, he could handle such a situation. Everything depended on the opponent. However, the man was tall and muscled.

"If I'd intended to kill you, you'd already be dead," the stranger said.

"An unusual introduction for a friendly chat," Lazar retorted. He thought of his gun, but the man seemed to read his mind.

"Leave your gun where it is, and no one gets hurt." The man smiled. "I had a busy day, and that makes me nervous. But to avoid any misunderstandings, I'm Jasmina's brother. You know Jasmina as Zumra."

Lazar frowned. "Wow. But why didn't she tell me about you?"

"Because she thinks I'm dead, just as I thought she got killed years ago. It's only since yesterday I'm aware she lives in Sarajevo and has problems. I guessed that I'd find her here. Do you know where she is?" His voice suddenly sounded threatening.

"I talked to her about an hour ago. What's your name?"

"They call me Edhem, but my real name is Kamal. That's all you need to know for the time being. We all have something to hide, don't we, Chief

Inspector Magas?"

Lazar got cold. What did this man know about him? *Does he play poker?*

"So you know where Jasmina is?" Edhem lowered his weapon.

"Yes, but what proves to me that you're her brother?"

"We're both from Srebrenica. In 1995 she worked there as an interpreter at Dutchbat 3 where she met a Dutch officer named Bram Ruyter. This man tried to save our family, but a certain Cees Visser had him locked up for obstruction. Cees wanted him out of the way to rape Jasmina, but he failed. Out of revenge, he threw her out of the compound. That's all I know. When I could neither find Jasmina, our sister Azra, nor our parents in Tuzla, I assumed that they were dead and buried in an anonymous mass grave. Yesterday, by chance, I met a girl having my sister's features. Jasmina has a child and gave it the name of our sister. Is that enough?"

He's seen Jasmina's daughter! His heartbeat increased. Where was Timka, her son and Azra now? Was the man in front of him involved in their disappearance?

Lazar tried to hide his shaking hands by sliding them between his thighs.

"Was Azra alone when you met her?" he asked.

"Timka, her son Hadar and Azra are safe with Bram."

Lazar shot up. "Bram Ruyter?"

"Yes, the man you're hunting is innocent of everything you want him to blame. Or do you think he sent you those three pictures? More about that later. Where's Jasmina?"

Lazar kept quiet. How did Edhem know about the photos?

"Lazar, we don't have much time for games. You're looking for the truth, as I do, and I'm willing to collaborate. I'm going to take you to Bram, but I want to talk to Jasmina first."

Lazar shook his head. " Jasmina is in the hospital and requires some rest."

The man jumped out of the armchair.

"What, what happened?" he excitedly shouted. "I know about Loverboy. Timka told us, that's Bram and me, that you're her boyfriend. That's why I'm here. Is Loverboy responsible for what happened to her?"

Lazar could read Loverboy's death sentence in the sparkling green eyes.

"Loverboy took Jasmina to a hotel room," he began.

"Yes, I know. Eurotel. Timka admitted that she'd to go to the rendezvous, but that she was unwell. That's why Jasmina replaced her. Since Tuesday afternoon, she hasn't given a sign of life."

"Well, I believe you're telling the truth. Why did you take care of Timka, her son and Azra? And where?"

Edhem sat down again. "We all have something to hide, including Timka."

Lazar listened attentively to the staggering story about Suada who'd relinquished her son to her sister Timka, the bastard of a British general. The irrefutable evidence of misconduct and perhaps of a conspiracy involving

Serbs, UNPROFOR officers and a general of the Bosnian army.

"Unheard of," Lazar growled. "How can you be so sure someone's after Timka's adopted son?"

"Until yesterday I didn't know anything about it." Edhem took a break. "Timka got in danger when Mayke, that's Bram's wife, showed up here."

"The reporter who got killed in an accident last year," admitted Lazar with a grin.

"That's right. But as you probably know, it wasn't an accident. Mayke had met Suada as part of her investigation on misconduct at UNPROFOR. Misconduct that translated into the rape of Muslim women in captivity. Suada told a staggering story, and from that moment Mayke started a crusade against General Flower, the highest British commander here in 1994. This son of a bitch appears in several reports established after the war. But all the time he denies the accusations, claiming that testimonies from revenge-seeking women have no value at all. He demanded substantial evidence and added gloriously that such evidence didn't exist. Mayke tried to interview that man, but he refused. Eventually, she came here, met Timka's mother, then Timka and her son. She first wanted to make sure Suada's story was not a fake, before publishing it. Then she drove to Pale to get concrete evidence, knowing where Suada had hidden General Flower's wallet. Flower wouldn't be able to deny it any more."

Lazar nodded.

"Did Flower think he'd destroyed all evidence with the death of that reporter?" he asked.

Edhem shook his head. "I don't think Flower knew anything about his son, at first. Otherwise, he would have found him already."

"But how did Flower know that Mayke possessed evidence?"

"A few days before Mayke left for Pale, she visited a party at the EUMM. She spoke to several people there. One of them was Derek Fleming."

Lazar immediately thought of Emir Besic's neighbour.

"What does he have to do with it?" he asked.

"We don't know yet, but Bram thinks that Fleming knew Mayke's plans, that he got killed her, or that he passed on information to General Flower. That's why Bram asked Emir Besic to keep an eye on Fleming."

Lazar sat up. New pieces of the puzzle fell into place.

"I am Bram's friend," Edhem said. "He told me everything. We were both in Srebrenica, and he did everything he could to save not only my sister but my whole family. That forges a close bond."

Lazar sighed inaudibly. Through Edhem's explanations, he started to see the light through the forest. He suspected that more revelations would follow.

Edhem leaned in. "Before we go on, I want you to tell me what happened to Jasmina."

Lazar told him everything Jasmina had revealed to him. When he'd finished his story, he looked at a trembling man. Meantime, Edhem had put away his Glock, which didn't mean that it would be easy to take him by surprise. However, he wasn't going to do that. Edhem might be an excellent collaborator.

"You said Emma Badora was there too?" Edhem said.

Lazar nodded.

Edhem continued. "Bram has managed her record. It bothered him enormously that those criminals had got her back into their hands, what turns out to have been a wrong assumption."

"I know that Bram took a leave after Emma Badora's abduction."

"Is that a crime? He was affected by Emma's disappearance."

"Furthermore, Emma Badora knew Daria Bazila, who in turn got murdered by a foreigner. Everything points to a Belgian IT on EuPol's payroll."

Lazar did the whole story about his murder case and what Stone had revealed about the relationship between Daria and Emma.

Edhem frowned. "A teddy bear would be the cause of Emma's abduction and torture. And of Daria's murder?"

"Murders are seldom complicated," Lazar said. "Usually, we find the perpetrator in the immediate circle of acquaintances or family members. Far too many clues convince me that the real perpetrator has staged a passionate murder to make Stone the prime suspect. I see the absence of his laptop as sufficient proof of his innocence."

Edhem stayed quiet.

Lazar continued. "I know that your friend Bram had visited Greg Stone shortly before Daria got killed." He briefly explained what Stone had told him about this meeting.

Edhem frowned. "So Stone mails pictures to Bram and shortly after his visit Daria gets murdered, and the perpetrator steals Stone's laptop."

Lazar nodded. "That's right. We may now rule out a passionate murder."

"It's no coincidence that either Emma and Daria got murdered. What do you have on the Frenchman of whom Daria thought he wanted to kill her?"

Lazar shook his head. "I tried to track him down, but he doesn't seem to exist. No one under the name Dragon Borjan works for EuPol."

FIFTY-THREE

I SHOULD HAVE BEEN MORE SUSPICIOUS. I'VE BEEN CARELESS. VERY CAUTIOUSLY Bram laid his holster on the table. But why didn't the Watson brothers come in earlier? Then he remembered that Tim knew he'd got a gun. Being masked, he would never get unharmed into the house. So he'd explored the surroundings to prepare his action, waiting for the early morning to take his chance. Someone who's done a night shift got tired and wasn't so vigilant any more.

Bram heard a car stop. A door slammed shut, and someone entered the house. Gazing over his shoulder, he saw a second Watson emerge into the kitchen. A man with a head injury and an arrogant grin on his face, holding a gun. Tim Watson.

"Hello, Bram," Tim chuckled amused. "You've already met my brother Sam."

At that moment, another door swung open.

"Mummy, Mummy..." Hadar yelled in a faint panic, searching for his mum.

Tim Watson grinned and stepped into the living area. Bram tried to get up, but Sam's wild waving with his gun withhold him.

"So you're Hadar," he heard Tim saying.

Another door opened, followed by Timka's scream. His muscles tighten, but Sam Watson shook his head.

"You won't get very far," he warned.

Bram believed him.

"Enter the room," he heard Tim shouting.

The fear was bubbling up in him, but he wasn't afraid of himself. *They are here for Hadar*. He also had no illusions about the fate of the others.

"Where's your notebook?" shouted Sam in his face.

Bram got confused. *Notebook?*

"I don't have a laptop here," he retorted after a brief hesitation. Sam stepped up to him and slapped him hard in the face. Bram could well bear the pain; his whole life had been a succession of all kinds of pain. When he heard Hadar and Azra crying, he jumped up but got pushed back into the armchair with brute force.

Madness.

Timka called out his name.

Sam hit Bram again.

"Where's your laptop?" he shouted in anger. "Should we get Timka her?"

Bram felt like a snorting lion on chains, trying to understand. But no matter how well his neurons did their best, they didn't produce answers. *Damned, my laptop doesn't contain anything valuable.*

"Why do you want my laptop?"

In response, he received another blow.

"What would I do with a laptop here?" roared Bram in powerless anger. "I left it on my desk."

A new blow. *Yes, come closer, Sam, one more step and your brother, will lose his twin.*

Sam made another step.
Bram knocked the gun hand aside and rammed his fist into Sam's stomach while he jumped upright. Sam looked like a boulder, although he stepped back and gasped for breath.
Bram kicked to his knee but only hit the upper leg. Sam screamed in pain and stumbled backwards. But he was a trained fighter who instinctively understood that he'd to get out of Bram's reach.
I have to take his gun. Then he felt metal in his neck.
"Stop it, immediately," Tim called out behind his back.
Bram had lost his chance, the fight was over. Tim had been reacting faster than he'd expected. *I'm not good enough against those highly trained bastards.*
Sam got furious, ready to kill. But Tim stopped him with a shorthand gesture.
"We still need him," he said.
A blow in the hollows of his knees brought Bram down. One moment later, Tim turned him on his stomach.
"Put your hands on your back," he yelled.
Lying on his belly, he was utterly defenceless. Fear started to overwhelm him. He heard one of the brothers moving out. A door slammed, and footsteps were coming back.
"Sam, to you," Tim snarled.
When Sam pressed his ankles together, starting to wrap them with tape, he thought that the end was imminent. His situation became hopeless. In a few minutes, Sam finished wrapping his lower legs and his forearms.
Bram was lying on the floor near the couch. As he lifted his head, he saw Tim going into the kitchen, dragging Timka by the hair. The kids were crying in the other room.
"Where's your notebook?" asked Sam once more.
"I don't have a laptop here. If not in my office, it should be at my home."
Timka screamed when Tim squeezed one of her breasts.
"We searched your house. It's not there," Tim said impatiently, getting ready to hurt Timka even more.
"Have you checked the wardrobe?" Bram asked desperately.
"We have…"
"But you didn't find the double bottom, on the left side. That's where I hide my gun and laptop. So, you didn't find any ammunition either." He hoped that the answer would satisfy him. Bram needed time, a lot of time. He hoped that the police would catch these guys if they ventured into his lodging. The brothers seemed not being aware that the police was searching for him.
Tim frowned. "A hiding place?"
"Yes, or do you think I'd leave my gun on an unsecured place, being in a

country where burglary is part of everyday life? It's a plank that falls into a groove."

"Well, I'll believe you, but if we don't find anything, I'll kill you. By the way, how did you come over here?"

"A friend brought us."

"And where is your friend now?"

"I don't know. Tomorrow I would have come down to your house to arrange food delivery."

"And where's your duty car?"

"In town, near Central Café."

"Hum." After a short pause, he raised his eyebrows. "Do you have the code of the garage?"

Bram shrugged. "The envelope containing the code is in my office safe and must only be accessed in case of an emergency, as you probably know." Tim didn't know that the deputy also knew the code. Anyway, he'd always managed his own rules, as having keys near the safe houses.

But Tim seemed satisfied and left him alone, getting the kids out of the room. Hadar seemed terrorised while Azra tried to appease him, holding his hand while following Tim to the kitchen. She looked terrified. Hadar desperately clung to his mother.

"Can I change clothes?" Timka begged.

"You don't need any clothes where you're going," answered Tim with a broad grin. His words betrayed their fate. They left the house, and Bram heard car doors slamming.

The twins stayed away for minutes. When they returned, Tim made a tour of the rooms, examining all the furniture, including the command post.

He's still looking for the laptop.

Then Sam appeared in his field of vision, holding a syringe in his hand.

That's it, then. But Tim's earlier remark echoed through his head. *'We still need him.'* They still needed him, letting him there because it was the safest place. Winston wasn't aware. But they would come back, kill him and bury his body in the woods.

Unfortunately, Bram didn't have his fate in his own hands. He felt the sting in his buttock, and his surroundings became blurred.

Until he lost all memory.

FIFTY-FOUR

LAZAR SAT BEHIND HIS DESK, SIPPING COFFEE FROM A HUGE MUG, CONTEMPLATING if whether or not he'd release Greg Stone. He looked around, leaned back and glanced thoughtfully at the window, sensing the strong smell of coffee that filled the room. Stone was innocent, but if he released him, Daria's killer would soon find out, and that would put Stone in mortal danger. Those guys didn't take any chances. On the other hand, keeping Stone in custody could lead to diplomatic difficulties.

I'll hold him for a few more days, he decided, hoping Stone would accept his justification. He sipped coffee again, fidgeting with his hair as he always did when thinking. His gaze roamed over the report sent by the forensic department and a small envelope next to it. But his thoughts were not yet focused on a new day. He yawned loudly, thinking about his nocturnal visitor. Soon they'd gather at Kamal's home. Edhem or Kamal, whatever.

His night had been far too short, and he'd given up a day off. He'd also skipped breakfast, and hadn't shaved. Over coffee, he'd listened to the radio and suffered a slight shock when he'd heard the news of Ivar Ragnarsson's death, which had touched him deeply, for, despite their complicated relationship, he'd always respected Ivar for his integrity.

The secretary found his body behind his desk. Heart attack due to stress, the reporter had concluded, after EuPol had published a communiqué.

What an inglorious ending for such a great man, he thought. He hardly knew Normand Montpetit, the deputy commissioner designated as the Viking's replacement.

Zumra and her brother flashed through his mind. How must he go on with their story? He contemplated Edhem's proposal to involve Stone since there was a link between Daria Bazila and Emma Badora. *No, there are already too many deaths in this case*. Stone had to be kept in secure custody. Moreover, he wanted to meet with an arms dealer first.

Then he thought of Bram with mixed feelings, studied the brown folder for a while, picked it up and extracted its contents, clearing his mind. A list of the telephone company, a report about the cell phone found in Ahmed's car and a picture of its owner. Lazar cursed internally. He had assumed that the cell phone found in Ahmed's gloves compartment belonged to Emir Besic. But now he found out that it belonged to Safet Begovic. This got him confused for a moment. He grabbed the phone list of which were notified the conversations of the whole month until the day of Begovic's dead. After going through the list, he leaned back, closing eyes. *A familiar number, several conversations*, he thought.

After a while, he took his phone and called Drazen.

"Hi Drazen, this is Lazar. Can you arrange a meeting with Trifko this morning? It's a matter of life and death, also for him."

Few police officers knew that the restaurant owner Drazen Korac was a confidant of the federation's most fearsome arms dealer: Trifko Petrovic.

"I'll call back," replied Drazen, and he broke the connection.

Lazar called Fadila. "Collect everything you can find about *White Wolves*. It's urgent."

Hardly had he hung up, or his phone buzzed.
Message from Drazen.

At ten o'clock. Alone.

The envelope on his desk caught his attention, and he picked it up. There was nothing written on it. Curiously, he tore it open. A CD fell on the desk.
Mirsad.
He inserted the CD in his notebook, selected the video file and stiffened, watching the scene.

Jasmina steps into the room. Loverboy says something and moves out. After a while, a guy emerges into the suite and unexpectedly slaps her in the face. The blow staggers her, and she falls, her head touching the corner of the table. She keeps motionless. The man hesitates, pick her up, put her over his shoulder and leaves the room.

He had the scene played three times.
Everything fitted with what Zumra had told him in the hospital. Finally, he put the cover with the CD in the bottom desk drawer, put his head in his crossed arms and wept silently.

FIFTY-FIVE

BRAM GENTLY PULLED UP HIS EYELIDS, SAW DUSK AND HEARD BIRDS SINGING beyond the walls. He couldn't move his arms, recalling they got tied behind his back, and his lower legs taped together. Inside his head, drums were hammering to the rhythm of his heartbeat.
Sunrise.
Gradually his neurons began to function again. Moving his head caused a spinning sensation. He groaned, being glad that his mouth was not stuck shut. His lips felt like dry cardboard, and he yearned for water.
The Watson faces flashed through his mind.
"Timka, Azra, Hadar," he yelled.
No reaction. Cursing in frustration, Bram started to remember. Any attempt to move his body caused pain bumps electrocuting his brain. The man who'd taped him knew his trade. The dizziness and dry mouth were the aftereffects of the anaesthetic he got injected. However, they'd miscalculated the dose; he wasn't supposed to wake up before their return. *Stay calm. There is a solution to everything.* There wasn't much time left, Azra's life was at stake. His concern for that vibrant child who was his daughter exceeded the fear of his future. He also thought of Hadar and

Timka, who were in even greater danger. Being alive meant that they still needed him. Why? He closed his eyes and took a deep breath. *I'm lying in the kitchen. How do I get out of here?*

Even if Edhem showed up, he had no way of getting in. Without keys, this was only possible by operating the electrical installation from the command post. *Perhaps Edhem won't come back.*

He'd been a trained military man in another life. A long time ago, but he'd kept his body fit, more or less. Every day he ran ten to fifteen kilometres if he had the time. At least four times a week. He ate healthily and didn't show a gram of obesity. But the way Watson had wrapped him up, it was almost impossible to get on his feet.

Then he heard footsteps stopping at the rear door, followed by a loud knock on the door.

"Bram, it's me." It was Edhem's voice.

"They've robbed me," he shouted. "I'm tied up, lying on the floor."

"What about Timka and the kids?"

"Abducted by Watson," he yelled. "I'll try to get free." The words shot out his mouth like an irregular salvo. Thirst tormented him. Holy shit, he must have slept for hours.

"Can I force the door? Maybe by car," shouted Edhem.

"I doubt it. Wait and see. Are you armed?"

"Don't worry."

"If someone comes, don't trust him! Not even if he claims to be from *Last Hope*," Bram yelled, struggled to lift his head to have a look at the sink.

A block of knives.

After taking a deep breath, he rolled like a sausage across the floor toward the fridge and the sink, which was more difficult than he'd hoped. Every time he lay on his stomach, he'd got to concentrate on tilting his weight sideways before overturning his entire body again. He fell back twice. The sweat was pearling on his forehead, pricking in his eyes and blinding him. He continued to roll over. Arrived at the fridge, he took a short rest. Then he turned on his back, retook a deep breath and shifted his body until it lay perpendicular to the sink. He slowly lifted his feet to the doorknob, and after four attempts, he got the door ajar. Eventually, he got the door fully open with a lateral foot kick.

The exercise had absorbed a lot of energy. For minutes, he kept on his back, heavy panting. Then he hooked his heels behind the sill of the cupboard, pulling his body forward. After another pause, he bowed his knees against his chest, stretched his lower legs in the air and let them descend against the edge of the metal sink. Using his heels again, he pulled his body somewhat closer to the cupboard, until his shoulders found support on the floor, while his calves were hanging over the sink.

The knife block stood to the left of his feet. He knew that the first attempt had to be the right one. His limbs hurt, and he couldn't hold this position for long. Closing his eyes, he let his body tilt to the left until gravity took it over from his will. Everything went very fast. As his body lost balance, his feet slid in the right direction, hitting the wooden block that started to shove to the edge. Then it was diving, followed by his legs. He tilted to the side, felt a painful jolt in his loins, while the wooden block hit the ground with a dull blow. From the corner of his eye, he watched two knives flying out. It took a lot of effort to get on his back again.

The tilted block lay next to the cupboard door, which he shut with a head kick.

"Are you all right?" Edhem shouted,

"Yes, be patient."

Bram rolled aside, moving his head toward the knives. He grabbed the handle of the longest knife between his teeth, pulled it out of the block, took a deep breath, and cautiously turned his body around until his head reached the sink. After pausing for a time, he proceeded, pushing his feet on the floor and moving his bottom toward the lower cabinet until his back leaned against it. His daily relaxation exercises now proved their worth. Sucking air into his mouth along with the knife handle, he bent his upper body forward, pressed the blade between his shins into the tape and made careful sawing movements. Although the knife was razor-sharp, it laboriously cut through several layers of tape. His jaw muscles got cramped, and his mouth opened. The knife fell clattering next to his feet.

His heart was beating fast, and it took him a few minutes to catch his breath again. With an extreme effort, he got up. His jaws, his back, his calves and his thighs were aching. Along the backside, the tape still glued his lower legs together, but after some prying and squeezing, they got free. Eventually, he stood in a spread position.

"I can move," he shouted.

"Can you open the door?"

"I'll try that now."

He rushed to the command post and saw to his surprise that the screens were still on. *They have been in a hurry.* On one of the screens, he saw Edhem looking at the camera. He bent over the switchboard, counting several buttons, pushed his forehead on one of them and heard a buzzing sound. On the screen, he saw Edhem opening the door.

The adrenaline was gone.

His whole body began to tremble, and dizziness took him by surprise.

Everything got blurred.

The faintness was short-lived. Fortunately, Edhem had turned up on time, catching and holding him upright when he stumbled out of the command room.

Totally extinguished Bram sat down on the couch in the living room. All his limbs hurt. Edhem immediately loosened the tape, but Bram could barely move his arms, while his legs felt like concrete.

Edhem found the rest of rakija in the kitchen and gave him a half-filled whisky glass. "That will get you back on your feet quickly."

Bram swallowed the moisture, and shudder pierced his body. A pleasant lightness as if he'd been smoking hashish, pushed the heavy feeling away.

"I reacted too late," he said, and he told Edhem how the twins had surprised him. When he got up from the couch to stretch his legs, Edhem asked, "Where's your laptop?"

Bram smiled. "In the trunk of my car, I put in the garage."

"They'll get their hostages to a hideout. After that, they'll go to your house. For whom do they work?"

Bram shrugged. "I employed Tim as a security guard. I didn't know he had a twin brother. I'll have to inform Winston."

"Why did Tim Watson take a job at *Last Hope*? Because you were there? If I've understood everything correctly, he also knew that your laptop wasn't in your office. How did he get access to it?"

"Our files don't contain state secrets, and we don't wage war on human traffickers, other human rights corporations do. We give accommodation until the women return to their country. Why should we lock our offices during duty time? We've got no secrets from each other. What Tim Watson is looking for in my computer is a mystery to me."

Edhem frowned. "You'd better check your notebook, Bram. I've visited Chief Inspector Magas, and he gave me a lot of information. He has spoken to Jasmina in the hospital."

Bram listened tensely to Edhem's story about Jasmina's experiences.

He shook his head. "Tortured in a medieval cellar. Your sister is a survivor. First Srebrenica and now this? Furthermore, she has spoken to Emma Badora. Holy shit, what's all that supposed to mean?"

"Bram, what did Greg Stone tell you?"

"How do you know I've visited him?"

"Magas has arrested Stone on suspicion of the Daria Bazila killing. That would have happened after you'd visited him. Did he e-mail you pictures?"

Bram looked puzzled. "They were in love with each other. I've talked to Daria as Stone was away. No, Stone didn't kill her."

"So those photos are now on your laptop?"

"Not exactly, they're in my mailbox. Why all these questions? What does Stone have to do with my laptop?"

"That's what I'm wondering. At least the Watson brothers are looking for your laptop. I suggest we take a look at those photos as soon as possible."

Bram hit himself against the forehead. "Of course, Tim Watson, the torture cellar, the place where Jasmina got under the car..."

Edhem interrupted him. "All right, we'll drive to my place. I have the internet."

"I hope I'm right. I think I know who's behind the abduction."

FIFTY-SIX

LAZAR PASSED A LARGE STONE ARCH, THE ENTRANCE TO ONE OF THE LARGEST AND most famous market places in Sarajevo. People loaded with carrier bags were walking in both directions. Every day early in the morning, the two massive iron gates opened, and they closed late in the evening. An attraction for natives and foreigners who met in the various cafeterias for various reasons.

But this place was also the working area where merchants sold illegal cigarettes and other products. Vegetable stalls offering tomatoes filled with drugs. That trading empire was part of a shadow economy, presumed harmful to the state, however, of vital importance to the population.

Everyone was aware of it, and the local police allowed it, which EuPol was watching with a crooked eye. Some police officers doing their rounds there came to collect their financial compensation for their blindness or protection.

Lazar knew what was going on in this prominent market place and he bit his lower lip, turning up a narrow road alongside the entrance gate. Fadila was following at fifty metres. Finally, he'd decided not to go alone. But his colleagues would stay outside.

Two hundred metres farther, Lazar turned brusquely into a dead-end road. This place was known to many, but no one talked about it. Only insiders ventured into this area. Behind the verge on the left side were a few houses, while the right side of the path, over a length of more than fifty metres, was bordered by high concrete plates. In the middle of it was a heavy iron door with a spy.

He drove down the cul-de-sac, turned and came back until the iron gate, stopping in front of it. Fadila came to a halt at a car length behind him.

Lazar glanced at Senad. "You stay in the car. If I haven't sent a text message within ten minutes, come and get me." He didn't expect any problems because he'd got an appointment, and as long as he respected the unwritten rules, there would be no problems. But in this environment, where both politicians and notorious gangsters were guests, you could never be sure. Yet he did not expect any surprises at this hour. Drazen Korac was not an idiot.

Before he got out, he checked his Sig-Sauer P228, the gun he'd also used at the FBI. *Always be prepared.* He moved firmly toward the iron door, found the small bell button in the doorpost, and gave the agreed signal.

As he waited, he looked in Fadila's direction and nodded briefly. Everyone was tense.

Behind the green door, it remained quiet. No footsteps, no voices. Lazar repeated the signal and heard the sound of ringing in the distance. Impatient, he looked up and down the street to each side, glanced at the low houses across the meadows, spun around and put his ear against the door. He didn't catch a noise.

He checked his watch; he was on time. Had Drazen discovered he wasn't alone? He impatiently pushed the handle down, and the door opened squeakily. Grabbing his gun, he turned around and beckoned his friend to join him. But Senad had already reacted and stood next to the car.

Lazar pushed the door fully open and pointed his gun into the gap, gazing to all sides in the garden. He walked inside, staring at the wooden benches and tables dispersed over the whole area. Once the others had joined, he proceeded. A path of concrete tiles led to the porch of which the double sliding door was open. Odd. Senad stayed close behind him while the other team members scattered across the grass where a few benches stood under the treetops of chestnut trees.

Drazen would never have left the door open.

Reaching the porch, he hesitated; it could be dangerous to go inside, although it was the only way.

They crossed the porch and halted at the entrance of the restaurant. Lazar knew this place well. He beckoned Senad to cover the right side, also fearing the left-wing since he would be an excellent target. When Fadila joined him, he took a deep breath, jumped through the doorway, made a rollover and came to a standstill against the counter.

I'll have at least a few blue spots.

Senad followed his example.

Seconds ticked away but nothing happened. Lazar kept lying flat on his stomach, the barrel of his gun pointed at the corner of the bar.

"NTR," Senad called out.

Fadila rushed into the room, jumped to the left and toppled a table. She halted alongside the short wall next to the toilet and aimed her gun at the bar.

Nijaz ran to the right side, covered by Nizet.

"NTR," he shouted.

While Fadila was holding the counter and the kitchen door at gunpoint, Lazar grabbed a chair, swung it over the bar, and sprinted around its corner, where he rolled sideways across the floor. He lay on his belly, aiming his weapon at the room behind the tap cabinet, noticing nothing else than shattered glass.

He crawled up and pointed his gun to the toilet doors. While Nijaz and

Izet were holding the kitchen door at gunpoint, Fadila opened the doors one by one. Lazar didn't have to shoot. He turned toward the kitchen, the last place to check. Draze didn't live here but in one of the buildings across the fields. He beckoned Nijaz to take position near the portal and then glanced shortly at Senad who fiercely nodded. Nijaz grabbed the handle and threw the door open. Lazar quickly took two steps forward, while the barrel of his pistol described a large arc. For a second he stood there as paralysed. Then he lowered his weapon, the moment Senad was joining him. A coppery odour of blood hung in the air.

It was a classic kitchen with wooden tables, large refrigerators and cookers with countertops alongside the long wall. Lazar saw a couple of things sticking out beyond the door. He stepped forward and halted. A large red-coloured man lay sprawled on his back half-hidden behind the door, against the high shelving full of kitchen utensils.

Throat cut. The head was bathing in a pool of blood that slowly ran away to a floor grid. Blood and particles from Drazen's skull stuck to one of the shelves. Someone had shot a bullet through his head from behind.

Lazar stepped toward the refrigerators, shuffled along the front of the table and stopped at a body, stretched out on his back. A long, muscular guy without a head, which lay in a large blood puddle a step away. A thin bloodstream flowed alongside the stoves toward a gutter on the floor. The stench of blood was pungent.

Lazar spun around.

"We have to get out of here," he shouted. "This is a matter of the Organized Crime Department." Making this decision was a professional mistake, but he thought of Edhem and Bram, convinced that their lives were in danger.

Fadila did not seem to understand. "And what happens in this case?"

"You'll return to headquarters," Lazar snarled. "Did you see the beheaded man? That reminds me of the war. I have an important appointment now. And not a word to Egzon. We've never been here, is that clear?"

"I got it."

They emerged from the house, rushing toward their cars.

"Who are these guys?" Senad asked.

"The fat one was the owner, Drazen Korac. The other Trifko Petrovic."

When they got into their seats, Lazar caught Senad staring at the entrance.

"How did the perpetrators know that we would come here?" he asked.

Lazar frowned.

After a few seconds, his features became grim. "I have two answers to that." He was thinking about what he'd said to his team the day before. *I have to contact Trifco.*

"But I reject the first," he continued.

"And the second answer?" Senad asked.

"Microphones in my office or our team meeting room."
He grabbed his cell phone and typed a message.

I'm coming. Lazar.

FIFTY-SEVEN

BRAM HAD ALL THE PHOTOS WHICH STONE HAD SENT HIM BY E-MAIL, STORED ON HIS notebook. While managing the viewer, his heart started beating of excitement. *Randomly shot pictures in the EUMM banquet hall.* Those photographs were showing people at the tables and the bar.

"That's not going to work," he murmured when he'd checked half of the stuff.

Edhem looked over his shoulder. "Stone had got these images on his laptop," he clarified, "which Daria's murderer has stolen. That can't be a coincidence. Why else did Tim Watson want your laptop?"

Edhem was right. The answers had to be found in the pictures. If soon he didn't find a trace, they'd never see Azra, Hadar and Timka alive again. He had an idea, but he needed proof.

Fully concentrated, Bram reviewed all the pictures.

"That's crazy," he said.

"What do you mean?"

But Bram didn't answer and scrolled for the third time through the images. Then he focused on three of them. He knew that a wrong interpretation would resume in the death of three people he loved.

"How could I be so blind?" he murmured. Arriving in Sarajevo, he'd only been interested in people who'd posed with Mayke, shown in the photographs she'd sent to him. A big mistake. He should have known that Mayke had met other people. All that time, the solution had been in front of him, and he hadn't seen it. What Edhem had told him about Jasmina's experiences in a creepy house, had given him the first hint.

"I know the person who's in control," Bram said. "And I'm afraid of Azra, Timka and her son. We can't waste any more time."

After a short delay of reflection, he told what he'd discovered, showing Edhem the concerning pictures. "Do you see the man trying to hide behind the ambassador's back? That's Tim Watson." He stabbed his finger on a person among a group of five people.

"And that is our key person." The designated man was sipping of a whisky glass that was hiding half of his face, voluntarily or not.

Edhem nodded. "We must go there immediately to free them. The longer we wait, the less chance to arrive there on time. If I may believe Lazar's testimony, those people killed Emma."

Bram fully agreed. '*Where you go, you don't need any clothes*,' Tim Watson had told Timka while dragging her out of the shelter.

Jasmina had been naked in a cell.

Bram hesitated. "It could end badly if we go there right away. We should make sure that we don't endanger the hostages. I hope it's not too late because they've got already locked up for almost a whole day. However, I've got a plan."

During minutes he explained how they could neutralise the Watson brothers with a minimum of risk for the hostages.

Edhem agreed. A few minutes later, he handed him a new Glock and a syringe of which he briefly explained how to handle it. Bram gazed surprised, but there was no time for questions.

Five minutes later, he left.

Bram took a deep breath after the security guard had let him in. He walked with long steps down the hallway and entered the office without knocking.

Winston sat at his desk and looked puzzled as he recognised the visitor. He smiled, but his features were cramped.

He cleared his throat. "Hey, Bram, what are you doing here? You didn't want to come back to work until Monday, anyway."

Bram looked at the adjacent office, greeting the secretary behind his desk. Peter Camden waved shortly and returned typing on his keyboard.

Bram stepped toward the wooden desk and stopped in front of his chief.

"Something terrible has happened," he said almost in a whisper. "You should come with me. But it's confidential." His upper body slightly bent over the desk.

Winston looked suspicious. "Did you know that the police were here for you?"

"Yes, but that was a misunderstanding. I didn't kill Cees Visser. I'm here because someone urgently needs help. You give me your word that if you don't agree, you immediately forget what I've been asking you."

Winston hesitated. "What do you want?"

Bram noticed that he was always staring at the connecting door, scratching his fingers through his beard.

"I made a blunder, Winston. I should never have employed Tim Watson."

The older man's eyes widened. "Why? Because they got him by surprise?"

"No, no. I told you about my friend Jasmina in Srebrenica. I thought she was dead, do you remember?"

Winston didn't answer.

"Jasmina is alive! Do you hear? Jasmina is alive, Winston."

The man occasionally glanced again at the connecting door, as if he feared that Peter Camden could be listening to their conversation. But Bram saw that the secretary didn't show any interest.

"Watson knows Jasmina and her girlfriend. Therefore I've given three people shelter," Bram said.

Chambers's eyes narrowed. "What did you do?"

Bram knew Winston wouldn't tolerate such initiatives. He sighed. "I wanted to tell you, but I didn't have time. Watson is a psychopath working for the traffickers. He staged Emma's abduction. And now that cunt has Jasmina's girlfriend Timka and two children in his power. He surprised me, injected me an anaesthetic and left me gagged. I don't know why, either. But I do know that he has tortured my Jasmina." Bram told him what had happened in the shelter.

"Have you been drinking? Tim would have a twin brother?" Winston shouted.

"Believe me, you have to." Bram stared at him beggingly. "I can prove what I say, but you've got to come with me to my car. There's something in the trunk that you've got to see. After that, you decide for yourself whether you help me or not. However, you're my only hope."

Winston narrowed his eyes. "If Tim strapped you, how did you get out?"

"The twins were in such a hurry that they didn't tie me up so well. The dose of anaesthetic was probably too weak."

Winston stood up. "I hope your accusations are justified," he said grumpily. "Otherwise, you can forget your job here. I don't have time for games. On Monday, we're going to talk about the fact that you've used a woman's shelter for personal purposes."

"You'll thank me for it, Winston."

He noticed that Winston was still hesitating. "Tim Watson has made a huge flutter, but it's up to you to decide how to proceed."

"Well, let's get this over. But I hate riddles."

"I can't bring the evidence in here, because if you don't agree, no one should know about it. Then I'll go straight to the police."

Winston sighed, visibly not entirely convinced, and went into the next room.

"I'm off for a while, Peter, keep an eye on things."

"Yes, chief, it's okay," said Peter Camden quietly.

Bram walked out, followed by Winston. At the guard booth, Chambers asked the guy if everything was okay.

"No problem, chief," answered the man after scrutinising all the screens.

When they were through the front door, Bram stopped and looked Winston straight in the eye. "That psychopath abducted Emma to rape and torture her. When did you see Watson for the last time?"

"Yesterday, I think. I didn't notice anything unusual about Tim's behaviour. You'll have to make these accusations hard, Bram; otherwise, you'll be up to your neck in shit. And given your mental problems in the past..." The rest of the sentence got stuck in his throat. "By the way, why are you so secretive about what's in your car trunk?"

As they walked alongside the staff's cars, Bram saw him looking around. "Tim has ugly beaten up Jasmina," he said.

Winston's eyes narrowed, but he kept silent.

When they reached the car, Bram halted behind the trunk. "Did you know that Jasmina lives here under the name Zumra?" he asked softly.

The older man shook his head.

"Winston, I need your help. Jasmina had a harrowing experience. She was taken to the hospital but chose to leave because she was afraid that Watson would find her. That's why I promised to keep her in a shelter until we've Watson taken into custody. Please, Winston, without your help this poor woman is lost. Do it for me."

Bram glanced at the building. From where they stood, he couldn't see the entrance because his car was parked backwards.

"Is she in the trunk?" Winston asked with an expression of displeasure and disbelief in his eyes.

"Don't be alarmed. You've never seen anything like this. My girlfriend got tortured by a beast. That's why I had to put her in the trunk..."

Bram opened the boot lid.

Winston took a step forward, stared with big eyes at the red blanket under which he noticed the shape of a body, and he bowed forward to reveal what lay underneath.

Bram pushed the barrel of the Glock into Winston's neck. "Immediately into the trunk," he ordered.

"You fucking bastard, do you know who I am?"

Bram thrust him hard in the back before the man could react. Winston felt half inside the trunk, while his body effortlessly flattened the wire work that had shaped a human body. Bram jabbed a needle into his thigh while holding the barrel against Winston's genitals. '*Every man gets willingly when his natural jewels are in danger*,' a military instructor had once told him.

'*The serum paralyses the muscles very quickly*,' had Edhem assured him. He hadn't exaggerated. Winston stopped struggling, his eyes turning blank. Bram put his gun away, swayed Winston's legs into the trunk and shut the boot lid, while his eyes quickly roamed the surroundings. He took a deep breath, got into the driver's seat and started the engine, his gaze focused on the building.

No one came running out.

He turned onto the road and accelerated. Everything had gone according to the plan, without arousing suspicion. The first part of his reckless plan had succeeded.

For the staff, Winston had left with Bram Ruyter.

The security guard hadn't seen anything suspicious.

FIFTY-EIGHT

LAZAR AND SENAD FOLLOWED EDHEM TO THE LIVING ROOM, WHERE THEY GOT introduced to Bram. They shook hands, and Lazar studied his striking face a moment, struck by those stinging green eyes accentuated by the black eyebrows, eyelashes, ring beard and shiny black hair. *A sorcerer*, he thought. On the picture he got anonymously, he couldn't see well his long hair, while the strength of his eyes got lost. The cap also hid half of his face. Bram had a firm handshake and endured his gaze with a mocking smile on his lips.

"Until yesterday I wanted to take you into custody," Lazar said with a faint smile. "But you're still on my list as a witness." His eyes wandered across the room toward the intermediate door where Edhem was waiting.

Lazar stepped into an adjoining sparsely furnished room. He frowned on seeing a naked man sitting in an armchair, his hands strapped with plastic strips behind the handrail and ankles on the chair legs. Next to the man lay a pile of clothes with a cell phone on the top. Instantaneous he recognised Winston Chambers, the director of *Last Hope*.

"That's Jasmina's torturer," Edhem said, and he told him why they had abducted the man.

Lazar halted in front of Chambers. A naked man feels particularly vulnerable. Only in novels and films, heroes or criminals are strong enough to let their genitals cut off to keep a secret. Chambers didn't look much the fatherly person whom he'd spoken on Wednesday. Lazar thought of Winston's heartbreaking statements on television about the suffering of the women victims of trafficking. But naked in that chair, the hypocrite looked like a cornered predator with a hateful eye.

Lazar chuckled humourlessly. "As a policeman, I can't approve of this method," he said to Edhem, his head full of conflicting feelings. He'd enjoyed a peaceful American upbringing, but he couldn't deny his Slavic ancestry. Three years of war and Jasmina's agony in mind chased his last merciful feelings. *Any minute lost can be fatal to the three hostages*.

Edhem went behind the prisoner. "A naked man is malleable as clay. This monkey tortured my sister, your girlfriend, Lazar. You've seen what he's done to her. We'll have to exchange him for saving two kids and a woman, but I don't trust his accomplices. SAS people always find ways to turn hopeless situations into their advantage. They're professional killers, and after the handover, they'll try to kill the hostages and us. Hadar's disappearance is their highest priority."

Lazar squeezed his lips together and walked around the poorly furnished room. A chimney without a stove, some old couch next to the window and a wooden table with four chairs.

"Winston is an eminent person who's a good reputation among the humanitarian aid organisations," he said. "Jacques Klein will not be happy." In other circumstances, he would have taken everyone in this house into custody. But the events of the last few days and the certainty that his desk was under surveillance demanded unusual methods. "If Winston is responsible for Jasmina's torture, he'll die."

Bram waved toward the table in the living room, and Edhem got a glass of rakija for each guest before he sat down.

"No doubt, Chambers is Jasmina's torturer," Bram emphasised.

Lazar nodded and reported what Jasmina had told him about the house of horror.

Bram leaned in. "No matter how vague her description, it corresponds to what I've seen on Sunday on my visit. Besides, Winston also has my wife killed."

He speaks excellent Serbo-Croatian, thought Lazar, understanding that Bram didn't want Winston Chambers to hear what they had to say to each other.

Bram gave a brief account of his experiences from the moment he'd taken the children and Timka to the safe house until Chambers's abduction. He described how the twins had kidnapped Timka and the kids, and how he'd managed to get free. He also talked about the photographs he'd found in his mailbox.

Lazar's face brightened up. "Finally, something concrete," he said. "Are you talking about the photos Greg Stone has been sending you?"

Bram nodded.

"When did that happen?"

"Wednesday evening. He sent them to my e-mailbox. Even if the twins had succeeded in stealing my laptop, the pictures weren't on it."

Stone's statements are correct.

"These photos must be significant because some people are killing for them," Bram continued.

Lazar could barely hide his impatience. "Can I see those pictures?"

Bram got up and led him to the living room where he opened his laptop. After starting up a photo viewer, he let his seat to Lazar who sat down and started scrolling through the photo album.

"By the beard of the Prophet," he exclaimed seconds later. "What did Miralem Lulic do at the EUMM?"

"Who?" Bram obviously didn't know that man.

"Lulic is a suspect in one of my homicide cases." Lazar passed to the following image. "Emir Besic," he called out, staring at the screen as if he saw a ghost.

"Yes, I know that guy," replied Bram.

Lazar called Senad, who'd stayed in the other room with the prisoner. When Senad appeared next to him, he reacted in amazement.

"Besic," he muttered.

"Lulic and Besic," Lazar admitted, zooming in on a new photo. The image was blurred, but they could recognise Chambers talking to a woman. That woman was also on the following picture, in conversation with an oriental-looking man.

"Ahmed Salah," Lazar growled.

Bram coughed lightly to get attention. "I saw that woman Sunday at the window of Chambers's house."

Lazar glanced up to him. "Jasmina has probably killed that woman."

Two images later he saw Miralem talking to Salah. He noticed that the woman was on several pictures and always in Chambers's immediate vicinity. *Greg Stone has depicted a secret meeting without realising it. That woman and Chambers must be the central figures.*

Lazar turned to face Bram. "How is it possible that Besic attended a party in the EUMM HQ? This also applies to a few other gloomy individuals."

Bram shrugged. "All aid organisations are invited on St Patrick's Day party. There is no real checking; you enter with someone who has a pass. But Besic certainly had an official invitation. Furthermore, everyone who works for the EU has an EU pass. SFOR has its ID card."

Lazar scrolled through the whole series of images again.

Bram's finger touched the screen. "That's Mayke talking with Chambers," emphasised Bram. "And there Tim Watson and Chambers in a wide-open space, discussing. You recognise them by their clothing."

Lazar's brain was working at full speed. He recognised the man he'd seen on Mirsad's CD. "At the Beard of the Prophet," he shouted. "Tim Watson has abducted Jasmina! Or his double. These photos must have caused Daria's death, and they also explain why Stone had to be the scapegoat." He paused for a few seconds.

"People, we need to free the hostages as quickly as possible," he snarled, turning toward Bram. "Who knows you've taken Chambers hostage?"

Bram shrugged. "No one yet. The employers will be surprised he didn't come back, but there's no reason why they would be alerted."

"When the Twins discover that their boss has left his office with you, they'll assume that you got aid to get free. Or they've already established that by now. We have no time to lose. Probably we still can get the hostages released without much risk. We know Winston's dwelling place, and we're four armed men, enough to invade the house and overpower both inhabitants. But before we go, I'd like to know how his henchmen will behave in the absence of their chief." He beckoned Edhem who was leaning against the doorposts to interrogate the detainee.

Lazar straightened his back. "Winston Chambers probably get the support of the SFOR-group *White Wolves*. He's a psychopath looking for Flower's bastard son to kill. There's little time left for us. Bram, can you make a drawing of Chambers's house with as many environmental details as possible?"

Bram nodded with a grim face. "I know what Chambers wanted from me on Sunday. Giving time to his men for scavenging my house. I was wondering why he lived in the woods, close to a road but invisible. That's now clear. He can torture and kill undisturbed, and make the corpses disappear into the woods. Chambers is a suspicious jerk, and it wouldn't surprise me that he installed cameras. From what Jasmina has told you, we know that there's a descending path at the rear. So someone will set up a diversion on the front side, while the others approach the house from the rear."

Lazar smiled. "It could be more comfortable if we employ Chambers as a diversion. Too bad, we don't have his car. One of us takes him to the front side. Not you, since the twins know you and if they smell danger, they'll use the kids as a shield. Neither can I because my face sometimes appears on television. So Edhem must do it, he speaks excellent English."

Edhem emerged from the adjoining room. "Chambers is the only one who gives orders," he explained. "Tim Watson is his right hand, but he does nothing as long as there is no emergency. If Chambers is no longer able to give orders, Colonel Brubaker of the *White Wolves* must be informed."

"What do you know about those *White Wolves*?" asked Bram.

"We should avoid them," Lazar replied, telling what Mirsad had revealed. He turned to Edhem. "Let Chambers get dressed. We'll take him with us."

Edhem nodded and headed into the other room.

Bram took a paper from the computer table drawer and started drawing a map while Lazar studied all the photos again.

"Bram, is Azra your daughter?" Lazar asked all of a sudden:

Bram nodded. "Yes, she is. I don't know how Jasmina will react when we gather, but Azra is undoubtedly my daughter."

"You know she's with me..."

"Lazar, I knew her in Srebrenica, seven years ago. I have been blaming myself for her death until I've got married. I've been changing. However, Azra is the best thing that ever happened to me. She's still my daughter, and there's nothing we can do about it." They looked at each other until Edhem appeared in the room.

"Chambers is ready for our mission," Edhem announced. "I'll get some equipment." He walked to another door and disappeared into the hallway.

"Bram, you have to hide this laptop in a safe place," meant Lazar. Then he turned to Senad. "You don't have to come with me. It can be dangerous. Besides, I do this entirely unofficially. If Egzon finds out, I'll have to leave the police. I don't want to jeopardise your career."

Senad grinned. "Egzon is a jerk. I'm in."

Bram gave Lazar the paper.

Lazar looked at it and smiled. "Done with military precision. Recognition points, orientation and distances. All right, time to define our strategy."

Fifteen minutes later, two cars drove off the Humska plateau.

FIFTY-NINE

BRAM WAS READY TO KILL. THE MOMENT HE'D AGREED TO FREE THE HOSTAGES, HE knew that no witnesses were to be left behind. Edhem had made that very clear to him. If Lazar resisted, they would take him out. This operation would never have taken place.

The house stood on a hilly plateau in densely wooded surroundings. A narrow path, winding through tall conifers, led to it. Bram and Lazar climbed the steep slope slowly, both holding a gun, while Lazar was also carrying a small suitcase. They had left Senad behind with the car, tucked away among the trees alongside the paved main road; Lazar was afraid that, sooner or later, *White Wolves* would show up and if that happened, Senad had to warn them. It all depended on what the twins had decided in the last few hours. Meantime, they must have understood that something had happened to their boss. *Tim will prepare for a confrontation with me.*

Bram was convinced of Tim's narcissistic personality disorder. Tim would try to solve the problem himself. He had already overpowered Bram once and probably thought that a SAS officer shouldn't fear anyone, certainly not an amateur.

It will never occur to him that I get help.

When he'd shared these considerations with Lazar, the latter got a slight smile on his face. "Maybe you're right, Bram. But it may be dangerous to rely on emotions. We're dealing with an unpredictable guy."

"That's why we'll keep the risks to a minimum," answered Bram without looking at him. He could feel the curious gaze burning on his neck.

"And what does that mean?" asked Lazar with a deep harsh voice.

"My daughter is in their hands. And I don't take any chances, any more than Edhem does. We agreed to kill those arseholes."

Lazar kept quiet.

Bram checked his watch. "Five more minutes," he warned.

Lazar cleared his throat. "These men committed several murders, Bram.

Don't worry, I will not interfere. Anyway, they would soon be free again. These guys get protection at the highest level."

"Edhem and I share that opinion. This operation never happened," Bram growled.

"What will you do after that? Leaving *New Hope*?"

"I doubt if I'm suitable for that kind of work. How many of those girls do you think we've repatriated?"

"I have no idea."

"Not enough. But what can you expect? I can understand that local police officers are corrupt, but not that there are so many rotten apples among the international police observers. The system works poorly. They should screen the candidates better. But that's a national issue, and each country has its proper method of selecting observers. The Americans employ a private organisation for this purpose. DynCorp."

"Bram, IPTF practically belongs to the past. There are police officers from the most corrupt countries in the world, Pakistanis, Malaysians, Russians, and so many others. Those officers don't earn as much as their western colleagues. Can you blame them for trying to exploit as much as possible their opportunity?"

Bram shook his head. "And do you think EuPol will do better than IPTF? They send senior officers for working at the highest level with your Ministry of Internal Affairs, and with the senior police officers, hoping that corruption will disappear. No way. Since when do politicians solve problems?"

Lazar kept silent.

Bram rechecked his watch. "Edhem is moving to the entrance now, let's hope he attracts enough attention."

They increased the pace on the last but steepest part of the path, and a few moments later they reached the rear side of the house. Everything remained quiet. Bram put his ear against the heavy door and listened tensely.

"The kitchen seems deserted," he said muffled.

Suddenly they heard screams on the other side of the building. "The signal," murmured Bram. As planned, Edhem and Winston stood at the front door, and the twins were reacting as expected, probably surprised that not Bram showed up, but a stranger with Chambers as a hostage.

Lazar started to examine the rear door. "It has a robust suspension and an old but solid key lock. The wood is excellent even though it's a few centuries old. Look at the bottom of it."

Bram squatted, seeing what Lazar meant. There was a large gap under the door edge.

"That's the weak point," Lazar explained. "I'll employ the old method."

They heard another voice yelling. Edhem had started a lingering negotiation using Winston as his living shield.

Lazar took a thin rubber mat out of his suitcase and shoved it under the door edge. "Magnetic," he whispered. From a toolbox, he took a pair of pliers that ended in a hollow cylinder with frayed walls.

"I can clamp the rod behind the beard into this pair of pliers. If the mechanism is rusted, I won't be able to exert enough force to turn the key. But then I'll thrust it out of the lock, and it'll fall on the mat that I pull back." Bram hoped Lazar's optimism would turn out to be justified. However, before he could make an ironic remark, he heard a click.

Lazar threw his tools back into his suitcase, took out a pouch he put in his jacket, closed the bag and put it against the wall. Both knew what to do. The Watsons indeed held one of the hostages with them, and he was afraid it was Azra.

Bram pressed the latch down and slammed the door open, while Lazar pointed his gun at the opening. The kitchen was empty. But the door giving access to the corridor was open, and they heard loud voices at the front door.

He recognised Tim's voice. "Who are you? Where's Bram?"

"Bram got arrested for the murder of a fellow countryman," retorted Edhem. "But you already know, don't you? You sent incriminating pictures to the police, didn't you?" Edhem was playing it cunningly.

"If you don't release Winston, we'll kill her," Tim called out, "We have three hostages. If you hurt Winston, we'll kill the rest."

"Well, what are you going to do if you don't have anyone to kill any more? What do you think I'll do with Chambers then?" He was gaining time so Lazar could bring the hostages into safety.

Lazar stepped through the basement door. "Good luck," he hissed.

Bram nodded, waited one minute and progressed cautiously through the hallway toward the entrance, gun at shoulder height. Although the voices sounded loud, he didn't see anyone. He recognised Edhem's voice in the distance. "Don't be a hero. You're alone. There's no need for wasting blood. Hand me over the hostages, and you get Chambers. End of story."

Approaching the hall on his foot tips, a noise behind him made him stiffen. He swivelled around and watched Lazar enter the kitchen, followed by Hadar and Timka who hesitated for a moment. But after he made a fierce gesture, Timka moved and disappeared in the kitchen.

They're holding Azra. His heart was pounding as he halted in front of the hall, fearing for Azra's life. Sam might be next to the staircase on his left. The open front door faced out to the parking lot, but he could catch sight of neither Tim nor Edhem and Chambers. Bram reckoned they were standing out of sight ten to twenty metres from the entrance. To take out Sam, he had to enter the hall, exposing himself to both brothers. The element of surprise would give him at least a second. He hoped Edhem could take out Tim. His hands felt clammy. The longer he waited, the more dangerous it got for Azra. His opponents had nothing to lose.

It is incomprehensible that they left the rear side unguarded. Bram took a deep breath, preparing himself to commit two killings. Shoot to kill, there was no other option. They wouldn't wear bullet-proof jackets.

Then two swishing sounds, followed by a sharp scream, made his heart rate go up. *Azra got struck*! Stepping forward like a raging bear, he saw Azra coming around the doorpost, yelling. She stopped abruptly, clasping to his legs. "Daddy, you've come." She started sobbing wildly.

He lifted and pressed her against his chest, pointing his gun at the staircase. There he saw a pair of legs stretched out on the floor. He put Azra in the hallway and told her to be quiet. Then he rushed forward, discovering in amazement Sam's lifeless body sprawled on his back, with a dark hole in his forehead. *Holy shit, who has shot him?* He turned toward the door, his gun heading in the same direction. Outside, beyond the doorposts, lay Tim Watson's lifeless body.

"Edhem," he called out. Something was wrong. A rifle had shot the brothers, and Edhem did not carry such a weapon.

At that moment two black-clothed men emerged in the doorway, aiming their shouldered automatic weapons at them.

SIXTY

LAZAR SAW BRAM TIPTOEING TOWARD THE HALL. AFTER TAKING A DEEP BREATH, HE descended the stairs. A bulb in the ceiling spread a weak light across the cellar floor. He gazed through a gloomy corridor with a vaulted ceiling and three barred fences aligned on both sides. On his left was an iron door that, according to Zumra's description, led to the torture chamber. He pressed a switch on the wall, and the basement got bathed in a sea of yellow light.

After a few steps, he got struck by a smell of sweat, urine and faeces and a shudder crossed his back. It was worse than he'd imagined.

"Timka, Hadar, Azra," he called out. "Have no fear. I'm Chief Inspector Lazar."

He heard a metallic sound and ran down the corridor, seeing a woman appear at the bars. She looked terrible with swollen eyes and cracked lips, trying to keep her torn nightgown together, wearing shorts in which a trembling little boy was clutching.

"Don't worry," he whispered. "I'll get you out of here. Don't make any noise, and everything will be all right."

He put his gun away, opened his pouch, grabbed a unique burglar tool with which he got the lock open in less than one minute. The chain fell crackling on the grey floor, and he pulled the barred door.

"Follow me. Whatever you see, don't make noise and stay close to me. I'll take you outside into the forest. Then we're going to walk toward a road where a colleague waits with a car."

"Inspector...they have Azra..."

"I know," he interrupted her. "From now on, you keep quiet and follow me close." As he started walking, he grabbed his gun. Beneath the stairs, he paused for a time to listen. Then he climbed the stone steps. Once in the hallway, he nodded toward Bram, who stood near the entrance. There was some yelling outside.

Meanwhile, Timka and the boy had joined him. He gestured to the kitchen door and rushed inside, closely followed by the little boy. He saw Timka hesitate, glancing in the direction of the hall.

"Come here," he snarled.

When Timka got into the kitchen, he waved toward the outside door, which was still open. Then he emerged outside into the forest, picked up his briefcase and walked up the path, closely followed by the boy and Timka. The hardest part was done. Now Bram had to get Azra out.

But he didn't get far. Before he realised what was happening, he stood with his face against a tree.

"Not a word," he heard in his ear. Some hands grabbed his gun and suitcase, then slipped over his body. "Turn around."

His breath stopped when he faced a masked guy who pointed an automatic weapon at him. Two individuals in the same black uniform and balaclava were holding Timka and the boy.

"Don't make a sound, and nothing will happen to you. We are here to help you," hissed the man standing next to him.

Lazar noticed that they were wearing earplugs. *A military operation.* He didn't know whether to be relieved or afraid.

"Stop," snarled someone. The robot-like men in front of him didn't move until a short scream came from the front side.

"We're moving in, now," said the nearest guard in a microphone. He started moving, followed by Lazar, the woman and the boy, and behind them the other two warriors. They stepped through the door and entered the adjacent living room through the connecting door.

Lazar felt relieved as he discovered Bram at the far end. They had to sit next to him but weren't allowed to talk. Azra had put her thin arms around Bram's neck, pressing her wet cheeks against his unshaven face. She hugged him as if she was afraid that he would walk away. Lazar wondered what was going on, fighting upcoming panic. If these men were the *White Wolves*, they all had to fear for their lives.

Why didn't Senad warn us?

Hadar was trembling all over his body but had stopped wailing. Azra had finally disengaged herself from Bram and had settled down between him and Timka.

"Everything will be all right," Bram whispered. "These men are not criminals or terrorists. They belong to the government or such an organisation."

Lazar hoped he was right.

At that moment, two masked men brought in Edhem who had to sit in front of him.

"They took Chambers," Edhem murmured.

That didn't look good. A black-clothed man stood there like a vertical stone pillar, looking at them, while heavy footsteps roared through the whole house.

After half an hour, someone brought a few bottles of water and plastic cups. Azra had recovered very quickly, remaining close to Bram. Her eyes followed every movement of the black-clad militiamen, who occasionally walked through the dining and sitting room.

"Are they SFOR soldiers?" asked Timka after a while.

"I don't know," replied Lazar muffled. He had heard short sentences in English upstairs on the first floor.

After two hours, he became impatient.

Timka and the children were allowed to go to the toilet under supervision. Barely back, a big, sturdy man with a gun belt came to them. He pulled his balaclava off and glanced at each of them. *In the fifties,* thought Lazar. He had friendly features, grey hair, a flat nose, fleshy lips and an angular face. His dark eyes were staring at Bram.

"Who's the spokesman here?" He spoke English with a massive voice.

The house had become ominously quiet, noticed Lazar. *We're alone with a few guards*. That could mean the worst.

He cleared his throat. "I am Chief Inspector Lazar Magas. These are..."

The man interrupted him with a waving gesture. "I know who you are," he snarled. "I am the commander of *White Wolves*."

The heavy bass voice gave Lazar chills. All his hopes of getting out of this adventure in one piece flushed away.

SIXTY-ONE

THEY HAD TAKEN THEM ON THE FIRST FLOOR TO WINSTON'S INCIDENT ROOM, AS they called it. The room was spacious with four white painted walls and two tall windows facing out into the parking lot. The military commander was sitting at the head of the long table in a modern high-backed leather chair with handrails, surrounded by six high-backed chairs on either side. To his left were Lazar, Bram and Edhem in front of three men in blue suits.

CIA or MI6, thought Bram, convinced that the *White Wolves* had purged the house of anything that could compromise Chambers. It was a bad sign that the criminal had vanished.

We're witnesses. Bram was afraid of Timka and the kids, who had got to stay in the living room. He estimated the man in front of him a high-ranking official. He turned toward the military commander who cleared his throat and opened the séance.

"For the avoidance of doubt, this meeting never took place," the man said. He first glanced up at Lazar, then at him. "Everything that would have taken place here is pure imagination." His loud bass voice echoed through space. "Anyone who dares to spread gossip about this house and Mr Chambers will be severely punished. Chief Inspector Lazar, I understand that you're here in the context of a murder investigation. Take my word, Mr Winston Chambers is not involved, and I hope that you'll clarify that during a press conference. Or do you have a different opinion?" He stared sternly at Lazar, which features became strangely agitated.

"What do you like to hear, Mr Joe Doe?" retorted Lazar. "I hate authoritarian foreigners who come to threaten us in the name of their nation and a free world. Obviously, you know my name, but I don't know yours. In this country, politeness demands that you introduce yourself before you start negotiating."

Bram caught his gaze and nodded approvingly. Who cares, those cunts had already decided about their fate.

The man arched an eyebrow, visibly disturbed.

"David Brown, Secretary of the Ministry of Foreign Affairs," he answered solemnly. "Mr Chambers is a British citizen, and there is no question of negotiating."

Bram doubted it was his real name.

"And where have you transferred Chambers?" asked Lazar not at all intimidated.

Brown pointed to Edhem, who kept staring at him provocatively.

"He needed some medical care as a result of this gentleman's injection here," he grunted. "After recovering, he'll get a few months off."

"Chambers, or whatever his name is, has been guilty of rape and murder," countered Lazar.

Brown raised an eyebrow. "Explain yourself."

"A girlfriend managed to escape from this house, you know?"

"Has she met Mr Chambers?"

"No, but she has seen this house and its basement with the cells and the torture room. And there was another woman who got killed here!" Lazar sounded furious.

"Blame the Watson brothers for all the crimes done in this house, but they committed those atrocities without Chambers's knowledge. They've paid for their sins. Dead and buried." Brown smiled smugly.

"And tell me, what happened to the corpse of the black-haired woman?"

"What black-haired woman? I assure you we haven't found a single corpse in this house. Neither a torture room."

Bram felt disillusioned and angry. *The White Wolves have cleaned up all traces of their criminal activity.* Jasmina's testimony had become worthless. Easy to refute, given her physical condition.

"I understand," replied Lazar with a raw laugh. "But I'd like to get answers on a few questions. You come here to lecture us, whereas you're protecting compatriots who don't respect our traditions. I don't bother as Westerners kill each other, but since Tuesday some of my compatriots have died in bizarre circumstances. No doubt, Chambers is involved. Do the names Besic, Dzeko, Begovic and Lulic mean anything to you? Or Salah and Moon?"

When Lazar pronounced the last names, Bram got confirmation in Brown's eyes.

The secretary leaned forward.

"We recently found two colleagues in a ravine," he said fiercely. "Chambers has nothing to do with those murders, so who does?" He looked alternately at Edhem, Lazar and Bram. "Those two soldiers got murdered shortly after they met Mr Ruyter. I'm wondering what happened in his lodging."

"I have no idea. Where did those bodies go?" Bram asked with determination.

Brown shrugged. "Whatever," he said forgivingly. "They are dead and buried. Annoying, because they were close to cover up a conspiracy. They were watching Besic because he belonged to a fundamentalist organisation. Ever heard of the Free Islamic State. FIS?"

Bram shook his head.

Brown straightened his massive body. "We could have killed you easily. But I believe that too many people got killed by misunderstanding. We have that clarified. Little Hadar no longer needs to worry for his life, as long as his mother keeps her mouth shut. We know who he is and where he lives. Don't make the mistake of thinking that you can protect him. General Flower hasn't raped a single Muslim woman, is that clear to all of you? He can't defend himself, so do not defile his name and honour. Concerning Chambers, he's on leave and will retake his place as *Last Hope* office commander whenever he's ready again. Mr Bram Ruyter, you can keep working for him, or you can leave. But don't do anything stupid. Wherever you go, we'll find you. Forget about this case and live a healthy life. If you think the media should know, make your testament first. That's all there's to say. You can take the woman and the children wherever you want. You're free."

Brown stood up and addressed Edhem. "Your weapons are in the trunk of your car," he said. Then he glanced at Lazar grinning. "Your colleague or assistant is attached to the wheel. He waits very impatiently for you."

All the men stood up, while Brown left the room.

Lazar sighed deeply. "I can't believe it's over," he said, somewhat trembling.

Bram didn't say a word but left the meeting room. He stormed into the sitting room and let out a sigh of relief. The guards were gone, and Timka was sitting on the long couch with the two children. She raised her head. Then her face features relaxed.

Azra had noticed her reaction, glancing past her.

"Dad," she shouted, and in two jumps, she lay in his arms.

Bram felt like the happiest man in the world.

SIXTY-TWO

NEVER BEFORE HAD JASMINA SEEN LAZAR SO EMOTIONALLY. HE WAS WAILING AND made no effort to hide it. *That's new*, Jasmina thought. Always so businesslike and full of self-confidence as if nothing could hurt him. The war had made him that way, she assumed. He held her hand, continuously stroking it.

"Everything will be all right again," he whispered in her ear.

Liar.

"Azra, Hadar and Timka are in security." He'd told her about Hadar's biological father and what General Flower had planned.

"Can I see Azra?" she begged.

"Soon, my dear, she's on her way with Timka. And I have a surprise for you."

She carefully moved her muffled head toward him, glancing questioningly. She didn't have time to play games, wanted to see her daughter, advise her and make sure she was in good hands.

"Lazar," she stammered, "it's all my fault. If I had told you the truth right away, none of this would have happened." Her voice sounded weak. "After all, I've got survived Srebrenica, and now this."

Spilling tears wouldn't change anything.

"I just want to see Azra and hear you promise that you will take care of her," she said softly.

"Jasmina, do you love me?" He seemed shocked by his proper voice.

"Of course, stupid question."

"And what would you do if you meet Bram again?"

That question amazed her. "Bram? He returned to his country a long time ago," she murmured. "Why should I see him again?" Was Lazar jealous of a ghost from the past?

She looked into his eyes. "Lazar, Bram is a phantom from another life. Well, we were in love then. But a lot has happened since. In Srebrenica, I only experienced poverty, illness, death and sometimes a bit of luck in the Dutch compound. Bram was a nice guy, and I think we've loved each other. Azra is proof of that, isn't she? But Bram doesn't belong in Bosnia. He doesn't even know he has a daughter. He may have a wife and children now. Lazar, Bram is history. I want to go through life with you, with no one else."

Why am I telling such nonsense? The long speech had been exhausting, and she took a deep breath.

Lazar looked at her with concern. "Azra is in good hands. But you weren't mistaken then, Bram is indeed a nice guy."

"How can you know that?"

"I think Azra's waiting outside," he said with trembling voice, as he stood up, and paced toward the door, wiping his eyes dry.

Timka came in with Azra and Hadar at hand. The children loosened themselves and ran to bed. Lazar had to pull them back because they were almost ripping the infusion tubes out of her arm.

"Calm down, Azra, Hadar," Zumra said happily, and she pulled her daughter with her free arm against her. Then it was Hadar's turn.

"You have a lot to tell me, I've heard," she said. She tried to laugh despite the pain in her belly.

Then she looked up. *That's impossible.*

"Kamal," she whispered but glancing as hypnotised at the man she once had loved. "Bram, what are you doing here?"

Azra had made way for her father, coming along the bed, while Edhem stood on the other side.

Jasmina looked from one to the other and let her tears run free.

Edhem reacted first and hugged her carefully. Then Bram leaned forward and kissed her on the cheeks.

"It's been a long time." His voice sounded light-hearted. But she saw how difficult it was for him to control his emotions. She looked at Lazar, who had taken a few steps back.

"Lazar, you knew, why didn't you tell me?" Her voice was hoarse.

He shrugged, starting to walk out of the room.

"Lazar," she called out, "come next to me, please."

She saw him hesitate, then reluctantly approaching her. Bram took a step aside, and she took Lazar's hand, squeezing it hard.

"You are my future husband, Lazar, and your place is next to me. Are you eventually going to tell me where you found these two ghosts?" Her attempt to be light-hearted failed; she began to wail.

"Let's give you a moment..." Bram said.

"No," she called out. "You stay. I just want to know what..." She saw Azra grabbing Bram's hand, and she got silent. Her gaze went from Lazar to Bram and back.

"You know," she murmured, and she saw him nodding almost imperceptibly.

Lazar squeezed her hand. "He has saved Azra, Hadar and Timka from certain death," he said. "Without him, we would never have arrived in time to get them out of the hands of...".

He got silent.

"And who told Azra?" she asked sobbing.

"She's a smart girl," answered Bram with a broad grin. "She understood before we told her. She has been listening to our conversations and figured it out."

Jasmina smiled sweetly. "What did you think when you heard that you had a daughter?"

"No one told me, but I knew it as soon as I saw her. She looks so much like her mother..."

He kept quiet, and she noticed tears rolling down his cheeks. Timka, in turn, went to greet her and they both wailed quietly in each other's arms.

Then there was a long silence.

Jasmina got very tired but forced herself to stay awake. She was afraid to close her eyes. Lazar sat on a chair next to her, while Bram and her brother were at the foot end. Timka was standing beside her. The children were next to Lazar as if they felt that she was not feeling well.

Oh Allah, if you exist, I beg you, help me.

Bram seemed to notice the despair in her eyes.

"I promise you that I will take care of Azra," he said.

Didn't Allah exist? Seven years earlier, *He* had pushed Bram into her arms and blessed their love with the birth of a beautiful daughter. *Why did you not help Bram when he wanted to save my family and me?*

It became blurred in her head. Praised be Allah, *He* has shown Bram the way to Sarajevo. *He* had sent him to save their daughter, had him meet Kamal, and made them friends. In this way, they tracked her down and saved her. She had been in Shaitan's claws.

Everything became right, and Azra had now her father. But what about Timka, her dear friend, with whom she'd shared love and sorrow?

"Timka, I love you too," she murmured.

Timka's fingers were like velvet on her cheeks; they softened the pain. She'd noticed that Timka was secretly lurking at Bram, quickly turning her eyes away when he looked at her.

Jasmina tried to smile, but her muscles were protesting.

Allah, hear me one last time, make sure that Timka and Bram find each other. What an idiot I am. Jasmina had long ago stopped believing, but now she was calling on Allah. Was she in such bad shape?

"Jasmina, I will keep an eye on her," she heard Lazar say as he leaned his head over her.

"I love you," she whispered, hoping that he could understand.

Dizziness engulfed her. It was as if all the power was draining from her body. She got cold despite the fire in her belly. The voices around her faded into an unintelligible cacophony. She had more and more trouble concentrating on her surroundings.

"Timka, I thank you for everything, without you I would never have made it. Take care of Azra," she murmured. "And of Bram," she added.

"I promise," she heard from far away.

"Mummy, Mummy..." *Why is Azra screaming?*

"Bram, take good care..." She wasn't sure he could hear her voice. She closed her eyes when her belly seemed to explode. She opened her mouth wide to squeeze all the pain out of her body. In the distance, she caught the sound of a chaotic concert of screaming and shouting. She couldn't understand the words, but she felt the desperate pressure of Lazar's hand.

Then her world ceased to exist.

Weeks later

SIXTY-THREE

THE MESSAGE WAS ALARMING. ANNOYED, BRAM WAS WONDERING WHY LAZAR HAD called for this meeting. What did Lazar have to discuss with them so urgently? And why gathering in Edhem's lodging? Or did he have something in mind choosing that place? He arrived as of last.

I'm even more suspicious than I used to be.

After hugging each other, Edhem poured a shot of plum alcohol and placed a beer in front of each. *First, some drinking to open the party.* Bram doubted it was a part. Standing around the table, they talked about the latest news, and Lazar was continually joking about EuPol and its new commissioner. After the first round, they all settled down in an armchair. *Three different men around a lounge table*, he thought. On top of it two large bowls of snacks. They drank plum alcohol and beer, telling what they had done since Jasmina's funeral. Lazar informed them of Greg Stone who'd finally returned to Belgium.

Time was going on, and there was a cosy atmosphere, but Bram did not believe that Lazar had organised a lovely party just to talk about good old times. Rather a dramatic period that had brought them together. He recalled Edhem's unexpected message that morning on his cell phone.

Lazar wants to catch up with us. Tonight, at seven o'clock at my house.

After Jasmina's funeral, he'd only spoken to Lazar and Edhem on the phone. But every day he'd visited Timka because Azra suffered greatly from her mother's death. She was also afraid that her dad would disappear from her life. After a few days, Timka had asked him to come live with her temporarily. What he did.

Azra had calmed down. After three days, she could smile again and think of other things than her mother's death.

Hadar had tried to distract her, avoiding bullying her.

Bram spent the day at the office replacing Winston Chambers, who was still on leave. Initially, after a day's work, he drove at home, took a shower, changed clothes, and headed to Timka's dwell. In the morning, before driving to the office, he went back to his lodging.

For a week, he and Timka were sleeping under the same roof but in separate rooms. Then in the ninth night, Timka crawled in his bed. They held each other silently like drowning people at sea, looking for a passing ship. Then, in the early morning, they got closer, sealing their love in a passionate unification.

Bram had planned to stay with *Last Hope* for the remaining time, considering quitting his job as soon as Chambers was back. Although his responsibility as a father and his promise he'd made to Jasmina had got prevented him from planning Chambers's killing. However, he was afraid that sooner or later, the temptation would become too high. Committing revenge meant putting Timka, Azra and Hadar in mortal danger. Brown's words kept echoing through his mind, and he didn't doubt for a second that the threat was real. That's why he hesitated to continue working with Chambers when he came back.

He shook off all those dark thoughts, poured a shot of plum alcohol in his throat and washed away the flavour with a large sip of beer. He wondered when Lazar would come to the point.

That happened after he'd opened his fourth can of beer. All of a sudden, Lazar's features became severe.

"I finally want to put an end to the past," he opened solemnly. "I haven't just been sitting on my ass, you know. I couldn't find rest until I'd got all the answers. In doing so, I became aware that Bosnia is changing. Our ethnic disputes have led to a bloody civil war, and the Westerners believe that we should now forget the past and start again. They are blind to a new threat, jihadism."

Nobody spoke.

Bram had hoped he'd got put the past behind him for good. He'd managed to forget the horrors of the past, glad to start a new life, no longer tormented by nightmares. He'd found new luck and happiness with Timka, Azra and Hadar. Why did Lazar want to reopen healing wounds?

Lazar glanced from one to another.

"We all thought that Winston Chambers, by order of General Flower, has committed a series of crimes of which he has finally escaped trial," he grunted. "We know his crimes, but what were his secrets? Too many questions kept unanswered. That's why I continued my investigation in secret." Lazar paused, eating a piece of cheese. "A colleague had bugged my desk and my team's meeting room, so I had to be very careful. Eventually, I found out that two different cases got entangled by chance."

"Sounds mysterious," reacted Edhem laughing.

Lazar chuckled.

"It started with the Besic case," he went on. "The murder at the *Princip Bridge*." He glanced at Bram. "You've got Besic persuaded to spy on his neighbour Derek Fleming because you thought that he was involved in the murder of your wife, Mayke."

Bram nodded. "That's right. It was on Tuesday the 8th I recall. I was on leave walking around in town when Besic sent me a message. He wanted to meet me urgently. We often met to exchange information, usually in the park where we sat on a bench for a chat. On Tuesday the 8th, after making an appointment, he wasn't in the park as usual. However, I found him strangulated behind the wheel of his car."

"You also noticed two men in a car," added Lazar.

Bram kept quiet.

Lazar chuckled again. "In Chambers's house, Brown has mentioned that two employees being tracking jihadists, were discovered in a ravine. I didn't get the meaning of it." He glanced at Bram. "Can you maybe clarify?"

Bram shrugged. *'Dead and buried,'* Brown had said. So he didn't have to fear persecution. He exchanged a brief look with Edhem before explaining what had happened in his home that night and why.

As Bram had finished his story, Lazar just continued his speech with an expressionless face. "You wrongly thought that those MI6 agents killed Besic. They had placed a transmitter underneath Besic's car and were watching all his movements remotely. But they didn't kill him. Ahmed Salah did."

"Wow, I didn't know that," reacted Bram surprised. "But as they entered my lodging, it wasn't to have a hot drink with me."

"We'll never know for sure." Lazar's fingers traced the contours of the rim of his can of beer, and he changed the issue. "In Bogusevac, we found four bodies. Safet Begovic, Miralem Lulic, and the foreign mercenaries Ahmed Salah and Alistair Moon. Miralem Lulic and Ahmed Salah belonged to the Free Islamic State. Safet was a little rascal, a follower, a loser."

Bram interrupted him. "You mean everything has to do with FIS?"

"Not quite. I started to understand the game when I received the list of Safet Begovic's phone calls from his cell phone. Safet had been on *The Mountain*, an outlier of the Igman from where, if you have an off-road vehicle, you can drive onto a narrow path to Pale. Safet was there when he tried to call Besic, but he never got a communication. I think Safet got compromised after discovering something he wasn't supposed to see and he had to flee. Whatever, shortly afterwards he called Besic, who was in the Glass Tower, from his dwelling place. My men searched Safet's home and found traces indicating that Safet had fled through his bedroom window. But another event proves that Safet was in a panic. A man speaking Bosnian with a foreign accent called the reception of *Digital Future* using Safet's cell phone, and that conversation came from Safet's house or immediate surroundings. No doubt, the caller was Ahmed Salah. We found Safet's cell phone and some iron wires in his car. The same type of cable with which Besic got strangled. So no doubt, Salah is the perpetrator."

"But how did Safet's phone end up in his car?" asked Bram frowning.

Lazar looked from one to the other.

"I've got based my reconstruction on the traces Safet left in his lodging. So that's my conclusion: Salah emerges in Safet's house, but Safet can escape, leaving his cell phone behind. Salah calls with that phone to *Digital Future* to find out where Besic is. The receptionist gives him that information. Besic seems to be the second target. Salah quickly drives to the Glass Tower, waits until Besic leaves, follows him to the Miljacka and strangles him. Anel Dzeko has stated that his friend Emir Besic left the Glass Tower in a hurry after he got a few calls.

We have also received from Telecom a list with the connections Safet's phone has made with the nearest antenna. Further, we found strangling cables in Salah's car. So I conclude that after Salah has strangled Besic, he drives straight to Bogusevac to kill Miralem Lulic, the third on his hit list. He parks his vehicle among the trees, covering it with branches. Miralem, however, is not at home. Salah breaks in and sits inside waiting. As Miralem arrives, he notices that the front door is damaged and rushes into the forest. Salah must have heard the car, and when Miralem doesn't show up, he realises that something must have alarmed him. Salah emerges from the house into the forest, discovers Miralem and follows him until he steps on a landmine."

Lazar tipped a glass of rakija backwards.

"But how did Safet end up in Bogusevac?" asked Bram with a raised eyebrow. "He escaped an assassination attempt at home, why not disappear?"

"As I said before, Safet fled from his home," Lazar replied. "He jumped out of the bedroom window at the rear of his house and ran into the woods. Salah didn't chase him."

"How can you be sure it happened that way?" Bram didn't seem convinced.

"There were stains on the window frame, and footsteps beneath leading to the woods," Lazar riposted. "Later Safet returned to pick up his car and his gun. Then he tried to meet Besic. That proves he had no idea that Besic was already dead. I saw Safet pass by at *Digital Future*, but seeing me, he drove away. He must have decided to move toward Bogusevac to warn his friend Miralem.

"I think that once Safet escaped the boss decides to get rid of all those involved. Thus he calls in Alistair Moon. Anyway, Moon expects Safet at *Digital Future* and follows him. When Safet drives up the path to Miralem's house, Moon stops, apparently surprised, and staying on the roadside, he fires at the target. Several bullets shatter the rear window, and Safet gets one into his back. As for Miralem Lulic, the clothes we've found in his bathroom contains blood and human tissue. But only Salah's. No blood or tissue from Miralem Lulic. That proves that Lulic was close to Salah, but lay in a ditch when the landmine exploded."

"What a lucky man," grunted Bram.

"Miralem put the landmines there himself during the war," Lazar replied.

"So when he runs away from Salah, he knows very well what he's doing. It's his only chance, because Salah holds a gun, whereas his weapon is in his house. So he lures Salah into a minefield."

"A clever man," Bram said.

"A landmine rips Salah apart," continued Lazar with a high voice. "Miralem, unharmed, heads back to his house, changes clothes quickly and gets ready to go into hiding. In any case, he prepares weapon and spare ammunition for use, which indicates that he's afraid of another murder attempt. But Safet's unexpected arrival disturbs his preparation. He grabs his gun from the table and runs outside, where he finds the deadly wounded Safet lying on the ground. As he tries to help him, Moon appears on the edge of the clearing facing his house.

Meanwhile, Moon had parked his car between two trees and rushed through the woods toward the edge of the clearing where he threatens Miralem. And now it gets even more bizarre. Somewhere between the road and the house lies a sniper who shoots Moon. Miralem goes into cover, but when he jumps up and runs toward the forest, he gets a bullet.

"How do you know all this so exactly?" asked Bram astonished.

"The magazine and the ammunition lay on the table in Miralem's living room. That indicates that Miralem runs out when Safet arrives and never gets back inside. The footprints next to Safet's car, the bullet impacts in the window frame, the fresh grooves on the mudguard of Safet's car and the traces of crusted blood going from Miralem's car along with the house into the woods, indicate that Miralem has run away bleeding."

"Holy shit."

"Exactly. Miralem is severely wounded and tries to reach Salah's hidden car he'd discovered earlier. He dies about ten metres from it."

Bram scratched his hand through his beard.

"How do you know there was a sniper lurking?" he asked with a smile. "What was his goal? And why not killing Miralem earlier when he emerged from the woods after getting rid of Salah?"

Lazar pulled his mouth crooked for a moment. "According to our technician," he said slowly, "there was a two men's team: a sniper and an observer who caught the shells. Those men arrived there whereas Miralem was changing clothes after Salah had stepped on a mine. But before Safet and Moon showed up. Their arrival was a surprise for everyone. But the sniper has not hesitated to shoot Moon. Miralem got hit but could run. Then the sniper team burned Moon's body."

"Damned, how can you prove that?" interrupted Edhem.

Lazar chuckled. "The report of the forensic institute."

"Be clearer," grunted Edhem.

"We have rifle bullets extracted from the window and Miralem's footsteps along with Safet's car. Moon got killed by a rifle bullet, just like Miralem.

Besides, our technicians found the place where the team had been lying. Enough to paint a credible picture, don't you think so?"

Bram shook his head. "Unlikely that all these men belonged to the same group?"

Lazar paused, glancing from the one to the other.

"Except for those two shooters and Alistair Moon," he continued, "all of them belong to the FIS. Ahmed Salah served during the war with a group of mujahidin, Moon with the Arkan Tigers, although they were on the same payroll. MI6. One infiltrated the Serbs while the other one infiltrated the Bosnian troops. In this way, the British government knew what was going on on both sides. But also in our case, they worked for Chambers, as we now know."

"But why to kill each other?" asked Bram with apparent astonishment. "I cannot see the motive."

"I believe Safet Begovic, Emir Besic, Miralem Lulic, Ahmed Salah and Alistair Moon originally belonged to the same group. But their goals were different.

"Telecom telephone lists have got answered a lot of questions, allowing me to establish the chronology of the events. It starts with Safet calling Trifko Petrovic, the arms dealer. After that call, he rushes to *The Mountain*. Why?"

"He has vital information for his employer. But his visit is not planned," answered Bram, arching an eyebrow.

"Exactly," acknowledged Lazar with a mocking grin. "When Safet reaches *The Mountain*, he witnesses something he didn't expect, and he tries to warn Besic. But he got interrupted because the call took only twenty seconds. Anyway, he succeeds in getting away. We know the sequel."

"What did he see on *The Mountain*?" Bram asked, straightening his back.

"I come to that. You know, if there is something that can go wrong, it will go wrong. That visit is the turning point that resulted in a series of murders. All of a sudden Chambers must abandon his plans, and he doesn't hesitate to do that, giving Salah and Moon the order to kill Safet, Besic and Lulic. Then he sends another team to eliminate Salah and Moon."

"But what did Safet see on *The Mountain*?" Bram insisted.

"I've made a trip to that place and found there an empty shed," answered Lazar with some bitterness. "But at the rear, I've discovered a path leading to Pale. Good enough for a 4x4 of which I've found fresh tracks."

Edhem frowned. "Do you think a famous person out of Pale has been in that shed?" he asked gruffly.

Lazar nodded. "Safet caught sight of a famous Serbian talking to Moon, signing his death warrant when he got spotted. It was also the end of his group," replied Lazar, squeezing his empty can together.

After a short delay, he continued. "Safet did business with Petrovic for the group. The arms dealer got murdered on Friday the 11th, shortly before I came to visit you. The pieces of the puzzle are slowly but surely falling into place. Remember, we're dealing with jihadists, a weapons supplier and a remote shed in the mountains. All that smells like a FIS operation."

Bram wasn't entirely convinced.

"General Flower has tasked Winston Chambers," he exclaimed. "Killing the kid and then making the body disappear. His proper son, being proof of his scandalous behaviour in 1994 on the Jahorina. Fortunately, I've discovered Chambers in conversation with Mayke on the photos Greg Stone had sent to me. Winston had never told me he'd met my wife. That's where I started suspecting him as the originator of Timka and the children's abduction. As a result, we were able to save them in time. But what has Chambers to do with FIS?"

Lazar smiled mysteriously. "You now know who is behind all those murders and why Chambers decided to kill his proper people. But do you know what he'd planned with his team?"

Bram shrugged. "Whatever Chambers's plans, Stone's photographs could have betrayed the conspiracy, exposing him and his team. I already understood that when you recognised Salah, Moon, Lulic and Besic on the pictures. Besides, Chambers and that woman seemed to be the central figures. The entire group got exposed on several photos, except for Safet, a poor, stumper who would have been out of place. You have very convincingly demonstrated that Salah and Moon killed the three Bosniaks after Safet's visit on *The Mountain*. Also, another sniper team eliminated Salah, Moon and Miralem. I think that those mysterious killers were the Watson brothers. They have the profile of such a sniper duo, and they both worked in Chambers's assignment." He beckoned to Edhem, who listened very attentively.

"That's approximately right," answered Lazar, amusement written all over his face. "But why did Chambers order such a massacre? Why not just cancel his plan and only get Safet killed? Safet was the only one who'd witnessed what happened on *The Mountain*."

Bram rubbed his beard. "There must be more. While I was visiting Chambers, his men have searched my house, stealing three pictures from my desk drawer, photos of Mayke talking to Derek Fleming. I discovered that later when I started suspecting Chambers. However, Chambers was not interested in what those three pictures showed; they proved that Stone possessed other images which might betray him. They could also put me on his track as the potential perpetrator of Mayke's death.

"Moreover, they proved that he knew all those men, that he knew Mayke. If he wanted to go ahead with his original plan, he first had to make these pictures disappear. When Safet discovered what game he was playing, Chambers decided to cancel the whole operation. But that wasn't enough.

He had to erase all traces for different reasons. After he'd got Greg Stone's laptop stolen, he discovered that Stone had mailed all the photos to me. That's why he sent the twins after me. First, find my laptop, then kill me."

"Exactly," said Lazar. "Go on."

"On my visit, Winston commented on my writing activities. Only Edhem knew about it. But on my laptop, there's a folder with all my writing. Thus Chambers had examined my notebook earlier, what he could only have done in my absence in the office because, after duty, I take my computer at home. That's how he found out about Timka's existence because I'd made notes about Suada and Timka in preparation for a story. Fortunately, Timka's address or that of her mother was in my mailbox, and he couldn't get in it."

Lazar nodded. "You know that Chambers was looking for a kid - the evidence of the general's bad behaviour during the war - to let him disappear," he said. "But he had another secret to preserve."

"I'm getting more and more curious." Bram got the feeling that Lazar was ready for the conclusion of his thrilling story.

Lazar glowed. "Without you, I would never have discovered the conspiracy. The Bosniaks admire Ahmed Salah as a Mujahid who fought at their side. They trust him. So Chambers had no trouble persuading FIS supporters to participate in his operation."

"I don't get it," interrupted Edhem with confusion. "What operation?"

"Kill Karadzic and Mladic." Lazar looked as if he'd unveiled the last secret of Tutankhamun.

"That's insane," called out Bram.

"You say it," replied Lazar enthusiastically. "Winston Chambers wanted to ambush the Serbs and have them killed. And that's the moment to bring Alistair Moon in the headlights. Moon had served with the Arkan Tigers and knew Mladic personally. They had met in Srebrenica.

"Moreover, Mladic had also met Flower in 1994. Mladic is an arrogant jerk who thinks he's invincible. He accepts Chambers's proposal to deliver Karadzic to the *White Wolves* in exchange for not being prosecuted for his war crimes."

"I thought Mladic was an extremely suspicious guy," groaned Edhem. "He only negotiates with people of his rank. Winston Chambers is a citizen for whom Mladic would only pick up his nose!"

"You're right, Mladic only negotiates with the people he chooses. That's why the plan was so Machiavellian, having every chance to succeed. Mladic trusted Chambers because he met him during the war."

Bram felt an icy chill running down his back.

"So, you're saying Chambers met Mladic during the war?" he repeated, looking as if he'd seen a ghost.

"Yes. In 1994, on the Jahorina," Lazar stated.

"Impossible, in 1994 he was in England," Bram retorted. "He told me."

"Sorry, Bram. When Mayke confided Chambers during that EUMM party, she couldn't know that he was the man she wanted to destroy."
Bram stiffened, realising what Lazar meant.
"Chambers is General Flower," whispered Bram with dismay.

SIXTY-FOUR

LAZAR'S LAST REVELATION CAUSED A LONG SILENCE. EDHEM AND BRAM exchanged glances but kept silent.

Lazar slammed another shot backwards and cleared his throat.

"After a severe traffic accident in London 2000, General Flower got a new face of plastic surgery and a new name, Chambers. Together with the full grey beard and a thick moustache, his face had become unrecognisable, which suits him and the government well because his name got mentioned in several Bosnian reports. A few Muslim women had testified that he'd abused them. So officially Flower disappears after that accident, which was only realisable with the involvement of the highest authorities. Chambers appears while Flower has become a ghost. It's unclear whether or not the government sent Flower to Sarajevo to get rid of Mladic and Karadzic. But as long as both war criminals are alive, he would never be secure, and the general Flower, the national hero, would finish in dishonour. However, he went to Sarajevo and started establishing a Machiavellian plan. First, he must convince Mladic that Chambers is Flower. They gather for a private conversation, probably on *The Mountain*. General Flower, alias Chambers, makes Mladic believe that he's acting in the name of the British government, which is partly true. Officially Flower doesn't exist any more. He has drawn up a plan to silence Mladic and Karadzic forever because he fears that sooner or later they'll betray his secret if they ever get arrested. So it's not just about the rape of Timka's sister and killing his bastard son, but also about the secret deals that he has made with Karadzic during the war. Especially about the abandonment of the eastern enclaves."

Edhem straightened his tall body. "You mean that there were agreements made to give up Srebrenica?"

"Yes. In 1994," Lazar confirmed. "Even though Flower's successor, who was hating the Serbs, pursued a different policy, a French general did in 1995 what General Flower had agreed with Karadzic. However, this is mainly about what General Flower has done, and what will never appear in the history books. To bury any evidence of this agreement forever, Flower has set up a Machiavellian conspiracy."

Bram shrugged. "In the name of his government?" His voice went up. "Is that why Brown has destroyed all traces of Flower's criminal behaviour in his rented house?"

"No, Brown had another reason to do so. But first, let me explain what Flower has done."

"Is there more?" asked Bram with some consternation.

"As I said before," continued Lazar with a slight grin, "Flower persuaded Mladic to extradite Karadzic. Mladic hates that politician, and if Flower also promised him that nobody would ever know that he'd extradited the hero of the Bosnian Serbs to the West because there would be no witnesses left, he agreed. Then Flower revealed his monstrous plan to him. Partly; he made Mladic believe that FIS would be held responsible for the massacre."

"Massacre? What massacre?" asked Edhem with raised eyebrows.

"The Karadzic massacres. Slaughter of the whole family clan. At his meeting with Mladic, Flower introduced his right hand. Alistair Moon. Mladic knew and trusted him. From now on, Mladic would organise the implementation of Flower's plan with Moon. Flower wanted to stay in the background. I think that Safet has observed Moon with Mladic on Tuesday, October 8. That explains everything that followed."

Bram shook his head incredulously. "Slaughter a family?" he called out. "How was Flower going to realise all that? Not with that small group of veterans, or with some FIS supporters and two mercenaries. The great warrior Mladic also had to understand that."

Lazar opened a new can of beer.

"You forget the *White Wolves*," he countered. "This unit was under Brubaker's command." He looked amused. "I found out that Brubaker is Flower's bastard son. Yé, another one, the result of an affair with a general's daughter. After his wife's death, Flower cared a lot about Brubaker who was making a quick career. I recently got that information from the State Security. I guess Mladic wanted to trap the whole Karadzic family. FIS supporters would slaughter Karadzic and all his companions with the help of the *White Wolves*. Decapitate everyone! Then the *White Wolves* would shoot the mujahidin. Safet, Emir, Miralem, Salah and Moon. But also, Mladic! Beautiful staging. The local authorities and the international community will blame the FIS fighters. After all, decapitation is a mujahidin speciality. The whole world will clap in the hands while the military high command celebrates the *White Wolves* as heroes."

"Flower is a psychopath," Bram grunted. "When that prick had to abandon his plan, he got killed all his fellow workers. Mayke has told him what she was going to do in Pale, and he got her killed. Later, I got a job at *Last Hope* because Flower wanted to find out what Mayke could have revealed to me. They probably have been watching me after Mayke's dead." He stopped and stared ahead of him, pondering. "But if he controlled the *White Wolves*, why are we still alive?" asked Bram after a short pause.

"We were just lucky," replied Lazar grinning. "After SFOR had found the bodies of the two MI6 agents, the British Ministry decided to intervene. They'd given Flower plenty of leeway to destroy Karadzic and Mladic. But the corpses piled up, and public critics increased, pointing to the British. The death of those two MI6 agents might be the reason why we are still alive. Or the authorities in London found out that Flower was serving another master. In any case, they replaced Brubaker. When the new commander discovered what Flower, he only knew as Chambers, was up to, he decided to intervene. Several team members were aware of his relationship with Miloska Stambolic, Follum's interpreter.

"Besides, Greg Stone found pictures of that bitch, dressed as Jasmina's torturer, on the EuPol network. Scenes with Miloska and Follum playing sexual games. But she was also exposed in Stone's photographs."

Lazar let out a deep sigh.

"Jasmina had to kill her to get out," he said tonelessly, "and Flower probably made her body disappear. I don't know since how long the new commander was watching Flower's house, but he knew of the hostage-taking. When Edhem and Flower arrived there, the *White Wolves* were already in position. The new commander did not hesitate to have the Watson brothers killed. The scapegoats. Perhaps by order of the higher authorities. The twins now get all the blame. After that, the new commander has made all traces of Flower's misconduct and criminal activities disappear. But he was ordered to release the man he knew as Chambers. According to the State Security, Flower may have signed an agreement with MI6, and now he'll betray his former masters. London had to avoid a scandal. There were rumours that Flower has been working for some shadow organisation, which knew him as Chambers. That was the reason why he'd got to kill all the people involved in his plan. Officially, nothing has happened, and we can't prove otherwise."

Bram looked straight at him. "It's strange that he can keep his post at *Last Hope*."

Lazar nodded. "He has a lot of influence on the highest level, and we can't harm him. Remember, Flower has officially vanished. But now I come to the second case. That's where your name pops up." Lazar made a desperate hand gesture, facing Bram sharply.

"I'm a busy man," replied Bram ironically.

Lazar grinned. "Listen to another amazing story. Greg Stone saves Daria Bazila from human traffickers. The woman comes to live with him, and he gets fired, accused of inappropriate behaviour. Daria tells him that in Mitrovica a compatriot has confided a secret to her. It's about a Western commissioner who had two colleagues got killed because they blackmailed him." Lazar did a brief account of what Greg Stone had told him during his interrogation.

"When Daria gets employed in the *Florida Bar*, she still owns that little bear with inside a terrible secret. She doesn't know what to do with it, and when she moves in Greg Stone's lodging, she hands that bear to Emma Badora." He glanced over at Bram, who knew the story. "But Dragon Borjan, a French policeman, follows Daria from Mitrovica. Daria is afraid that he wants to kill her for the contents of a bear she no longer owns. Emma, the new owner of that secret, is on her way to her homeland Romania. That poor girl makes Tim Watson her confidant, and he takes her straight to Flower's house. We know the sequel. Emma got imprisoned in Flower's home, and Dragon Borjan disappears without a trace. Stone has described this guy very well. But at EuPol, no one talks. Could be ordered by higher up. But I did some neighbourhood research where the French deputy commissioner lives. There, one of the neighbours spotted Borjan, who has vanished since Wednesday, October the 9th. I don't think we'll ever see him again either."

Edhem's features hardened. "Why investigate the neighbourhood of the Deputy Commissioner?"

"I found out that the EuPol commissioner, the former deputy, has worked in Mitrovica. After two subordinates got shot to death, he lost his function. His commissioner was the Viking, Ivar Ragnarsson."

"Wow," Bram exclaimed. "Not hard to guess why Montpetit had got Greg Stone fired."

"But it doesn't explain why Tim Watson kidnapped Emma Badora."

Bram chuckled. "Someone wants to avoid that Normand Montpetit gets accounted for his behaviour in Mitrovica."

Lazar nodded. "You say it. Anyone who's a threat to Montpetit must be eliminated. Borjan is looking for Daria and the content of the bear. Stone is Daria's lover and has seen Borjan's face. Both represent potential threats to the deputy commissioner. Dragon disappears. Emma is kidnapped by someone who at first sight isn't linked to Montpetit. But Emma has received something from Daria. Both women know each other! Moreover, Daria lives with Stone, the man who made some revealing photographs. The circle is complete."

"The links," Bram agreed.

"Yes. I found out that Commissioner Ragnarsson had become suspicious. Wednesday night, October 9th, he has called Montpetit at his home. I've spoken to Ragnarsson's wife. When she heard I was investigating the right circumstances of her husband's death, she was willing to collaborate. She revealed to me that Ivar wanted to force his deputy commissioner to resign. If Montpetit refused to get out voluntarily, Ivar would send information about the Mitrovica incident to the media. Strangely, Ragnarsson died of a cardiac arrest the next day, Thursday, October 10th ."

"That doesn't mean anything," countered Bram with a crooked grin. "Stress."

"Possible. But I also spoke to Ragnarsson's secretary. Shortly before his cardiac arrest, he got the visit of a young French diplomat who showed an ID card with the name of Louis Grandjean. The meeting lasted twenty minutes. When the woman had to get into Ragnarsson's office sometime after Grandjean had left, she found the Commissioner dead in his chair. I investigated that French diplomat. Unknown, and the French Embassy is formal, no one has called Ragnarsson, and the real Grandjean was much older. Nowhere did I find that fake Grandjean in Sarajevo. Montpetit is now the EuPol Commissioner. Do you recognise the pattern?"

Edhem walked pacing through the room.

"Is something wrong, Edhem?" asked Bram with a suspicious look.

"What Lazar says, sound crazy," replied Edhem. "I don't see how Emma Badora's kidnapping fits into the overall picture. Tim Watson was Flower's fiduciary. What links him with that girl?"

Lazar chuckled. "Not directly, my friend. However, if you put everything together, you can see a network of links, a spiderweb. The Besic case is about Flower, who wants to get rid of his past. But we also believe that Flower worked for some other organisation. The British found out and made a cleanup. They cleared him of all blame. After all, they have no other choice because they have created Chambers, who will be their informant in this secret organisation. Our second case concerns Montpetit. If his image gets jeopardised, the cause has to be removed, the same modus operandi as with Flower. Emma and Daria have jeopardised Montpetit's and Flower's career, which results in the assumption that Flower and Montpetit are working for the same organisation because both girls are linked."

An awkward pause stretched into an embarrassing silence. Finally, Bram broke it.

"Who has Daria killed?" he asked after a few seconds.

"One of the twins ordered by Chambers-Flower," Lazar answered. "A double blow: getting rid of Stone, including his laptop with the photos, and killing Daria because she knows Emma Badora and Montpetit's secret. Stone is the common denominator. He is a threat to Chambers because he has taken pictures of him and his fellow conspirators. But he also is a potential risk to the French deputy commissioner because he lives with Daria, who has proof of Montpetit's criminal behaviour in Mitrovica. To avoid any suspicion, Stone has to pay for the murder. A double blow."

Bram frowned. "You mean that this mysterious organisation for whom Chambers or Flower works, has ordered the killing of all those who were a threat to Montpetit or Flower, and also set up a conspiracy to catch Karadzic and Mladic?" He didn't seem convinced.

Lazar shook his head. "No, no," he replied loudly. "Your first assertion is correct, but Flower used this organisation against its knowledge to get rid of the two Serbian war criminals. The organisation I'm talking about fighting the FIS in absolute secrecy."

Edhem sat down again.

"That's right," he said with a deep sigh. "We have suspected for quite some time that a secret organisation fights the political Islamisation. We don't have any concrete evidence, but since FIS got established, we've determined that Islamic investors got regularly killed in all kinds of accidents. Last year Bush talked about the New World Order, and the wildest rumours started to circulate. Check out YouTube, and you'll find dozens of videos about this subject. Politicians are shouting "fake" while they continue to deny the Islamic siege of Western Europe. I am Muslim but abhor fundamentalism. As if we haven't suffered enough in the name of our different gods. For months, we have noticed that Bosnia has not escaped the influence of politicised Islam. The West is to blame for this. They have given us little support, only making the rich wealthier. The poor remained poor. Give those poor people some money and hope, and they will follow you without asking questions. That is what the investors from the rich Arab countries are doing. They're building every day a new mosque somewhere." The tone of his voice was bitter.

"You say "we" all the time," remarked Lazar, who observed Edhem sharply.

Edhem chuckled. "You know, my friend, I'm part of the State Security."

Bram showed a pseudo-smile. "I'm not surprised any more," he replied with a touch of faint sarcasm. "At last, an answer to questions I never dared to ask. Like, wherefrom do you get those modern handguns and stun guns? Well, we're a big family now, and I hope you won't let me go to jail right away."

"Lazar is right," returned Edhem laconically. "For months, a unit of fundamentalists have been active in Sarajevo. Safet Begovic, Emir Besic and Miralem Lulic were part of it. We have been looking for the leader of this unit. It might be a high-ranking official. Also, we think Flowers known as Chambers is here to fight FIS. However, we don't know for whom or for which organisation he works. As Bram just remarked, Flower is a psychopath. In his sick mind, he wanted to kill two birds with one stone, solving his proper problems and destroying a fundamentalist group. Success or not, Flower has deceived this mysterious organisation. I'm surprised he's going to stay in Bosnia. As far as FIS is concerned, they will have to set up a new unit. We reckon that jihadism will be our new enemy soon. In the previous war, three different ethnic groups fought each other, and in the next war, Muslims will kill other Muslims. We must avoid that."

Bram suddenly showed a lot of interest.

"A fundamentalist Muslim organisation without the West knows anything about it?" he exclaimed in disbelieve. "Terrorists do seek publicity, and they do so with terrorist acts. They want to deliver a message. The war has been over for seven years now, and I don't know anything about terrorist acts in Bosnia."

"That's what makes them so dangerous," reacted Edhem with great firmness. "Several Islamic leaders have understood that you can't get anywhere when using violence. A new generation of jihadists wants to increase its influence, here as in all European countries, which can only be done by infiltrating the leading politic parties and by having favourable immigration laws voted so that as many fundamentalist Muslims as possible can immigrate. To achieve this, you have to lobby the current politicians. That means infiltrating the prominent political parties with jihadists who publicly pretend to be moderate, placing pawns everywhere and becoming part of national politics. They already have made the first step. FIS started with this in Bosnia and dispose of unrestricted financial resources. Few Arab countries can finance such operations, and I think Saudi Arabia is behind it. In any case, FIS is the greatest enemy of true Islam."

"This is madness if you're right," Bram groaned.

Edhem's features became severe, and he glanced over at Lazar.

"Egzon Subic belonged to the mujahidin during the war. He even met Osama bin Laden, together with our leader Izetbegovic. Now he's wealthy and on his way up to the top. We can't prove anything, but we suspect that he is one of the wealthiest influential FIS leaders in Bosnia." He lifted a fresh can of beer. "Let's remain optimistic and hope it doesn't take that way. It's time to enjoy and drink at our little private society. Lazar, you are one of those who can steer this country in the right direction, starting as the next police chief." He glanced over at Bram. "In your country, you are an outcast. Here you have a beautiful family, a future. You speak our language very well. Help us to make sure that in ten years, we'll still be able to chat here as freely as today. On a prosperous Bosnia."

They toasted silently, but Lazar had not finished yet. He coughed into his hand.

"Bram told us earlier that the Watson brothers were the snipers who killed Moon and Miralem Lulic. That's partly true. Tim Watson worked for *Last Hope* or better for Chambers, and kept as much as possible in the obscurity. He was a reserve pawn. The sniper team consisted of his brother Sam and Miloska Stambolic.

Bram and Edhem stared at him in disbelief.

"Are you sure?" asked Edhem after a short silence.

Lazar nodded resolutely. "Until recently, I refused to believe the Cleaner-story in Srebrenica," he said. "I was wrong. Miloska Stambolic was *Cleaner*. As a young woman, she lived in a village that got burned down by Naser Oric. After his men killed all the inhabitants, beheaded essential villagers and let themselves be photographed with them. Naser has even shown such photographs to the media. Miloska escaped the massacre because she had a romantic rendezvous with a Serbian soldier. While Miloska was fucking, Naser's commandos killed her whole family. When the young woman saw the bodies, she almost went mad with grief. At the funeral, she swore revenge. A few days later, she murdered a Muslim woman, put on her clothes and entered Srebrenica. That happened at the beginning of the war. That day Miloska started her career as a murderer. However, she kept in contact with a Serbian unit. There she met Alistair Moon. In the beginning, she killed randomly, later she carried out assignments. After the war, she left Srebrenica and turned up in Pale. She became Mycroft Follum's interpreter. One day she ran into Moon, who persuaded her to meet Chambers. What she did. And there was a click between them.

"Chambers placed Miloska with Sam Watson in a team. Her work with Follum was beneficial to him, so Chambers could have an eye on the British activities. One day Miloska got recognised by a Srebrenica survivor. The man wanted to make a lot of money with the information. But before he could talk to the State Security, Miloska silenced him. He probably tried to blackmail her first. Her life ended on Wednesday, October 9th, when Jasmina killed her in Chambers's house. After her death, the twins worked together again. They killed Anel Dzeko. At first, I thought that a woman was involved, after a neighbour had said that she had heard a woman's voice in the hallway when two people went to visit Dzeko. But Tim has a rather high voice. They killed Anel because he was Besic's friend, and they wanted to exclude all risks. Knowing that we were investigating both freaks, they tried making us believe that computer software was the motive for the murders. Anel took the hard drives out of Emir's apartment, but the Watsons waited outside for him, and he got shot. They took everything from him except his identity papers, wrapped the corpse into plastic bags and dropped the package in the Miljacka. After that, they turned his house upside down. There, too, they stole the hard drive to deceive us."

Bram shook his head.

"Psychopaths, just like Flower," he humbled. And I have to work with that jerk. Impossible!"

Edhem winked at him. "Come working for us. But the payment is terrible."

They were both laughing until Lazar took their attention with a hand gesture. "To finish," he said. "I have an unsolved case, the Vitruvian Man-mystery-case.

He looked closely at Bram.

"Did you kill the Dutch military attaché?"

SIXTY-FIVE

BRAM GLANCED OVER AT LAZAR. DID THE INSPECTOR BELIEVE HE'D KILLED VISSER? "I'll tell you the whole story," he said with a sigh. "The photos you received anonymously are real; I was in the hotel that night, and one of the Watson brothers must have photographed me. I waited until Cees Visser was alone. Then I went to his room to kill him." A shudder went through his body as he thought on that night.

Sunday, 6 October 2002

The lobby was not that big, and he estimated the reception barely ten metres away from him. He accelerated his pace and walked next to a man walking to the lift. A short glance sufficed: that was the right guy.

Bram had pulled his hockey cap deep over his forehead.

"Hi," he said, laughing.

The man turned to him with a suspicious look and put on a sullen face.

Bram didn't discourage, keeping pace. "You are the striker of Zeljeznicar Sarajevo. Uh, Stankovic?" he asked in Serbo-Croatian. He feigned being an excited football fan who unexpectedly bumps into his idol. Stankovic was a well-known national football player.

Bram looked at him beggingly. "Can I get an autograph?" He had a small notebook in his hand and a felt-tip pen that he wanted to hand to the other one. Everything well prepared.

The man's eyes narrowed.

"Do I know you?" He also spoke Serbo-Croatian.

"Oh sorry, I'm Pieter Vanbon, a Belgian sports journalist."

They passed by the reception desk.

"I don't know you," snarled the man annoyed. "I'm not a footballer either."

Bram knew that his interlocutor wasn't a footballer, but a pimp. Emma had told him. He made a disappointed face.

"Don't you play football?"

"No, I don't."

"Sorry for the disturbance." Meantime, they'd reached the lift. Bram got in first and stood in the farther corner. The American no longer showed any interest in him. On the third floor, they got out. The man turned to the right, Bram to the left. At the end of the corridor, he stepped through the emergency exit and left the door ajar.

Three minutes later, he saw a young woman and the American pimp leaving the chamber. They rushed toward the elevator, whispering. When the cage started whizzing down, Bram stepped into the hallway and ran to the number 308. He knocked on the door, hoping that the resident would think that his late visitors had forgotten something. Who else would knock on the door at that time?

The man opened the door unsuspectingly, and before he realised his mistake, Bram jabbed the barrel of his gun under his nose.

"Inside," he commanded.

"You," the man stammered in bewilderment.

"Hello Cees," retorted Bram without losing sight of him, as he slammed the door shut with a backward foot movement.

Sarajevo, November 2002

Bram sighed deeply. "I just wanted Visser to explain what had happened to Jasmina in 1995 in Potočari," Bram said to Lazar. "After I'd left the army, I met Wim, the non-commissioned officer and chief of the shed, who had helped me have some undisturbed moments with Jasmina. After Cees had got me locked up, he had tried to rape Jasmina, which Wim had prevented. Wim had also witnessed Cees and a couple of Serbs, leading Jasmina and family to the white house near the camp. I've asked Cees what happened there. He trembled like a leaf in the wind, convinced that I was going to kill him. He told me that the Serbs only wanted to question the family, but that the father had intervened, which provoked the killing of the whole family. I have not dared to kill him, leaving him with a promise that I would kill him if he didn't keep his mound shut. The next day I heard that he'd got murdered."

"Do you really think I'll believe that nonsense?" snarled Lazar.

"He's telling the truth," groaned Edhem, opening another can of beer. After having swallowed half the content, he put the tin can in front of him, glancing with a challenging look at Lazar.

"Bram is innocent, I've killed Visser."

SIXTY-SIX

THE TWO MEN WHO WERE FACING HIM KEPT SILENT. THEIR FEATURES WERE TENSE. Edhem didn't care what they thought about him; he didn't regret his act at all. He poured a shot plum alcohol down his throat and straightened his back.

"Bram had told me what happened at the fence of the Dutch camp in 1995," he said slowly. His alcohol consumption begun to affect his vocal stability.

"Cees Visser was responsible for the death of my parents and sisters. As I killed him, I didn't know yet that Jasmina had survived. When suddenly Bram emerged from the hotel, I'd been there for a while, hesitating whether or not going to Visser's room. Surprised and fearing that he'd got killed

Cees Visser, I rushed to his room. That jerk was not suspicious when I knocked on the door, introducing myself as a police inspector searching a Dutch fellow I described as Bram. He let me in. Then I told him who I was, forcing him to drink with me a glass of plum alcohol, which I enriched with a vegetable transparent liquid. He was so frightened, he didn't see what I poured in his glass. After his muscles had become so weak as a broken-air balloon, I informed him he was going to die. After that, I bared him up, inspired by some Leonardo Da Vinci drawing. A symbolic representation which ought to divert the police. I'm a Leonardo da Vinci fan, you know, and that drawing has always puzzled me. So, why should it not puzzle the investigators?"

"This *Vitruvian Man* gave me a lot of headaches," retorted Lazar. "I thought a serial killer was at work."

"I rather wanted to leave a message, making Visser's death a memorable story of a punishment for what he'd done in 1995. A thin needle through his ear and brain finally ended his sinful life. I hoped the police would conclude that he got murdered either by a woman, out of revenge, or by someone from Srebrenica who had known him there, which would provide thousands of potential killers. I was right, you couldn't resolve the case." He laughed aloud.

"Why a woman?" Lazar asked.

"Well, for whom else would Visser have voluntarily stretched out in that position? Everyone knew he loved young women. There were no traces of violence, and the poison I've been using leaves no traces. So, everything was pointing to a sexual crime. There was enough evidence, including the woman in the lobby. So the police would quickly find out that Visser had got a hooker's visit. First, they had to resolve the question of how it was done." Edhem paused and glanced at each other. "Possible conclusion: a woman sits on him, he closes his eyes, enjoying what she's doing to him, and then she jabs the needle in his brain. Enough evidence to explain how the perpetrator could have committed the murder. In any case, Visser deserved death."

He paused briefly. "By the way, that day, I also found out that someone got Bram watched and photographed."

"Don't be afraid," interrupted Lazar with a vague smile. "You're Jasmina's brother."

Edhem shrugged. "My good friend Lazar, we all have secrets, haven't we? You know, Loverboy will never bother women again."

"That's why you've got on the road so long, whereas the killer brothers visited me," Bram talked with a heavy tongue. "But who'll mourn Loverboy?" Plum alcohol started having its effect.

"What about your secrets?" Edhem turned toward Lazar. "Are you as pure and unblemished as you're pretending?"

Lazar didn't answer.
Edhem smiled mysteriously.
"I also have a fascinating story for you," he whispered mysteriously.
Lazar narrowed eyes. "I'm curious," he answered after a short pause.
They all kept silent, listening with great interest. Edhem sipped beer, looked around and smiled.
"Long before the war, a young man goes abroad," he started, "does university studies and starts a brilliant career. Then the Bosnian war breaks out. Caring about his parents, he returns home where he ends up in a dirty civil war. And he arrives too late; Serbs have been killing his parents. But it wasn't just anonymous Serbs: due to rumours, his parents got killed by friendly neighbours with whom they had barbecued before. Those friendly neighbours hung the elderly in their garden on a thick branch with their heads down. First, they pulled out their eyes, then cut off their tongues, her breasts and his penis, while they're still alive. After hours of torture, they killed them like sheep.
"The poor man suffers from terrible nightmares triggered off by the terrifying story a witness told him.
"After the war, he decides to stay in the country. With his diploma and his knowledge, he quickly starts a new career within the police. A new life begins.
"But he can't forget what happened to his parents. As a kid, he'd known his neighbours, and he can't believe they're killers. He doesn't think they're capable of such atrocities. He needs to know the truth. Why not ask them?
"One evening he goes to visit them. Although he moves into Serbian Republic territory, he tells the elderly couple that he's Bosniak looking for their neighbours. They don't recognise him, and cautiously he gives another name, pretending to be a friend of the family.
"The couple remains very kind, alleging with great enthusiasm how well they got along with their neighbours. No, they don't know where the family fled, probably abroad. But not a word of killing.
"After a pleasant afternoon, eating and drinking a lot, he gets convinced they're innocent. He's about to reveal his true identity when his gaze focusses on the beautiful carpet. Before he left for America, he'd seen that carpet in the living room. But not in this house.
"At that moment something's breaking into him. He grabs his gun and reveals who he is. Fear appears in their eyes, especially when he takes a meat knife from the kitchen and asks the man to show him a set of strong ropes he uses to hang up sheep before slaughtering.
"They beg his forgiveness. *'It was war, please forgive us. Our leaders had misled us,'* they yell.
"But he remains merciless, puts a gag in their mouths and binds their arms and legs. One by one, he carries them to the backyard next to a tall, sturdy

tree.

"You can guess the sequel. The angry man recalls how they got killed his parents, and he set the same staging, hanging them upside down on a thick branch. Finally, he cuts their throats and waits until they have lost all their blood. Then he crawls into his car and races back to Sarajevo.

"But he doesn't see Nezir, a sneaky guy in Egzon's service who has been following him, witnessing everything."

Edhem glanced sharply at Lazar and their eyes locked.

"Nezir is no longer," said Edhem with a big smile. "I've given him eternal peace after he'd confessed all his sins. However, Egzon has become a threat to the entire Muslim community. Take care of him." He lifted the beer can. "Now let's put the past behind us and drink to a better future."

Lazar knew what he had got to do.

SIXTY-SEVEN

THE POLICE CHIEF OF CANTON 9 WAS ABOUT TO OPEN THE FRONT DOOR. IN THE ceiling of the porch hung a large lamp that attracted mosquitoes. The stench of their charred bodies was almost unbearable.

"Good evening, Chief."

Egzon turned around.

"Lazar, what gives me the pleasure?" His voice sounded grumpy.

"I think we should finally put an end to it," snarled Lazar. His gaze wandered across the almost unfathomable darkness, in which he spotted countless dancing lights. The house looked like a grey, lugubrious mini-castle. The paved road running along its domain was a barely visible black-and-white line. Lazar caught the noise of the murmuring water caused by the river beyond the house.

"What does that mean, Lazar? If you've something to say to me, come to my desk tomorrow."

"I'm afraid that will too late, Egzon."

The man pivoted toward him. "Have you lost your mind? Get out of my sight..."

"I know you're the Head of FIS in Sarajevo," interrupted Lazar. "It took a while to find out the truth. You've placed microphones in my office and also in my meeting room. So, you knew about Anel Dzeko. Also that I wanted to catch up with Trifko Petrovic. I know that both Trifko and you were in the same battalion. That's why you killed him, just as you killed Drazen. You feared I would find out for whom you are working. For a moment, I thought of Chambers, but no Westerner could approach Trifko that close to allow what the perpetrator did; you belong to the same group. I guess he trusted you!"

"What nonsense are you telling me there?" Then his eyes spotted the gun with a silencer in Lazar's hand along his thigh.

Lazar raised the weapon until the barrel pointed at Egzon's chest.

"You had me watched by Nezir when I went to see my parent's neighbours," he said softly.

"I've never threatened you with that!"

"When were you going to present me the bill? What special plans does FIS have for me?"

Egzon shook his head, but before he could answer, several dull bumps sounded. Egzon flew against the door, slid down and kept lying convulsing in front of the doorstep. He was still alive, and his eyes beggingly looked at Lazar. When he tried to say something, blood flowed between his lips and his words went lost in an unintelligible gargle.

Lazar aligned the barrel between his eyes and squeezed the trigger. The head fell aside.

Lazar gazed around, saw no trace of life, dropped the gun next to the body and turned around. He quietly walked to the road where his car stood. One last time he looked around him.

Feeling satisfied, he got behind the wheel. His gaze wandered to the house while he took off his gloves and threw them over his shoulder in the back seat. He sighed deeply, started and drove off.

Now I am free.

SIXTY-EIGHT

BRAM DECIDED TO SPEND THE REST OF HIS LIFE IN SARAJEVO. HE WAS HAPPY WITH Timka, and the children were kind to him. He hadn't yet seen Chambers, wondering how this first meeting would go. After their last gathering with Lazar a few days before, Edhem had asked him not to turn his back on *Last Hope* right away and wait with his decision until their next meeting. Edhem still had a few things to take care of State Security, but he possibly had a proposal for him. Their gathering took place in private.

Edhem greeted him warmly and guided him to the lounge. He gave each of them a glass of beer and sat opposite him.

"Everything okay at home?"

"Excellent. I hope I can stay in Bosnia, even if I leave *Last Hope*."

Edhem took a big sip and leaned back. Bram resisted his piercing gaze, wondering what his friend had in store for him. He understood that this was more than a friendship meeting.

"I can assure you of your stay here," Edhem suddenly said.
Bram held out his gaze. "But... there's a but, isn't it?"
Edhem chuckled.
"As long as you're at *Last Hope*, we'll extend your visa without a hitch. That's our wish, too."
"You mean State Security." Bram was uncomfortable. He had always feared that his experiences in Bosnia wouldn't get a happy ending. You got nothing for nothing. And he was controllable.
"My country, our country now, is still vulnerable, as you know. Especially the Muslims will have to make difficult decisions in the future. Fundamentalism is growing and has become a severe threat to our future. I am an infidel in their eyes. If medieval writings dictated by a god determines a man's life, then we become the plaything of any dictator acting in the name of these writings."
Bram nodded. "We've already talked about that."
"It's necessary to understand the current situation here, and why there's a role for you, too."
Bram raised his eyebrows but remained silent.
"You probably heard the police chief got murdered?"
Bram chuckled.
Edhem's features betrayed a certain unease. "Egon Subic was a leader of a FIS cell designed to infiltrate politics and industry. But FIS has a counterpart on an international level."
"Lazar mentioned that on our last meeting. You also did."
"But there's no hard evidence that an anti-FIS organisation exists," Edhem replied.
"I know that the right-wing extremism is flourishing. Every new terrorist attack somewhere in Europe increases the number of right extremists."
Edhem chuckled. "Indeed, but extreme parties only create chaos and violence, not solutions. We discovered that there's a mysterious organisation operating under the name *Nemesis*. This organisation employs elite soldiers who quietly fight radicalism. So not with drones or other guided machines. There are no more murders, only accidents."
Bram straightened his shoulders. "Are you talking about a conspiracy theory?"
Edhem smiled. "The *Nemesis Brotherhood* is not an illusion but a reality, even though we have no concrete evidence."
Bram shook his head. He followed international politics and was aware of a massive influx of immigrants into Europe with more than 80% of Muslims. The EU politicians saw no problem with this. On the contrary, they fought critics and changed laws to facilitate mass immigration. He did not concern himself with politics.
"How can you be so sure?" he asked with squeezed eyes.

"Together with Lazar, we unveiled a Machiavellian conspiracy and solved the murders related to it. The mysterious group mentioned was supposed to be responsible for murders which got classified as accidents."

"The Swedish Commissioner. Or a French gendarme, Dragon Borjan."

Bram thoughtfully scratched his beard. He'd never heard of *Nemesis*. On the other hand, he knew Edhem wasn't a liar.

Bram frowned. "Dragon Borjan. Wasn't he killed by someone from Mitrovica?"

"Lazar thinks so, but we don't. Why would the man from Mitrovica make the body disappear? It's an additional risk of getting caught. The Commissioner got murdered by a person who vanished. Officially the Swede died of a heart attack."

"The Swede wasn't a fundamentalist Muslim."

Edhem grinned. "Lazar assumed that the French deputy and Chambers got protected by a mysterious organisation. I investigated further on that. And Lazar was right, the Swede stood in the way of the French deputy, wanted to drop him off. *Nemesis* works like FIS; they too infiltrate governments and military institutions to fight radical politicians who are slowly but surely taking up ministerial posts. *Nemesis* identifies possible dangers and removes them. The French colonel was an essential pawn in their network. In France, for example, all people representing a danger to Montpetit's career got eliminated."

"A peculiar way of defending democracy."

"Collateral damage, negligible if one can avoid chaos and wars in the future. We don't want a repetition of what we experienced in 92-95. But we reject assassins in our territory who are killing politicians they consider radicalised. We don't need Inquisition methods to get rid of radicals."

"And how do you intend to deal with the problem?"

Edhem went to get a new pair of beers. Back in place, he swallowed a mouthful of beer and leaned in.

"You have contacts in the EU. You visit their clubs, and you know essential people. You've got to maintain those connections, go to their parties and memorise the people you meet. If newcomers show up, you'll quickly notice them. Members of the *Nemesis Brotherhood* behave as inconspicuously as possible. Try to identify them. There are high-level commanders, but there are also their protectors. Identify them. All you have to do is observing and informing. We'll have them followed by our people."

Bram shook his head, his features betraying disgust. "So you want to make me a spy for national security?"

"You belong with us, and we defend the same values. Help prevent Muslims from killing other Muslims in the future. If there's a God, then all humans are his children. So why would *He* want some of his children got killed because they don't want to listen to what the other children say? Is that the case, we're talking about fratricide. Religion should help a man to simplify his life, not to sour his life or to spill innocent blood. My people are Muslim because, in 1389, the Turks forced us to become so, but we never let our religion determine our lives. We do not stand in the way of marriages with infidels or others. We do not want to conquer the world and to impose our religion. Believe me, we like to keep it that way. So we're fighting fundamentalism, but we don't want strangers in our country randomly killing important people because they're radicals."

"And what about the *Nemesis Brothers* you identify?"

"They will be expelled from the country or forced to cooperate. We, too, want to identify the real enemies."

"And what about Winston Chambers?"

"We both know who he is, but we can't hurt him. We assume he's part of the *Nemesis Brotherhood.* There's nothing he can do to you either, so you'll have complete freedom of movement. Keep an eye on him and try to find out who his protector is, with whom he has contacts, his relationships, and so on."

Bram drew a deep breath; he'd never expected this upcoming, thinking about Timka and the children. Did he have another choice? He would do the job he did before and keep his eyes open. Smiling, talking and listening to everyone. That wouldn't take him in any particular danger. He wasn't eager to become a target of the *Nemesis Brothers*, whoever that might be. He still doubted the authenticity of the story.

"It wouldn't surprise me if Chambers's protector got also employed at *Last Hope*," Edhem said thoughtfully.

"The Watson brothers, but they're gone."

"I'm just thinking. Those twins were too primitive. Anyway, maybe you'll find out. Besides, you get a monthly allowance, not high, but also not negligible."

Edhem grinned wide. "And finally, we can make sure you get the Bosnian Citizenship. You could marry Timka."

Bram hesitated for a moment. "All right, I'll talk to Timka about it."

Edhem shook his head disapprovingly. "Women don't have to know everything. "You're responsible for her well-being and that of the kids. The less she knows, the better. Officially, you're an aid worker. Stay loyal to your new motherland, and nothing will happen to you. You'll be protected. But beware, you may be approached by *Nemesis*. Stick to your story. Only you and I know what you're doing. A document on our cooperation will be kept safe with State Security. I'm the only one who'll stay in touch with you. You don't know anyone in our organisation either. If anything happens to me, the head of Section "D" will contact you."

"That sounds terrifying," groaned Bram. "Well, I don't have any other choice. And as you say, nothing's going to change my life."

"Good decision."
A handshake confirmed the agreement.
Edhem roared with laughter. Bram had never seen him so excited.
As they left his house, he understood that he was starting a new chapter in his life.

SIXTY-NINE

THE VISITOR LOOKED AROUND, SCRUTINISING THE EDGE OF THE SURROUNDING forest. Knowing that Chambers could be watched, he didn't take a risk. During one hour, he'd observed from different spots all possible approaching places and possible observation posts. Clean. Then he'd returned to his car, put his electronic environmental scanner in the security box integrated into the trunk. Then he had taken the regular road, parking his car in front of the entrance.

Winston Chambers opened the door and frowned. "You," he called out. "You're the last person I'd expected. Come in."

The visitor nodded with a slight smile and passed him. He waited in the hall until Winston had shut the door. Then he followed him silently to the sitting room.

"What can I do for you?" asked Winston with a quick look at the elongated dark box that he was carrying under his left arm. "Have a seat."

"A few glasses will do the job," answered the visitor while opening the box and taking out a bottle that he lifted in the air: rectangular shape, gold content. At the top of the label, in large white letters, was written *Bushmills 21*. He sat down in an armchair and put the box carefully on the tabletop in front of him.

He gave Winston a broad smile. "I've come to drink at a farewell."

The grin on Winston's face faded. "What makes you say that?"

The man shrugged apologetically. "Everything has an end, and I have a new task," he answered. "I called the office in Apeldoorn, which has already arranged my transfer. You don't have to worry about the paperwork."

Why should I make it difficult for him? The elderly man wrongly thought he was working as his protector.

Winston's gaze darkened. "Nice to come here and tell me."

The visitor ignored the irony, still smiling. "I'm leaving early in the morning, so I thought I ought to say goodbye properly. Everything has been managed by phone since the Head of Apeldoorn wanted an immediate decision. I've come to apologise, and I've thought of this." He waved to the box.

Winston's face brightened up again. "Well, I won't refuse Bushmills 21."

The visitor knew that Winston was considering this whisky to be the best product Ireland ever had produced. "*I don't drink much, but if I drink a glass, then only quality*," he used to proclaim at parties.

I couldn't have chosen better.

Winston rushed to the bar and put a little later two whisky glasses and a box of cigars with scissors on the table.

"Does it bother you if I light a cigar?" Winston almost begged, knowing his visitor wasn't a smoker.

"Not at all, I love the smell of cigars. It matches this whisky," the younger man answered. He took the glasses, put them next to each other, opened the bottle and carefully poured in the golden liquid until each glass was a quarter full. He couldn't have served nitroglycerine more carefully. Winston cut off the tip of his cigar, lit a match, held the flame at an angle under the end and then sucked with tucked out lips at the other end.

The visitor grabbed one of the glasses between thumb and fingers and placed it in front of Winston.

"On a short but fruitful collaboration," he said solemnly.

"Cheers." Winston inhaled the smell of honey, chocolate and black mocha. "That's the end." His face expressed delight as if he was listening to singing angels above his head.

The visitor nodded in agreement. He was not a whisky drinker, but for this special occasion, he made an exception. He sipped the golden liquid, wondering how such a bitter product could make a man happy, put his glass on the tabletop, observing the elderly man leaning back and blowing smoke rings to the ceiling.

Extraordinary moment.

"Who's replacing you?" asked Chambers all of a sudden.

"Not my business," replied the visitor. "I think he's already in Sarajevo."

Winston Chambers nodded and had a sip. After a while, the visitor started grinning, seeing Winston's eyes turning dull.

"Such a whisky is indeed the end," he grinned. "A good ending of a long career and a short collaboration."

"What do you mean?" stammered Winston, struggling to get some words over his lips. His arms fell limply, and his fingers were losing their strength. The visitor, knowing these symptoms, smiled broadly. The glass tilted in Winston's lap, spreading out the precious liquid over his thighs. Seconds later, the cigar fell on the floor next to the armchair. Winston's eyes were changing, expressing countless emotions. Misunderstanding, anger, hatred. He was trying to say something, but no sound came over his lips.

The visitor reckoned Winston was beginning to understand.

"Accidents happen, Winston," the visitor said slowly, giving him time to realise how hopeless his situation was. Winston always kept on his guard. Even when he'd poured whisky in the glasses, the elderly man had watched every movement he made, feigning to fully concentrate on his cigar. Winston didn't trust anyone, not even his amiable visitor and protector. And he was right. However, he'd been deceived and was wondering what mistake he'd made.

The visitor grinned. "While you were looking at my hand pouring the whisky into my glass," he said, "I was pouring with the other hand a transparent, odourless liquid into your glass, a simple magic trick. The product is vegetable-based, a miracle drug that leaves no trace. It paralyses your muscles; however, it gives you enough time to say goodbye to this world. You still have ten minutes, I reckon." The visitor closed the bottle and shoved it back into the box. Then he poured the rest of his whisky over Winston's crotch and slid the glass into his pocket. *You can't be too careful.* Science could reveal traces that you wouldn't suspect.

Winston did not move a fine, but his eyes were embers.

"Have you not guessed who I am yet? I'm Brother Lynx, an *Executioner*." Winston's eyes flickered. He understood. Usually, a protector only used violence if the *Chosen* was in immediate danger. An *Executioner* was killing in order. However, after taking out the Viking, he'd got to stay any longer as Winston's protector.

"Now you know who ordered your death," continued the *Executioner* with a deep sigh. "The Council is very disappointed. You've caused a lot of negative publicity, putting our goals at risk and drawing the jihadist's attention to us."

He noticed Winston started breathing more difficult. *He will not make it for long.* Winston's death meant a significant loss since the man was brilliant and could have slowed down the advance of fundamentalism in Bosnia by identifying their top managers and financial resources. He was a *Chosen*, but he hadn't been honest with his superiors, having a dark past that he'd concealed.

The visitor shook his head. "Even a *Chosen* ought to respect the rules. Otherwise, there's chaos leading to anarchy. You betrayed the *Brotherhood* to save your ass. Or do you think we don't know about your agreement with MI6? We have ears and eyes everywhere." He looked at his watch. "In a minute or so, your heart will stop beating, as did Ivar Ragnarsson's heart. But that was a good man, contrarily to you. A pity he wasn't one of us."

Winston's eyes had turned glassy, and the visitor stopped talking. He'd accomplished his task. Winston had been endangering the *Brotherhood*. A massive blow for *Nemesis*, which placed its hope on the last *Chosen* still being in this damn country. Normand Montpetit, the new EuPol commissioner.

The visitor put on his gloves, cleaned everything he'd touched before, grabbed the box and left the house. Outside he took off his ugly dark-framed spectacles, shoved them in his inside pocket and opened the door. Then he pulled off his black wig, revealing a bald skull, and threw it with the gloves in the backseat. *I don't need them any more.* He got into the driver seat of his Volkswagen.

Bye-bye, Peter Camden.

The silent secretary had ceased to exist.

Characters

"Last Hope" is a non-governmental organisation

Winston Chambers is the office manager
Peter Camden is secretary
Bram Ruyter is a Dutch social worker.
Tim Watson is the safety officer

Edhem Hasic is a survivor of Srebrenica, Bram's friend

Sarajevo Police District.

Egzon Subic, Police Chief of Canton 9.
Lazar Magas, Superintendent of the Sarajevo Homicide Department.
Senad Mujdza, an inspector at the Sarajevo Homicide Department. Lazar's partner.
Fadila Piric: Team Lazar
Nijaz Bolic: Team Lazar.
Izet Neoric: Team Lazar
Zumra Abdic: friend of Lazar Magas.

The State Security Service, Sluzbi Drazvne Bezbednost.

Mirsad Pejic: Head of Division "D" of the State Security Service

Forensic team Sarajevo.

Ferid Munic: Tracker
Mila Delic: Pathologist atom

EuPol.

Ivar Ragnarsson is EuPol Commissioner
Normand Montpetit is EuPol Deputy Commissioner.
Mycroft Follum is Political Advisor
Derek Fleming is Operations and Planning
Greg Stone is a Belgian computer scientist

Anel Dzeko is part of IT team Stone.
Miloska Stambolic is the interpreter of Mycroft Follum.

Emir Besic is a computer scientist at “Digital Future”, an IT company doing business with EuPol and friend of Anel Dzeko.

Mercenaries.

Ahmed Salah: mercenary of British nationality
Alistair Moon: mercenary of British nationality

War Veterans.

Safety-Regovic: Bosnian war veteran
Miralem Lulic: Bosnian war veteran
Trifko Petrovic: Bosnian arms dealer
Emma Badora: victim of trafficking in women
Daria Bazila: victim of trafficking in women

Suada Omarovic: victim of rape during the war. Lives in Belgium.
Timka Omarovic: Suada’s sister, lives with her mother in Sarajevo.

Fictional organisations.

FIS: Free Islamic State
“Last Hope”: NGO that deals with the repatriation of victims of human trafficking.
EuPol: European Police
Nemesis: a British private organisation

Historical characters.

Radovan Karadzic: Serbian politician, President of the Republic of Serbia during the Bosnia War
Ratko Mladic: Military commander of Serbian forces in Bosnia.
Naser Oric: Commander-in-Chief of the Bosnian Armed Forces in Srebrenica.
Alija Izetbegovic is a Muslim activist and President of Bosnia and Herzegovina following the 1993 referendum.
Rasim Delic: Chief of Staff of the Bosnian Army (ABIH).

Jacques Klein: Special Representative of the Secretary-general in BiH. He was involved in a human trafficking scandal in Bosnia 2000. When Kathryn Bolkovac submitted several reports on IPTF observers engaged in human trafficking, she was dismissed and did not receive any support from SGSg Klein who refused to deny or prosecute the American IPTF observers. He will also be involved in a similar scandal later on in a post in Liberia.

Existing organisations.

IPTF: International Police Task Forces
EUMM: European Union Monitoring Mission
EUPM: European Union Police Mission
IOM: International Organisation for Migration.

BUTMIR CAMP.
Butmir is a district in Ilidža, in the canton of Sarajevo of Bosnia and Herzegovina. The international airport of Sarajevo belongs to Butmir. Although it is now part of Ilidža, it was an independent town for a long time. SFOR troops got stationed in the Butmir camp

The author.

I have spent almost four years in the Balkans, carrying out several tasks such as "*Civil and Military Cooperation Officer*" in Banja Luka and Albania (during the Kosovo war), mainly concerned with the refugee issue. I was involved in the reception of Kosovar refugees in Kukes (Albania-Kosovo border) and their return, immediately after signing the peace agreements. After that, to end my career, I spent a year and a half as a EUMM observer and six months as a EUPM IT expert. The experience I've gathered has been helping me enormously in writing this story.

During the Bosnian war, the Serbs detained Muslim women on the Jahorina. Hundreds of Muslim women have accused several UNPROFOR officers of rape and sexual abuse during their imprisonment in Serb camps. The *Research and Documentation Centre of the League of Prisoners in Bosnia* has recorded and documented their statements, quoting an English and a Canadian general.

The fall of Srebrenica has caused a lot of flowing ink, and I did not want to write yet another version of it.

"The Vitruvius Inspiration" is a human story about four war victims, happening seven years after the war. I have chosen this period deliberately because I have been living in Sarajevo from 2001 until 2003, knowing the situation well. Besides, I have worked for the police mission for six months, witnessing the way IPTF was working.

Although the story is a fiction, insider knowledge, real events, historical facts, testimonies and the political situation I experienced it in 2001-2003 inspired me. I wrote the first manuscript in the period 2011-2012.

EuPol, "Last Hope", FIS just exists in my imagination. However, I have based their functioning and structures on similar existing organisations and used the real names of historical characters and events.

There are numerous indications that Islam is increasing its influence in the West. In Bosnia, since the end of the war, 130 new mosques have been built in Sarajevo alone, while throughout the country of 6 million inhabitants, 1,400 new mosques have emerged like mushrooms. The economy is weak, and the enormous Arab investments are aiming for an increase of the Islamic influence, causing a proportional increase of radicalisation. Islam has become more visible everywhere. Coincidence?

At the moment I am writing these phrases, four known villages openly raise the IS flag. The “Fifth Column” is no longer a populist fabrication.

To avoid tiring the reader with complicated structures, I have used names for the Bosnian judicial system, which are customary in our country. In the meantime, the Bosnian police got wholly restructured.

Henri Patrik, 2015

Documentation consulted

"Ich Flehte um meinen tod" by CID (Centar za Istrazivanje I documentaciju)

"The Srebrenica Diaries" by Charlef Brantz

"Leaving the void behind us" by Selma Leydesdorff."

"Memories of Srebrenica" by Hendrina Praamsma, Jet Peekel, Toni Boumans

Srebrenica. Witnesses to mass murder, Bob van Laerhoven.

"The Whistleblower" by Kathryn Bolkovac

"Gesloten Gezelschap" by Henri Patrik.

Internet.

Thanks

Thanks to Frans Esselink, my friend and first reader for his tireless support and resolve. He gave me the motivation to become a writer.

Without Alexander Cammans, my publisher, I would never have been publishing. I'm also thanking him for his patience and help.

Bob Van Laerhoven, a famous Belgian writer, who wrote the first book about the Srebrenica disaster 1995: "Srebrenica, witnesses to a massacre", became my literary example. His comments, advice and beautiful foreword were of inestimable value.

Thanks also to my Bosnian friend Edhem Bezdrob, with whom I've spent two unforgettable years in Sarajevo, learning a lot about the country and the people. He and his family will always be in my memory. I'll never forget this period, neither our gathering in 2005. And I hope the Bosnian people will eventually find peace and prosperity without giving up their identity.

Werner Donné, provided me with a fantastic program which allowed me to convert my books decently and quickly in epub-format.

I also thank my wife Marie-France, for her understanding, patience and strong coffee that helped me overcome challenging moments.

And to all my readers: you are fantastic.